The Badminton Library

OF

SPORTS AND PASTIMES

EDITED BY

HIS GRACE THE DUKE OF BEAUFORT, K.G.

ASSISTED BY ALFRED E. T. WATSON

GOLF

THE CLUB HOUSE, ST ANDREWS

GOLF

BY

HORACE G. HUTCHINSON

WITH CONTRIBUTIONS BY LORD WELLWOOD,
SIR WALTER SIMPSON, BART., RIGHT HON. A. J. BALFOUR, M.P.
ANDREW LANG, H. S. C. EVERARD, AND OTHERS

*WITH NUMEROUS ILLUSTRATIONS BY THOMAS HODGE
AND HARRY FURNISS*

ASHFORD PRESS PUBLISHING
SOUTHAMPTON
1987

Published by   ASHFORD PRESS PUBLISHING 1987
                1 CHURCH ROAD
                SHEDFIELD
                HAMPSHIRE SO3 2HW

First published in 1890
Republished 1987

Introductory Note © 11th Duke of Beaufort 1985

All rights reserved. Except for use in a review, no part of the Introductory Note may be reproduced or utilised in any form or by any means, electronic or mechanical, including photocopying, recording or by any information storage and retrieval system without written permission from the publisher.

British Library Cataloguing in Publication Data

Hutchinson, Horace G.
    Golf.—(The Badminton library of sports and pastimes).
    1. Golf
    I. Title   II. Series
    796.352   GV965

    ISBN 1-85253-018-9

Printed and bound in Great Britain

Introductory Note

My great great-grandfather, the 8th Duke of Beaufort, was always proud to say that he had been instrumental in bringing about one of the great sporting achievements of this century. In 1882, he and his great friend, Alfred Watson, set about compiling The Badminton Library, a series of books that would attempt to highlight, examine and explain all of the many great sports that this nation enjoys. The aim was simple; the Library was to become an encyclopaedia of sport that would supply basic information to all amateur sportsmen.

As a result of their work some 23 volumes were published that covered all sorts of activities: Hunting, of course, a subject always very close to my family's heart; Fishing; Racing and Steeplechasing; Lawn Tennis; Shooting; Driving; Athletics; Football, and even Cycling and Motor Driving. For each volume the most influential specialists were asked to impart their particular expertise, and indeed many of these are still remembered today for their sporting achievements. I think particularly of Lord Brassey on Yachting, Lord Walsingham on Shooting and the 8th Duke of Beaufort himself on Driving and Hunting – but the list of names is endless and each has a claim to our attention.

The finest illustrators were also eager to add their contribution: Archibald Thorburn and A.C. Sealy are notable examples. And so a magnificent sporting library was born, created from the greatest talents and with the immense tradition of Badminton firmly behind it. As might have been expected, the Library was a huge success. During the years it has gained great respect and instant recognition all over the world, and the books, although somewhat rare now, are still very much sought-after.

My great great-grandfather was more than the notional editorial figure-head that some might wrongly imagine. He worked enthusiastically to cull the best talents available and to edit them into a series of readable, entertaining volumes. He was rightly very proud of his part in commissioning and compiling the Library: it has remained one of his greatest achievements.

The reissue of the Library is long overdue; it could not have come at a better time. Far from losing its popularity, sport is now once again at its height. Television has had a major impact and modern day lifestyles have enabled many more people to participate in and enjoy sport at both amateur and professional levels.

At the same time, sport in its truest sense is threatened today by many evils that my great great-grandfather would never have imagined – hooliganism, financial influences, drugs, politics, and even terrorism. Let us hope that the best of sport will survive and that the reissue of the Badminton Library will remind us of at least some of what is best in sport.

The Badminton Library offers lifetimes of experience gained by a host of illustrious sportsmen, and provides a fascinating insight into the traditions and rites of the sports as they were enjoyed so many years ago.

It has now fallen to me to follow in the family tradition, and I take great pleasure in being able to help re-launch the Badminton Library. In introducing it I hope I have managed to convey just a fraction of the enthusiasm with which my family has always regarded these volumes.

I commend the Badminton Library to a new generation of sportsmen and women; hopefully they will gain as much pleasure from reading these volumes as I have; and undoubtedly they will increase their abilities by listening to the great mass of advice and anecdotes offered by such an esteemed selection of our great sporting forebears.

The 11th Duke of Beaufort
June 1985

DEDICATION

TO

H.R.H. THE PRINCE OF WALES

———•◆•———

BADMINTON : *March*, 1890.

HAVING received permission to dedicate these volumes, the BADMINTON LIBRARY of SPORTS and PASTIMES, to HIS ROYAL HIGHNESS THE PRINCE OF WALES, I do so feeling that I am dedicating them to one of the best and keenest sportsmen of our time. I can say, from personal observation, that there is no man who can extricate himself from a bustling and pushing crowd of horsemen, when a fox breaks covert, more dexterously and quickly than His Royal Highness; and that when hounds run hard over a big country, no man can take a line of his own and live with them better. Also, when the wind has been blowing hard, often have I seen His Royal Highness knocking over driven grouse and partridges and high-rocketing pheasants in first-rate workmanlike style. He is held to be a good yachtsman, and as Commodore of the Royal Yacht Squadron is looked up to by those who love that pleasant and exhilarating pastime. His encouragement of racing is well known, and his attendance at the University, Public School, and other important Matches testifies to his being, like most English gentlemen, fond of all manly sports. I consider it a great privilege to be allowed to dedicate these volumes to so eminent a sportsman as His Royal Highness the Prince of Wales, and I do so with sincere feelings of respect and esteem and loyal devotion.

BEAUFORT.

BADMINTON.

PREFACE

A FEW LINES only are necessary to explain the object with which these volumes are put forth. There is no modern encyclopædia to which the inexperienced man, who seeks guidance in the practice of the various British Sports and Pastimes, can turn for information. Some books there are on Hunting, some on Racing, some on Lawn Tennis, some on Fishing, and so on; but one Library, or succession of volumes, which treats of the Sports and Pastimes indulged in by Englishmen—and women—is wanting. The Badminton Library is offered to supply the want. Of the imperfections which must be found in the execution of such a design we are conscious. Experts often differ. But this we may say, that those who are seeking for knowledge on any of the subjects dealt with will find the results of many years' experience written by men who are in every case adepts at the Sport or Pastime of which they write. It is to point the way to success to those who are ignorant of the sciences they aspire to master, and who have no friend to help or coach them, that these volumes are written.

To those who have worked hard to place simply and clearly before the reader that which he will find within, the best thanks of the Editor are due. That it has been no slight labour to supervise all that has been written he must acknowledge; but it has been a labour of love, and very much lightened by the courtesy of the Publisher, by the unflinching, indefatigable assistance of the Sub-Editor, and by the intelligent and able arrangement of each subject by the various writers, who are so thoroughly masters of the subjects of which they treat. The reward we all hope to reap is that our work may prove useful to this and future generations.

THE EDITOR.

CONTENTS

CHAPTER		PAGE
I.	THE HISTORY OF GOLF	1
	By Andrew Lang	
II.	GENERAL REMARKS ON THE GAME	29
	By Lord Wellwood	
III.	CLUBS AND BALLS	53
	By H. G. Hutchinson	
IV.	ELEMENTARY INSTRUCTION	73
	By H. G. Hutchinson	
V.	ON STYLE—VARIOUS STYLES	151
	By H. G. Hutchinson	
VI.	OUT OF FORM: A CHAPTER FOR ADEPTS	170
	By Sir Walter Simpson, Bt.	
VII.	HINTS TO CRICKETERS WHO ARE TAKING UP GOLF	203
	By H. G. Hutchinson	
VIII.	ON NERVE AND TRAINING	209
	By H. G. Hutchinson	
IX.	HINTS ON MATCH AND MEDAL PLAY	225
	By H. G. Hutchinson	
X.	ETIQUETTE AND BEHAVIOUR	256
	By H. G. Hutchinson	

CHAPTER		PAGE
XI.	ON GIVING ODDS AND HANDICAPPING	277
	By H. G. Hutchinson	
XII.	PROFESSIONALS AND CADDIES	293
	By H. G. Hutchinson	
XIII.	SOME CELEBRATED LINKS	311
	By H. G. Hutchinson	
XIV.	SOME CELEBRATED GOLFERS	332
	By H. S. C. Everard	
XV.	THE HUMOURS OF GOLF	410
	By the Rt. Hon. A. J. Balfour, M.P.	
XVI.	THE RULES	433
XVII.	GLOSSARY OF TECHNICAL TERMS EMPLOYED IN THE GAME OF GOLF	445
INDEX		451

ILLUSTRATIONS

(REPRODUCED BY J. D. COOPER AND MESSRS WALKER & BOUTALL)

PLATES

	ARTIST	
THE CLUB HOUSE, ST. ANDREWS	*T. Hodge*	*Frontispiece*

		TO FACE PAGE
AN OLD DUTCH PICTURE	*From a picture in possession of Col. Boothby*	24
A GOLF WIDOW	*H. Furniss*	44
MODERN GOLF CLUBS	*T. Hodge*	62
THE 'HEADSMAN' STYLE	*H. Furniss*	162
THE PICNIC ON THE PUTTING-GREEN —'JUST THE PLACE FOR IT'	*H. Furniss*	178
'OH! WHAT A SURPRISE!'	*H. Furniss*	182
'ARRY. A SKETCH ON LONDON LINKS	*H. Furniss*	204
'KEEP YOUR EYE ON THE CAMERA'	*H. Furniss*	214
FINISH OF A BIG MATCH	*From an old picture*	226
THE DAWN OF GOLF	*T. Hodge*	248
'APPROACHING THE LAST HOLE'	*T. Hodge*	264
FIGHTING THEIR BATTLE OVER AGAIN	*H. Furniss*	288
A CADDIE'S DUTIES	*H. Furniss*	298
THE WINDMILL, WIMBLEDON	*From a photograph by A. Lubbock, Esq.*	312
THE SEA HOLE, ELIE	*T. Hodge*	320
THE POND, WIMBLEDON	*From a photograph by A. Lubbock, Esq.*	328

		ARTIST	TO FACE PAGE
THE MAIDEN, SANDWICH		*From a photograph by Mr. Goodman, Margate*	330
ALLAN ROBERTSON AND TOM MORRIS		*T. Hodge*	336
MAY AND DECEMBER		*H. Furniss*	410
THE WORST OF SEASIDE BUNKERS IN THE SEASON		*H. Furniss*	418
OLD TOM TELLING HIS STORY		*T. Hodge*	430

WOODCUTS IN TEXT

	ARTIST	PAGE
VIGNETTE	*From an old missal*	1
A TILE		3
A TILE		5
AN ENCAUSTIC DISH		10
AN ENCAUSTIC TILE		12
A TILE		17
SPINDLE ROCK	*T. Hodge*	29
A BAD CASE	*H. Furniss*	31
DRIVEN INTO	*T. Hodge*	39
VIGNETTE	*T. Hodge*	53
FOSSILS OF THE PAST	*T. Hodge*	55
GOLF BALLS	*T. Hodge*	69
VIGNETTE	*T. Hodge*	73
POSITION FOR THE DRIVE	*C. L. Shute, from a photograph*	75
POSITION DIAGRAM		77
AT THE TOP OF THE SWING (AS IT SHOULD BE)	*C. L. Shute, from a photograph*	82

ILLUSTRATIONS

	ARTIST	PAGE
AT THE TOP OF THE SWING (AS IT SHOULD NOT BE)	C. L. Shute, from a photograph	85
AT THE END OF THE SWING (AS IT SHOULD BE)	C. L. Shute, from a photograph	88
AT THE END OF THE SWING (AS IT SHOULD NOT BE)	C. L. Shute, from a photograph	91
MR. LESLIE BALFOUR	C. L. Shute, from a photograph	98
THREE-QUARTER STROKE	C. L. Shute, from a photograph	112
POSITION DIAGRAM		115
THE POSITION FOR THE APPROACH SHOT	C. L. Shute, from a photograph	116
POSITION 1	From a photograph	118
POSITION 2	From a photograph	119
POSITION 3	From a photograph	120
BEGINNING OF THE HIGH LOFTING STROKE	C. L. Shute, from a photograph	126
FINISH OF THE HIGH LOFTING STROKE	C. L. Shute, from a photograph	128
OFF THE LEFT LEG	T. Hodge	130
MR. A. F. MACFIE	T. Hodge	137
AN ALTERNATIVE STYLE OF PUTTING	C. L. Shute, from a photograph	142
IN A SAND BUNKER	T. Hodge	145
A CHAMPION IN DIFFICULTIES	T. Hodge	149
VIGNETTE	T. Hodge	151
THE ST. ANDREWS SWING	T. Hodge	154
AGRICULTURE	T. Hodge	167
ST. ANDREWS CATHEDRAL	T. Hodge	170
FIG. 1—A SMALL OR FULL SWING		186
FIG. 2—A BIG, OR SHORT, OR HALF SWING		187
VIGNETTE	T. Hodge	203
VIGNETTE	T. Hodge	209

		ARTIST	PAGE
The Last Hole (St. Andrews)		*T. Hodge*	211
Indoor Practice		*T. Hodge*	221
Vignette		*T. Hodge*	225
Key to Lord's Picture of the Game of Golf			226
The Man to Back		*T. Hodge*	254
Vignette		*T. Hodge*	256
Understudies		*H. Furniss*	275
Stone Bridge, Swilcan Burn		*T. Hodge*	277
Vignette		*T. Hodge*	293
A Good Caddie		*T. Hodge*	303
Bell Rock Lighthouse		*T. Hodge*	311
The Himalayas, Prestwick		*T. Hodge*	323
Hole-cutter		*T. Hodge*	332
Old Daw		*T. Hodge*	363
Jamie Anderson		*T. Hodge*	363
Willie Campbell		*T. Hodge*	369
Willie Fernie		*T. Hodge*	377
Mr. Pat Alexander		*T. Hodge*	384
Mr. James Condie		*T. Hodge*	384
Mr. Sutherland		*T. Hodge*	384
Sir Robert Hay, Bart.		*T. Hodge*	386
Mr. George Glennie		*T. Hodge*	389
Mr. Robert Clark		*T. Hodge*	391
Mr. John Ball		*T. Hodge*	403
Golfing Extraordinary		*T. Hodge*	408
Bass Rock		*T. Hodge*	410
'He looks at the Hole from the Ball'		*T. Hodge*	423
Vignette		*T. Hodge*	433

GOLF

CHAPTER I

THE HISTORY OF GOLF

BY ANDREW LANG

THE history of golf, as of most games, has still to be written. As a rule, these topics have been studied either by people of letters who were no sportsmen, or by sportsmen who had little tincture of letters. Golf has so far been fortunate in receiving the attention of Mr. Robert Chambers. The editor of 'Golf, an Ancient and Royal Game' (R. and R. Clark, Edinburgh, 1875) was deeply versed in Scotch antiquities, and communicated his learning with unstudied grace. But 'Golf' is undoubtedly incomplete, sketchy, and scrappy, a collection of documents and odds and ends. It is not here, in a single chapter, that the history of golf can be exhaustively written. But we may try to show its relations with other ball games, its connection with foreign forms most nearly allied with itself, and we may lightly trace the antiquities of the sport.

The name *Golf* is usually thought to be akin to the German *Kolbe*, 'club,' and may be a Celtic form of that word. M. Charles Michel, Professor of Sanskrit at the University of Gand, writes : 'As to the etymology of "golf," I fancy none but Scotch philologists are puzzled by it. At a first glance I do not think we can connect it with the French Chole.' (This was a guess which I submitted, being no *grand clerc en philologie*, to M. Michel.) 'This is what I find in the "Etymologisches Wörterbuch der deutschen Sprache" (1889, p. 181), under *Kolben*, Old High German *Cholbo*, Icelandic *Kolfr*. It presupposes a Gothic word, *Kulban*=stick with thick knob (probably=English *club*). The word *Golf* might readily be Celtic, for the Germanic form Kolbe demands a *g* and a *f* in the other Indo-European languages. The word *chole* (Belgian for a club) might well be a Germanic term, surviving in Walloon, and *Golf* may be the Celtic form, surviving in English.'

While leaving the question to scholars, I am inclined to agree with M. Michel's probable theory, and I would note that *Golf* occurs in some Celtic names of places, as Golf-drum.

So much for the word golf. It is not necessary to dispute the absurd derivation from 'the Greek word κόλαφος,' which appears in several treatises. And, in passing, it may be observed that though golf, or something like it, was played in the Low Countries, there is no specific resemblance whatever between golf and the Dutch game called kolf. This is proved by the following account of kolf, from 'The Statistical Account of Scotland,' 1795, vol. xvi. p. 28 :—

KOLF

The following account of the Dutch game, called *Kolf*, was very obligingly communicated by the Rev. Mr. Walker, one of the ministers of the Canongate, whose former residence in Holland has enabled him to give a very satisfactory description of that

ITS HISTORY

game. The Dutch game called kolf, from which the word golf is derived, as both are probably from the Greek word, κόλαφος, is played in an enclosed rectangular area of about 60 feet by 25. The floor, which is composed of sand, clay and pitch, is made as level as a billiard table, and the inclosing walls are for two feet above the floor faced either with polished stone or sheet lead, that they may cause the ball to rebound with accuracy. At about 8 to 10 feet from each end wall, a circular post of about five inches diameter is placed precisely in the middle of the area with regard to breadth, consequently opposite the one to the other, at the distance of 40 feet or thereby. The balls used in the game are about the size of cricket balls, made perfectly round and elastic, covered with soft leather and sewed with fine wire. The clubs are from three to four feet long, with stiff shafts. The heads are of brass, and the face, with which the ball is struck, is perfectly smooth, having no inclination, such as might have a tendency to raise the ball from the ground. The angle which the head makes with the shaft is nearly the same with that of the *putting* club used at golf. The game may be played by any number, either in parties against each other, or each person for himself; and the contest is, who shall hit the two posts in the fewest strokes and make his ball retreat from the last one with such an accurate length as that it shall lie nearest to the opposite wall of the area. The first stroke is made from within a few inches of what is called the *beginning post*, and the player directs his ball as precisely as he can on the opposite one, that he may hit it if possible, computing at the same time the force of his stroke, so that, should he miss it (which from the distance may be supposed to be most frequently the case), his ball may rebound from the end wall, and lie within a moderate distance of the post, and before it, *i.e.* between the two posts, rather than between the post and the end wall. The reason of preferring this situation of the ball will appear by reflecting how much easier it is in that case to send the ball, after striking the post, back again towards the other one. The skill of

FROM A TILE

the game consists in striking the post in such a way, whether full or otherwise, as may send the ball towards the place where you wish it to rest. It combines the address required both in golf and in billiards. Five points make the game; and such is the difference between a capital and an ordinary player, that the former will give four points of the game and frequently be the winner. This superiority of play I experienced myself at a *kolf baau* near the Hague, after I had considerable practice in the game, and was, in fact, no mean player. With the advantage of three points I was completely beaten, and even when I got four, I could hardly preserve any tolerable equality.

A great advantage of the game of *kolf* is, that it can be played at all seasons, and in all weather, as the place is as close as a house, while, at the same time by opening the windows, which are very large, you may have a sufficiency of air. There is generally a kind of apartment at one end of the *kolf baau*, two or three steps higher than the floor, where spectators may enjoy the sight of the game, so far as the clouds of tobacco smoke, with which they commonly fill it, will allow.

Clearly golf is no more kolf than cricket is poker.

The essence of golf is the striking by two parties, each of his own ball, to a series of given points—in golf 'holes.' This is clearly distinct from any game in which each party strives to strike the same ball to opposite points, as in hocky or shinty. But we shall see that, in the form of golf still played in Belgium, both parties play with the same ball. One endeavours to reach the given point in a certain number of strokes. The other is allowed one back stroke out of three. Here we touch the place where golf is differentiating itself from such games as hockey and polo. Let each party have as many strokes as he can get, and we have hockey. Let each play his own ball, and neither of them touch his opponent's ball, and we have golf, or pell mell, *jeu de mail*.

Now forms of this intermediate stage, *chole*, still surviving in Belgium and Northern France, are of extreme antiquity on the Continent. They represent golf in the making. The game might develop into golf, or pell mell, or remain arrested at a stage between golf and hockey, as in Belgium now. If the point played to was a hole in the ground, golf arose : if you played to a stone, tree, or rock, or through an iron hoop elevated on a post, pell mell, *jeu de mail*, *Pila-Malleus* was the result. In the Low Latin dictionary of Du Cange, we find that *Choulla* (French *Choulle*, or *Chole*) was *globulus ligneus qui clava propellitur*, 'a wooden ball struck by a club.' This occurs in legal documents of 1353, 1357. Under *crossare*, to play at *crosse*, or at *chole*, we learn that the clubs used had iron heads, like niblicks and irons. An engraving from a missal of 1504 is printed here, showing peasants engaged at *chole*, *choulla*, or *crosse*. In the original coloured miniature the heads of the clubs are painted of a steely blue. It has been remarked that the game, as represented, is a kind of hockey rather than golf. It must be noted, however, that the artist may have introduced the iron-headed clubs of one game into the other. The confused descriptions given by a learned but muddle-headed writer in the old *Mercure de France*

FROM A TILE

show that he got all the possible games mixed in his mind. The oldest mentions of *chole* and *choulla* seem usually to have been made because a quarrel arose at the game, and one player hit another over the sconce with his iron-headed club.[1]

There is nothing to show, as far as I am aware, that these early Flemish golfers putted at holes. They do not do so now, but play to a given mark, a stone, a church gate, a pot-house door. M. Charles Michel thus describes the game as it exists in Belgium :

[1] The missal from which we borrow our engraving is in the possession of Sir William Gibson Carmichael, at Castle Craig. Mrs. T. G. Carmichael has kindly copied the miniature.

The players divide into two parties, after fixing the point on which they are to play, sometimes two or three, or even four leagues distant from the tee.

It is as if you played on Dourie Castle door from the first hole at St. Andrews.

The game is to reach and touch with the ball, say the right-hand pillar of the door of a church in such or such a village. The captains of each side choose a player alternately, till all the company are divided into two parties, each under its captain. Then the number of strokes in which the distance is to be covered is, as it were, put up to auction; the side which offers the lowest estimate wins, and strikes off.

Thus, if one side bets it will reach the goal in six strokes, while the other can only offer eight, the sportsmen who think they can do it in six strike first from the tee.

Then off they go, across field and meadow, hedge and ditch, the game being usually played in autumn, when the fields are bare. Each man of the striking-off party swipes at the ball alternately, but, when they have had three strokes a man of the other party *déchole* (hits back). Then the first side plays three more strokes, then comes another *décholade* by the opponents. Thus each of the original strikers has three strikes for one strike by the adversaries. The *décholeurs* try to hit the ball into every kind of hazard. If the ball is hit into an impossible hazard, say over a wall which cannot be climbed, the players settle among themselves where a new ball is to be put down. In short, impossible hazards are replaced in a possible position.

M. Michel's authority tells him that a strong player can drive about four hundred yards—a rare feat. The Belgian club which M. Michel kindly sent me is a very rude weapon, with an extremely concave iron head, hafted on a stiff handle. The Belgian golfer thinks that with our clubs we ought to be able to hit further. The Belgian ball is an egg-shaped one of beechwood. Experiment shows that English golfers cannot make a long drive with Belgian weapons.[1]

[1] I gave the Belgian driver to the Wimbledon Club.

ITS HISTORY

Thus M. Michel's account corroborates that of M. Zola in 'Germinal' (p. 310). M. Zola's description, however, reads somewhat romantic. An excellent tale of Belgian golf is M. Charles Deulin's 'Le Grand Choleur,' founded on tradition. It was translated by Miss Isabel Bruce, and published as 'The Devil's Round' in 'Longman's Magazine' (June, 1889).

Apparently the robust Flemish game has become mixed in an American's mind with our golf, as appears from the following quaint notice of golf, from the 'Philadelphia Times' of Sunday, Feb. 24, 1889.[1]

Up to this time golf has made little way in the United States. It is occasionally played in Canada, although even there it has not assumed the importance of a regular department of sports. It is a game that demands at once the utmost physical development upon the part of the player as well as a considerable amount of skill, and it arouses the interest only of those who go into sports for the love of action. It is far from being a 'dude' game. No man should attempt to play golf who has not good legs to run with and good arms to throw with, as well as a modicum of brain power to direct his play. It is also, by the nature of the game itself, a most aristocratic exercise, for no man can play at golf who has not a servant at command to assist him. It is probable that no sport exists in the world to-day or ever did exist in which the services of a paid assistant are so essential as in this national game of Scotland. The truth is that the servant is as essential to the success of the game as the player himself.

To play golf properly there is needed a very large expanse of uncultivated soil, which is not too much broken up by hills. A few knolls and gulleys more or less really assist to make the game more interesting. In Scotland it is played generally upon the east coast, where the links are most extensive. Having selected a field, the first thing necessary is to dig a small hole, perhaps one foot or two feet deep and about four inches in diameter. Beginning with this hole a circle is devised that includes substantially the whole of the links. About once in 500 yards of this circle another hole is dug. If the grounds selected cannot include so large a circle as this, the holes may be put at as short a distance

[1] This is borrowed from the *Edinburgh Evening Dispatch*, March 21, 1889.

as 100 yards from each other; but the best game is played when the field is large enough to include holes at a distance of 500 yards apart. The game then may be played by two or four persons. If by four, two of them must be upon the same side.

There are eleven implements of the game, the most important of which is the ball. This is made of gutta percha, and is painted white. It weighs about two ounces, and is just small enough to fit comfortably into the holes dug in the ground. Still it should not be so large that it cannot be taken out with ease. The other ten implements are the tools of the players. Their names are as follows: the playing club, long spoon, mud spoon, short spoon, baffing spoon, driving putter, putter, sand iron, cleek, and track iron. Each of these is about four feet long, the entire length of which in general consists of a wooden handle. The head is spliced on, and may be either metal or wood. The handle, as a rule, is made of hickory covered with leather.

At the beginning of play each player places his ball at the edge of a hole which has been designated as a starting point. When the word has been given to start he bats his ball as accurately as possible towards the next hole, which may be either 100 or 500 yards distant. As soon as it is started in the air he runs forward in the direction which the ball has taken, and his servant, who is called a 'caddy,' runs after him with all the other nine tools in his arms. If the player is expert or lucky he bats his ball so that it falls within a few feet, or inches even, of the next hole in the circle. His purpose is to put the ball in that next hole, spoon it out and drive it forward to the next further one before his opponent can accomplish the same end. The province of the 'caddy' in the game is to follow his master as closely as possible, generally at a dead run, and be ready to hand him whichever implement of the game the master calls for, as the play may demand. For instance, the ball may fall in such a way that it is lodged an inch or two above the ground, having fallen in thick grass. The player, rushing up to it, calls on his 'caddy' for a baffing spoon, and having received it from the hands of his servant he bats the ball with the spoon in the direction of the hole. An inviolable rule of the game is that no player shall touch the ball from one limit of the circle to the other with his hands. All play must be done with the tools.

In this the caddy really gets about as much exercise out of the sport as his master, and he must be so familiar with the tools of

ITS HISTORY

the game that he can hand out the right implement at any moment when it is called for. If a player has succeeded in throwing or pushing his ball into a hole, his opponent must wait until he has succeeded in spooning it out before he begins to play. Obedience to this rule obviates any dispute as to the order in which a man's points are to be made. For if one player has his ball in a hole and his opponent has his within an inch or two of it, he must wait before he plays until the first player has gotten his ball clear of it and thrown it toward the next hole. Following this general plan the players go entirely about the circle, and in a large field this may involve a run of several miles. If the ball is thrown beyond the hole, it must be returned to it and carefully spooned out again.

The aim of the sport is not necessarily to complete the circle as quickly as possible. There are no codified rules according to which the game is played. As a general custom the players make the entire circuit of the circle and the one who gets his ball in the hole at which they began first wins the game. Nevertheless it is sometimes agreed that the game shall be won by him who makes the largest number of holes within a given number of minutes, say twenty or thirty. In either case the principle of the game remains the same; and if partners are playing, it simply means that if A strikes a ball and B is his partner, B must run forward and make the next play, and A must run after him and make the next, and so on, while D and C, who are on the other side, are doing the same thing. In the partnership game there is actually more exercise to the players than in the single game, and the servants or 'caddies' are equally busy.

Spectators sometimes view games of golf, but as a rule they stand far off, for the nature of the implements employed is such that a ball may be driven in a very contrary direction to that which the player wishes, and, therefore, may fall among the spectators and cause some temporary discomfort. Moreover, it would require considerable activity upon the part of the spectators to watch the play in golf, for they would have to run around and see how every hole was gained, from one end of the game to the other. There may be as many as thirty spectators at one game, but seldom more, and a good game is frequently played without any at all.

The principal qualifications for the game are steady nerve and eye and good judgment of force, with an added ability to avoid knolls and sand-pits, which, in the technical terms of the Scotch game, are called 'hazards.'

It is not a game which would induce men of elegant leisure to compete in, but those who have strong wind and good muscle may find in it a splendid exercise for their abilities, and plenty of chance to emulate each other in skill and physical endurance.

This astonishing nonsense about a familiar game may,

FROM AN ENCAUSTIC DISH

perhaps, suggest distrust of the accounts which travellers give of savage religions.

If one may judge by the old Dutch tiles in the possession of Mr. W. L. Purves, and most kindly lent by him for reproduction here, the Dutch played a more golf-like and less frantic kind of golf than the Belgians, a game more suitable to men of elegant leisure. Engravings of the seventeenth century show Dutch skaters playing on the ice. I am informed that in an old picture at Neuchâtel there is actually a representation of *putting*.

A more genteel and courtly foreign game, sister to golf, is *Le Jeu de Mail*. The great authority on this is Lauthier's rare 'Jeu de Mail.'[1] An early but inadequate and contemptuous account of the *Jeu de Mail* is given by Hieronymus Mercurialis.[2] He calls it *Pila-Malleus*, and says:

> Hunc procul dubio inter exercitationes tardas atque remissas collocandum esse omnes affirmant, cumque virgis illis pilas in circum ferreum impellentibus agatur, necnon modo stando modo ambulando exerceatur.

Hieronymus, who perhaps had never played, and I do not see how he *could* play at Venice, thinks jeu de mail a game for old men. But this was not at all Lauthier's view, and he was a professional. Lauthier describes the attitude and 'swing' at pell mell in words that apply equally well to golf. The boxwood ball could be hit 400 yards, probably, on a smooth hard surface like that of the Mall in London, where Pepys saw the Duke of York play. The Duke was a golfer. The club was a light supple croquet mallet. A few heads of clubs of this sort are in the little museum of the Club House at St. Andrews. The game of pell mell is probably older in Scotland than England, and was borrowed from our 'auld ally' of France. Queen Mary Stuart played both golf and pell mell at St. Andrews after Darnley's death, whereas the Mall was only made in London after the restoration of Charles II. Madame de Sévigné refers to the jeu de mail several times.

[1] I have only once seen a copy, in the Beckford sale. It was purchased by a bookseller, and offered in his catalogue for ten guineas. Not expecting to write a history of Golf, I did not buy it at this ransom. In M. Cohen's catalogue of French illustrated books of the eighteenth century, it is priced at five francs. But M. Morgand has not succeeded in procuring a copy for me. The matter is reprinted in 'L'Académie des Jeux,' without the interesting plates. Some of these are reproduced in Dr. Prior's work on *Croquet*.

[2] *De Arte Gymnastica*. Venetiis, 1573. Published by the Junta. There are earlier editions.

St.-Simon says, 'le mail est un jeu presque oublié.' The rules of the game need not be given here; generally speaking the aim was to 'loft' the ball, in fewer strokes than your adversary took, through an elevated iron ring, the *circum ferreum* of Hieronymus Mercurialis. This is clearly the same game as golf in idea. But the course was narrow, and sometimes, apparently, bordered by a palisade.

Such, then, are the foreign games, cousins or sisters of golf. But whether golf was developed in Scotland only out of one of these, or whether it was carried hither from Holland (where a picture by Cuyp shows us a little girl armed with regular clubs, on links by the sea),[1] or whether, again, Holland borrowed from Scotland, are difficult points. It is certain that, in the reign of James VI., the Scotch bought their balls from Holland, so that James put on a prohibitive tariff, as it was not then the crazy fashion to encourage foreign at the expense of home manufactures. This looks as if golf had its native seat in Holland. However this may be, to write the history of golf as it should be done demands a thorough study of all Scottish Acts of Parliament, Kirk Sessions records, memoirs, and in fact of Scottish literature, legislation, and history, from the beginning of time. Unfortunately it is not possible for me to devote the whole of my declining years to this research. A young man must do it, and he will be so ancient before he finishes the toil that he will scarce see the flag on the short hole at St. Andrews from the tee. A briefer, a more hasty survey is the most that can be attempted

FROM AN ENCAUSTIC TILE

---

[1] The picture was seen in a French shop by a Scotch player, but was sold to some one in Amsterdam.

by one who has resigned the ambition of being the Gibbon of golf. As an earlier student remarks,[1] golf was popular, a game of the people, as early as 1457. Even then Parliament was trying to 'put it down' in the interests of archery. The English were our masters at this pastime, which was more important than golf before the general use of firearms. *That the fut ball and golf be utterly cryit dune* was the stern ordinance of an iron time, in which, however, we have no documentary evidence that 'irons' were used. About every twenty years afterwards, for some considerable period, golf was thus denounced. But it was to no purpose. Golf has thus historical records far more ancient than cricket can display. As to its *Origin*, that, we have seen, is as dark as all other origins. The game, in idea, is very simplicity. A number of holes are made at irregular distances, and he wins who can put the ball into the hole in the smallest number of strokes. All the variety comes from the nature of the ground, now rough, now smooth, now grassy, now sandy.

Golf was a *popular* game, as we have said ; this is proved by frequent denunciations of golf-playing on Sunday. In 1592 and 1593 the Town Council of Edinburgh contributed to the pious gloom of their country by forbidding this harmless and healthy amusement on Sundays. John Henrie and Pat Rogie, early martyrs of the club, were prosecuted for 'playing of the Gowff on the Links of Leith every Sabbath the time of the sermonses.' At Perth, Robert Robertson suffered in the same cause, and sat in the seat of repentance, in 1604. There is a seat of repentance in the town kirk of St. Andrews, the City of Martyrs. I have looked on it with reverence, and sat in it with pious pride. Many a long driver, many a 'fell' putter must have consecrated by his weight this inestimable relic. The old Church, the Catholic Church, never persecuted anybody for playing golf. The early Stuarts, on the English throne, wanted their Scotch subjects to play after church, but, of course, that was enough to prevent a true Scot from playing. What ! amuse

[1] *Golf*. Edinburgh. Clark, 1875.

oneself by royal command? Death sooner. But Mr. Hay Fleming points out to me that Prelates as well as Presbyters persecuted Sunday golf.

April 27, 1651.—The which day James Rodger, Johne Rodger, Johne Howdan, Andrew Howdan, and George Patersone, were complained upon for playing at the golf upon ane Lord's day; were ordained to be cited the next day.

May 4.—The which day compaired the aforementioned persons, and confessed their prophaning of the Lord's day by playing at the golf; were ordained to make their publick repentance the next day.[1]

January 30, 1621.—David Hairt.—The quhilke day David Hairt, prenteis to Gilbert Banhop wrycht, confest prophanatione of the Sabboth in playing at the goff in the park on the Sabboth aftirnone in tyme of preaching; and therefor is ordenit to pay *ad pios usus* vjs. viij*d*. &c.[2]

Golf was a royal, as well as a popular, game, and was played by the gentry. In 1503, in the Royal Accounts, we find 2*l*. 2*s*. 'for the King to play at the golf with the Earl of Bothwell.' Only nine shillings were paid for the Royal club and balls; probably he had a bet on with Bothwell. Clubs cost a shilling each, and balls were four shillings the dozen. Needless to say that these balls were of leather, stuffed with feathers.[3] In 1603, James VI. appointed William Mayne to be royal club-maker, and in 1618 he gave James Melvill a monopoly of ball-making at four shillings (Scots?) each ball. Balls from Holland, as we have remarked, were pretty heavily taxed, for this was before the delightful discovery that it is good for a country to be undersold by foreign cheap labour. From a Harleian MS. we learn that the ill-fated Prince Henry, bemoaned by Chapman and other poets, was a golfer, and that the play was 'not unlike to pale maille.' An earlier account of golf as a student's game at St Andrews seems to have escaped

[1] *Register of the Kirk Session of Humbie*, printed in Maitland Miscellany, i. 440.
[2] *Register of the Kirk Session of Stirling*, printed in Maitland Miscellany, i. 458. [3] Clark, p. vii.

the diligence of Mr. Clark; it is given by Melvill in his 'Autobiography' (Edinburgh, 1842). Melvill was in his fourth year at St. Andrews, in 1574.

And I haid my necessaire honestlie aneuch of my father, but nocht else; for archerie and goff, I haid bow, arrose, glub and balls, but nocht a purs for catchpall and tavern, sic was his fatherlie wisdom for my weill.

'Catchpall' was a kind of rackets. If Melvill had only one 'glub' he must have been sadly to seek in bunkers. Melvill, who was taught the game at Logie Montrose by the minister, Mr. Wilyam Gray, became Professor of Theology in St. Andrews. Perhaps he kept up his play, but no clubs are mentioned in the inventory of his possessions. He speaks of a queer feature of the Reformation: the kirk-rents of the priory were 'spendit at the goff, archerie, good cheer, &c.'[1]

A bishop had once worse luck with the devil at golf than M. Deulin's *Grand Choleur*, at least it may be presumed that the two men whom the bishop saw, though nobody else saw them, pursuing him with drawn swords at golf, were diabolical. He cast away his clubs, went home, 'tooke bed instantlie, and died, not giving any token of repentance for that wicked course he had embraced.' So says the Presbyterian Row, but he does not tell us what particular mistake about his 'course' the bishop had made. Anybody may heel a ball, and have to play an unconventional 'course;' it is not a hanging matter, unless, indeed, he played a 'hanging-ball.' This bishop was he of Galloway, Gavin Hamilton, 1610–1612. Before his time, in 1585, golf had reached the Orkneys; James Dickson, writing from Kirkwall, says, 'Ye will remember to bring with you one dozen of common golf ballis to me and David Moncrieff.'[2]

Among illustrious golfers it is inspiriting to find the great Montrose, who patronised St. Andrews, as well as Leith Links.[3]

[1] P. 127.   [2] *Correspondence of Sir Patrick Warn*, 1882, p. 341.
[3] 'On May 19, our hero (Montrose) is hard at golf on the Links of St. Andrews; but the 24th of that same month is noted as "the beginning of my

These were of old the metropolitan Links of Scotland, and of the world, being 'within a mile of Edinburgh Town.' That a good many clubs were used then as now, appears from Montrose's purchasing a set of six, besides having some 'auld anes' mended.[1] The anecdote of Charles I. breaking off a match at Leith because news came of the Irish Rebellion is very well known.[2] The King might have remembered how Drake finished his game of bowls, with the Armada signalled. If his Majesty had holed out, like a resolute sportsman, the rebellion would neither have been better nor worse, but, perhaps, Charles would have been a different man, with a different fate. Possibly he was four down with six to play, but even that would be no excuse.[3]

lord's sickness." For the last month the boy had been feasting like an alderman, and riding like an Arab. The scene changes, and now he is disclosed to us in a sick chamber, passing through the phases of an alarming illness to convalescence and cherished with various delicacies, bespeaking the well-cared-for invalid; such as chickens, jelly, sack and sugar, and possets, the daily purveyor of the same being "James Pett's dochter," that is to say, the daughter of the man who provided him with golf clubs and bows.'—Napier's *Life of Montrose*, p. 38.

'"Six bowstrings to my lord (Montrose's father) cost nine shillings;" and "ane dozen goiff-balls to my lord," three pounds. This last would seem to have been rather an expensive indulgence; as "the tailor that made ane stand of claiths to my lord" is only paid four pounds. Thus, so far as the exterior man was concerned, the value of the old earl as he stood in a new suit was not much beyond a dozen golf balls.

'This vigorous prosecution of archery was no less vigorously diversified with golfing, tennis, hunting and hawking. A week rarely passes throughout which we do not discover the young collegian distributing liberally, one day "to a boy carrying my lord's quiver and bow that day," and another "to the boy who carried my lord's clubs to the field." Sometimes, when on his return to St. Andrews from Edinburgh, he passes a day at Leith, where we find him expending ten shillings "for two golf balls, my lord going to golf there," and also sixteen shillings "for balls in the tennis court at Leith."'—*Ibid.* p. 48.

'On the ninth day after his marriage there is a sum paid "to ane going to St. Andrews for clubs and ball to my lord;" and also for "sax new clubs, and dressing some auld anes, and for balls." Immediately follows another payment, "my lord being in Montrose at golf, for stabling the horse."'—*Ibid.* p. 70.

[1] Napier's *Memoirs of Montrose*. Edinburgh, 1856.
[2] *Transactions of Society of Antiquaries of Scotland*, 1792.
[3] Campbell's *History of Leith*. 1827.

In the time of his son, James II. (then Duke of York), we hear of the 'fore-cadie' who ran in front, to mark the ball down. Such a minister is needed at Wimbledon, and very much more at Bungay Common, but at St. Andrews the decay of the whins makes the 'fore-cadie' superfluous. Dickson, the cadie, or caddie, became a club-maker, and founded a house which did well in the last century. Professionals were then unknown apparently, for when James wanted a Scotch partner to play a foursome with two Englishmen, he was recommended to choose John Paterson, a shoemaker. Paterson's house, the Golfer's Land, is figured in Mr. Clark's book. It is 77 in the Canongate. The cognisance of the lucky shoemaker who won the match for James is a hand, dexter, grasping a club, with the motto 'Far and Sure.' The inscription by Pitcairne, a Scot who wrote elegiacs, is dated 1727. I know not on what authority he makes the first syllable in *Patersonus* long.

FROM A TILE

The Duke of York may have made golf known in England. In the 'Westminster Drollery' (London, 1671), p. 28, occurs:

> Thus all our life long we were frolick and gay,
> . . . .
> At Goff and at Football, and when we have done
> These innocent sports we'll laugh and lie down,
>   *And to each pretty lass*
>   *We will give a green gown.*

The betting in those days was considerable, in pounds Scots, and may have reached the modern half-crown on the round. But no less than twenty guineas were competed for by Porteous, of 'The Heart of Midlothian,' and Alexander Elphinstoune. Carlyle of Inveresk was present at the Porteous troubles, and was himself a great golfer. His account of play in England, 1798, deserves to be extracted from his 'Autobiography' (Edinburgh, 1860).

Garrick was so friendly to John Home that he gave a dinner to his friends and companions at his house at Hampton, which he did but seldom. He had told us to bring golf clubs and balls that we might play at that game on Molesey Hurst. We accordingly set out in good time, six of us in a landau. As we passed through Kensington, the Coldstream Regiment were changing guard, and, on seeing our clubs, they gave us three cheers in honour of a diversion peculiar to Scotland; so much does the remembrance of one's native country dilate the heart, when one has been some time absent. The same sentiment made us open our purses and wherewithal to drink the 'Land o' Cakes.' Garrick met us by the way, so impatient he seemed to be for his company. There were John Home, and Robertson, and Wedderburn, and Robert and James Adam, and Colonel David Wedderburn, who was killed when commander of the army in Bombay in the year [1773]. . . . Immediately after we arrived we crossed the river to the golfing ground, which was very good. None of the company could play but John Home and myself and Parson Black from Aberdeen. . . . Garrick had built a handsome temple, with a statue of Shakespeare in it, in his lower gardens, on the banks of the Thames which was separated from the upper one by a high road, under which there was an archway which united the two gardens. Garrick, in compliment to Home, had ordered the wine to be carried to this temple, where we were to drink it under the shade of the copy of that statue to which Home had addressed his pathetic verses on the rejection of his play. The poet and the actor were equally gay and well pleased with each other, on this occasion, with much respect on the one hand, and a total oblivion of animosity on the other; for vanity is a passion that is easy to be entreated, and unites freely with all the best affections. Having observed a green mound in the garden opposite the archway, I said to our landlord, that while the servants were preparing the collation in the temple I would surprise him with a stroke at the golf, as I should drive a ball through his archway into the Thames once in three strokes. I had measured the distance with my eye in walking about the garden, and accordingly, at the second stroke, made the ball alight in the mouth of the gateway, and roll down the green slope into the river. This was so dexterous that he was quite surprised, and begged the club of me by which such a feat had been performed. We passed a very agreeable afternoon, and it is hard to say which were happier, the landlord and landlady or the guests.[1]

Forbes, of Culloden, the judge, was also a keen amateur, and his name brings us to 'The Goff,' an Heroicomical poem in three cantos.[2] The author was Thomas Matheson, a 'writer' or attorney. The piece answers, in golfing history, to 'The Kentish Cricketers,' also to Love's poem, quoted in the Badminton book of 'Cricket.' The piece is in the mock heroic vein, but throws some light on the game and its terminology. For example, 'hot sandy *face*' is used, meaning a bunker. 'These old faces of our infancy' still give much trouble, as a ball lying immediately under one of them is apt to hit it, when played, and lose all its velocity. The great players then, at Leith, were Duncan Forbes of Culloden, Dalrymple, Rathsay, Crosse, Leslie, Aston, and Biggar. The club was 'of finest ash.'

> Pond'rous with lead and fenced with horn, the head,
> The work of Dickson, who in Letha dwells,
> And in the art of making clubs excels.

This Dickson was much more probably a descendant of the Duke of York's caddie than the veteran himself, who must have been at least a hundred. The ball-maker was Bobson,

> Who, with matchless art,
> Shapes the firm hide, connecting every part.
> Then in a socket sets the well-stitched hide,
> And through the eyelet drives the downy tide;
> Crowds urging crowds the forceful brogue impels,
> The feathers harden, and the leather swells.
> He grins and sweats, yet grins and urges more,
> Till scarce the turgid globe contains its store.

---

[1] *Autobiography of Alexander Carlyle.*   [2] Edinburgh, 1743.

Bobson was a St. Andrews man.

> Such is famed Bobson, who in Andrea thrives,
> And such the ball each vig'rous hero drives.

In the match one of the heroes hits a sheep, the shepherd kicks the ball into 'a gaping face,' and the player throws his iron at the shepherd, and hits his dog. He then plays out of the bunker. One player lies within two club lengths of the hole, playing the one off two. The other lofts over the road, and holes out, a gobble. As for the opponent,

> Seized with surprise th' affrighted hero stands,
> And feebly tips the ball with trembling hands.
> The creeping ball its want of force complains,
> A grassy tuft the loitering orb detains ;

and the hole is halved, as far as history can deduce fact from divine song.

Golf, by the way, enters the history of a person more romantic than great Bobson—namely, Dame Margaret Ross, the original of Lady Ashton, in the 'Bride of Lammermoor.'

There is a tradition [writes Colonel Fergusson] that she found means to convert herself into a golf-ball for the express purpose of spoiling her political adversary's game. Can you conceive a meaner trick? Thus when a hole was about to be 'halved' and a gentle touch with the putter was all that was wanted to hole out and so divide, her ladyship, by rolling the eighth of an inch to one side, caused the hole to be lost!

I don't believe the tradition ; for this reason. To act in this way she must, I should say, have retained a certain amount of sense, and sensation. If so, fancy her feelings when teed and sent hissing through the air with a *skelp* of a cleek, *côté de pile*, or still worse, being hacked to pieces in a bunker with a sand-iron laid in with strong arms and lost temper.

The only references I have to this are, 'A Satyre on the Familie of Stairs'—a very bitter piece beginning

> 'Stair's neck, minde, wyfe, sons, grandsons and the rest,
> Are wry, fals, witch, pests, parricid, possesst.'

That is to say, respectively.

> 'He *jure postliminii* did transub
> Himself to ball, the Parliment to club
> Which will him holl when right teased at one blow;
> Or els Sir Patrick will be shinnie goe.'[1]

What that means I don't know; but you may find the context in a *Book of Scottish Pasquils*, by J. Maidment, pp. 181-184.

So much for Dame Margaret of Balneil.

Colonel Fergusson has also kindly recalled my memory of a passage, 'The Muses Threnodie, or the Mirthful Mourning for the Death of the Gall,' 1638. This was the book whence Sir Walter got the name 'Gabions' applied by him to old *bibelots* in general, hence 'Reliquiæ Trotcosienses, or the Gabions of Jonathan Oldbuck,' a catalogue of his treasures at Abbotsford.

At p. 18 of 'The Muses Threnodie' the author, Henry Adamson, writes:

> And now I must mourn for Gall since he is gone
> And ye, my *Gabions*, help me him to mone.
>
> . . . .
>
> And ye, my clubs, you must no more prepare
> To make your balls flee whistling in the Air,
> But hing your heads, and bow your crooked crags,
> And dress you all in sack cloath and in rags;
> No more to see the sun and fertile fields,
> But closely keep you mourning in your bields.
>
> . . . .
>
> And when you cry make all your crags to fall
> And shiver when you sing. Alas! for *Gall*.[2]

A note on this makes the earliest mention I know of 'Bushwhacking' on the long grass and whins of *inland* greens, as Wimbledon, Ascot, and, pre-eminently, Bungay Common. A

---

[1] 'Sir Patrick Murray wes the representative of Stranraer in Parliament, put in there be the Lady Stairs, to whom she promised Old Nick's assistance if he voted her way in Parliament, and accordingly she ordered his ball (as in the preceding leafe) while at golfe.'—R.M.

[2] Craigs = necks. The *crooked craigs* of the golf clubs is, I think, idiomatic.

note in the 'Threnodie' says, 'the pastime is interrupted during the summer months by the luxuriency of the grass . . . milch cows, &c.'

Returning to the eighteenth century, and apologising for having driven into the whins of seventeenth-century anecdote, we read [1] about golf just before the invasion of our rightful king, Charles III. :

On application of several persons of honour skilled in the ancient and healthful exercise of the goff, an act of the town council of Edinburgh was passed on March 7, appointing their treasurer to cause make a silver club, of 15l. value, to be play'd for on the links of Leith the first Monday of April annually. The act appoints that the candidates' names be booked some day of the week preceeding the match, paying 5s. each at booking ; that they be matched into parties of two's, or of three's, if their number be great, by lot; that the player who shall have won the greatest number of holes, be victor; and if two or more shall have won an equal number, that they play a round by themselves in order to determine the match ; that the victor be stiled 'Captain of the Goff ;' that he append a piece of gold or silver to the club ; that he have the sole disposal of the booking-money, the determination of disputes among goffers, with the assistance of two or three of the players, and the superintendency of the links. Accordingly, the first match was play'd on April 2, by ten gentlemen, and won by Mr. John Rattray, surgeon in Edinburgh.

Here, next, is an extract on early Musselburgh practice :

The golf so long a favourite and peculiar exercise of the Scots is much in use here. Children are trained to it in their early days, being enticed by the beauty of the links (which lie on each side of the river between the two towns and the sea), and excited by the example of their parents. To preserve the taste for this ancient diversion, a company of gentlemen, about eighteen years ago, purchased a silver cup, which is played for annually in the month of April, and is for a year in the possession of the victor, who is obliged to append a medal to it, when he restores it to the company. The inhabitants of Musselburgh had need to watch over this precious field for health and exercise, lest in some unlucky

[1] *Scots Magazine*, vi. 197. April, 1744.

period the magistrates and council should be induced to feu it out, on pretence of increasing the revenue of the town.

At present it is a common, to which every burgess has a right of pasturage; although part of it has already been let off in feu, which has made the entry to the town, both from the east and west, less free and open than it formerly was and greatly decreased the beauty and amenity of the place.

When speaking of a young woman, reported to be on the point of marriage, 'Hout!' say they, 'How can she keep a man, who can hardly maintain herself?' As they do the work of men, their manners are masculine, and their strength and activity is equal to their work. Their amusements are of the masculine kind. On holidays they frequently play at *golf*; and on Shrove Tuesday there is a standing match at *football*, between the married and unmarried women, in which the former are always victors.[1]

We next turn to the history of Leith golfing, which was not 'dour' and solemn, but gay and convivial :

Leith was scarcely more famous for its races than for its golf-playing, the great extent and inequalities of the Links ground being peculiarly well adapted for the practice of this healthful and ancient Scottish game. Like the former, however, the golf playing on the Links of Leith has grievously degenerated from its pristine character. In the days of yore, it was conducted with a degree of frank and free hilarity which has long since ceased to animate the modern practice of this manly pastime. The solitary parties of players which may now occasionally be seen wandering over the Links, go through the business of the game with a coldness and heartlessness of manner which sufficiently announces that the true and ancient spirit of the sport is gone. They play as if it was an act of condescension to be pleased with so vulgar and simple a recreation, and stalk over the ground with a gravity which would be an acquisition to a funeral procession. No energy, and scarcely any interest, appears amongst the gentle, melancholy-looking sportsmen, who resemble more a parcel of love-lorn shepherds with crooks in their hands, than a band of jovial young fellows engaged in an active and exhilarating pastime. Matters were differently managed in the last century. Then, the greatest and wisest of the land were to be seen on the Links of Leith, mingling

---

[1] *Statistical Account of Scotland* (Inveresk).

freely with the humblest mechanics in pursuit of their common and beloved amusement. All distinctions of rank were levelled by the joyous spirit of the game. Lords of Sessions and cobblers, knights, baronets and tailors, might be seen earnestly contesting for the palms of superior dexterity, and vehemently, but good-humouredly, discussing moot points of the game, as they arose in the course of play.

There were, in particular, somewhat later than the middle of the last century, a batch of lively active old fellows, who made this good ancient pastime almost the sole business of their lives. Each of these veterans, according to Smollett, was turned fourscore, and never went a night to bed without having under their belts the best part of a gallon of claret. Before the present golf-house was built, which was in the year 1768, the merry golf-players of Leith used to frequent the house of one Straiton, who then kept a tavern at the head of the Kirkgate, on the west side, and near to the junction of the new road with the foot of Leith Walk. Here they were wont to close the day with copious libations of pure and unadulterated claret, brought, in shining pewter or silver tankards, fresh from the butt.

The manners of caddies, at this period, are commemorated by no one less than Smollett, in his 'History of Humphrey Clinker,' the history which Rebecca Sharp read with her young charges at Queen's Crawley. But he mainly speaks of street caddies, not of golfers.

The period of Bobson, and of 'The Goff,' saw the giving of a challenge prize, a silver club, by the City of Edinburgh, to the gentlemen golfers, and in 1754 a club was given at St. Andrews, and the club then more or less formally became an institution. *Stet Fortuna domus!* The early consecration of the Links to golf is vouched for on a parchment.[1] The Earl of

[1] A parchment marked on the back, in not very ancient hand, 'Licence by the city of St. Andrews to John Archbishop of St. Andrews, for making cunnig-gairs in the north part of their links, &c. dated 25th January 1552, No. 275,' which is of the following tenor, viz., 'We John, by ye mercie of God, Archbyshop of St. Andros, primat and legat notour of the haile realme of Scotland, grantis us to have obtenit licience and allowance by ye free consent of our lovitts, provest, baillies, conseill and comtie of our cittie, Sant Andros, *to plant and planis cuninggis* wtin ye north pairt of yair comon linkis, next

AN OLD DUTCH PICTURE

Elgin, and many Wemysses and Leslies, Bethunes, Cheapes, and Spens's, were among the donors of the St. Andrews silver club. Mr. David Young and Mr. John Young, professors of 'philosophy,' were also in the list. St. Andrews professorships were kept very much in certain families, during the last century. In 1766 it is interesting to see that the golfers dined at Glass's Inn, where Dr. Johnson found good entertainment, agreeably served, says Boswell, after a cold drive across Fife.

In these days men were undeniably good golfers. We cannot compare at cricket Harris with Lohmann, nor Beldham with Barnes, because the grounds of old and the style of bowling were so different from those of our time. But we do know that (considering the course as it then was) a round of St. Andrew Links, on medal day, at 94, is excellent. The green was then very narrow, and much beset with heather

adjacet to the Watter of Eddin; and yat it sall be leegim to us *to tack ye profitt of ye said cuniggis*, and to uss yaim *to our valitin and pleseur*, referring always to our said provest, balleiss, consell, and communtie, all mainer of ryt, and possessioun, privtie and communtie of ye said linkis, *bait in pastering of yair gudis, casting and lading of divott and sheratt to yair uss and profit, playing at golf, futball, shuting at all gamis* wt all other mainer of pastyme as ever yai pleiss, als weill quhair ye *said cuniggis sal be planted and plainsit as otheris pairtis of ye said linkis wtotin only closing or dyking to be maid be us of ony pairt off ye said linkis*, or ony privtie to be had be us and our successouris of ony pairt thereof; bot alawane we to tak ye profitt of the said cuniggis for our time alanarlie, sua yt nay persone sall *tak, destroy boll or delf furth*, any of ye saids cuniggis; bot the linkis and *cuniggis* to be usit in mainer foirsaid; And we thairfoir, be yir presents for us and our successouris and with consent of our chaptour, confermis, ratifeiss and approviss ye rycht and possessioun, propertie and comtie of ye said linkis in *pastering of gudis*, casting and lading of dovett and sherett, *playing at golff*, futbal, shuting at all gamis, wtt all other mainer of pastyme als weill quhair ye said cuniggis sal be *plantit* as *otheris pairts* of ye said linkis as said is; *To pertein* and *remain pecebill* and *perpetuall* with ye said *provest*, balleiss, consell, comtie, and inhabitaris of our said cittie, *without any dyking* or closing of ony pairt yairof fra them, or impediment to be maid to yaim yairuntill, in ony tyme cuming. In witnessing heirof to yir prests subscrivit with our hand, our rond feill, togedder with ye comoun seill of our chaptr, as appendit at our cittie of Santandrs ye twinty-fyve day of ye moneth of Januar, in ye yeir of God ain thousaind fyve hundreth fyftie-tua yeris, befoir yir witness, Maister Alexainder Forest, provest of Lady Moutrey; Robert Eadmylton, chalmirain, Robert Forseyth, with otheris.'—*From Session Cases, St. Andrews University*, 1804-1809.

and whin. To-day the course is perhaps a dozen strokes easier than it was only forty years ago, from the decay of Hell and other bunkers, and from the disappearance of whins. But James Durham of Largo won the silver club at 94, on September 3, 1767. This also proves the excellence of the feather balls, while they lasted. About 100 to 105 was then an average winning score. Dances were already given at the autumn meeting, and a *fête champêtre*, which apparently was *not* held in the open air. There is little joy in St. Andrews picnics, without sun, or trees, or brooks. The patronage of St. Andrews by William IV. is hardly part of the sportive history of golf, but the Royal Medal endures. The arrival of Tom Morris as green-keeper on the death of Alan Robertson, of great Bobson's line, in 1864, is also a point of interest.

Other important clubs are Musselburgh (1774) and Blackheath. At Musselburgh, Dr. Carlyle, he who saw the Porteous Riot, and the fight at Preston Pans, was winner of the medal in 1775. This club used to present the local schoolboys with golf balls, and offered 'a creel and shawl' to the best golfer among the fishwives. Such gallantry is rare among golfers, who have excellent reasons for objecting to the flutter of petticoats on the green. The Edinburgh Burgess Golfing Society claims the date of 1735. They drank rum chiefly, and rum which paid 44*l.* of Government duties, in July 1816, was drunk out by October 2, 1817. So whisky was laid in.

The history of the Scotch game in foreign parts, England, France, India, Canada, Texas, need not detain us long. The game at Blackheath may have begun in the time of James VI.; the regular minutes of the Knuckle Club were kept very much later, and are, or were, quite as much convivial as sporting. We find entries of 'bets of gallons of claret;' the round was done in such figures as 132, 125. In 1822 it was proposed to alter the mystic name of 'Knuckle Club' to 'Blackheath Golf Club.' This was carried, and the ἀπόρρητα of the Knuckle Club were destroyed.

The club at Pau was informally existing early in the fifties.

In 1857 the Duke of Hamilton gave a gold challenge medal. The club was now formally constituted, and the ground on the haugh laid out. The old rent was 25 francs to the poor box, now it is near 1,000 francs. The Ladies' Club began in 1874.

Majora canamus!

Blackheath was the mother of Bombay, Westward Ho, Wimbledon (with its two clubs),[1] and Hoylake. Thence sprang golf all over England, by seaside links and on deplorable commons, where the hazards are whins, and the 'green' is a foot deep in vegetation.

The historic evolutions of golf have few of the changes which we trace in cricket. Clubs, and balls and rules were always pretty much what they still are. In the *reliquaire* at St. Andrews are weapons of the last century: they are like ours, but heavier. The club heads are bigger, and much more curved. The irons are like battle-axes, and extremely scooped. A first sketch of the brassy, a wondrous weapon with iron socket, iron foot, and head made of leather in layers, may be seen there. The balls are excellent, the sewing of the seams is extremely neat, but they were expensive—when gutta-percha came in (about 1848), and made the art of Bobson obsolete. Dr. Graham sang in 1848:

> Though gouf be of our games most rare,
> Yet, truth to speak, the wear and tear
> Of balls were felt to be severe
>   And source of great vexation;
>
> When Gourlay's balls cost half a crown,
> And Allan's not a farthing down,
> The feck o's wad been harried soon
>   In this era of taxation.
>
> Right fain were we to be content
> Wi' used up balls new lick't wi' paint,
> That ill concealed baith scar and rent—
>   Balls scarcely fit for younkers.

---

[1] It is needless, and might be dangerous, to say *why* there are *two* clubs.

> And though our best wi' them we tried,
> And nicely every club applied,
> They whirred, and fuffed, and dooked, and shied
>   And sklentit into bunkers.

As for the gutta-percha balls,

> Ye're keen and certain at a putt—
> Nae weet your sides e'er opens up—
> And though for years your ribs they whup,
>   Ye'll never moutt a feather!

Well may the poet cry,

> Hail, gutta percha, precious gum!

The earlier 'gutties' took on paint badly, and were not hammered in the now familiar way, but they were undoubtedly better, cheaper, more durable, than the old productions of Bobson and Gourlay. Changes in the rules, and the difficulty of making an œcumenical set of rules for a game in which so much depends on various accidents of ground, are dealt with elsewhere. Elsewhere, too, are legends of great old golfers and 'singles' long ago. It does not become the mere archæological duffer to describe heroes who were seen by living eyes, and are appreciated by living memories.[1]

---

[1] The writer of this chapter has to thank Monsieur Charles Michel, Mr. Hay Fleming, Colonel Alexander Fergusson, Miss Isabel Bruce, and Mrs. Ogilby for much information and some original research. His obligations to *Golf* (Messrs. Clark) are considerable. For French games like golf, the student is referred to an essay, *De quelques Jeux populaires de l'ancienne France*, by M. Siméon Luce, Académie des Inscriptions et Belles-Lettres.

CHAPTER II

GENERAL REMARKS ON THE GAME

BY LORD WELLWOOD

SPINDLE ROCK

IT is no light matter in these days to undertake to make general remarks on the game of golf, as we cannot but feel that upon this subject we follow very exhaustive writers. That golf has a history and a literature of its own was demonstrated about fifteen years ago, when much antiquarian and statistical information, and many articles and songs written by lovers of the game, were collected in an interesting and handsome volume by the skilled hands of Mr. Robert Clark. Then, as the game spread not only in Scotland but throughout England, a succession of manuals appeared; frequent descriptive sketches were published in newspapers and magazines, and lately instructive works on the theory and practice of golf have been written by players of distinction and experience. It is thus impossible to make general remarks on the game without the risk of repetition or without trenching more or less on the province of one or other of our colleagues. We undertake the duty on the distinct understanding that we are permitted to roam at large over the whole subject, and, at the same time, not be held responsible for the accuracy of our history or our science.

Golf affords a wide field of observation for the philosopher and the student of human nature. To play it aright requires nerve, endurance, and self-control, qualities which are essential to success in all great vocations. On the other hand, golf is occasionally peculiarly trying to the temper, although it must be said that when the golfer forgets himself his outbursts are usually directed against inanimate objects, or showered upon his own head. It must also be admitted that in some aspects golf is a selfish game in which each man fights with keenness and calculation for his own hand, grasping at every technicality and glorying in the misfortunes of his opponents. It will thus be seen that, whether the philosopher's views of life are rose-coloured or cynical, he will find ample material to interest him while he watches the game. We must warn him, however, that if in the pursuit of his study he insists on accompanying matches, he may find that he proves an excuse for many a miss, and possibly for some bad language. He must certainly be prepared for this.

It is not difficult to account for the popularity of the game. It affords, as few other games (if any) do, moderate yet sufficient exercise for all; sufficient for the young and strong, and yet not too violent for those who are older or less robust. While it is simple enough for the unambitious to play with pleasure, it demands, if it is to be played really well, quite as high a degree of skill as cricket, tennis, or any other first-class game. It is thus a game for players of all degrees and ages; for the veteran of seventy, as for the boy of seven. It cannot be learnt too soon, and it is never too late to begin it. It is a touching sight to see one who has grown grey in the service of his country, in the army, at the bar, or in the church, sitting meekly at the feet of a professor of the art, patiently practising the same stroke again and again, and humbly asking to be told what he has done wrong. It is a game for both sexes—we say this with a mental reservation. It does not require

A BAD CASE

numbers; you can play it if you can find an opponent, or even by yourself, although we do not recommend a solitary game. It can be played all the year round, except when snow is actually lying on the ground; and even then enthusiasts play it with red balls. Lastly, it is not necessarily an expensive game, provided always you do not break your clubs, or lose or maltreat your balls, or bet too much and lose your money.

The fascination which the game possesses for those who play it is only equalled by the indifference, bordering on contempt, with which it is regarded by those who do not understand it. It must have fallen to the lot of most golfers to endeavour to get a visitor to take an interest in golf. After the theory of the game has been carefully explained to him, he is led out to witness, say, a first-rate professional match. All is in vain; the longest drives, the most deadly putting, the wonderful smallness of the average number of strokes taken to the hole; all these things excite not the slightest surprise. He sees nothing in them except an unnecessary expenditure of energy and care upon a very simple and easy game, and you are lucky if you have not to withdraw him with shame on account of his making audible and comic criticisms on the players' attitudes:—

'What is the matter with the man's legs?' or some such remark.

The truth is, the game is not so easy as it seems. In the first place, the terrible *inertia* of the ball must be overcome. Until it is properly 'addressed' it will not move on; and many are the rejected addresses which fall to the lot of the beginner. At cricket, the ball, if you fail to hit it otherwise, may come against your bat, or your leg, or your head, for that matter, and thus make runs for your side, and at the worst you are bowled or caught out, and there is an end of you, but the game goes on. But at golf, until you can personally (if you are playing a single) induce the ball to move in the right direction, the game is at a standstill, and the green is blocked. Besides, you must deal with a ball as you find it, and the beginner must distinctly understand that he will not (or should not) always find it neatly perched on a little pyramid of sand.

Now, wherein lies the difficulty of hitting that unresisting little piece of gutta-percha? Everyone knows that there are about twenty-two things to attend to in making a drive, but it may suffice to mention three or four. For instance, grasp, balance, keeping your eye on the ball, and letting your arms follow the ball.

A beginner's natural inclination is to grasp a golf club as he would a cricket bat, more firmly with the right hand than with the left, or at times equally firm with both hands. Now, in golf, in making a full drive, the club, when brought back, must be held firmly with the *left* hand, and held more loosely with the right ; because, when the club is raised above the shoulder and brought round the back of the neck, the grasp of one hand or the other must relax, and the hand to give way should be the right hand and not the left. The common failing is unconsciously to grasp the club too tightly with the right hand, the result of which is that the grasp of the left hand is relaxed, and when the head of the club reaches the ball, its nose is turned in, and the face is not brought squarely against the ball. If you examine gloves that have been worn by a good player, you will find that the left-hand glove shows more signs of wear and tear than the right-hand glove, across the palm, and between the fore-finger and thumb.

The difficulty in keeping one's balance lies in this : in preparing to strike, the player necessarily bends forward a little. In drawing back his club he raises, or should raise, his left heel from the ground, and at the end of the upward swing stands poised on his right foot and the toe or ball of the left foot. At this point there is a risk of his losing his balance, and, as he brings the club down, falling either forwards or backwards, and consequently either 'heeling' or 'toeing' the ball instead of hitting it with the middle of the face. Accuracy of hitting depends greatly on keeping a firm and steady hold of the ground with the toe of the left foot, and not bending the left knee too much.

To 'keep your eye on the ball' sounds an injunction easy to be obeyed, but it is not always so. In making any considerable stroke the player's body makes, or should make, a quarter turn; and the difficulty is to keep the head steady and the eye fixed upon the ball while doing this.

But it is not enough to keep your eye on the ball and to hit the ball with the proper part of the club. If you draw in your arms at the moment of striking, and do not let the club go freely out in the direction which you wish the ball to take, the drive will lose not only direction but force; and a cut or spin will be put upon the ball which will prevent it from lofting or running far.

All this will be explained more fully and authoritatively hereafter; but we have said enough to indicate some of the difficulties of the game which escape the notice of the uninitiated.

A fine day, a good match, and a clear green! These words sum up a golfer's dream of perfect happiness. How seldom is it fulfilled in this imperfect world of ours! He cannot command the weather. Wet is destructive to his clubs; and wind, if gusty, leads to wild driving and fills his eyes with tears when he tries to putt—a pitiable and humiliating condition. A clear green! No man can understand what land-hunger means until he has played, or tried to play, on a green which is too small for the number of players. Whatever his political views on other matters, he will at once become a rank socialist as to this, and call loudly for the compulsory allotment of those stretches of shore ground which are crying aloud to be converted into golfing greens. To make a good match, however, is to some extent in his own power; and he must be a weak or very good-natured man if he often makes a bad one. But the match once made, let him make the best of his partner. And here is an opportunity for the study of character and the exercise of tact and self-control. Never scold; if your partner is timid, it will make him nervous; if obstinate, he will sulk; if choleric, he will say unpleasant things or break his clubs. If you praise, do so sparingly and judiciously and without seeming to patronise, or his pride may take alarm; and give as little advice as possible unless you are asked for it. It is wonderful how much can be got out of even a bad player by good management and good feeling.

It must not be supposed that in order to make a good foursome match all four players must be equal. Some of the closest and pleasantest matches are those in which two first-class players have each a good second-class player as his partner. An admirable partner of the second class was the late John Blackwood, whose death was a grievous loss to the cause of golf in Scotland. He was not, and did not pretend to be, a long driver. But he scarcely ever went off the line, and his short game was deadly, especially his putting. He had the rare faculty—it could not be termed chance, because it happened so often—of holeing putts of six or eight feet. The moral effect of two or three of these in the course of a round may be imagined. Best of all, he knew exactly the limits of his own powers ; and he played to win the match, and not for his own glory. He helped to win many a match which on paper looked a certainty for the other side simply through his great qualities as a partner.

In a single, the players should be as nearly as possible equal, as giving or taking odds inevitably diminishes the interest of the game.

Singles and foursomes are both excellent in their way ; but of the two to play regularly we prefer a good foursome. It must be remembered, however, that partnership involves an accounting ; and although an erring partner at golf is not subjected to such severe and systematic heckling as at whist, he must expect to hear a good deal directly and indirectly about his shortcomings if the match is lost.

To those who look below the surface of things the scene on the teeing ground represents the land question in miniature. The order of playing off depends on priority of seisin duly taken with a pinch of sand ; the player whose ball is teed first being entitled to play first, and so on. The balls as they are teed in succession represent first, second, and third bonds (mortgages). The prior bondholders regard the postponed bondholders as squatters, and the latter retort by denouncing the others as land-grabbers. On some greens a system of registration of teeing rights has been introduced which has been found to work well. Parties who wish to play give in their names and approximately the hour at which they wish to start to the greenkeeper, and they are enabled by inspecting his list to select a vacant place and thus know when to be prepared, and are not kept waiting. Where this system does not obtain the teeing ground is a very uncomfortable place, full of malice and all uncharitableness, especially if a searching north-east wind is sweeping the course. The undignified work of scrambling and wrangling for precedence should be done by deputy; and it is a distinct advantage to have an experienced, nay, a masterful caddy at this juncture. An unprincipled player affects to know nothing whatever about his turn to play; and thus, alas! is able to take advantage of his caddy's sharp practice, if successful. Your ball being teed and your turn come, the next thing is to strike off. There is much loose talk about the length of drives. In the absence of wind an average player will do very well if he can loft his ball 120 to 140 yards. A fine player and powerful driver told us that he once tested his driving power by driving a dozen balls backwards and forwards on a day when there was little or no wind. He found that the average loft of a good drive was 140 to 150 yards; but one or two balls which were hit exceptionally cleanly flew 170 to 180 yards before landing.

A drive from the tee at the first hole is not usually very successful. The player is too much hustled and agitated by his struggles for place, especially if some one else is trying to strike off at the same moment, to take very accurate aim. It is a matter of some importance, however, that one of the party should make a fairly long drive. Each side is entitled to play their second shot before the next party can start; so much law is allowed. But whenever the second shots have been played there is a shout of 'fore!' and the cannonade from behind begins.

'Have they played their second?' 'No, only one of them.' 'Now then drive into them, touch them up!' 'Oh, let them out a bit, poor devils!' as if they were cheeping partridges and would not be fit for the table if they were taken too close. It may be noted that this feeling of contemptuous pity rapidly vanishes with each successive hole. Such are some of the exclamations to be heard on the teeing ground while a couple of short or unfortunate drivers are endeavouring to make good their escape.

The course between the teeing ground and the putting-green is called *par excellence* 'the green,' the putting-green being considered, as we shall see, a sanctuary by itself. Playing through the green is the most difficult part of the game, because you must play your ball as you find it, without any adventitious aids. There must be no patting of the ground, or teeing of the ball, or marking the sand in a bunker. It is almost against human nature not to mark the sand, but it must not be done. There was once a privileged person to whose offence in this respect all were with common consent blind. It was said that he bitterly repented of his irregularities every night; but he invariably repeated the offence next day, if necessary. One day a stranger to the green was playing in a foursome in which this gentleman was one of his opponents. The latter disappeared after his ball into a favourite bunker, and as he was absent rather a long time without any visible result, the stranger walked forward to the edge and looked in. He immediately returned with a very pale face and said to his partner in a horrified whisper, 'I say, that old fellow is teeing his ball!' to which the other replied, 'Of course he is, the dear old boy! he always does it there; what does it matter?' Then seeing his partner's face grow long he added, 'But he won't do it again this round; there's not another bunker between this and home where he can't be seen.'

In playing through the green there is full scope for the golfer's skill. If anyone doubts the necessity of skill of a high order, let him try to make a full drive with his ball in a cup, or loft a hanging ball, so as to fall dead. Many players of no mean order spend their golfing life in the vain endeavour to master such strokes, for they require wrist power and manipulation which are given to few. It is a grand sight to see the ball shoot out of an apparently impracticable cup, skim not far from the ground for sixty or eighty yards, and then soar gradually upwards till the strength of the drive is spent. This is not the place to describe the arts by which this stroke is made; but it can be made, and sometimes the ball flies nearly as far as a ball struck from the tee. Again, what sweeter sound is there to the golfer's ear than the metallic ring of the iron which accompanies a well-played approach shot! Irons are difficult to handle, but they are worth the study of a lifetime, requiring as they do a firm grasp, a supple wrist, and the eye riveted on the ball. In skilled hands they surmount difficulties which no wooden club can overcome, but in unskilled hands they are worse than useless, and serve only to cut up the turf, ruin the temper, and promote bad language.

We at one time proposed to ourselves to write a golfer's progress for the instruction and warning of youth, but the work proceeded no farther than the headings of the chapters, which ran as follows: (1) The Topped Tee-Shot; (2) The Bad Lie; (3) Driven into; (4) Passed on the Green; (5) The Black Spoon; (6) Bunkered in Port; and (7) Picked up.

Those headings tell their own sad tale—the tale of a badly-played hole, a bad start, a bad course, and a bad finish, or rather no finish at all—in short, an allegory of a misspent golfer's life. On some of the headings little need be said. We have already touched on the topped tee-shot and the bad lie, and will only add that there seem nowadays to be more bad lies than there used to be. Being 'driven into' does not necessarily imply being hit; indeed, the most refined and effective form of cruelty is not to hit the party in front, but to keep dropping balls just behind them from a long distance. The effect on the nerves of a ball landing behind you with a thud after a flight of 150 yards, just as you are addressing your ball, will be readily understood by anyone who has endured this persecution. The usual result is that after a few holes played in this fashion you beseech your tormentors to pass on and leave you in peace. It is a remarkable fact that very few people are badly hurt, or even hit, at golf, and it is equally remarkable that seldom, if ever, is there a serious breach of the

DRIVEN INTO

peace in consequence of being driven into. There is a great deal of shouting and bawling and gesticulation and waving of clubs, but it all comes to nothing. We remember a very hot-tempered man being driven into and smartly hit on the calf of the leg; but all that he did, after giving a yell caused by the pain, was calmly to order his caddy to tee the offender's ball, which he thereafter drove firmly into the sea. The man whose ball it was was also quick-tempered, and at first there was a good deal of shouting, but it all ended in words. The truth, we suppose, is that the 'driven into' to-day knows that he may be the 'driver into' to-morrow, and that it is wiser to agree that there should be give and take in the matter.

Passed on the green! The golfer's cup of humiliation is now full. He knows that the party behind mock themselves of him, and regard him as a slow-coach and a foozler, on whom it is unnecessary to waste the courtesies of golfing life, and hold him up to public ridicule and contempt as a creature to be hustled off the green with impunity. Yet this calamity should seldom occur, because, on the one hand, no party should try to pass another on the green unless the latter are playing with unreasonable deliberation; and, on the other hand, a really slow party ought to have the good sense to allow the quicker party to pass them with decency at one of the holes. A collision usually occurs in consequence of one man in the slow party being not only slow, but obstinate, and determined to take his time and stand upon his rights. Then the unseemly scrimmage begins; there is nothing like it except a bumping boat-race, in which the following boat perpetually overlaps, but cannot make its bump—save the mark! It often happens that in their burning anxiety to get past, one of the quick party misses his ball, or sends it into a bunker. Then the slow party rally, and there is a neck-and-neck race for the putting green. Even if the quick party succeed in reaching the putting green, they reach it breathless and in disorder; and the slow party pick up their balls and hurry on in hopes of having at least one parting shot from the tee at their conquerors, if one of the latter happens to make a bad tee-shot. We gladly drop the curtain on this painful scene.

The 'black spoon' requires a little explanation. If you hear your partner call for his 'black spoon,' or whatever club is his

GENERAL REMARKS ON THE GAME

equivalent for that instrument, you may take it as a signal not merely of danger, but of despair; and if you are so disposed, as a studied reflection, for such it is, upon yourself. We venture to explain our meaning by quoting a description which we gave elsewhere of this ill-omened club :—

It may be explained parenthetically that this same 'black spoon' was a name of terror, especially to Mr. Burton's partners, as it was only invoked when the Burton cause was *in extremis*; and then not so much as a helpful *deus ex machinâ* as a solemn protest and last dying testimony that everything that man might do had been done to retrieve his partner's mistakes. It had a head like a canoe bottomed with brass, and the shaft like the piston of an engine; and when in full swing boomed through the air like a cannon ball. It was created by a well-known maker towards the beginning of this century (the brass bottom was comparatively modern), and doubtless would have seen the next, for a *force majeure*, which no mortal spoon cold have resisted.

'Bunkered in port' and 'picked up' may be taken together : the one almost inevitably follows the other. We all know the tremor with which we confront the frowning face of the bunker which lies between us and the hole; and we all know the anxiety and terror with which, under the same circumstances, we see our partner confidently attempting a lofting-shot—a stroke which, to our knowledge, he never yet succeeded in doing properly. There he goes! just as you expected, either digging up a square foot of turf and leaving the ball in the hole thus made, or catching the ball clean, and driving it hard into the face of the bunker, where it lies half buried, like a sugar-plum on the top of a cake. A smothered growl, a wild blow with the niblick, which drives the ball out of sight, and the ball is picked up and the hole is over.

But a ball may be picked up under circumstances still more painful. A match had run to the last putt. One player had holed out and secured a half of the hole, but the other, who was dormy, had an easy, short putt for the match. Whether it was that the sight of his enemy's ball lying snugly in the hole displeased him, or that it took his eye off his putt, he walked away from his ball and said to his caddy, an inexperienced lad, 'Pick up that ball.'

Instead of the ball in the hole, the caddy promptly picked up *his master's* ball ! There are some griefs which are too deep for tears. Without a word or a sigh the bereaved golfer turned his face to the wall—and went to lunch.

Once upon the putting-green the slowest party is safe from persecution for the time. According to the present law and practice, the putting-green is a sanctuary ; no man may drive into or molest a party on the putting-green. You might as well shoot a partridge on its nest, or commit the terrible crime known to the law of Scotland as 'Hamesucken,' *i.e.* assaulting a man in his own house. Public opinion would not stand it ; and, conscious of this, the slow player is very deliberate in his movements. His methods vary. Sometimes, after a careful examination of the ground between the ball and the hole, he sinks into a cataleptic condition and stands, or rather crouches, with the face of his putter glued to the ball while you might count a hundred. At last a faint tremor of the limbs is perceptible, the putter is slowly drawn back and then jerked forward, and for good or evil the putt is made. At other times he spends just as much time squatting behind the ball examining the lie of the ground ; and then suddenly darting upon the ball, he takes it by surprise, as it were, and runs it in.

Meanwhile, what are the rest of the party doing? Some parties on the putting-green present the appearance of a cricket-field set for a fast bowler with all the fields behind the wicket. Some players cannot endure that anyone should stand in front of them, or indeed, within sight, while the solemn deed is being done ; and accordingly, all are waived aside with the exception of the player's own caddy, who is permitted to remain with him till the last moment, like a chaplain at an execution. Usually, however, players and caddies crowd to see the last of the ball as closely as the temper of the player will permit.

Now, why should the putting-green be inviolate any more than the 'green'? Why should the wielders of the putter have a close time which is denied to those who toil and dig with the long spoon and the niblick? We see no reason why, after an incubation of, say, forty seconds, the clôture should not be applied on a majority of both parties standing up in their places. The man who has to follow the squatter might be trusted to vote with the opposition.

Joking apart, putting is a serious, nay, at times, an awful matter. You are playing a match of, say, eighteen holes, and have reached the putting-green of the last hole. The match is all even ; your partner has laid you within three feet of the hole and one of your opponents playing the odds has laid his ball about a foot from the hole on the far side. This being the home hole, a large gallery is looking on ; and you know that there is a good deal of money on the match.

'You've that for the match !'

Who can hear these words unmoved? The result of a round's driving and lofting and bunker practice and putting hangs upon that 30-inch putt, long enough to miss and short enough if missed to disgrace. How absurdly easy it looks ! To all appearances a straight level putt. If you were not playing a match you would back yourself to hole it ten times running. But you *are* playing a match ; and now that you look at it you see that the ground is not quite level. There is an awkward side slope between your ball and the hole, and you must either borrow or put a spin on the ball and run it straight at the hole. But if you adopt the latter course you may leave your partner a stimy or run out of holing. What are you to do? You can of course secure a half, but in order to win you must play boldly. Your partner, with transparent bravado which ill conceals his anxiety, has handed his putter to his caddy as if the match were over and has half turned away towards the club-house, and you hear one of your opponents whisper, 'He's not in yet.' Your confessor is beside you, exhorting and directing.

'Take the putter, sir ; you can't miss it ; over that ; be up.'

Well, you cannot stand shivering over it much longer ; so

with tingling nerves you seize your putter and *address* the ball. The confessor retires and the silence deepens—at length the blow falls, the ball disappears, and the match is won. Your partner falls upon your neck, and the party breaks up and vanishes like a vision in a magician's mirror.

Or—but the alternative is too painful to dwell upon. The putt missed, the hole overrun, your partner hopelessly stimied. Such a moment suggests self-destruction, and makes even a man *constantis animi* feel that he had rather have been taken red-handed in crime than miss such a putt before the eyes of the golfing world. Even your own familiar caddy (who has probably lost a small bet by the miss) has not a word of consolation for you.

As to the proper position and mode of putting we do not pretend to speak with authority. In our opinion the knees should be bent as little as possible; the more erect the position the better will the view of the line to the hole be, and the more firmly you will stand—a matter of great importance in putting as in other parts of the game. In putting the work is done by the right hand, holding with firm but delicate grip. The left hand should merely guide the club. The putter should swing evenly and without jerking, like a pendulum, the length of the swing (we use the word in a very restricted sense) being proportioned to the length of the putt. We recommend that at the end of the backward swing a very slight pause be made before beginning the return movement. This, in our experience, is of great service, especially in long putts, in enabling the player to calculate or weigh the strength to be applied.

Having now conducted the golfer to the end of his round (the hole being the round in miniature), we shall proceed to say a few words on certain matters which hang on the fringe or skirts, so to speak, of our subject; and first and appropriately of:—

Women's Rights.—We do not know that a claim for absolute equality has as yet been made; but the ladies are advancing in all pursuits with such strides, or leaps and bounds,

A GOLF WIDOW

whichever expression may be thought the more respectful, that it will, no doubt, not be long before such a claim is formulated. How is it to be met? Now, it will not do for the men to take too high ground in this matter. Want of strength is not a sufficient objection, because everyone knows that clean hitting more than strength is required. And, besides, in the mere question of strength and endurance there are some men with whom it would go hard if they were pitted for a summer's day single against some ladies we wot of. Again, it will not do to urge that the game is unfeminine. It is not more unfeminine than tennis and other sports in which ladies nowadays engage freely. No ; if any objection is to be entertained, it must be based on more subtle grounds, some of which we shall, not without fear and trembling, attempt presently to shadow forth.

It will be convenient to consider this delicate question under three heads : (1) the abstract right of women to play golf at all ; (2) their right to play the 'long round' with or without male companions ; and (3) their right to accompany matches as spectators.

On the first question our conscience is clear. We have always advocated a liberal extension of the right of golfing to women. Not many years ago their position was most degraded. Bound to accompany their lords and masters to golfing resorts for the summer months, they had to submit to their fathers, husbands, and brothers playing golf all day and talking golfing shop the whole of the evening, while they themselves were hooted off the links with cries of 'fore,' if they ventured to appear there. We therefore gladly welcomed the establishment of ladies' links—a kind of Jews' quarter—which have now been generously provided for them on most of the larger greens. Ladies' links should be laid out on the model, though on a smaller scale, of the 'long round' ; containing some short putting holes, some longer holes, admitting of a drive or two of seventy or eighty yards, and a few suitable hazards. We venture to suggest seventy or eighty yards as the average limit of a drive advisedly ; not because we doubt a lady's power to make a longer drive, but because that cannot well be done without raising the club above the shoulder. Now, we do not presume to dictate, but we must observe that the posture and gestures requisite for a full swing are not particularly graceful when the player is clad in female dress.

Most ladies putt well, and all the better because they play boldly for the hole without refining too much about the lie of the ground ; and there is no reason why they should not practise and excel in wrist shots with a lofting iron or cleek.

Their right to play, or rather the expediency of their playing the long round, is much more doubtful. If they choose to play at times when the male golfers are feeding or resting, no one can object But at other times—must we say it ?—they are in the way ; just because gallantry forbids to treat them exactly as men. The tender mercies of the golfer are cruel. He cannot afford to be merciful ; because if he forbears to drive into the party in front he is promptly driven into from behind. It is a hard lot to follow a party of ladies with a powerful driver behind you if you are troubled with a spark of chivalry or shyness.

As to the ladies playing the long round with men as their partners, it may be sufficient to say, in the words of a promising young player who found it hard to decide between flirtation and playing the game : 'It's all mighty pleasant, but it's not business.'

But it is to their presence as spectators that the most serious objection must be taken. If they could abstain from talking while you are playing, and if the shadow of their dresses would not flicker on the putting-green while you are holing out, other objections might, perhaps, be waived. But, apart from these positive offences against the unwritten laws of golf, they unintentionally exercise an unsettling and therefore pernicious influence, deny it who can. You wish to play your best before them, and yet you know they will not like you any the better if you beat their husband or brother. Again, it seems churlish not to speak to them; but if you do the other players will justly abuse you. It may be stated parenthetically that one of the party is sure to speak to them; because (to their praise or blame be it said) few foursomes do not contain one ladies' man.

Thirdly, if they volunteer to score, they may, and probably will, score wrong (not in your favour you may be sure); yet you cannot contradict them. An outraged golfer once said to his opponent in a single who had brought his wife to score for him three days in succession, 'My good fellow, suppose we both did it!' This was in the circumstances a very strong and cogent way of putting the case; because there was no manner of doubt what the speaker's wife would do if she came. But the remonstrance was not well received, and the match was not renewed.

Betting.—What is to be said about betting in connexion with golf? It must be admitted that *theoretically* betting spoils, or at least does not improve, any good game. To some games and sports indeed such as cricket, football, and boating, it seems to be positively foreign and inimical; if we except the time-honoured annual bets between old university and public school men which serve to keep alive friendships which might otherwise die. But in other games it must be admitted that such is the infirmity of human nature, the normal man will not exert himself without the inducement of a bet. How would it be, for instance, with countless gentlemen of riper years if they were forbidden to play whist for money? Life would become a burden, and the club a howling wilderness. And so with golf: we fear the game would languish if the harmless and necessary half-crown were by law forbidden. It is too deeply rooted in the golfer's keen and acquisitive heart to be plucked out without injury to the game.

There is even high authority for the view that not to bet is a symptom, nay, a virtual acknowledgment, of moral weakness. We were once told by one who well understood the science and keenly appreciated the humour of golf, that he overheard a committee of caddies debating as to the reasons why certain gentlemen did not bet. The gentlemen in question were men of the highest respectability and the soul of honour. This indeed was an accepted condition of the discussion. But how came it that such men would not bet? That was the question. That their conduct proceeded from high-minded motives such as a conviction of the wickedness of betting, or a desire not to set a bad example to younger men, was scouted as simply incredible. Poverty and niggardliness were in turn put forward as explanations only to be summarily rejected ; as most of the men were known to be well off and fairly generous to the profession. The discussion languished and was about to drop, when a caddy (who subsequently rose to eminence) suggested with great subtlety : 'They daurna trust themselves to bet.' The plain English or Scotch of which was that in the speaker's opinion the said golfers knew too well that if they did bet they would certainly cheat ; and knowing this, and having a character for probity to maintain, would not expose themselves to a temptation to which they felt they must sooner or later succumb. This solution was at once accepted as correct, and became the judgment of the committee.

In the long run, not much money changes hands. A man's form is so quickly known that he is soon correctly handicapped, and unless he discovers a mine of wealth in the shape of a man whose vanity exceeds his regard for his pocket, he has not much opportunity of winning continuously. In a *single* such a windfall may possibly be enjoyed for a brief season ; in a *foursome*, never. A golfer may fancy his own game, but he will not permit his partner to over-estimate his ; at least, not a second time.

The golfer's life and habits, when not upon active duty, are very much what might be expected. Of course he talks shop and that incessantly. Now, all shop is intolerable to those who neither know nor care about the subject ; but we do not think that golfing shop is worse than any other.

We do not know whether it falls within the scope of this

chapter to give the golfer any advice in regard to his diet ; we presume not, because he would certainly pay no attention to the advice given. Thanks to the healthy nature of his occupation and the fine air he breathes, the golfer can and does eat and drink everything with impunity—for a season ; and nothing but a gastric crisis, or losing two or three matches in succession, will open his eyes to the fact that he is abusing his advantages. There is a weird story of a mysterious stranger who had been taken into a foursome, who was interrupted in the heroic attempt to putt *through* a large black retriever dog which was standing between himself and the hole. On being remonstrated with by his partner, the stranger asked him quietly whether that was a real dog ; and on being assured that it was, seemed much relieved. *His* explanation, which was received politely but without comment, was that he was suffering from indigestion produced by his having for two or three days been emboldened by the fine air to take a glass of port after his cheese—a thing which never agreed with him.

The golfer's home bears traces of his noble infirmity. For the sake of domestic peace our advice is, that he should not be permitted to take a club home with him. But he is very sly, and has a trick of walking about with a cleek and pretending to use it as a walking-stick ; and whenever he finds a bit of turf he begins at once to exercise his destructive art. If he possesses a lawn he is sure to have a round of short holes upon it. If his girls have a tennis-ground, he slily punches putting-holes in the corners ; and if he is driven from that, he practises wrist iron shots among the flower beds. Even within the house on a wet day he practises his swing in the lobby, and putts into tumblers laid upon their side upon the dining-room floor. That is to say, he does all these things if his wife permits him, or if he can escape her eye. If she is a wise woman, she will give in at once ; the disease is incurable and ends only with life. The golfer's night thoughts are even as his day thoughts, so far as the god of dreams will permit ; but golfing dreams are apt to be inconsecutive and grotesque. Our own special forms of nightmare are that we are driving or putting with an umbrella (the badge of a respectable professional man), or shooting rocketing golf balls. Others have been known to use a fishing-rod as a driver in their dreams. Now all this is magnificent sport, but it is not golf. Others, again, have protracted quarrels with their partners, or opponents, in which they get very angry, but never a bit nearer a satisfactory conclusion. To all at last comes oblivion till another golfing day dawns, and they begin the round of their daily work again.

If, at any time, we have seemed to treat the golfer with levity, our excuse must be that it is due to the same impulse which makes schoolboys, released from school, shout and gambol to work off the effects of the enforced restraint of the hours of tuition. The real business of golf is so earnest and exacting, that while it is in progress all joking and superfluous comment are sternly repressed; but, although we may not speak or laugh at the time, we see and hear a good deal which must find expression in some way. If any further excuse is required, it is just because we love and esteem the game and the golfer so well that we have ventured to deal so familiarly and 'faithfully' with him.

CHAPTER III

CLUBS AND BALLS

BY H. G. HUTCHINSON

THE present writer, when an undergraduate at Oxford, had the privilege of introducing his logic tutor to the royal and ancient game of golf. On the evening of his initiation the professional framer of definitions gave this account of the game — that it consisted in 'putting little balls into little holes with instruments very ill adapted to the purpose.'

Putting little balls into little holes—with the addendum that the victory is to him who achieves this object in the least number of strokes—may be taken as a fairly accurate general description of the game ; but, on the other hand, the accumulated experience of all the golfing ages, with respect to the instruments best adapted to this purpose, may perhaps be held of even greater value than the opinion of a professor of logic. And when we come to consider that these holes vary, in point of distance from each other, from a hundred yards to a quarter of a mile—that the individual strokes vary from a hundred and eighty yards, or so, to a few inches—that, after the first stroke to each hole (for which it is permitted to place the ball on a little eminence of sand, for greater ease of hitting), the ball has to be driven from every variety of lie, sandy, grassy, rushy, or stony, in which it may chance to rest—it will not appear so very unreasonable that there should be a more or less corresponding number and variety in the weapons which are employed for such diverse functions.

Mr. Jorrocks' biographer states that that sapient master of fox-hounds once propounded the query, 'Who shall advise a man in the choice of a wife or a 'oss?' Though couched in the interrogative form, it is clear enough that the question contains its own answer, and that in Mr. Jorrocks' opinion it is the part of the wise man to deem discretion in advising upon either of these delicate points by far the better part of valour. Mr. Jorrocks' principle is capable of extension to many another department of human life, and had Mr. Jorrocks been a golfer he would doubtless have phrased it, 'Who shall advise a man in the choice of a wife or a driver?'

In truth it is quite impossible to be dogmatic. We see very little men—first-class golfers—playing with such long clubs that, as with the dog with the big tail, the club seems to wag the golfer rather than the golfer the club ; and we see very tall men—first-class golfers no less—doubling down to a little short club so as to lose, as it would seem, all the advantage that their height could give them.

Nevertheless there are good clubs and bad clubs—good long clubs, and bad long clubs ; good short clubs, and bad short clubs—and the practised golfer will be able at once to tell, on taking a club, be it long or short, into his hand, whether it be one with which a player to whom its length is adapted will be able to strike the ball with fairly consistent power and accuracy.

The oldest clubs which have come down to us are probably those which are enshrined in a sort of golfing museum at the Royal and Ancient Club House at St. Andrews. There is no relic of golf clubs of the Stone Age, nor anything coeval with primitive man or the cave-bear. We find no palæolithic flint niblicks; in fact, strangely as the nineteenth-century niblick resembles one of the war-clubs of antiquity, it would appear that the niblick is a quite modern evolution. The specimens preserved at St. Andrews show the iron-headed golf club in a transition stage. We may there see evidence of a confusion of species which would greatly have delighted the heart of Darwin.

They have begun to depart from the primitive form of 'cleek'—in response to such altered conditions as roads and stone dykes—but they have not yet evolved the comparatively highly organised stage of 'niblick.' The functions of the various members of the Iron Club family have not yet become finely differentiated. In golf history, in fact, these clubs of the St. Andrews museum occupy the place of the Pterodactyl in world history —an intermediate form between the birds and the reptiles—or the Manatee, Duck-bill, or Ornithorynchus, intermediate between birds and mammals.

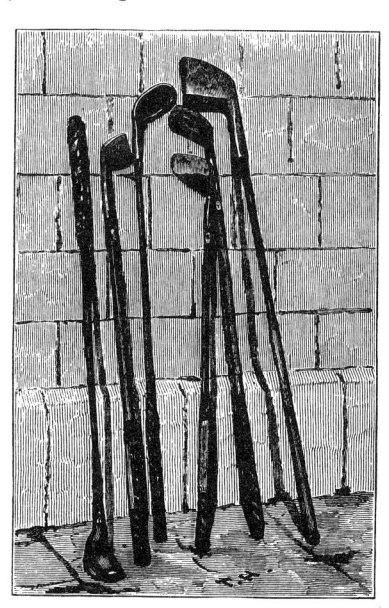

FOSSILS OF THE PAST

The wooden clubs in use by our ancestors of the time of the St. Andrews museum would seem to have been of a stubborn, stout, inflexible nature, bull-dog headed. Then arose a great master club-maker, one Hugh Philp by name, who wondrously refined golf-club nature. Slim and elegant, yet, as we of these days would say, of but insufficient power, are the specimens of his art which have descended to us. His true specimens, it should be said; for there is many a club boasting Hugh Philp as its creator which that craftsman never saw—nor can we expect it would have been otherwise, since it is a matter of common report that at least two subsequent clubmakers had a 'Hugh Philp' stamp with which upon the head of the club they would imprint a blatant forgery. The golfing connoisseur will inspect the time matured head of the old putter which claims Philp as its father with as cultured and microscopic a criticism as the dilettante lover of Stradivarius or the Amati will bestow upon their magic works.

But away with history, away with the fossils of the past into the nethermost bunkers, entombed amongst feather golf-balls, and let us see what best will serve us to smite the gutta-percha of to-day. Well, first as regards the driver. We have already hinted that length is to a great extent a matter of taste. It should be observed, however, that extremes should certainly be avoided. This is not a mere *à priori* statement. We have seen all sorts of extremes tried—we have tried all sorts of extremes ourselves—but none of them have ever answered. One gradually reverts to the established type again—was Darwin, after all, a golfer? A little depends, however, upon previous training. Should a man have suffered under the misfortune of being brought up a cricketer, to the entire neglect of his golfing education, and should he then take to golf comparatively late in life, he will probably do better with a short club. He can in this way stand to the ball with less outrage to his natural instincts, and make a sort of compromise between golf and cricket swing which may be very effective. We may mention Mr. R. A. H. Mitchell, as both the most successful and one of the most typical of the reformed cricketers.

The weight of driver that you will find best suited to your style of play must necessarily very largely depend upon the speed of your swing. A slow swinger will incline to compensate for the want of velocity by the increase in weight. The thing to be aimed at is a balance between the two—not such weight as to make your natural swing drag ; nor, again, such lightness that your natural strength is in part wasted, or the swing for a moment checked by the concussion of the ball. But the tendency of human nature rather inclines to assume too much than too little to itself—and the golfer is very human. He therefore has an ineradicable tendency to give himself just a little more weight in his club than he can swing with comfort. It is, therefore, the part of the adviser to endeavour to correct this by asserting, as we are quite prepared to do, that he—the golfer, typical of his species—would probably play better and more steadily if he were to play with a lighter club. True, he may now and again get a longer ball from his weaver's beam, but what difference does that make ? You do not want to hit the ball so very far. You want to hit it often—or, rather, the oftener you can hit it truly, the less the total hits that you will require. Moreover, it is quite amazing to see with what toys of clubs some drivers will hit very long balls. Mr. David Lamb is a most striking instance of this power.

Essentially bound up in this question of the weight of clubs is the question of their suppleness, or flexibility. For each of the two depends greatly on the other. A heavy head may bring just the right amount of life—of what Tom Morris calls 'music'—out of a very stiff shaft, while on a flexible shaft it would waggle it to pieces and be utterly useless. In fact, once you have made up your mind to the standard of weight you require in your driving clubs, the weight itself will in a great measure determine for you the springiness of the shafts. A fine steely spring is what the golfer wants to feel, a spring that will bring the club back, quick as thought, to the straight. Then it feels, in his hands, like a living thing, full of energy— of controlled, obedient energy—to do his service.

And not only is the amount of spring a matter of import, but also the location of the spring. It ought not to make itself felt too far up the club, 'under the hand,' as it is called, but ought to be situated chiefly in the six or nine inches of shaft just above the whipping which binds head and shaft together. Yet the spring must not be there, and nowhere else, so that one can point with the finger and say the spring comes up so far and no farther; but it must gradually and imperceptibly die away into the comparatively unyielding upper part of the handle. There is a further word to be said with regard to the proper relation between the speed of the swing and the suppleness of the club. But, for the clear understanding of this, it is necessary first to have a clear understanding of the principles of the swing; and for its consideration we therefore refer the reader to Chapter IV., 'Driving,' under Elementary Instructions in the Art of Driving.

The principle of the lever is tolerably well known to most people, and it is therefore scarcely necessary to point out that the longer the shaft, the heavier—for practical purposes—does the head become; so that a man who plays with a short club may play with a far heavier head than a man of equal power and similar speed of swing playing with a longer club. It is not a bad thing to keep in your set a short, stiff, and heavy club, with a very flat face—'putter-faced,' as it is called—to play with upon very windy days. Speaking practically, rather than mechanically, we may say that the short stiff club hits the ball a more solid, firm blow than the more supple, flimsy club. The ball flies with more determination, so to speak, and is not blown aside with every wind at cross purposes. Moreover, the stiff club and the flat face keep the ball low, so that it skims over the ground and cheats the gales that are expecting it aloft. This is the style of driving especially to be cultivated in the wind's eye.

Next, an important consideration is the 'lie' of the driving club. It is an untrustworthy weapon only too often, but in this instance the expression has no moral sense. The 'lie' is the result of the angle formed by the head with the shaft. When head and shaft are at an obtuse angle the club is termed a 'flat-lying' club; when they more nearly form a right angle the club is said to be 'upright,' or to have an 'upright lie.'

The more upright the club the nearer his feet will the player need to have his ball, and, consequently, the shorter will be the club. The reformed cricketer style gives a good example of this. The flatter-lying club is more suitable to those whose swing resembles somewhat the action of a man mowing grass. Bob Martin's style offers an example. It will be found that with the flat-lying club, other things being equal, the ball will be sent with a flatter trajectory than from the more upright ; therefore, as a rule, it is found that those who play with these flatter clubs are more successful than others, comparatively speaking, in a wind.

Thus far we have been dealing mainly with drivers, or, at least, driving clubs. A few years back the golfer did not deem himself armed at all points unless his equipment included a graduated series of 'spoons'—from the 'grassed club,' which was in reality nothing but a driver with a slightly filed-back face, down to the 'baffy,' very short and stiff and with face very much laid back. Between this Alpha and Omega was a long series, quite as numerous as all the letters of the Greek alphabet which most golfers can remember, of spoons of different degree. There was the 'long spoon,' the 'mid spoon,' and the 'short spoon,' with their various modifications, shading off into each other and into each extreme. Nowadays the array of wooden clubs is commonly much curtailed. The 'baffy,' with which the golfer of old used to approach the hole, is now replaced by the lofting-iron—much to the detriment, as the old golfer is so fond of telling us—and truly telling us, may be— of the turf of the links, from which the iron skelps up such divots. The practised iron player is always ready with the retort that the reason that men ever use the baffy now is because they cannot play the iron. One of the most finished exponents of the old style of baffy 'approach' was the late Sir Robert Hay.

But in place of the numerous spoons of a nearly bygone age there has come into very general use a club that is named the 'brassy.' This weapon is shod, or soled, with brass, whereby its wielder is enabled to play off roads and hard lies without injury to the head. Moreover, whereas this club is sometimes made very short in the head, it then is given the name of the 'wooden niblick,' from its family likeness to that bulldog-headed specimen of the iron club species, the niblick proper. This small head enables it to fit into many a rut where its more elegant brethren could not follow it, and to cut with greater ease through grass and that accumulation of mossy annoyance which the Scotchman and the golfer call 'fog.'

The 'brassy,' then, whether wooden niblick or brass-shod spoon, should be somewhat shorter and stiffer than the driver, for it will be called upon to do execution under rough and trying circumstances, and the more it partakes of the character of the wooden niblick, the more you will probably find it will require to be spooned. It is the usual custom of club-makers to screw on the brass sole beneath the little strip of horn which, in the driver, runs along the base of the face of the club. There is, however, something to be said in favour of dispensing altogether with the 'horn' in the case of brass-soled clubs. No golfer can fail to be aware of the unsatisfactory feeling, and the no less unsatisfactory flight of the ball, which result from striking the ball on the horn. It jars the hand, and the ball does not go off sweet. The brass is in itself a quite sufficient protection for the face of the club, and the dispensing with the horn will render available an additional eighth of an inch or so upon which the ball may be struck without the unsatisfactory results above mentioned. It is even possible that this advantage may come to be held of such importance that brass-soled hornless drivers may come into fashion, though it must be borne in mind that the greater weight thus attached to the bottom of the club-head must be counteracted by a less weight of the lead behind the point of impact—which is the point at which weight is of most value.

There is a great 'fashion' in golf clubs. In the old days of baffy spoons, golfers used to putt almost exclusively with wooden putters. These are now very generally superseded by iron putters. It is likely that there may be something more in this than mere fashion, however. It is a fact that most golfers will admit, though few will attempt to explain, that the ball seems to run closer to the ground—with a closer grip of the ground—from the iron than from the wooden putter. The ball is therefore more ready to catch and go down into the hole, when it meets it, off the iron putter; but it is also more ready to grip and shoulder up against any little roughness or obstacle which it may meet on its passage. This is of less importance than in days of old, for putting-greens, no less than wickets, are, generally speaking, in a better-kept condition than formerly. They have thus become more adapted for the use of a club which sends the ball closely biting to the ground. In further proof of our present contention, it should be noted how seldom, comparatively, a good golfer is seen to approach the hole from any distance, unless the ground be exceptionally smooth, with an iron putter. He will commonly call for his wooden putter, to approach over the rough ground, and will then exchange this weapon for his iron putter when on the true smooth putting-greens. There exists, indeed, a notable exception to the general statement here laid down, as exemplified in the iron-putter approaches of Captain Molesworth, R.N. ; but this may be fairly claimed as one of those exceptional instances which go to prove the rule.

But a few years ago this style of approaching with the putter was an offence in the eyes of the golfer. 'Eh, ye're safer with yer putter,' was a piece of advice often tendered to the hesitating and indifferent golfer by the canny and all too candid caddy, but was accepted as a reproach containing an implication of an incapacity for the true golfer-like stroke of lofting with the iron. But of late there has set in a reaction even in the *élite* of the golfing faculty. It was mainly Bob Fergusson, of Musselburgh, who initiated the movement, approaching with his putter over the level greens of Musselburgh with such deadliness that the stroke came into general use, and the facetious caddy will refer to the putter thus employed as 'the Musselburgh iron.' At yet greater distance an implement called the 'driving putter,' a modification between the putter proper and the short stiff driver above described as a useful weapon against the wind, is affected by some, though its use is not very general.

Your putter proper—and this applies alike to wooden and iron putters—should be the shortest of all your clubs, for all agree that you should stand near your ball for putting; its shaft should be very stiff, absolutely devoid of spring, but the main essential for a good putter is perfect balance. This is a quality difficult to describe, but even the tiro cannot fail to appreciate the difference between a well and a badly balanced putter on taking the two weapons into his hand. It is therefore advisable, in selecting a putter, to have a large number from which to make your choice. And, the choice once made, be careful of your putter. Preserve an old and tattered leather, rather than have a new strip put upon it on slight occasion ; for this balance is a delicate matter, which, once disturbed, it is very difficult to readjust. Above all, should such a misfortune befall you with your wooden putter as that the lead should come out, be careful to treasure up the bit of base metal for the guidance of the club-maker, whose business it will be to run in fresh lead of the same exact weight.

As to a further final comparison between wood and iron as material for putters, it would seem that the line of the face of the iron putter is more readily and exactly seen. This is a valuable merit, for a large part of the business of putting consists in getting the line of the face—your base line, so to speak—at right angles to the line on which you intend the ball to travel.

The perfection of balance insisted upon as an essential quality in putters is important also in drivers and in all clubs. With these latter, however, it is not so much a matter of absolute necessity as with the club which is intended for the more delicate stroke. The two chief malformations under which the practically abortive efforts of club-makers are prone to suffer are heads put on 'hooky,' or heads 'lying away'—that is to say,

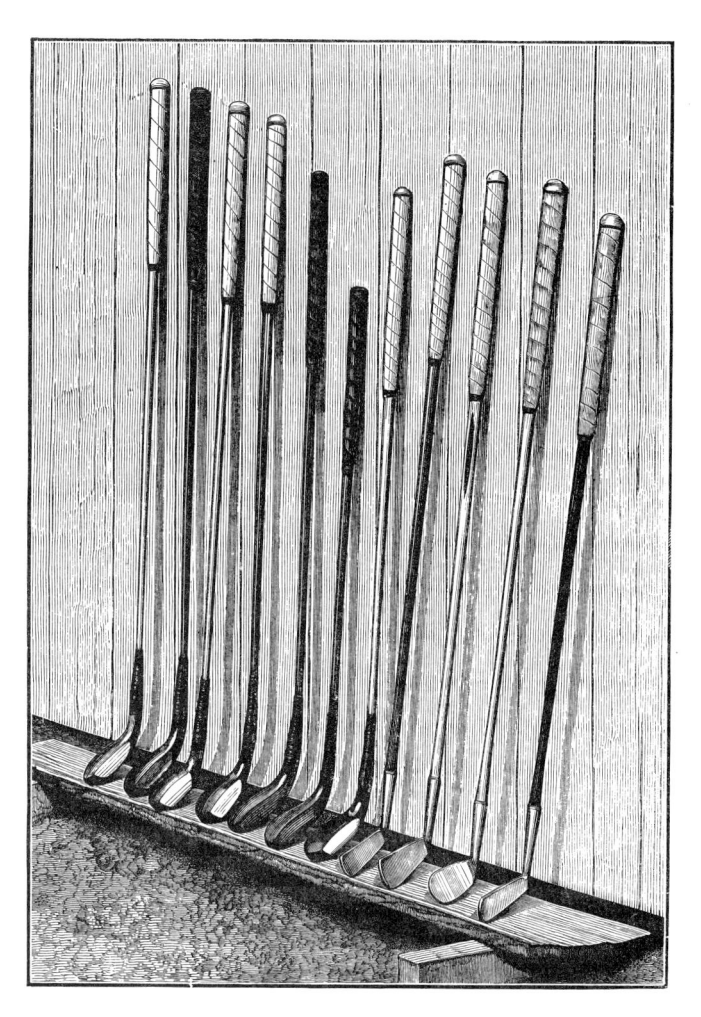

MODERN GOLF CLUBS

heads whose faces, instead of lying in the same vertical plane with the shaft, incline at an angle to the left or right respectively. This does not, of course, hold true, mathematically speaking, of any clubs with spooned faces ; but practically this test may be applied to them also, for their faces should so lie that if they were putter-faced they would lie in the same plane with the shaft.

When it is said that these two malformations are the principal ills which club flesh is heir to, it is not intended to imply that there are not many driving clubs made which are hopeless and impossible in other ways—such as clubs that have spring anywhere, clubs that have spring everywhere, and clubs which have spring nowhere. A plentiful crop of such wretches, whose diseases are too many to enumerate, issues from the clubmakers' shops. Likewise, heads that are brittle and shafts that are green ; but all these, and such like infirmities, are too obvious to be worth our while to dwell upon them.

It would not be right to close these notes upon wooden clubs in general without reference to a new departure introduced by Mr. Henry Lamb, and practised by him—and by many followed—with very remarkable success. His novel driving club, in all other respects similar to others, has a face which, instead of being a flat surface, bulges out at the centre. A complete analysis of his theory would involve a discussion of the causes which incline a ball struck upon the heel of the club to fly to the right of the proper line, and a ball struck upon the toe to go to the left. Such a discussion would here be out of place, but the bearings of this question have been exhaustively dealt with, in connexion with the curve in the air described by the baseball, by no less an authority than the late Mr. R. A. Proctor. For practical purposes, however, it may suffice to say that, in consequence of the inclination thus given to the face of Mr. Lamb's driver, the tendency of the 'heeled' ball to fly to the right will, upon his contention, be counteracted by the angle at which the slope of the face meets it, while the erratic disposition of the 'toed' ball will be no less controlled by the corresponding contrary slope given to the face towards the toe. Mr. Lamb aims, therefore, rather at a negative gain—a prevention of error—for it is clear that a ball struck perfectly correctly, i.e. on top of the bump, will be quite unaffected by the slope on either side of it. At the theory, and at the appearance of the club, it is easy to smile; but no one who had had experience of Mr. Lamb's practice of it can fail to acknowledge that it is difficult to beat.

But if the modern golfer has reduced the complexity of his manifold spoons almost to the simplicity of a single brassy, he has so fully made up for this in the number and variety of his iron clubs that the modern golfing stock-in-trade bears a striking resemblance to a set of elephantine dentist's tools. There are long cleeks and short cleeks, driving cleeks, lofting cleeks, and putting cleeks; there are heavy irons and light irons, driving irons, lofting irons, and sand irons. There are 'mashies' and there are niblicks. In this multitude of golf clubs there is perhaps wisdom—somewhere—but it can scarcely be that all of them are necessary.

The ordinary driving cleek is rather shorter in the shaft than the brassy. Later, however, it has become not unusual to play with a cleek with a very long and springy shaft, and a light head. Some players, notably Mr. Gilbert Mitchell Innes, have tried abnormal woods for the shafts of these long driving cleeks, such as malacca canes, and so forth; but probably nothing is better than the ordinary hickory. Split hickory shafts will, it is claimed, drive some trifle further, and last better than the sawn hickory, which has less length of grain. The really best wood for the shafts of iron clubs is perhaps the yellow 'orange wood,' for this preserves its straightness with wonderful consistency. For a player who is in the constant habit of striking the ground, the 'orange-wood' would, therefore, perhaps be the best possible material for the shafts of all his clubs. Lancewood, blue-mahoo, greenheart, and other varieties have been tried, with more or less success, for shafts —as also the common ash—and for heads, pear and apple tree, vulcanite, and other substances. On the whole, however, no improvement can be made upon split hickory for shafts, and well-seasoned beech for heads, with, perhaps, orange-wood for the shafts of the iron clubs.

But to return to our cleeks. The main trouble that the hard-hitting golfer will find about his cleeks is that the faces are so apt to get bent in with the constant hitting. In view of this danger, he should choose a cleek-head which has good thickness on the upper, as well as on the lower, edge of the blade. Moreover, the more weight that is given to the upper part of the blade, as compared with the lower, the more forward going power and the more run will the club impart to the ball. Other things being equal, the more the blade or face of the cleek is laid back, the higher will it send the ball, and the less distance will it drive it. With cleeks, as with other things, there is much virtue in the mean.

Of the modifications of the cleek proper there is not much to say. The putting cleek we have practically considered when treating of the putting iron, or iron putter. It differs from the iron putter only in that its face is slightly laid back. Balance is everything; and the besetting sin of the golfing Tubal Cain is to make the putter-heads too heavy. The most useful modification of the cleek is, perhaps, the short, stiff, and heavy approaching cleek. It appears to be coming somewhat into fashion, though it is, in point of fact, no novelty, but a revival of an old-fashioned type. Its face is much laid back, and its use is mainly in approaching the hole, for some forty yards or so, over ground which is rough at the start, and smooth when once the start is over-passed. The cleek will loft the ball, at no great height from the ground, over the rough ground, and allow it to run on over the smoother surface up to the hole. It is a particularly useful mode of approach in the teeth of a wind. Bob Martin is probably its best exponent; but he can play the stroke almost equally well with any kind of cleek. The power of long driving with the cleek has doubtless been a factor in the disuse of spoons. Douglas Rolland, of Elie, and

Mr. John Ball, Junr., of Hoylake, can both drive with a cleek very nearly up to their ordinary driver shot.

The names of the heavy iron, light iron, sand iron, driving iron, and lofting iron, to some extent explain themselves, and in a measure explain themselves twice over. Thus we may quite well include heavy irons and light irons under driving irons, of which they both are species. A slow-swinging golfer will probably play with a heavy driving iron, a quick-swinging golfer with a light one—that is all. And about driving irons there is not much more to say. They are heavier, shorter, stiffer, with faces more laid back, than the cleek, will drive the ball out of worse places, but will not drive it so far. They are the cart-horses of the golfer's team. The sand iron is practically a heavy driving iron with the face very much laid back. Its use has, however, been of late almost entirely superseded by that of the niblick and mashie.

The lofting iron is the most fascinating, the most coquettish, of all the golfer's following. Feminine, without doubt—so delightful on occasion; yet so exasperating, so untrustworthy, so full of moods and tenses.

There are two ways of playing the lofting stroke. Not merely a right way and a wrong way, but two ways which we may say are about equally right; and these two ways require different implements. Almost every professional gets his ball to stop comparatively dead—which is the purpose and essence of the lofting stroke—by means of putting cut upon it; which he does by drawing the club towards him, as its head comes to the ground, so that its face scrapes, instead of directly striking the ball. This imparts a twist to the ball which causes it to break to the right and bite close into the ground, instead of running freely on, when it pitches. Many amateurs, on the other hand, notably Mr. A. F. Macfie, succeed in preventing their ball from running far from the pitch by means of an accurately played, ordinary stroke with a very much laid back iron or mashie. Mr. J. E. Laidlay, who perhaps approaches with the mashie better than anyone else in the world, in a measure combines both these strokes, for he slightly cuts the ball with a very much laid back face.

At all events the beginner, who has not learned the cutting stroke early in life, will probably find it better to obtain the desired end by means of an iron much laid back—and constant practice therewith. The shaft of the club should be nearly without spring, and the head not too heavy. The great mass of the weight of the club should be towards the bottom edge of the blade, while the upper edge should be thin and light, for thus a slight stopping undercut is put on the ball without effort of the striker.

The mashie may be said to be a hybrid growth. But a few years back it was almost unknown. Now its use is universal. Some few golfers, when they wished to pitch the ball unusually dead, were in the habit of using the niblick. But since the small surface of the blade of the niblick head demanded almost greater accuracy of striking than the human hand and eye could master, it occurred to the same bold spirit to invent a modification—a compromise between niblick and iron—which, while allowing a little more scope for human error, should yet preserve the faculty of pitching the ball dead. Thus was the mashie evolved—an intermediate type called into being by conditions which specially favoured its existence.

Many golfers now carry a mashie to the entire exclusion of the niblick ; yet, though it be doubtful whether in the multitude of golf clubs there be wisdom, it is questionable if it is wise to discard the niblick altogether. For your mashie, for approaching purposes, should be essentially a weapon of balance, while your niblick, for digging purposes, should be essentially a weapon of weight. Your niblick should be heavy, to dig through obstacles ; your mashie should be comparatively light, to pitch the ball dead. In the niblick, no less than the mashie and lofting-iron, it is important to have the weight mainly upon the bottom edge of the blade, for thus will the ball rise straighter off the blade into the air. With a bunker cliff before you, this is a matter of some moment.

Moreover, your niblick is intended for coarse work. It is a heavy tough weapon. You may use it fearlessly among stones and railway lines, where you would shrink from risking your more delicate mashie.

We have thus traced a gradual descent of length and spring from the long flexible driver to the short stubborn putter or the stumpy-headed niblick. And as the clubs grew shorter their lies will have become more upright, and the ball nearer to us, till, with the putter, we are in some danger of cutting a divot off our big toe. So now that we have got the ball just under our very eyes let us take a look at it and see what it is made of.

A considerable number of years ago we should have found that it was made of a compact mass of feathers stuffed within a leather casing. This is, however, quite matter of history, and about the feather ball there is no need for us to trouble ourselves further. It is as absolutely obsolete as the flint arrowhead.

The feather ball was superseded by the gutta-percha ball. All golf balls at the present day are made of gutta-percha, of different qualities and by different processes, or of some compound into which gutta-percha largely enters. The first gutta-percha balls were made smooth, without any of the 'nicking' which we now see upon them. It was found that, though they possessed the advantages of cheapness and roundness to a degree with which the feather ball could not compete, they nevertheless did not, at first, fly so well as did the older fashioned ball. Some observant golfers remarked that they showed a remarkable tendency to fly better after they had been subjected to a little hacking with the iron. From this observation resulted the easy practical deduction of hacking the balls before they were painted. This was at first done with the reverse end of a hammer-head, broadened out for the purpose into something of a chisel-like shape. Then was devised a mould with ridges upon it which stamped the 'nicking' upon the ball in course of moulding. And these 'machine-made' balls, as they are termed, have now come into general use, to the almost total exclusion of 'hand-hammered' balls, as those nicked by the old process are called.

In explanation of the further capacity for flight which a ball most indubitably acquires as a consequence of this nicking, most golfers have been in the habit of asserting that it imparts a kind of rotatory motion to the ball, similar to that given to the rifle bullet in consequence of the grooves in the barrel. And every golfer enunciates this theory with a vague consciousness, or at least suspicion, that there is something not altogether satisfactory about it. Professor Tait, whose dictum may probably

be accepted in the matter, has maintained, on the contrary, that these nicks are absolutely an obstacle to the flight of the ball— by reason of the resistance they offer to the air. His contention is that their function and utility are as follows: Were the ball smooth and unnicked, that portion of it which is compressed by the impact of the club would spring out again with but dull and sluggish elasticity compared to the spring of the reaction of the numerous ridges and little knobs which are formed by the nicking. And this quicker spring is a gain of such importance as quite to overbalance the slight detriment to flight offered by the roughness upon the ball's surface. This, surely, is a more satisfactory explanation than the undigested hypothesis of the rotatory motion and the false analogy of the rifle-ball.

Then, besides the gutta-percha ball which issues from the club-makers' shops, there is the 'Silvertown' ball, as it is called, because it is constructed by the Silvertown Gutta-percha Company. This also is a gutta-percha ball, but it is subjected to greater pressure, by hydraulic power presumably, than the club-makers are able to apply.

Finally, there is the ball called the 'Eclipse,' but more commonly known among golfers as the 'putty,' because it is of softer substance than the gutta-percha ball, and because 'putty' rhymes with 'gutty.'

We may make a brief comparison of these three balls, taking the ordinary 'gutty,' which is the mean, as the standard.

The 'Silvertown' differs little from the ordinary ball. It springs away with rather sharper elasticity from the club; it is, in common parlance, harder. It has a slightly longer flight and carry, and it has the consequent compensating disadvantage of being somewhat harder to control in a high wind. It springs away with great liveliness from the iron or putter, and it is therefore somewhat more difficult to control in strokes needing delicate precision. For all these reasons it is a good ball for the weak driver, and for him who has a difficulty in getting his ball well into the air, as it rises quickly in the air. It is not a good ball against the wind, but it is a good friend to the club-maker, for it is liable to break the heads of wooden clubs. The ball will itself stand ill-usage better than the ordinary gutta-percha ball, always keeping its shape, and showing less marks of iron hacking.

The 'Eclipse' is the very opposite in its qualities to the 'Silvertown.' It is a soft india-rubbery ball, and goes off the club with the silence of a thief in the night. It will not 'carry' so far as the ordinary gutta-percha, but on good running ground it will make this up in its 'run.' It is a very good ball in a wind, for not soaring like the 'gutty,' and being heavier size for size, the wind affects it less, and it is less susceptible to the erratic influences of 'toeing' and 'heeling.' It is far easier to keep straight. It is a fine ball for putting, though it requires a harder knock to start it, for it recovers itself from any little roughnesses or obstacles it may encounter with india-rubbery light-heartedness. It is a very economical ball, showing scarcely any sign after the most severe ill-treatment upon the head. Nevertheless the 'Eclipse' ball, amongst good golfers at least, is going fast out of fashion. On a very keen green it is undoubtedly useful, and where the putting-greens get glassy-keen, as sometimes at Hoylake, it is infinitely easier to putt with it than with the livelier 'gutty.' But when the green is at all heavy, the loss of the few yards of 'carry' is a severe handicap. Moreover, it will not rise quickly from the club, and with an Eclipse ball lying behind a bank it is often necessary to take an iron, where the brassy would have got the gutta-percha well away. Further, whether with a greatly lofted iron, or with cut upon the ball, it is impossible to play a lofting shot with the Eclipse with anything like so dead a pitch as could be given to the gutta-percha.

It is not easy—it is scarcely possible—to go off after playing for several days with a gutta-percha ball and at once play equally correctly with the Eclipse ball. The difference is apparent with the driver, it is yet more manifest in the approach shot, and when it comes to the delicate operation of putting, it is apt to make itself most painfully evident. Thus, two years back such a remark as this was frequently heard: 'Oh, I cannot play as A's partner, he always plays with those soft balls,' or 'Of course we lost our foursome, B made me play with "gutties."' At one time this grievance became so distracting that there was some thought of petitioning Parliament for the abolition of one or the other style of ball; but the matter seems now to be righting itself again on the Darwinian principle of the survival of the fittest, and we owe a debt of gratitude to the inventors of the Eclipse ball in that they have made the club-makers exert themselves in a keener struggle for existence, to supply us with 'gutties' of a higher quality. The Eclipse was dead against their interests, for it not only took the ball-making profits out of their hands, but one could go on driving away at an Eclipse for months, and the face of the club looked as smooth and innocent as if it had never seen a golf ball.

Have your golf balls made of good gutta-percha, by a good maker, have them made not too small, say 27's at smallest, keep them for six months before playing with them, and if they do not win you matches the fault will not be in the ball.

CHAPTER IV

ELEMENTARY INSTRUCTION

By H. G. HUTCHINSON

(A) DRIVING

GOLFERS are very fond of insisting, and with great justice, that the game is not won by the driver. It is the short game — the approaching and putting—that wins the match. Nevertheless, despite the truth of this, it may be quite safely asserted that if there were no driving there would be very little golf.

In the volume of the Badminton Library which treats of Cricket, Mr. Lyttelton brackets together three sensations as the supreme delights which games can afford: 'the cut stroke at tennis, when the striker wins chase one and two on the floor; the successful drive at golf, when the globe is despatched on a journey of 200 yards; a crack to square-leg off a half-volley just outside the legs.'

Now, 200 is a nice round number of yards, and it has frequently been very greatly exceeded, under especially favourable conditions of wind and ground. Still, under ordinary fair conditions, 200 yards cannot be accepted without the assistance of a few extra yards from the long-bow, as the standard measure of the good golf drive. Let us call it 180 yards, which is dealing not illiberally with it, and we shall still find it quite sufficient to account for the fascination of the golfing devotee.

'Putting,' which is really so infinitely more difficult, is a matter of the purest simplicity to the spectator who is seeing for the first time a game of golf. He cannot think how you can possibly miss a putt of five yards. And very often, to your intense irritation, he takes his umbrella and knocks the ball into the hole from a yard or two away, almost without aiming at it, and you feel that in his crass ignorance he deems himself to have established a right to furtively, if not openly, make fun of you when he sees you settling yourself down upon your haunches to study a putt of a few feet. But for your driving he will always evince a certain respect. He is not likely to appreciate the fact that it demands any skill in its accomplishment, but he will, perhaps, go so far as to admit, with a certain air of patronage, that he had no idea 'the club would send the ball so far.' Do not *offer* to lend him a club, or he will suspect a trap, but insidiously put one in his way, in the manner of jugglers who force a card: he is sure to take it up. You may openly offer him a ball, unless he is singularly suspicious; and then he will begin to find out that the club does not always 'send the ball so far.' He will find that sometimes club and ball do not meet at all; he will be laughed at, and he will get hot and angry; he will perhaps break your club; but from that moment he is a golfer—nothing can save him; and his days are occupied with topping balls along the ground, and his nights with dreaming of balls flying through the air. From a state of insolence he will have fallen into a condition of desperation, to be shortly succeeded by that frame of reasonable humility which is the proper mental attitude in which to approach the shrine of the Goddess of Golf. He will now assimilate with thankfulness such of the esoteric mysteries as the initiated shall deem him worthy to receive. His first instructions shall then refer to the *position in which he should stand, relatively to the ball which he intends to drive.*

Now this will in part depend upon the length of club which his fancy shall have determined to be the best adapted to his physical anatomy. Instead, therefore, of taking our measurements in feet and yards, we will measure by means of

POSITION FOR THE DRIVE

the driver itself. The ball, then, we may say, should be at just such a distance from the player that when the club is laid with its *heel*—not the *centre* of its face—to the ball, the end of the club shaft reaches just to the player's left knee as he stands upright. But even this mode of measurement is liable to many exceptions, for the proper distance of ball from foot is in a great degree determined by the 'lie' of the club—by the angle which the head makes with the shaft. With flat-lying clubs the ball will be farther from the player than with clubs that are more upright ; but the rule of a club-length's distance (measured from end of shaft to heel) between ball and knee, when the knee is straight, is a good useful rule with a club of fair medium angle of lie. The ball should be just opposite the hands—that is to say, in more exact mechanical language, that ball, club-shaft, and hands should be all, as nearly as possible, in the same vertical plane. Avoid, when learning, a tendency to 'knuckle over' the ball—to get the hands away in front of it, and, on the other hand, do not get the ball away in front of the hands. Let the whole length of the club-shaft, when the head rests behind the ball, be in one vertical plane, and let club-shaft, face of the club (presuming that we are speaking of a flat-faced driver), the player's hands, and the player's left eye be all, likewise, in one and the same vertical plane ; finally, let this vertical plane be at a true right-angle with the line in which it is proposed to drive the ball. The player's hands, as they grip the club placed in position behind the ball, will thus be a little in advance—or to the left—of an imaginary vertical line drawn down the middle of his body.

Here, then, we have, in proper relative position, hands, club, ball, eye, and left foot. It remains to discover the proper position, relative to these other arrangements, of the player's right foot. Most treatises on the art of golf lay it down as with a yard measure that the distance between the golfer's feet in position for the drive should be one foot six inches. This is manifestly somewhat arbitrary ruling, and will necessarily require some modification to fit the different anatomy of different human frames. Nevertheless, it is, perhaps, roughly speaking, as near a measure as can be arrived at of the most comfortable and best straddle for a medium-sized man. Any attempt to lay down the distance with mathematical accuracy should take into its calculations the fact that since both feet turn somewhat outward, the distance between toe and toe is likely to be some inches greater than that from heel to heel. It is generally seen

ELEMENTARY INSTRUCTION

that the left foot is turned but slightly outwards, the right foot somewhat more so—and this not without reason ; for, as the blow is struck, a forward impetus is given from the right foot, and impinges upon the left.

Having then arrived at this rough conclusion with reference to the proper distance of the right foot from the left, it remains to fix its position by taking another angle of measurement. Let us take a line, at right angles with the vertical plane in which we have placed shaft, hands, and left eye, running from the player's left toe towards the right of him, a line parallel in fact, though we are producing it the opposite way to that in which

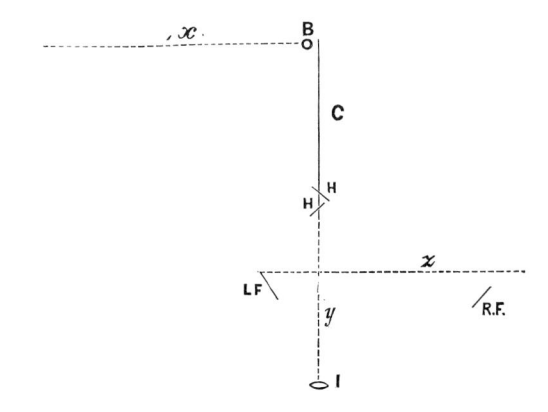

he is intending to drive—his right toe should be some three inches in rear (farther away from the ball) of this imaginary line. Stand up, club in hand, on your drawing-room carpet, which has probably some lines in its pattern, or on the kamptulicon in the hall, choosing your position not without reference to the chandelier, and you will oon contrive to persuade your untutored members into the positions herein indicated ; which relative positions will be more readily comprehended by a glance at the above diagram. Herein, I is the player's left eye, at H H are his hands gripping the club C, which lies with its head behind the ball B; and the vertical plane in which these all lie is a right angle with x, the intended line of flight of the ball. The dotted line z is drawn from the toe of the left foot, L F, at right angles to the plane in which the club shaft lies, and parallel with x. The right foot R F is two or three inches short of this line.

And having thus dogmatically laid down the position for the drive, it next devolves upon us to justify it by reasons. For it is not universally conceded that this position is the right one. One golfing instructor who is very worthy of respect, actually advises that the right toe be placed as much in advance of the dotted line z as, in our diagram, it appears in rear of it. He claims for this position a gain in power, and points to certain gifted players who, with, or in spite of, this style of stand, are of the very foremost rank. Yet these, as has been contended elsewhere—in the chapter upon 'Style'—partake rather of the nature of the exceptions which go to prove the rule. For let us resolve the golf swing into its ultimate purpose—what is it? To give oneself the best possible chance of hitting the ball surely and swiftly, to combine the far and the sure. The clubhead wants to be travelling, when it meets the ball, in the direction in which it is intended the ball should go; and it is exceedingly obvious that the longer the club-head is so travelling, the longer will be the space—the longer the segment of that rough circle which it describes—in which it is possible for it to meet the ball correctly. And this requires to be combined with sufficient speed. It may therefore be stated that the aim of the ideal golf swing is a combination of the utmost possible speed in conjunction with the utmost possible length of movement of the club-head in the desired line of flight of the ball.

This much being granted, let a man now proceed to take his stand in the position indicated by the preceding diagram. In this attitude let him take an easy natural swing at the imaginary ball, noting carefully the course of the club-head. Let him then vary his position by bringing forward his right foot in advance of the line indicated by the dotted line z in the diagram, and in this attitude let him again take an easy swing and again note the course of the club-head. It will be at once apparent that in the latter case the club-head rises and falls more vertically, with less of a sweep, than in the former case ; in other words, that it does not travel so long in the intended line of flight of the ball. The reason of this is that in the upward stroke the arms are less able to swing freely away from the body in the latter than in the former attitude ; and that in the downward stroke there is as it were a corner to be passed in the swing, the arms have to be drawn in again a little towards the body as the club-head descends. This is what some professionals mean when they tell the learner that this standing with the right foot advanced tends to 'check the swing.' In point of fact, it does produce a moment of check in it, preventing the swing from coming evenly through. Moreover, quite apart from such deductions from first principles, it will be seen that the very great majority of fine players stand with the right foot slightly in rear of the left, that those who adopt the alternative position are quite remarkable in their departure from the normal rule, and that the great mass of professional players instruct the learner to stand in the attitude shown in our diagram, which is also the position which is recommended in the golfing manuals of Mr. Chambers and of Mr. Forgan. With this weight of testimony in favour of the mode of stand which we have indicated, we may confidently proceed to the further details which go to compose the driving-swing, starting from this basis as the first position.

Before going into the matter of the course which the club-head ought to pursue on its upward and downward journeys, we will first consider the general nature of the intended stroke. Above everything, the golfing drive is a swing, and not a hit. These are very short and simple words, and contain a truth universally admitted—universally, almost, forgotten. If only a man can show practical full appreciation of their depth of meaning, he is not far from a finished driver. It may be almost termed a sweep : the ball is to be met by the club-head at a certain point in the swing, and swept away ; it is not to be *hit at*. The word 'hit' ought to be a misnomer for the stroke—too often it is not—and the word 'drive' should be scarcely less so. There is much in a name, in its effect upon those to whom it appeals; and the golfer, holding fast to the idea of 'driving'—as if driving in a pile, or, at all events, driving through a dense medium, which is really the notion which the word suggests—is unconsciously misguided into errors from which the idea conveyed by a 'sweep' or 'swing' would have probably preserved him.

But what, precisely, is the difference, it may be asked, between a hit and a sweep or swing? Just this, that the former is delivered with a jerk and with tightened muscles, the latter is a motion whose speed is gained by gradual, not jerky, acceleration, with the muscles flexible. This is, to the golfer, an enormously important truth; and one whose full appreciation would probably go far to improve the play of even the very best of golfers. It does not in the least preclude the application of great strength and great effort to the swing; it only precludes their misapplication. The muscles of the left hand are the sole exception to this rule of general flexibility; for the grip of the left hand must be firm, since it is the main connecting link between the human swinging machinery and the hickory machinery it wields. There must be no such weakness in this important joint between man and club as to permit the slightest falling out of gear on the concussion consequent on the meeting of club and ball.

The swing is, of course, made up of two parts, the upward and the downward swing; and the downward swing has a wonderful tendency to be, in point of direction, a reproduction, in reverse order, of the upward swing—that is to say, that the club-head will tend to trace the same course in its downward flight as it did in its upward. This is a fact so well known that professionals take every pains to see that the learner gets the upward swing correctly, knowing by experience that a correct downward stroke will naturally follow. Thus, when you are driving badly, a professional will often tell you that you are bringing your club up too straight. Of course, strictly speaking, what he means is, that you are bringing your club down too straight ; but he knows that if he can induce you to correct the former, the latter can be trusted to correct itself. So true is this, that an experienced observant player can nine times out of ten foretell, by watching the course of another's upward swing, whether or no he will make a correct swing of the downward stroke—that is to say, whether or no the shot will be a good one. Let us then give every due attention to this upward swing. The essential of the stroke, in point of direction, is that the club-head should travel as long as possible in the intended line of flight of the ball—this we have laid down as a maxim. In leaving the ball, therefore, the club-head should swing back as far as possible, but without too forced and painful straining after this object, upon a line which would be given by a production through the ball, and to the player's right, of the ball's intended line of flight. The club-head ought to sweep back along the ground, away from, rather than towards, the player. And how is this to be accomplished? By allowing the arms to go to their full length as the club-head swings away from the ball, or as nearly to their full length as is possible without forced stretching. In order to prolong this horizontal sweep back of the club some players fall into the error of swaying the body towards the right as the club swings away ; but this is a mistake, for the extended sweep is thus attained at too great an expense—at a sacrifice of accuracy. The driver's body should move on its own axis only ; the shoulders working round as if the backbone were their pivot. Let the club, then, be swept well away from the ball, the arms swinging freely away from the body, the left hand gripping firmly, the right hand holding lightly—which leads us to a somewhat *vexata quæstio*, the manner of this grip.

Certain points may be noted about the grip, but it is a mistake, in striving after a prescribed fashion, to work the hands into a position of discomfort. In the first place, a few inches of the shaft should be allowed to project above the left hand, for thus a greater command over the club is acquired. Secondly, since, as will be shown later on, the club has to turn in the right hand at a certain point in the swing, it should be held lightly, in the fingers, rather than in the palm, with that hand. In the left hand it should be held well home in the palm, and it is not to stir from this position throughout the swing. It is the left hand, mainly, that communicates the power of the swing; the chief function of the right hand is as

AT THE TOP OF THE SWING (AS IT SHOULD BE)

a guide in direction. The back of the left hand should be turned towards the direction in which it is intended to drive the ball—turned upwards, rather than downwards; for if at all turned downwards, it is almost impossible, as anyone may at once see for himself, to swing the club back round the head without shifting the grip. No less should the back of the right hand as it grips the club be somewhat upward; for if too much under a difficulty then presents itself (the difficulty, namely, of getting the club to follow easily through after the ball) at another part of the swing, at the moment that the club hits the ball. On the other hand, some professionals so exaggerate the upward turn of the back of the hands as to run a considerable risk of torturing their pupils into writer's cramp. The thumbs should lie in a natural position across the shaft of the club, not straight down it.

The two hands should be as close to one another as conveniently possible, for the object is not to strike the ball what Sir Walter Simpson calls a 'heavy' blow, but a swift one—not the sort of blow you strike a dynamometer, but the sort of blow with which a schoolboy flicks, with his fore-finger, a pill of paper across the room.

So much, then, for the grip. Now, when the club, in the course of its swing away from the ball, is beginning to rise from the ground, and is reaching the horizontal with its head pointing to the player's right, it should be allowed to turn naturally in the right hand until it is resting upon the web between the fore-finger and the thumb. At the same time the right elbow should be raised well away from the body until, when the club is horizontal *behind* the head, this right elbow is considerably above the level of the right hand. The club will have turned so freely in the right hand that the right wrist will be straight— in a natural easy manner—and the back of the right hand will be uppermost. The slight crook which will have been given to the left elbow, as a natural result of the slight upward turn of the back of the left hand, will have allowed the left hand to come up above the level of the right shoulder without any fumbling of that elbow against the striker's chest; and the left wrist will have been turned back to allow the club to come to the horizontal behind the head—for it is behind the head and above the right shoulder, not *round* the shoulder, that the club must be allowed to swing. To let the arms swing well away from the body, and to let the club turn freely in the right hand, are the two great points to bear in mind.

Such, then, should be the course of the upward swing—roughly approximating to an arc of a circle with a somewhat flattened circumference towards its base. And—remember this—it is a *swing*.

How many times has it been inculcated upon the young player that he is to bring his club slowly back, and how many has it led astray? For the golfer, hearkening to these words of his mystic oracle, 'Slow back,' has a tendency to lift his club with a stealthy painfulness of motion, as of a man—as Sir Walter Simpson humorously has it—striving to grab a fly upon his ear. So slow, so painfully, deadly slow—and then—whang! with a jerk. This is fatal: a cruel instance of the vile uses to which an excellent maxim, misunderstood, may be turned. There should be a certain even harmony about the golfing swing. The club should swing back quietly, without jerk or effort—slowly, if you will; but it must be a swing, and not a lift. It must swing quietly back, and it must not be arrested before it has done swinging back. The real meaning of the advice 'slow back' is that the club is not to be hurried back so that it cannot travel well out from the body. The advice called 'quick back' means being in such a hurry to get the club up that it is swung up too perpendicularly. The tiro who has this advice drummed into him is apt at last to turn in desperation and say, ' Why, every good player brings his club up quick!' This is true, but he does not bring it up so quickly that he has not time to sweep out his arms, as the tiro will inevitably do if he try to raise it equally quickly. Whether the swing be long or short, let the gentle force of the swing expend itself naturally, without effort of your muscles, and then, without dwelling, let the club begin to return again, so that the two swings shall appear natural parts of the one easy movement.

Now as the club came to the horizontal, behind the head, the body will have been allowed to turn, gently, with its weight upon the right foot. The knees, when addressing the ball, should have been slightly bent, at an easy natural angle, and in order to allow the body to make this half turn, without effort, the left heel should be allowed to rise slightly off the ground, so that, with an inward bend of the left knee the whole body will turn, naturally, upon the left toe. This raising of the left heel should not be an artificial action, so to speak—it should not be exaggerated with the view of *encouraging* the

AT THE TOP OF THE SWING (AS IT SHOULD NOT BE)

club to come round, but it should rather follow, as a natural sequence of the disposition of the rest of the frame. Some good drivers do not raise the heel at all, but this immobility is very little short of fatal to freedom. As in most other cases, the virtue is in the mean.

All these instructions should, of course, be read with frequent glances at their accompanying illustrations. It will there be seen that when the club is at the horizontal, roughly speaking, behind the back—i.e. at the top of the swing—the left forearm will be almost vertical from elbow to wrist, with elbow the lowest point, and will be brought round to what was the striker's front, as he stood when addressing the ball. It will be seen, too, that the left shoulder has been allowed to swing round underneath the head, while the right shoulder is above. As the club comes down, these positions should be almost reversed, and the more completely they are reversed—the more freely the right shoulder is allowed to swing away under, as the ball is struck—so much the more truly will the club-head swing through and follow the line of flight of the ball. Those who remember the style of young Jamie Allan will recognise the truth of this—how the shoulders came swinging round upon the backbone as if it were a pivot on which they revolved, and how beautifully true, in consequence, despite that peccant right foot forward, his swing came through! So the backbone must be steady, approximately speaking—for the body is not to be swung back, away from the ball (that, as has been pointed out, is a frequent error), but rather the shoulders are to swing round, upon the backbone, between the shoulder-blades as their pivot—working freely on a steady pivot.

Now, as the club comes near the ball, the wrists, which were turned upward when the club was raised, will need to be brought back, down again. It is a perfectly natural movement; but where many beginners go wrong with it is, that they are apt to make this wrist-turn too soon in the swing, and thereby lose its force altogether. The wrists should be turned again, just as the club is meeting the ball—otherwise the stroke, to all seeming perhaps a fairly hit one, will have very little power.

And the head is to be kept steady—as steady as if the line of vision from the two eyes to the ball were a rod of steel, rivetted at either end. All through the upward swing of the club the eyes are never, for the fraction of a second, to be seduced by the temptation of looking to see where it is going. It is a temptation—most of all a temptation, so poor young Tommy Morris used to tell us, with the attractive glitter of the well-polished iron. The eye is apt to go wandering after it, and sometimes it really never gets back upon the ball at all, or, if it does, only in a catchy, hazy sort of glance, which is a very vague guide for the free swinging club-head. Of course the swing is more or less mechanical; but it is far from being entirely so. Without the very keenest and most attentive assistance from the corrective eye, the most accurately swinging golfer cannot hope to bring down the club swinging in a perfect course, to sweep the ball away. All through the process of the upward swing the eye must be kept glued to the ball, until, at the height of the swing, it will be peering down, right over the left shoulder; and then, as the club swings down again, it should look at the ball harder than ever. As in a quarter-mile race the ideal to be aimed at is to start well nigh at the top of your speed and to go on increasing your pace until the finish, so, in the golf swing, begin by looking at the ball as hard as you can, and go on looking at it harder and harder, until it has been struck away—not only so, but go on looking at it, or at the place where it was, after it has gone; for this is the most seductive of all temptations to the tiro golfer—to take a glance, as from the top of Pisgah, at the land whither he promises himself he will send the ball; but whither he is very unlikely to send it if he look away from it a fraction of a second before its journey has begun. To guard against this, endeavour to keep on looking at it, even after it has been driven away. 'Keep your eye on the ball'—that is what all the professional droners keep on reiterating. It is immensely important. If you are looking anywhere else than at the ball, you might as well be as blind as Cupid; and it is quite marvellous how frequently attentive observation will show that a golfer is sometimes lifting his eye towards the hole just a trifle too soon, and sometimes seeming to think he is giving himself a fair chance if he gets a focus of anything within a foot of the irritating little bit of gutta-percha he is aiming at. And as the object is not to hit the ball upon the top, but on the side, let us remember to fix our eyes upon that spot of the ball which we wish to hit. Acting without thought of this, we are apt to fix our eyes upon the top, on which point it will be but a true correspondence of hand and eye if our club-head direct its severe attention likewise.

Correspondence of hand and eye—properly trained corre-

AT THE END OF THE SWING (AS IT SHOULD BE)

spondence—will, at golf, as at all kindred games, bring highest success. This is the unconscious genius with which the sportsman, gazing hard at his bird, brings his gun to his shoulder, without glancing along its barrel, with almost instinctive precision. But we have to help out this natural correspondence with studied mechanical measuring means. And this, mainly, is the function of the golfer's preliminary 'waggle.' By this little, almost playful, movement of the club over the ball we assure ourselves that our body is at the right angle of inclination to bring our hands at the proper distance, with regard to the length of club, from the ball. In addition to this, the preliminary 'waggle' is a means of seeing that all the machinery is in proper working order ; that the wrists, arms, muscles generally, are flexible, not tightened ; that the stand has been taken at a comfortable distance from the ball, and that the left hand is gripping tightly, while the right hand allows for some play of the club. The 'waggle' is, in fact, to the golfer, at each stroke, just what a trial trip is to a man-of-war or to an ocean steamer. It is apt to appear to the uninitiated a mere ornamental finish, but it is really of the greatest assistance, and can be dispensed with by no one. Golfers have golfed successfully in manifold improbable attitudes, but none have presumed to do altogether without the 'waggle.'

Your course of proceedings when you propose to drive the ball should be as follows :—When you approach the ball, you should first rest the head of the club upon the ground, just behind the ball, with the maker's name (stamped on the head of the club) just opposite the ball. With the club thus resting on the ground, and gripped in your two hands, you will then adjust your distance from the ball by shuffling with your feet. It is to be hoped that when you find yourself standing in tolerable comfort, and at a comfortable distance, you will also find yourself standing approximately in the position, and according to the measurements, indicated in our previous instructions and illustrations. These adjustments made, you should lift the club off the ground and execute the 'waggle.'

But you should not 'waggle' too much. Not only is it ungainly, but it is probably detrimental to accuracy. The present writer can speak feelingly upon this subject, as one who is grievously conscious of error in the shape of exuberance of 'waggle.'

The ideal 'waggle' consists in a gentle swaying to and fro, once or twice only, of the club over the ball, and in the same vertical plane as the arc which the head of the club ought to describe in the actual stroke. But the 'waggle' takes in but a small segment of this arc. These preliminary little trial swings should be given with the wrists working flexibly, and with the wrists alone. The upper arm should have nothing to do with it. Nevertheless, though the wrists should do all the active part of the 'waggle,' every joint in the lissome body, from the knees upward, will be affected by the movement of the 'waggle,' and will thus learn to spontaneously adjust the body at the right inclination. The club-head should swing forward, but a foot and a half or so in front of the ball, and about three feet away from it behind. Nevertheless, the length of the swing of a properly executed 'waggle' will depend largely upon individual lissomness of wrist.

Now this ideal 'waggle' is so smooth and quiet a performance as almost to belie the name which it has, in common parlance, earned, from its exaggeration. Even such a brilliant player as young Tommy Morris used to 'waggle' his driver with such power and vehemence in his vigorous young wrists as often to snap off the shaft of the club close under his hand before ever he began the swing proper at all. But genius is superior to rules of grammar; and yet its superiority is far from proving that, for the ordinary learner, such rules are superfluous. The 'waggle' of most of the slashing young St. Andrews players is a very much more athletic operation than the smooth swing we have been trying to indicate. None the less for that is it true that the learner will do better, in his days of inaccuracy, to handicap himself as little as possible by any such preliminary feats as must certainly tend to disturb the balance of his aim—to distort the true arc of his swing. Let the 'waggle' be executed quietly, with all the joints, except the grip of the left hand, loose (as in the actual swing), but with the wrists alone taking part as active agents in the preliminaries. And let the club-head travel in a plane, vertically, with the arc which it is to be hoped it will describe in the actual swing itself.

And, the 'waggle' thus concluded, let the club-head rest again for a moment, as a final measurement of distance, upon the ground behind the ball, before being smoothly swept away from it in the commencement of the upward swing.

It is important that the club should travel before the ball in somewhat the same arc as it shall describe in the stroke itself —no less than behind the ball—for this reason, that it is very

AT THE END OF THE SWING (AS IT SHOULD NOT BE)

little less important what becomes of the club after the ball is hit than before. The head must be following the ball along after it has been struck. It is with this object that we have advocated the free swinging down of the right shoulder to allow the arms to swing away after the ball. But whereas there is a constant tendency on the part of every unlearned golfer to swing his club round his body, after the stroke, which is wrong, instead of away from his body, which is right, it therefore is no unwise precautionary measure for the young player to slightly square his left elbow, which will be of great assistance in getting his arms away. This must be done in moderation, and must not be allowed to become a fetish, as it has with some—this crook of the left elbow. It is not by any means a panacea. It can but, as the doctors patronisingly say, 'help nature'—poor nature! The best illustration of the virtue of this left elbow crook is to be seen in the driving of Mr. Macfie.

We have, then, the left elbow a trifle crooked, the right elbow at an easy angle. How far should the hands be held away in front of the body—should they be held high up, or forced well down? The angle of the arms should be an easy, natural one—so, and no otherwise, do we feel most tempted to describe it ; but perhaps this will convey but little, or something far different to the intention, to the untutored golfer. In point of fact the illustrations will explain the angle of the arms and the angle of inclination of the body far better than words could do. But undoubtedly the tendency of the tiro golfer is not to get his hands down low enough. 'I drive like an auld wife cutting hay,' Bob Martin, then champion, remarked, one day, to the present writer ; and really this caricature does not convey a bad suggestion to the tiro golfer of the style of stroke intended. You need an almost scythe-like sweep of the club, but without that sway of the body which gives weight to the stroke of the scythe. Because, for the stroke of the golf club, we do not require weight, but speed. This sway of the body falls, together with rising off the left heel, and sundry other little peculiarities, under the head of what we may term false encouragements to the swing. They are deliberately adopted to give added length to the swing, and, as such, they are essentially vicious. Swaying with the body is a vice, absolutely—the shoulders should work freely upon the backbone as their steady pivot. The rising from the heel is not a vice, absolutely, but it becomes a vice when misused as a cause—with the object of elongating the swing back over the shoulders—instead of following as an effect resulting from the length and freedom of this backward swing as a natural growth.

Let the hands then be brought low down, as they place the club to address the ball. When we say that the shaft of the club should point at, or even almost below, the bottom waistcoat button, as executed by an ordinary tailor, we shall have perhaps given the most exact indication possible of the proper relative angle of hands, body and club.

Remember the instructions, that though the shoulders should work freely, the backbone is to be firm, and do not let yourself be led away by yet another insidious form of 'false encouragement' to your swing—letting yourself bend up, from the small of the back, as the club comes away from the ball. The back must remain throughout the swing at the same inclination at which you adjusted it when addressing the ball at the 'waggle.' If you let it unhinge itself at the small of the back, or if you let it rise up from the hips—in either case alike you throw all your measuring arrangements out of gear, and a 'top' or 'sclaff' will be the almost certain result. Though it has been insisted that the muscles must be flexible, it is no less true that they must not be uncontrolled—they must be supple but not loose. Your body, your arms—all the members of your frame—ought to be in the same relative positions at the moment of striking as when you addressed yourself to the ball. This is the secret of accuracy—of bringing the club back into the position in which you laid its head behind the ball ; and this can best—we had almost said only—be accomplished by keeping under firm control all parts of the body whose free movement is not essential to speed of swing. *This is the great secret.* These are big words to use, but they are not too big— for they are truth, and truth is great. Possibly the most general sin that cultured golfing flesh is heir to is a tendency to 'fall over' the ball as the club comes down to it. This is the result of inadequate control over the too freely working muscles, so that, in the player's exclusive attention to the speed of his swing, he does not so steady himself as to find the club and the jointed complications of his anatomy returning to the ball in the same relative positions in which they commenced the swing away from it.

And here it is that the question of the proper degree of suppleness in the shaft of the club most naturally suggests itself; for if a quick swinger play with an excessively supple club, his hands and body will have returned to the position in which they should be at the moment of club meeting ball, while the club, from its excess of suppleness, will be so bent, sickle-shaped, that its head will be still several inches from the ball. By the time the head does meet the ball the hands will be away in front of the ball, and all the mechanism just an atom out of gear. With a slower swing, however, the club would either have never been so bent at all, or would have regained its straightness before the head met the ball. Of all good players, old Tom Morris is probably he who plays with the most supple club; which he is able to do only by reason of the comparative slowness of his swing. Choose your clubs, therefore, of a proper suppleness with reference to the pace of swing which shall seem to you most easy and natural. And begin with stiff ones.

'But here,' the puzzled student will be apt to exclaim, 'here you have got us into a regular knot. You say that we are to get the club to the horizontal, or thereabouts, behind the back —very well. You admit that the shoulders may work freely; but you insist that the body is not to turn, except on its own axis—that is to say, neither from the small of the back nor the hips. How, then, is it possible for a human being to get the club horizontal behind his back, and to bring his left shoulder to the front, in the manner shown in the illustrations, when no turning is to be done on any joint below the shoulders?'

This is what the would-be golfer is likely to ask in his haste. We would point out to him that he has not interpreted our instructions rightly. We do not say turn on no joint below the shoulders. There are yet lower joints, below the hips—the knees; and it is from the knees that every good golfer allows his body to turn, as he drives. As the club rises, the left knee is bent inward and downward—as the left shoulder comes down—and the right knee is bent, somewhat more slightly than the left, and outward. Thus it is that the body is enabled to turn in the manner shown in our illustrations.

Now what, after all, is the meaning of the word 'swing,' which we have so often had occasion to use? It has a meaning which it is useful to fully realise. The upward swing should be slow and even, downward swing even and swift. But though the upward swing should be slow, it should, we have said, be a swing, and not a lift. And the essential difference between a swing and a lift, and between a swing and a hit, is this :—that in a swing one is all the while conscious of—one can all the while feel in one's hand—the weighty thing, the head of the club, *swinging* upward or downward, at the end of the shaft. We are to feel that the weight of the head has its influence upon the movement of the club—we must rather try to follow and be guided by this influence than to interfere with it with our tautened muscle; for this it is that produces jerkiness, and unevenness, and misses, and disaster. Encouraging and accelerating the speed of this swinging thing at the end of the club means hard driving, in its true sense—above all, accelerating the pace to its utmost at the moment that the club-head meets the ball. But directly we begin to force the swing out of its harmony —to over-accelerate the pace—from that instant it loses the true character of a swing and becomes a hit, a jerk—and this is 'pressing.' *Festina lente*—'Don't press.' Let the club swing *itself* through. Help it on, on the path of its swing, all you can, but do not *you* begin to hit with it. Let it do its work itself, and it will do it well. Interfere with it, and it will be quite adequately avenged.

And now we have finished, immensely, probably, to the student's relief, our didactic treatise upon the normal driving swing. We will now relate, for his recreation, a little golfing fable, a true story, not without its moral :—A certain Anglo-American, a true and zealous golfer, commencing the game at the time of life when autumn tints are seen among the hairs of the head, engaged for his instruction a well-known professional player, one Lloyd, surnamed 'The General.' After six weeks of hard study on the part of the pupil, and of painstaking tutorship on the part of the instructor, the former was mortified to discover that he played worse than on the very first day of his apprenticeship. Remarking on this singular fact to his tutor, the latter, for the first time, lost his much-tried patience, and exclaimed in accents of despair, 'Eh then, just tak' and throw yer club at the ba'.' This advice the would-be golfer put into immediate practice, if not in the letter, at least in the spirit, by striking at his ball almost without aim at all. What was his astonishment and delight at feeling the club strike the ball with perfect accuracy, and seeing the globe fly through the air to a greater distance than he ever, save in his dreams, had struck it in his life. And so it continued : by letting himself go, and playing with careless freedom, he found himself able to accomplish feats of which in his days of 'taking thought' he had almost come to despair.

Now what is the moral to be learnt from this true story? That all the intervening weeks of tuition had been wasted?—by no means. Without them he would never have been able to 'throw the club at the ball' and strike it as he did. We may be very sure that he swung no differently, on this his first occasion of free-striking, than in all those carefully studied failures which had preceded it. But he swung without thinking, without consciousness of the mechanical adjustments—just as a well-ordered stomach does its work of digestion—with all his eye, thought, and energy concentrated on the ball. But the tuition was necessary in order to give effect to the intuition. And this is the moral which we wish to point. It is necessary, in order to become as good a golfer as your natural gifts permit, to go through all this laborious and careful training while your style is in course of forming ; but when once your style is formed, when you are engaged in a match, and not occupied with the painful eradication of some darling fault, then you should let your style take care of itself. You must concentrate yourself then upon hitting the ball. If you get thinking of how you are going to do it, you will not do it well. But, until your style is formed, you will do far better to go conscientiously through this hard course of training, for it will well repay you in the end. Not only so, but after you consider that your style is really fairly formed, you should still practise—at balls at off moments, at daisies as you walk between the strokes, at imaginary golf balls in your front hall—in studious observation of all the rules of correct driving. Then, when the match comes, think about the ball and the hole ; and the laboriously acquired series of adjustments will reproduce itself spontaneously.

But, on the other hand, you must not allow yourself to be so puffed up with pride at the success of one or two such 'throwings' of the club at the ball as to think that you may indulge your muscles with a perfect joyous freedom, and smite away as hard as you can. This is a frequent temptation—very fatal. *Quem Deus vult perdere, prius dementat.* The one or two successful shots have filled your heart with a sort of insane jubilation, and you are very apt to think that you are sure to hit the ball provided only you hit carelessly enough. In fact, you are seduced into slogging : and it will take many a weary round of the old too-familiar treadmill to bring you back to such semblance of a game as you were just beginning to exhibit. In the words of the drill-sergeant, 'One, two, three, four—Now that you've got it, sir, see that you keep it, sir.' That is what you have to strive to do—to keep it, sir. Not to go to work to try and improve upon what is a legitimate subject of surprise to you that you should have done even so well as you have. Keep it—the good gift that fortune has sent—and practise with it, without trying too much, until you have made it your own and can keep it, even in fortune's despite.

A symptom unmistakable of a too free indulgence in this

joyous carelessness is that striking, or resting of the club, at the top of the swing, on the right shoulder, which is so pregnant a source of manifold disaster to the young golfer. It is an effect of stretching after an artificially long swing back, and as it causes a jerk and break in the harmonious movements of the swing, it is only natural that it should be so disturbing to the aim. In the figure of Mr. Leslie Balfour we see the proper

MR. LESLIE BALFOUR

position of the club as it comes horizontal behind the head. It is there seen to be high above the right shoulder, so that it would have to travel many inches from its normal course to touch the shoulder at all. To keep the club as far away from the shoulders as possible is not a bad suggestion for the direction of the entire course of the swing; for it contains the good points of stretching the arms well away from the ball in the upward and downward swings, and the notion of letting the arms well away from the body after the ball is struck, so as to fetch the club round at the greatest distance possible from the left shoulder. Some golfers so wind their arms round instead of away from their body after the ball is struck as to break many a club upon their left shoulder. The more normal form of this fault—of which club-breaking upon the shoulder is an extreme—is shown in the illustration (p. 91) of how the arms ought *not* to go, after the ball is hit.

Let the swing, then, work itself out—do not seek to hurry it ; yet let it be free. You must not strive so painfully after accuracy as to lose all dash. But there is one point that is quite essential to accuracy, no matter how practised a player you may be ; and that is, that you should be looking at the ball the moment the club is meeting it. And this you cannot do if you let your eye wander away during any part of the swing. We are guilty of this repetition lest the learner, misled by our advice to combine freedom with his studied series of adjustments, should be tempted to strike at the ball, as, all unconsciously, he will be very sure to do, many a time and oft, while his eye is enjoying itself among the surrounding scenery.

But, finally, this advice which we have given is not to be carried out, in its fullest meaning, by all of you. Worthy old gentlemen who begin golf at a time of life when a sight of their toes is not obtained without an effort cannot hope to get their club—by any means at all easy or natural—to the horizontal behind their head. If they succeed in getting it into this position, it will be by means of some of these fatal 'false encouragements' which we have noticed. It will not be a truly long swing, but a swing pretending to be longer than it really is. For these old gentlemen, no less than for the others, the proper advice is to let the swing develop itself as far and freely as it will—with freely moving shoulders, if may be, on a firm backbone, and with play and turning on the knees—but this natural development of the swing will be but a short arc of the glorious curve traced by the head at the end of a shaft gripped by a supple youngster. Nevertheless for crabbed age too, which will ever grow less crabbed as it golfs, the swing must be in kind, if not in degree, as we have described it; for so only will the golfer, no matter of what age, evolve to the utmost the capacity that is in him of combining 'the far and the sure.'

(B) PLAYING THROUGH THE GREEN.

Long ere reaching this point it will have very possibly occurred to the intelligent reader to criticise in this wise :—'The principle of letting the club-head travel, during as long a segment of the swing as possible, in the desired line of flight of the ball may be most excellent as regards balls upon the tee, and clean-lying balls generally; but it is obvious to the meanest capacity that there are cases of certain unhappy lies where such a principle cannot possibly be applicable.' The criticism is just: it is quite obvious that, if we try to put in practice this principle when there is a lump behind the ball, the lump will receive the larger share of the energy which we would wish to devote exclusively to the ball; the club-head may even stop in the lump, and go no further.

It must be our object then, under these unfortunate circumstances, to swing the club-head down so as to nip in between the lump and the ball. This, therefore, will be a downward stroke—the scythe-like motion is no longer applicable. Now a downward stroke, descending with the full force of the swing, cannot be re-directed at the moment after it has swept down over the lump and is meeting the ball. It must continue in its somewhat downward course, even after meeting the ball, and must therefore plough into the ground. Thus meeting the ground involves a jerk: the whole mechanism is conscious of a concussion—the wrists more especially so—and it is from this jerk that the stroke takes its name. A ball thus played from a lie of this description is said to be 'jerked.'

It is a name that has doubtless given rise to misapprehension (against which we would put our reader on his guard) in the minds of many ; for it suggests the erroneous and very disastrous notion that there should be something jerky in the swing. Of course a jerky swing is, properly understood, a contradiction in terms. It is part of the meaning of the word swing that there should be nothing jerky about it. And the swing for the jerking stroke should be as true a swing—as absolutely free of jerk—as any other. It differs from the straightforward driving swing, which sweeps away the clean lying ball, only in point of direction. It is no less true of the swing of the jerking stroke than of the true driving swing that the downward swing will be naturally inclined to follow upon the track of the upward swing. If we raise the club correctly, it will descend correctly. It is scarcely necessary to instruct the golfer how to raise the club straighter from the ball than we have told him he is to do for the ordinary drive ; for it is part of the original sin of golfing nature to raise the club too straight, and he will be only too pleased to find any excuse for doing so. The arms, of course, must not be stretched away from the body so far as in the ordinary swing ; this is the obvious and natural means of swinging the club up more straightly. But there is this further point to be remembered—that the ball should be rather nearer the right foot than in the drive. The hands, however, must be kept in the same vertical plane with the eye, as in the other stroke ; whereby the hands will be somewhat in front of the ball, and the whole body more over the ball than in the drive. If these arrangements are not attended to, the ball will be almost inevitably sliced, in consequence of its being impossible, by reason of the lie of the ball, to give the club its normal sweep. As a further guard against slicing, the left elbow may well be kept slightly more to the front than is necessary in the drive. The club should be gripped firmly, in order that, as the head cuts or brushes the lumpy ground as it meets the ball, it shall not be turned, even ever so little, in the hand. It is even permissible, in this case, to grip firmly with the right hand, provided as a precautionary measure against pulling the right shoulder be allowed to swing down very free and loose.

In all other respects—except, of course, where they contradict the above remarks—the methods recommended for the common drive are perfectly applicable to the jerking stroke. It is a stroke which may legitimately be played with brassy, cleek, or iron—with a full swing—and it is a stroke which every golfer should aspire to acquire. It is not difficult; and to those who do not understand it, it is a mystery which fills their hearts with black envy of opponents who thus force the ball away from an unpromising lie almost, if not quite, as far as if it had been lying clean. We have considered it under its most typical aspect—a lie with a lump behind the ball—and it is applicable to every modification of this kind of lie, whether cuppy, 'foggy,' or what not.

It is a very common mistake with regard to this stroke to suppose that the club cuts into the turf *behind* the ball; though how this idea can be maintained by those who have seen the distance a ball travels off a stroke of this kind is hard to understand. As a matter of fact, the club hits the ball *before* it meets the turf, in its downward course—or it may be that the centre of the face meets the ball at the moment that the edge of the brass sole (supposing the club a wooden one) is meeting the grass. At all events, with a properly jerked ball the player is first conscious of club meeting ball—and *then*, and not till then, digging down and jerking in the ground. If the club hits the ground before it meets the ball the stroke is baffled, and the ball goes only a very wretched little distance.

A very great many good amateur players and nearly all professionals play almost all their full iron shots with this downward, jerking stroke—quite irrespective of how the ball may be lying. It is quite certain that it is easier to keep a ball thus jerked, on the desired line. Why this is so is hard to say, unless it be because it does not much matter, in this kind of stroke, what becomes of the swing after the ball is struck; whereas we saw that in the ordinary drive the after part of the stroke was of almost more importance than the former. But whatever the reason be, whether it be, as Sir Walter Simpson suggests, that the ball is thus struck what he calls a 'heavy' blow, it is certain that full iron shots can, taking the average all through, be kept straighter on this method than on the other, simpler one; and not only so, but the ball seems to fly away from a stroke of this description with a suggestion of a strict attention to business which conveys the idea that it knows what is required of it. It gives one the impression that the player has great command over it. The beginner's chief difficulty about the jerking shot is really an imaginary, a subjective one. He has got it into his head that there is to be a great jerk somehow, and he has a fixed idea that some superhuman effort on his part is required to bring this jerk about. Let him disabuse his mind of this fallacy, and he will find he gets on much better. Swing downward on the ball, letting your right shoulder work very freely down and round, as if there were no solid earth for the club to meet. Forget all about the jerk that is coming, and think of nothing but hitting the ball. The solution of the mystery of the stroke is that there *is* no mystery. Swing down on the ball, and let the club and the ground make their mutual explanations for themselves.

This method of playing iron shots of course cuts up many great fids of turf, and is therefore much deprecated by some of the players of the old school who were heroes in the days of the ' baffy '—in our opinion most unnecessarily. The truth is that a deep-cut divot—such as those we used to see hurtling through the air from the full iron strokes of Davie Strath, Bob Fergusson, Jamie Allan, and a host besides—if carefully replaced and trodden down, did not one mite of harm. It is the sclaffy little scrubs of the ground, which crumble to bits the piece they wound out, that do far the more damage; and such are quite likely to be scraped by the baffy. But the clean, deep-cut divot of the well-jerked iron stroke can be fitted in and will grow again as if it had had no such aërial journey, on the principle on which a gardener cuts deep and wide round the roots of a tree which he is about transplanting.

There are two points to be borne in mind when playing at balls lying in heavy grass. (1) You are exceedingly apt to pull the ball—therefore you should aim somewhat to the right, to allow for this tendency; and (2) your aim is very likely to be bothered by long wires of grass winding themselves about the club as you draw it back. The proper names of these wires of grass is windle straws, and the golfer commonly calls them 'wannel-stræs.' There can be nothing more exasperating than the maddening clutch in which they retain the club as you swing it back. The best way of fighting them is to draw the club back more slowly than usual, with a firm grip.

Of bad-lying balls, other than balls in a cup in the ground or the grass, the chief are the following : The ball with a face in front of it, the hanging ball, the ball lying above you, and the ball lying below you. In each of these circumstances the actual lie of the ball may be quite good, but it becomes for practical purposes a bad lie, by reason of its surroundings. The difficulty of getting away a ball with a face in front of it depends upon the nearness and the height of the face. If the face be very near, and high, and abrupt, it will be necessary to take an iron, whilst if it be 'a little farther away the obstacle may perhaps be cleared with the brassy. Of course the great object is to make the ball rise quickly off the club. This cannot be done without getting the club-head well under the ball, and therefore from a grassy lie it is often possible to clear a fronting face with the brassy where, had the ball been lying upon hard ground, it had been necessary to take the iron. But, in either case, whether the iron or cleek or brassy be used, the ball can be made to rise more quickly than its normal wont, off the club face, by slightly slicing it. All pulled balls start away low ; all sliced balls start away high. It is therefore advisable in such circumstances as these we are considering to play to slice the ball : to draw the club across the ball as it descends upon it. It will not thus, of course, go so far as if it could be got away clear of the hill with a perfectly true stroke ; but it will go a great deal farther than if it started by plunging into the hill. We, of course, have to remember that the ball so sliced will necessarily fly in something of a curve towards the right ; so that we shall have to make due allowance for the deviation. If the ball lie absolutely *on* the face—a cocked-up ball, as it is commonly called—the upward lie will so aid us in driving it high in the air, and over the brow of the hill, that we may take almost any club we please. The swing must be so arranged, however, that the club-head shall travel over the ground, in an upward sweep, conformably to the lie of the ground itself—and for effecting this it is advisable to stand well behind the ball ; that is to say, with the ball about opposite the left foot.

It is not, of course, very easy to slice the ball just when and how desired. You should stand with the ball rather in front of you. Now this, if you were to swing in the ordinary manner, would incline you rather to pull than to slice. But you must not swing in quite the ordinary manner—or rather, we should say, that your hands, as they grip the club, should be more in front of you (opposite the left thigh) than in the ordinary stroke. This will turn your club-face slightly outward. Your right foot should be slightly more forward, with reference to the line of the proposed shot, than in the ordinary drive, and these preliminaries of adjustment of hands and feet will predispose you to striking the ball with the required slice. It will, moreover, be found a great aid to this stroke if a slight pause be made at the top of the swing—not too laboured a pause, yet just so much as may assist in the accuracy of aim. The great fallacy that besets us when we address ourselves to a badly-lying ball is the fallacy that the harder we hit, the more likely we are to force it away. 'Force !' It is a word that is responsible for many an error of pressing and consequent awkwardness. The universal maxim that we should bear in mind as we play through the green, is that the worse the ball is lying, the more gently, the more easily, ought we to swing, for the worse the lie, the more need is there—not of force, but of accuracy. It is as unfortunate a term as 'jerk' for the shot that takes a ball out of a cup. There is a jerk, it is true, as the club-head meets the ground, but there must be no jerk in the swing as the club sweeps down with free downward swinging right shoulder. Now, as we come down to 'jerk,' as it is called, a ball from a bad lie, or, again, as we try to lift a ball over a face in front of us (with the idea of getting 'well under' it most prominent in our minds), in both cases we are very likely to make a mess of it through allowing ourselves to fall forward on the ball, the whole body and back bending down instead of the shoulders swinging round on the backbone on their pivot. There is a great tendency to do this, with that fixed idea of 'getting under the ball' in our minds; but it must not be, or the consequence will be disaster.

There is a great and horrible variety of bad lies. The one that has, perhaps, the most horrors of all for the unskilful is of very little consequence to the expert—it is the 'hanging ball' —a ball lying on a hill sloping towards the line in which we should like to drive it. How is it that the good player manages to get it away as he does? Well, in the first place, even he will usually take a somewhat spooned club. The straight-faced driver is scarcely the weapon for it, even in his hands, but it will make very little difference in the length of the resultant drive. How does he do it? It seems to be quite simple. He does not seem to bother himself particularly about 'getting under the ball,' which still, though this time with less reason, is the fixed idea in the mind of the poor player. His club seems to sweep over the surface of the ground just as if the ball lay on the level. That is a remark which anyone can make—the very remark that the envious poor player is most likely to make; but he will make it without any conception of the fact that in the truth of that remark lies the whole solution of the difficulty. You, have not to change your stand or your grip one iota from that in which you hit that last fine tee-shot; all you have to do is to let the club sweep over the ground as if the ball were lying smooth on the level. You may, if you like, turn the face of the club a little bit outward (your natural inclination will be to turn it rather inward, with some indefinite idea of making it 'clip in to the ball'). The outward turn will perhaps help you a little in getting the ball up into the air; but the real secret is not in this, but simply in the fact you yourself noticed in the stroke of the good player, that his club swept over the ground as if it were level. This is the answer to the riddle. Try to forget all about the inclination of the ground to the horizon. Take a club spooned at such an angle that the inclination of the face will compensate for the angle of the hill, and swing away as if the ground were level. You will find it very hard to bring yourself to realise that the stroke does not require some remarkable upward twist as the club meets the ball, but it is not so. The club must swing downwards over the ground, following the course of the latter until it meet the ball, and then (when the ball is struck), still on in the same line, leaving the spoon of the club to do the elevating. It is not, perhaps, as flattering to your pride as to think that by some extra unknown effort of wrist you can hoist the ball into the air, but still it is true—it is the club that must be left to do the hoisting. After all, it is far more humiliating to make a bungle. So just swing as if the ground were level, only remembering the universal maxim for all bad lies—that the worse the lie, the more quietly should you swing.

When we come to the consideration of balls lying on a hill facing you—or on a hill lying away from you—the difficulty is found to be not so much in getting the proper elevation on the ball as the proper direction. Some would say, take a short club for the ball that lies toward you, a long one for the ball that lies away from you; but for our part we have little belief in the value of this advice. Let us first discuss the ball on the hillside lying towards you—the slope of the hill at right angles to the direction of the hole. The great tendency with this stroke is to pull the ball, and to hit it on the toe of the club. Since the club is constructed primarily for ground that is approximately level, the toe is naturally that part of it which will first find its resting-place on the ground when we lay the club-head behind a ball thus lying facing us. Some might suggest a peculiarly upright club for this stroke, and a peculiarly flat one for the ball lying away ; but for our part we are not advocates for special clubs for special occasions. A new broom of this nature is not at all likely to sweep as clean as the old familiar stick. But we may perhaps manage to make our ordinary club address the ball satisfactorily by keeping our hands rather lower than usual, thus bringing the heel of the club lower upon the ground. But even when we have thus persuaded the club to fairly face the ball, there is the further tendency to 'pull' to be contended with. Shifting the position of the feet will be no good ; for if we bring the right foot forward we shall find it difficult to bring the club round clear of the opposing hill, and if we bring it further back, we do but encourage the pulling tendency. What is it that so inclines us to pull in this stroke? Undoubtedly it is that our arms are inclined to come back, round, down-hill towards us after we have struck the ball. It is an effort to induce them to go away from us, up-hill, after the ball—that is the reason of the pulling ; and it is by conscientiously making this effort that we may hope to overcome the vicious tendency. And how is the effort to be made? Certainly not by lunging with our body after the ball—that would be fatal ; but by letting the swing be very free and loose, especially by holding the right hand loose. Thus may we hope to induce the club-head to follow on properly after the ball. But, after all, it is very difficult—so difficult that many of the very best players seem to deem it the better part of valour to accept the pull as inevitable in the stroke. They stand so as to make allowance for the pull, which they know to be likely to follow. Nevertheless, it may to a great extent be obviated by attention to the special maxim of letting the swing and the right grip be free and easy, and to the universal maxim of swinging quietly at the bad-lying ball.

Now almost all this may be applied, conversely, to the ball

lying away from one. The heel is the portion of the club which now is naturally first to rest upon the ground ; therefore it will need that the hands be somewhat raised, in order that the club may fairly face the ball. Yet this is a stroke in which accuracy of direction is even harder to be attained than in the last ; nor can you so well forecast in which direction you will deviate ; for while it very seldom happens that a ball lying facing you is sliced, if truly hit at all, on the other hand it is often seen that a ball lying away is scandalously badly pulled. The chief tendency is, of course, to slice off the heel of the club. But when you make up your mind that you will sweep the club well round, and so avoid this error, you are very apt to rush into the very opposite extreme, and whirl the ball away to mid-on in a very astonishing manner. In truth, that is the lie of all others where the general maxims are of chief use, and for which no specifics are of value. Swing quietly, let the club (not your body) follow on the ball, and hope for the best.

Let us now briefly sum up the heads of the results so far attained :—

1. In cuppy lie : Swing evenly downwards so as to nip in between edge of cup and ball. Do not think about the 'jerk.'

2. With face in front : Play to somewhat slice the ball.

3. With hanging ball : Swing, with spooned club, over the surface of the ground, as if it were level.

4. Ball lying above, facing you : Swing freely, with right hand gripping lightly.

5. Ball lying below, away from you : Swing quietly.

The advice that we have given applies equally to wooden clubs and to full shots with cleeks and irons, and should your natural tendency be to somewhat 'jerk' the ball with the iron clubs, it will make no matter.

So much, then, for playing through the green.

(C) APPROACHING

'An approach shot' does not mean merely a stroke whose result is that the ball approaches somewhere near the hole—in some unfortunate but justly named 'approach shots' this is very far from being the case—but it means a stroke played with the intention of leaving the ball, which is as yet not on the putting-green, certainly on the putting-green, and possibly, somewhere near the hole. A full drive, with which the player smites with full vigour, not expecting to reach the hole, can scarcely be called an 'approach shot,' even though the ball, going farther than anticipated, lie stone-dead ; but it becomes an approach shot, even if played with the full driving swing, if the player had the expectation of reaching the hole, and therefore, as he should have done, calculated where the ball was likely to pitch, how it was likely to run after the fall, and generally paid more attention to nicety of direction than to length of drive.

Now, the great majority of drives are somewhat more sliced than pulled ; moreover, it is shown by experience that shots played as we have described—with special reference to direction rather than to length—are somewhat more apt to be sliced than others. Therefore, it should be borne in mind, in playing these full approach shots, that the ball is likely, on falling, to break to the right, and that it is therefore advisable (other things, such as the lie of the ground, &c., being equal) to aim rather to the left of the hole.

(In all these instructions we are, of course, presuming a right-handed player.) Further than this, it is not necessary to give advice with regard to the approach shot played with the full swing, for all the instructions with regard to the full swing in general are applicable. With regard to all approach shots, however, it cannot be repeated too often that the failing of the great majority of players is being short. For one shot that is past, you will see six that are not up. Therefore, when doubtful what club to take for your approach shot, it is a good rule to always take the longer of the two between which you are hesitating. For, remember, you base your calculations on the assumption that you are going to hit the ball correctly. No accident is therefore likely to make the ball go farther than your expectation, while the accidents that may possibly curtail its distance are, alas! only too many.

For the present, then, we may thus briefly dismiss the consideration of approach shots played with the full swing. The approach shot, in its common acceptation, conveys the idea of a stroke played with the iron, with something less than the full swing.

Approach shots, thus understood, differ from each other: (*a*) in point of distance, (*b*) in point of elevation, (*c*) in point of style.

(*a*) includes:—1. Three-quarter shots. 2. Half shots. 3. Wrist shots.

(*b*) includes:—1. Running the ball up, along the ground. 2. Lofting with run. 3. Lofting, so as to pitch nearly dead.

(*c*) includes:—1. Ball played with a straightforward stroke (club-head moving in the line of flight of the ball). 2. Ball played with cut (club-head moving across line of flight of ball).

These are not merely technical terms of difference, but denote differences, to understand which, in theory, will greatly help the golfer to accurately gauge the strength of his stroke, and execute it successfully.

The three-quarter stroke is the stroke required when at such a distance from the hole that a full swing shot would go just a little too far. (We may put aside, for the present, the question of elevation and of cut.) This three-quarter stroke distance is, perhaps, the most awkward of all—the shot at which most failures are made. If the golfer can understand rightly the difference between this stroke and the full swing stroke and the half shot respectively, it will greatly help him to play it correctly, instead of making a muddle of it, by trying to play a hybrid between a full swing and a half shot; for it differs from both. It differs from the full stroke mainly in this: that in the three-quarter stroke the shoulders do not swing round. It is a stroke played with the arms alone. The left shoulder does not swing down, nor, as a consequence, does the left heel rise

THREE-QUARTER STROKE

much from the ground. Let the iron swing back as far as the arms will take it, but do not let the shoulders go away after the club, or you will produce that kind of cross between full swing and three-quarter stroke—that kind of spoiled full shot—which is the pitiable fashion in which many golfers habitually miss their three-quarter shots.

So much, then, for the length of swing allowed to your three-quarter strokes. Wherein does the half shot differ from it? In this, that in the half shot, the right arm, from the shoulder to the elbow, takes no part in the stroke. It is a stroke played from the elbow only of the right arm—the upper part of that arm being kept closely to the side. Swing the club back as far as your wrists and the movement of your right fore-arm will take it, and no further, or, again, you make a hybrid between a three-quarter and a half shot, which is seldom successful.

If you can induce your club to recognise the difference between each of these strokes, you will have made a considerable step towards learning to play your approach shots. Meanwhile, your body must have been kept steady in the position in which you took your stand. Swing of the body will disturb your aim. The only assistance to the swing which the lower joints may give, is by the knuckling in of the knees.

The importance of appreciating these distinctions can scarcely be overrated. The great cause of the inexperienced golfer's failure to play his approach shots reasonably is that he has no definite idea of how he is going to swing his club at each distance—that there is no method about his stroke. The recognition of the distinction is one of the principles of the grammar of the approach shot. The other great one is that the golfer should learn to use his wrists. This he can best learn by practice at the wrist stroke proper—the stroke in which the iron is allowed to go back scarcely further than the turn of the wrists takes it, with hardly any movement even of the right fore-arm. Manifestly, it is only to be used for a very short stroke, and, in point of fact, it is not different in kind, but only in degree, from the half shot; for, for almost every wrist stroke, the right fore-arm is slightly used.

To say the truth, these iron strokes are less truly swings than is the full driving stroke. There is more of a hit at the ball—a hit given by a turn of the wrists at the moment the club is meeting the ball. For this the club has to be pretty firmly gripped. The turn of the wrists is, in point of fact, rather an upward turn, as the club is brought away from the ball, than a back turn; and as the club descends, the wrists have to be brought sharply back to the position in which they were held while addressing the ball. It should be part of the preliminary address to the ball, before striking, to bring the club away and back, once or twice, over the ball, with this upward and downward movement of the wrists, to see that they understand the movement they have to execute in the stroke.

In the full driving stroke the weight of the body is transferred from the left leg to the right as the club swings up, and, conversely, from the right leg to the left again as the club comes down. In half-swing shots this is not the case. In the three-quarter shot it is partly the case, but the tendency is to keep the weight more and more confined to one leg the shorter the shot. No really good golfer that we are aware of has his weight equally divided upon his two legs in playing his half and wrist iron shots. Some few rest their weight upon the left leg in playing approaches. The vast majority rest it upon the right leg. We will therefore obey this great consensus of opinion and strive to supply the learner with hints on this hypothesis— that the approach shot should be played off the right leg. In the drive we have placed our tiro, as he addresses the ball, facing very nearly at right-angles to the line of the proposed drive. For the half-iron shot we must ask him to make a half-left turn, so that he will be facing at an angle of 45° to the line of the proposed stroke. His left foot should point at a very similar angle to that line. And what about his right foot, then? In the first place, it should be half as near again to his left foot as in the driving stroke, and instead of being a little behind the line drawn from the left toe parallel to the proposed line of flight of the ball, it should be well in front of that line. Let us illustrate this by another diagram. Here, as before, x is the proposed line of flight of the ball, B the ball, C the club, I the striker's eye, H H his hands gripping the club, L F his left foot, and R F his right foot, in front of the line z, parallel to the line x. Now, comparing this with the position of standing for the drive, what differences do we note? Besides being in front of the line, the right foot is turned inward, instead of outward, to accommodate itself to the half-left turn of facing direction. H H, the hands, are represented on the nearer side to 1 of the line z, to indicate that they should be kept near in to the body. The position of B, the ball, is quite different. Instead of being nearly opposite the left foot, as is the case in the previous diagram for the drive, it is now nearly opposite

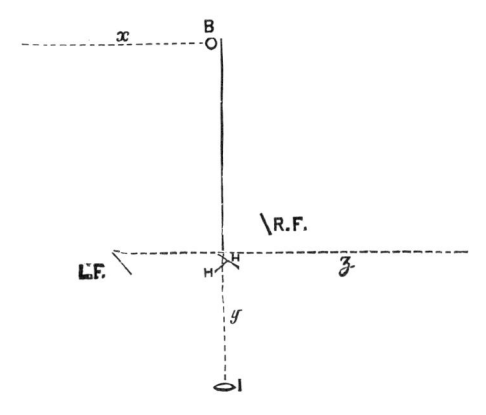

the right foot. Finally, though eye, hands and ball are still in one plane, this plane is not quite at a true right angle with the line of flight of the ball. The main other difference between the attitudes for this and the driving stroke respectively is that the knees are in this more bent, and the whole body in a more crouching posture.

The position we have been thus endeavouring to suggest is the attitude for a half-shot of medium distance and of medium loft—that is to say, a stroke which will loft the ball a certain distance and will then allow it to run ; it is the position for the typical half shot. It is also the correct position for the cutting strokes which make the ball stop dead, and similar elegancies which should not be exhibited in a match except under stress of necessity.

For the three-quarter stroke the position is very similar, but the right foot should not be so far forward, nor should the ball be so much to the player's right. The position for the three-quarter shot is, in short, a compromise between the positions we have indicated for the drive and the half-shot

THE POSITION FOR THE APPROACH SHOT

respectively. Roughly speaking, the shorter the shot the farther may the right foot be advanced and the nearer to it may the ball be placed.

The same attitude of standing is best suitable also for the running-up stroke with the iron, though the ball for this latter stroke will need to be yet more to the player's right, and is often seen quite opposite, or even outside his right toe.

Presuming, now, that we have these positions right, we must next consider the grip of the club and the angle of the arms. We have already said that the hands are to be nearer in to the body than was the case in the driving stroke. The right elbow is in fact to be close in to the side, and the right fore-arm (remember, we have said that the knees are to be considerably bent) almost resting upon the right thigh. This the illustrations will readily explain, and the position of the hands as they grip the club, relatively to the body, is thus sufficiently fixed. The left elbow ought to be slightly squared. A very high authority asserts that this squaring of the left elbow tends to produce slicing of the ball to the right, but in all deference to that high authority, we would submit that very many of the best iron players exaggerate this crooking of the left elbow to an almost fantastic extreme, and that in our own experience we have always found this crook to be highly helpful to straight steering.

We have very nearly come to the last hole in our account of these preliminary adjustments to our half-iron shots. It remains only to discuss the nature of the grip. It is a delicate matter, this iron stroke, it requires a nice tenderness of touch; our fingers are the most delicate instruments of touch we possess, therefore it is as much as possible in our fingers that we should hold our iron for the approach. Yet not gingerly— as if the weapon was a lady's fan—but with a firm close grip upon it, so that it shall feel like a part of our limbs. Even in the fingers of the right hand may we grasp it with loving firmness. For, see, in the driving stroke we had to let the club turn back in our right hand, upon the web between the forefinger and thumb. In this stroke, on the contrary, the club does not need, indeed should not, turn an atom in our grasp. The first section of the fore-finger of the right hand should press well home upon the leather, for this is the point that is going to give it the greater part of its guidance throughout the stroke. Firmly in our fingers then, so that we get a good feel of it, should we hold it, and yet, firm as is the fingers' grip, the wrists are to work well and supple. Practise the stroke first, without a ball, with the wrists only—the wrists bent back as shown in the three following illustrations as the club is brought back, and then forward again just as sharply as you can do it with comfort. Remember to hold the club well and firmly in the right forefinger ; the other fingers do not matter. Then take a ball and see whether you can hit it truly, using still the wrists alone.

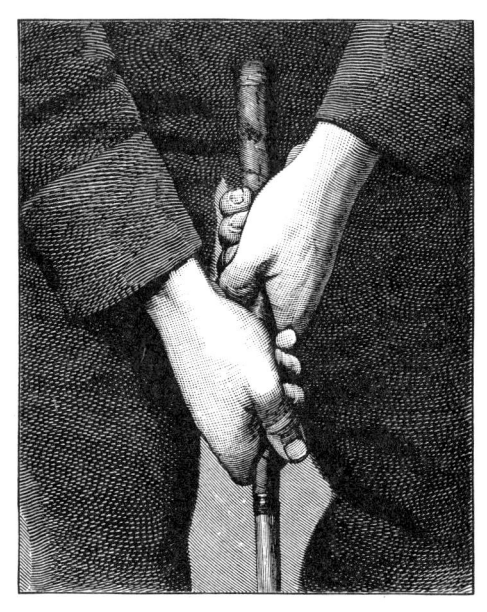

POSITION I

If you can accomplish this, treat yourself to a little longer shot—one wherein the right fore-arm is also brought into play. In order to bring the right fore-arm into play, though the right upper-arm be still kept close along the side, you will find yourself obliged to let your left hand follow the club away back, which it can only do by the straightening across the body of the left elbow. The stroke has now become a slightly different one from the pure wrist stroke. In the latter there was no movement of the club with the arms, which did not themselves move. But now the arms have gone away a little to give the club a little further swing than the wrists by themselves could allow. We have pointed this out especially because we would have you notice in particular the following advice—though the arms have swung a little back with the club, do not let them swing forward again any further than so as to regain the position in which they were when the ball was being addressed. Let the following on of the club after the ball be under control of the wrists alone. But it is not the extra length of swing thus given that in itself gives greater power to the stroke, but rather it is that this little additional length gives the wrists a little more time for accelerating the speed of the club—that is, the strength of the stroke.

These are true wrist strokes. We remember to have read in some didactic golfing work the remark that the name of wrist strokes was a misnomer. The writer even went so far as to say that he would wish the term abolished, and that it might be replaced by the term 'knee' strokes—the ancient name, as he averred, of this stroke. Now all this is pure misconception. The strokes we have been describing are wrist strokes in the most true sense of the term, and the golfer who does not play them with his wrists does not play the game at all. He does not play iron shots, technically so called, but he putts the ball up with the iron. Some men who 'play their iron,' as they call it, very well for an approach over level ground, are utterly unable to play a true 'iron shot' at all—are completely nonplussed when there is an intervening bunker and not ample running ground between it and the hole beyond. But these men could approach equally well with anything—with the putter, the spoon, it matters not what—or should we rather say, equally badly? If there were no other approaching to be done than that which these men execute, sometimes most successfully, it would be quite superfluous to attempt to learn to play the iron at all. Happily the great merit of the game is its surpassing variety, and one of its varieties is the stroke which necessitates true iron play.

Nevertheless, the name 'knee shots' is not without its meaning, to which we are now about to come. When the distance is just a little greater than that which we have been describing as negotiable by the wrists, aided by the slight extra allowance of swing obtained by the right fore-arm, and by

POSITION 2

straightening of the left elbow, then, while still keeping the right upper arm to the side, yet a little more length is given to the swing by letting the body sway on the knees. The left knee will knuckle inwards, the right outwards, as the club is swung back, and conversely as it swings forward. This is the origin of the term knee shots ; but, with this exception, the stroke is in every respect the same as the stroke played with the knees stiff jointed—that is to say, it is precisely the same until the ball is struck ; but after the ball is hit the motion differs slightly. The greater length thus given to the swing enables the club to be brought forward again with such speed that the wrists are scarcely able of themselves to control the follow on ; it would be too great a jerk for them. Therefore the arms have to be allowed to go a little way forward, in order to break

POSITION 3

the force of the jar on the wrists ; either that, or the body must be allowed to swing away, somewhat backward, with the same object—namely, to obviate the too great jar upon the wrists ; and the difference in result between the two methods here indicated is that the ball will run more off the stroke in which the arms have been allowed to follow on, than in the stroke which has brought the club rather more across the ball with a slice. And this brings directly before us one of the most crucial and vexed questions of iron play—the question of putting cut on the ball. Cut, as before intimated, is put on the ball by drawing the club, as it strikes it, across the line of its proposed flight. In those strokes in which the club follows along the flight of the ball, there is not cut put on it —in this direction, at least. We say 'in this direction' advisedly, for it is more than probable that, by using a very lofted iron, a cut is put on the ball almost without the intention of the striker. But in this latter case it is an under spin, not the side-ways spin that is given the ball by 'slice.'

Now the very great majority of good iron-players, and, we believe we may say, the professionals without exception, either intuitively or intentionally slice their iron shots. Following, therefore, our previous principle of adopting the wisdom of the multitude of counsellors, we will first see how this cut is communicated to the ball, setting aside for the moment the doctrine of those heretics whose schism consists in using with a straightforward swing an exceptionally lofted club to obtain the same result as the professional achieves by cutting the ball with his ordinary iron.

Standing in the position indicated in our diagram for the half shot, we see that if we raise the iron away from the ball by an upward turn from the wrist with the right hand, while holding it nearly in one position with the left hand, the iron will be brought up much straighter than when we bent round the left wrist also. And the club descending upon the ball in a corresponding straight downward direction, will chop it up very straight into the air with much back spin upon it. This up and down stroke is one method of putting cut upon the ball so that it will fall comparatively dead. This is the stroke which will pitch the ball deader than almost any other; but it requires great accuracy, and is scarcely applicable unless the ball be lying well, or, at all events, on soft yielding ground.

But there is another and more commonly practised method —to stand facing even more towards the hole than in the position indicated in our diagram ; then, with arms in the same position as for the ordinary half shot, to lay the iron behind the ball so that its face is at right angles to the line on which the ball should go ; whereupon, if the club be raised back with the wrists in the ordinary manner, and so brought to the ball again, it will be found to travel across the proposed line of flight of the ball. The ball will nevertheless fly on a line at right-angles to the face of the club as it meets it, and the result will be that the ball is sent straight forward, but is spinning all the while on its own axis from left to right. Hence, on pitching, it will not run straight forward, but, gripping the ground with its spin, will sidle off to the right. Therefore, more especially in playing this stroke, remember to always aim to pitch somewhat to the left of the hole.

This is the manner in which all the professionals (for they all play alike in this stroke at least) play their iron shots. They are all played with more or less of this cut upon them, and this is the manner in which it is executed. It is the stroke which is the despair of those who have taken up golf after years of discretion ; and yet it ought not to be difficult. It can practically be learned in a drawing-room. It is because learners will go out and try the game, the whole game, and nothing but the game, all at once, that so many of them never succeed in producing anything at all like the game. Those who learned the game young seem to have picked it up by intuition, but it was not so really. They picked it up by imitation. Boys are as imitative as monkeys, and if the golfer of mature years, but immature golfing experience, be not by nature similarly apish, he must rectify his degeneracy by assiduous study, or else he may indeed amuse himself, but will never make a golfer.

But to return to these professionals. One of them, of a past generation—Andrew Strath by name—was said to put such a tremendous amount of cut on his ball that it absolutely ran backward rather than forward. Those of to-day, you will observe, almost always seem to take some turf with the stroke, but do not you be seduced by that into thinking that you have to hit the ground before you hit the ball. We have seen it asserted in a grave treatise that it was by the inches of turf cut behind the ball that Jamie Anderson regulated the strength of his iron shots. Whatever you do, take stock in no such theory as that. All the turf that ever Jamie Anderson cut away before his iron met the ball was either on the very rare occasions on which he made a foozle, and the probably considerably more frequent ones on which he found himself in a very bad lie. The truth of this matter of turf-cutting is this—the cutting stroke with the iron is a sideways and a downways stroke; being a downways stroke, the club is apt to continue its downward course into the turf after the ball is struck. It thus becomes, for these purposes, similar to the jerking stroke described in our disquisition on playing through the green; and this brings us to another point for consideration in the matter of these cut iron shots.

The point may be thus briefly stated: It is very much harder to play these cut strokes when the ground is very hard than when it is comparatively yielding. The iron, when it meets the hard ground, is apt to start off it on the instant, before the ball has got clear away, and thus to make the ball go anywhere rather than where the striker wishes. What is the remedy? Well, in a measure, we have to confess ourselves beaten. It is not practicable to put cut on the ball to the same extent. Happily, however, the cases in which it is absolutely essential that the ball should stop at all dead are comparatively rare. But at all events the downward stroke must be abandoned. We may draw the club across the ball as much as we please, provided we hit it clean, but we must not strike that cruelly hard ground. These are the cases in which the exceptionally lofted club is especially admissible.

There is another quality of ground, though, which is very nearly as treacherous—very loose sand. However cleanly the ball may be lying on stuff of this perilous inconsistency, it must be charmed away with the greatest care and cleanliness. 'A table-spoonful of sand,' says a golfing scribe, ' is too much for the strongest arms.' The explanation probably is that a ball lying on turf is really a good inch or so from the solid mother earth, supported by sundry little wires of grass, while, on the bare sand, in its nakedness—there it is ! There is nothing between, no buffer. Be this how it may, it is a very delicate stroke. For our own part, we have found it a good rule, in playing off this loose sand, to shorten the grip of the iron ; it seems to help one in taking the ball fair and clean.

Now there is a certain way in which the ball may be made to stop even more dead than by any of the means we have yet noticed. It is by no means an easy stroke for even a first-class player, and we should never counsel its adoption except where no other stroke is feasible—for instance, with the hole close to the other side of an intervening bunker. The position is the same as for the ordinary half stroke, but the right hand is held loose ; for the club, wielded by the grip of the left hand and the turn of the left wrist, is allowed to turn up on the web between the right thumb and fore-finger, without the right hand itself moving at all far from the position in which it was when the ball was being addressed. The illustration on p. 126 will show what is meant far more briefly than any description and more plainly. The club is thus raised away from the ball straighter than by any other means. As it is brought down, the arms must not be allowed to swing any further than back to the position in which they were when the ball was being addressed, and the stroke, rather across the ball than straightforward, is to be finished off by the turn of the wrists alone. Although the club is seen to be brought so high and so far away from the ball, the ball will not travel at all further off a stroke thus played than off an ordinary half shot in which the club-head was drawn back but some three feet from the ball. There is little forward driving power in this up and down stroke. This is a shot, as we have said, which is not of general use, but only, if ever, to be attempted when in great straits. Nevertheless no chapter on iron-play could be complete without some notice of it.

Again, it should be observed that the more loosely the club

can be held in the hand, consistently with accuracy, the more dead will the ball fall, probably on the same principle that more 'side' can be put on a billiard ball if the cue be held loosely. But this is also a 'counsel of perfection' which it is dangerous to adopt as a common rule of golfing life.

BEGINNING OF THE HIGH LOFTING STROKE

And now 'why in the name of goodness,' the reader will be apt to exclaim, 'if there are all these perplexities and complexities about putting cut upon the ball—why, when we want it to stop dead, should we not escape from all these troubles by the back-door, by taking an exceptionally lofted club?' The answer is as simple as the question is natural: 'Because it is so very difficult to hit quite as you wish with a very much lofted club.' You may get the elevation pretty well, and you may get the dead fall, but it is very, very hard to get the distance. It is so very difficult to be sure of hitting the ball at the right height up the face. Say the faces of two irons are each two and a half inches broad at the centre, but one is fairly upright, while the other is excessively laid back. The upper edge of the uprighter one will be some two inches from the ground, when the sole is resting on the ground; whereas the upper edge of the other will be not so much as an inch, perhaps, from the ground. The same deviation in aim will therefore produce twice as much divergence in the point of impact with the one iron as with the other; and if the ball be hit near the lower edge of the iron, it will go far further than if hit near the upper edge. Hence the great difficulty of correctly gauging your distance with a very lofted club. You may hit the ball twice running with equal strength each time, and each time in the centre vertical line of the face, but the least divergence above or below the central longitudinal line of the face will make all the difference with your lofted club; while a similar divergence on the less lofted club would matter hardly at all. Yet some play fairly well with them. There are few directions to be given as to their use. The ordinary half shot—not the cutting stroke—rules are applicable to their use; and it is rather a question for the individual to settle for himself, whether he will prefer to take the responsibility of the greater accuracy of striking requisite for these very lofted irons, or the less accuracy, but greater complications, of putting cut upon the ball with an ordinary iron. To attempt to combine cut with a very heavily lofted club is a presumption upon which the Nemesis of the gods waits with speedy wing. Finally, we would repeat the observation with which we began, that the great majority of good players, and the professionals, we believe, without exception, prefer the cutting stroke with the ordinary iron.

And when you have struck your approach shot, be it what it may, do not be in too great a hurry to start away after it, before you have done playing it. This may seem a grotesque caution, but the grotesquerie which it is intended to meet is of frequent occurrence. Players often move off their position before the ball is fairly struck. Rather aim at the opposite extreme, and pause a moment in the position in which the finish

FINISH OF THE HIGH LOFTING STROKE

of the stroke left you—like a 'pointing' dog. It is one of the commonplace instructions of the professors of billiards, and ought really to be no less so with the professors of golf.

One of the features of St. Andrews is that many of the holes are on little plateaux with little banks leading up to them. The ground of the putting-greens is apt to be very hard, so that a ball pitched upon them, over the bank, would run off the green on the further side, unless most tremendously cut. A ball pitched in the ordinary manner would be killed by falling on the face of the hill. This feature is, of course, not peculiar to St. Andrews, though perhaps more frequent there than elsewhere, and it is these circumstances that call into play the stroke termed 'running up with the iron.' Though played from about the same distance as the half shot or wrist shot, it is not really a 'wrist'-shot at all. It might rather be called a body stroke. The position of standing is the same as for the half shot proper, but with the ball a little more to the right, and a little farther from the player. The right elbow is not to be bent in to the body, nor the right fore-arm to almost rest upon the right thigh, as in the ordinary wrist shot, but the hands are to be brought away out from the body, and a little forward—which has the effect of presenting the face of the iron more upright to the ball. The swing back is then made almost entirely by the body turning on the hips and the left knee, the joints of fingers, wrists, arms, and shoulders all rigid. The arms being still kept nearly straight, as when the ball was being addressed, the club will go back close over the surface of the ground. The club is brought back to the ball by a similar reverse turn of the body, and as the ball is struck the club follows on after it by the right shoulder being brought underneath (though rather by the body bending down off the right hip than by any slackening of the shoulder joints) and by the whole body being allowed to follow on, with inward bend of the right knee. The ball thus struck will be sent skimming close above the ground for the early part of its journey, and will then run on up the slope on to the putting-green—dead—perhaps in ! (why should we stint ourselves in the delights of a beautiful vision for which there is no charge?)

Bob Martin plays with his cleek a stroke that in appearance is the same as this, and plays it wonderfully well, but it is not the same stroke really; for though it goes skimming over the ground in the same way, it has a cut on it, and is played with the wrists. Of course, if we like, we too may run the ball up, with either cleek or iron, with a cut on it—though probably with rather less success than Bob Martin. But putting cut on this stroke is purely a work of supererogation. It serves no

OFF THE LEFT LEG

useful purpose, and though we may play it wonderfully well one day out of the work-a-day six, the other five are not

likely to be marked with a red letter. Possibly the cut slightly helps the ball to hold its way over unevennesses of the ground, but it is a stroke that requires an enormous deal of confidence to play with success—such confidence as we cannot expect to feel in ourselves consistently.

And now let us turn our attention for a moment to the half shot as played off the left leg. We have said that the very large majority of players play the stroke off the right leg. Is the other method, then, worth consideration? We should have said 'No,' were it not that one of the very best approachers of the day, Mr. J. E. Laidlay, habitually plays his approaches off his left leg; and this being so, and golfing nature being what it is—highly imitative—he is sure to have many disciples, at least in style, if not in execution.

The position for this stroke, then, is very similar to that for the drive (see diagram, p. 75). The ball is even rather more to the player's left—very nearly opposite his left toe—and since the lofting iron or mashy (the latter is the club with which, principally, Mr. Laidlay does such deadly execution) is shorter than the driver, the ball is proportionately nearer to the player. The weight of the body is thus mainly on the left leg, nor, in the half shot, is it transferred during any part of the stroke to the right leg. The knees are more bent than in the drive, the left knee being more bent than the right. The main business of the stroke is done with the left hand and wrist, it being necessary that the right grip and the right wrist should be loose, for otherwise the club cannot get away after the ball. Here, again, if the ball is to be lofted, the left arm must not be allowed to follow on, but the club be allowed to come through by the supple action of the left wrist only. It is possible to put cut on the ball, as with the stroke off the right leg, but, we are inclined to think, not to the same extent. Its votaries seem rather inclined to use clubs with a good deal of loft, Mr. Laidlay, as we have said, playing his approaches, when within range, chiefly with his mashy. Hitting the ball slightly upon the heel of the club is a means which they, in common with those who play the stroke off the right leg, employ as a further means of putting on cut. This heeling is more practised by the left-leg players than by the others, probably as a means of compensating for the greater difficulty in putting on slice by drawing the club across.

Further than this it is scarcely necessary to dwell upon this stroke, partly because it is not likely to be in general use, and partly because much of the instruction given for the ordinary half shot is applicable, with due modifications, to this stroke also.

To a golfer who has overcome the elementary difficulties of the iron approach shot, more trouble is apt to be experienced with the three-quarter stroke than with any other in the whole range of the game. We hope that we may have been of some use in helping him over these troubles by pointing out what a three-quarter stroke really is—that it is a stroke played with the whole swing of the arms from and below the shoulders. But we may warn him, further than this, that the wrists do not take part in this stroke in at all the same way as in the half shots and shorter wrist shots. The wrists need to be taut throughout the stroke, and after the ball is struck the club should be allowed to follow on after it by the following on of the arms. It is altogether a stiffish stroke. Even the elbows should not be allowed to be too lissome. The swing is given to the club almost entirely from the arms working on the joints of the shoulders—the shoulder-blades themselves being kept taut and not allowed to swing round as in the drive. The usual object of a three-quarter-shot is to send the ball as far as possible without taking a full swing at it—i.e. without letting the shoulder-blades turn. It is a shot played at a very uncomfortable distance. It is possible to take a full, very easy swing with a much lofted club, but this is a stroke which experience shows to be difficult to reduce to anything like certainty. Therefore we have to use the three-quarter shot—the club gripped firmly in both hands and the first section of the right fore-finger pressing hard upon the leather. For here again the club does not need to move in the right hand. We have already indicated the position of standing for this stroke, and there is little more to say. When the elementary principles of the stroke have been mastered, however, there is a point to be noticed which is of the greatest assistance in executing this difficult shot with fairly uniform success—to let the swing back finish itself well out before you attempt to bring the club forward again. Even dwell on the top of the swing—a little extra dwelling does not matter in this stroke, which is less of a true swing (demanding less harmonious timing throughout) than the full drive. It is more of a hit, and the dwelling on the aim when the club is back is a much-needed help to accuracy, and has no counterbalancing disadvantage.

It is not impossible that in certain cases of this stroke also supple wrist-work may be required. It is then, however, not possible to send the ball so far, and at the distance for which this stroke—a three-quarter shot played with cut—will be required it is more commonly advisable to play a strong half shot, without cut, which, in point of distance, will have much the same result. But supposing the uncomfortable necessity to arise of having to play up to a hole at the distance of a strong half shot (that is, a shot part carry and part run), but with a bunker close before it, the only way out of the dilemma is to play a three-quarter stroke with cut. Then it becomes really a 'knee' stroke. The whole body turns upon the knees, as the club is raised straightly away from the ball. Then down it comes with a reverse turn upon the knees, the arms not following on the ball, but the club being brought rather across the body by the free action of the left wrist, as before; this is the hardest stroke in all iron play, we might say in all golf. As such, it perhaps comes scarcely within the limits of instruction labelled elementary. We have therefore treated it briefly, but without some notice of it a chapter on iron-play and approaching would have been incomplete.

The strokes, then, to which for approaching the learner should especially apply himself are these : the ordinary three-quarter stroke, and the half stroke and wrist stroke played off the right knee, with as great a command of cut as he can manage to acquire. We say with as great a command of cut as he can manage to acquire; but we would counsel the learner, and even the adept, not to get into the habit of playing his iron approaches with more cut than is natural to his style or requisite for the special stroke.

And having acquired these, the elementary principles of iron approaching, we would submit, for the golfer's guidance, these four general and golden rules :—

1. Do not take your eye off the ball.
2. Do not aim too long.
3. Aim to pitch to the left of the hole.
4. (The greatest of all.) Be up.

With regard to No. 1, it was the opinion of the late young Tom Morris—than whose no opinion is entitled to greater respect—that the reason amateurs so often failed in their iron approaches was that they allowed their eye to wander back after the glitter of the iron face; and certain it is that taking the eye off the ball is a very frequent and very fatal cause of failure in playing approaches.

With regard to No. 2, the eye undoubtedly grows weary and loses gauge of aim and distance by too long gazing. Jamie Anderson, in his best days the best iron player then extant, was likewise the briefest in his style of address.

No. 3 was the great maxim of the late Mr. George Glennie (who for so many years held the record for the lowest medal score, namely 88, for the St. Andrews links), and is a reminder of the fact that almost every iron shot breaks to the right as it pitches.

As to No. 4, it requires no quotation of eminent golfer to certify its value, which is attested by the experience of every golfer eminent or otherwise who has ever striven to approach a hole. If a man always hit his ball hard enough, in approaching, to be up to the hole, he would probably never lose a match, even if he never approached with anything but a wooden putter.

Do we owe any apology that we have given not a word of instruction about approaching the hole with the baffy? We fancy not. For the few who in the present day practise this style of approach are without exception incarnate contradictions of the proverb that 'one is never too old to learn.' We have far too deep a respect for their years and their baffies to presume to intrude upon them our unsolicited advice.

(D) ON PUTTING

There is probably no golfer in the world at all worthy of the name upon whom any other golfer can gain a stroke a hole in driving, consistently all through the round. On the other hand, there are very many men who can, and uniformly do, gain a stroke off many other men in the short space intervening between the edge of the putting-green and the bottom of the hole. On a good and familiar putting-green to lay your ball dead, or within tolerable certainty of holing, at from fifteen to twenty yards, four times out of five, ought not to be difficult of accomplishment. Yet the man who can consistently do this is putting very exceptionally well. Putting is commonly and conveniently divided into two heads—'approach putting,' and 'putting out,' or 'holing the ball.' The respective strokes have gained their name rather in regard to the intention of the striker than to the result. A putt of twenty yards length is an approach putt, even though by a lucky chance it finish at the bottom of the hole. And no less does a putt of twenty inches come under the head of holing out, even though, as a matter of fact, it miss the hole altogether.

The great difficulty of all, in playing short putts, is to hit the ball quite true. It is just because it is such a gentle stroke that it becomes so hard to do this. And the greatest of all aids to true hitting is to keep the eye firmly on the ball. There is a special temptation in these short putts to take the eye off the ball at the moment of hitting, in the fact that the hole is so very near—inviting, as it were, a side glance at it. Or if it be not a glance at the hole itself, at all events a glance at the blade of grass over which the player has made up his mind that the ball should pass. For, in all putting, whether approach putting or putting out, there are these two methods—some men aim directly at the hole ; others, while standing directly behind their ball, so as to see the proper line, select a certain blade of grass or spot on the ground, over which they make up their mind the ball should pass. Having selected this, they dismiss from their minds the hole as an object of direction, and regard it only as an object for the calculation of strength. Of the two methods, our humble opinion is this—that the former will pay the better about one day a week, when the player is in exceptionally good correspondence of hand and eye, but that for the other five days of the week the latter method is by far the safer. The man who putts on the latter plan is not liable to such severe aberrations of the putting faculty.

The principal secret of good putting, as of good driving, is that the club should travel as long as possible on the line—or a production of it—on which the ball is to travel. For a player to find out for himself how best he may accomplish this is a problem that can be solved more readily in a drawing-room, without a ball—by seeing how the putter head may be best induced to move along a straight line of the carpet pattern—than on the putting-green. We give this advice to adepts and tiros alike ; for we are very sure that practice of this kind is a better lesson for true hitting of the ball with the putter than any amount of out-door play—though it, of course, teaches nothing of strength. We will first describe the manner in which, as a matter of fact, the great majority of good players do putt, and will then be guilty of the great presumption of describing an alternative method which, in the writer's opinion, is a better. Whichever plan, however, the tiro may adopt, we would say to him, stick to that. Change your club, if you like but not your style with the same club—and keep yourself continually in mind of your duty by taking your putter home and seeing that it works truly over the straight guiding line in the pattern of the carpet.

The favourite position for putting is very similar to the favourite position for iron play—*i.e.* off the right leg. This we believe to be, almost without exception, the position adopted by professionals. One of the very finest of professional putters

MR. A. F. MACFIE

was the late lamented Young Tommy Morris. His attitude was typical of the later professional putters. His right leg forward —the ball nearly opposite his right foot. The putter held with perhaps about equal grip with both hands—if anything, rather firmer with the right. If he were drawing the ball to the left of the hole at all, he would probably have told us that it was because he was gripping too tight with the right hand. If he were pushing it away to the right of the hole, he would have said that he was rather too firm with his left hand. And most likely he would have been right.

Let us take a glance at J. O. F. Morris, brother of the above, and a very fine putter. His style in putting is a modification of that of his even more famous brother.

In one point, though, we see that the latter is not typical of the run of good players. He seems to hit his ball much upon the toe of the putter. Doubtless he so does better execution than if he were to bother himself about striking the ball truly in the centre of the club ; but, for the learner, the centre is the place on which to strike it.

The great majority of good putters make great use of their wrists in putting. In fact, the stroke is made almost exclusively with the wrists. The wrists do not hit the club on to the ball, and then check it ; but the club is swung by a movement of the wrists. The best putters we have seen used their wrists greatly—Jamie Allan, in his best days, Mr. A. F. Macfie and Mr. W. T. Linskill, are the names that, among a host of fine putters, occur to us. All these players putted almost exclusively with the wrist, and let the club swing very far through after the ball. Any checking of the club as it meets the ball is fatal to consistent good putting.

Now supposing the tiro to be determined to form himself on the style of these putters—to putt off his right leg—our advice to him would be as follows. To take his putter with him into some room upon the floor of which the junction of the boards, or the pattern of the carpet, shows a clearly distinguishable straight line. With the face of his putter at right angles to this line, let him proceed to take up his position much in the attitude indicated by our diagram for the half-iron stroke, but with feet somewhat closer together. If he find it convenient, he may let his right fore-arm rest upon his right thigh. This will help him to be steady. Let him now, with his wrists, swing the putter-head backward and forward. If it work truly over the line, well and good; but at the first venture it is almost certain that it will not do so. If he find it working across the line—from outward, inward—he must advance his left foot and retire his right foot a little. If the club-head work from inside the line as he draws it back, to outside the line as he swings it forward, he must, conversely, draw back his left foot and advance his right foot. The hands must always work the putter as comes natural to them; the change in direction of travel of the club-head must be effected by changing the position of the feet. And after the right position is acquired—when the head of the putter is working straight and true along the line—then let the player be careful that he note very carefully the relative position of his feet and the supposed ball. The hands, gripping the club, as they have fallen naturally into position will not be inclined to alter, and when the player finds himself in a vein of bad putting he may pretty safely assure himself that it is something wrong in the relative position of his feet to the ball. Then, let him bring his putter home, and practise again over the pattern in the carpet to get the fault set right, and he may hope to go forth on the morrow and putt well again, and be happy.

Of the manner of the grip for putting, we should say that since putting is a very delicate matter, requiring great niceness of touch, the putter should be held well in the fingers—not home in the palm of either hand—and we would advise that the thumbs be laid down along the handle of the club. This gives a greater delicacy of power of guiding. 'Old Tom' used, at one time, to carry this tender 'fingering' of his putter to such a length, that he putted with his right fore-finger down the handle of the putter. But when, as we have elsewhere related, it was suggested to him on his missing a short putt, 'If you would have that fore-finger amputated, Tom, you might be able to putt,' Tom said he would not go the length of that, but that he would try the effect of holding it round the club, as most human beings do; and he has been putting in this, the normal fashion, ever since, with manifest improvement.

One of the great secrets of the putting stroke, as of every other, is that there should be no jerk about it. The club must be swung quietly back away from the ball, even if it have not to leave it by more than the space of nine inches. It must be let go quietly back for this brief length, and then be brought quietly and smoothly forward. Whether the club be held tightly or loosely in the fingers does not greatly signify ; but it must at least be held tight enough to prevent its loosening itself from the grip of the finger when the putter meets the ball. It was one of the great maxims of the late Mr. George Glennie, that famous old golfer, who for many years held the record for the lowest score for the St. Andrews medal, that the putter should be drawn well back, away from the ball, before the stroke was made. The point of this caution was that if the club be thus well drawn back, it tends to prevent any jerky, catchy hitting at the ball ; it goes far to ensure that it shall be struck a true blow. Mr. George Gosset, who was a very fine putter, was remarkable for this feature of his short game ; and it is noticeable with many who have brought putting to high perfection. A ball quite truly struck, even with a very gentle blow, gives out a peculiar sharp sound—it tells you that you have hit it clean. Many golfers will be able to bear us out when we say that we have been able to form a very good idea of how near the hole the ball will go by the sound it gives out when the putter meets it ; and there is no more convincing testimony to the rarity of the occurrence of a truly-hit putt than the rarity of hearing this clear-sounding sharp click.

Just before you make a golfing stroke of any kind, after the 'waggle' which forms part of the address, you should rest your club on the ground for a moment, just behind the ball, before drawing it back for the actual stroke. On each occasion, with every club (except in a bunker, where you are not allowed to 'ground' the club at all), you should form the habit of bringing the club-head close up to the ball, as you thus lay it behind it, for a second. If you loosely and carelessly lay the club-head several inches back from the ball, as we sometimes see done, you lose a valuable aid to accurate striking. And if this be true of all strokes, it is especially so of putting. Lay the club-head close up, almost touching the ball—nay, it matter not though you should touch it, provided you do not make it move—for this is never claimed as a stroke.

So much, then, for this, the normal attitude for putting—off the right leg. Now Mr. Glennie, a very deadly putter, used to putt with the ball about half-way between his two feet, and a long way from him. Mr. John Blackwood used to putt in an eccentric but most deadly style of his own, which quite defies description. But these are idiosyncracies.

Mr. J. E. Laidlay putts, as he does everything else, off his left leg, with the ball rather in front of him, and so do all those who imitate his style, and, as a rule, fall somewhat short of his execution. This putting off the left leg varies from putting off the right leg, as we have been describing it, only as playing the iron off the left leg varies from iron-play off the right leg. It is not necessary to give it a detailed explanation.

Most of the professionals, playing off the right leg, give a curious little knuckle inward of the right knee, just before they draw the club away from the ball. This is probably of no essential assistance to the stroke, but is more likely only an evidence of the imitative tendency of the golfer—a survival, we should fancy, of the dashing style of poor 'Young Tommy'— though it may date further back. And most of the professionals putt with a wooden putter. There is a mighty deal of discussion to-day as to the relative merits of wooden or iron putters. It is probably almost entirely a matter of the taste and fancy of the player. Fifteen years ago an iron putter was hardly ever seen. Now they probably have a majority. With the proviso that a man is sure to putt better with whichever of the two he may happen to fancy, we may indicate a few points of comparison.

Whether because they are generally straighter faced than their wooden-headed brethren, or from whatever cause, it seems that the ball runs closer to the ground off an iron putter than off a wooden one. And this quality, which is a positive advantage on a smooth green, and close to the hole, becomes equally a disadvantage where the ground is rough, as is commonly the case at a distance from the hole, and is too often the case quite close to it. Therefore we would say that for putting approach putts from any long distance, or over rough ground, a wooden putter is the better weapon ; for the ball not cleaving so closely to the ground as when played off an iron putter is

AN ALTERNATIVE STYLE OF PUTTING

less troubled by the roughness of the ground. But when the ground is smooth the ball which cleaves close to it has this advantage, that it is less likely to jump over the hole if it comes across it while going rather strong. Moreover, it is thought by many to be easier to see the line—the right angle—off the better defined face of the iron putter. Be this as it may, however, the choice is quite an open question, and may be left to the fancy of the individual player.

ELEMENTARY INSTRUCTION

Should the learner however adopt the less general, but, as we think, better style of putting which we are about to describe, it seems almost necessary that he should use an iron putter. For putting in the style to which we are referring, the player should have the ball almost half-way between his two feet—if anything, perhaps rather nearer the left foot. He should face at right angles with the proposed line of his putt, so that a line drawn from the toe of one boot to the toe of the other would be parallel with the line of the putt. The hands should be allowed to fall into a natural position, neither tucked in at the elbows towards the body, nor held out away from it. The putter should be held rather short, and, preferably, with a light grip, and should be worked backward and forward by the wrists —mainly, perhaps, by the left wrist. The left elbow may, if preferred, be a little crooked to the front. Our contention is that the golfer will find it easy, in this fashion, to keep his club going truly and straightly over the straight line upon the carpet pattern, will therefore be able to keep it going longer in the true line in which the ball should go, and thus be more likely to hit the ball correctly. The club-head will, on this method, be swinging somewhat after the fashion of a pendulum, and if the golfer gets the hanging arrangements of this pendulum correct, it cannot very well swing out of the true line.

At all events, we would say to the learner, make trial in your drawing-room of these two methods, and see in which it appears as if you could make the club to naturally pass longest and most truly over your guiding line. Then, having come to a conclusion, stick to it. Take up your position, and do not vary it. And remember for ever this golden rule—If you are putting consistently to one side or the other of the hole, try to counteract the divergence, not by different hitting with your arms, but by altering the position of your feet. In a certain position you will naturally putt in a certain direction. Get your position right, and you will naturally putt in the right direction. Now these methods are equally appropriate both for holing out and for approaching. For holing out, go directly behind your ball so as to see the proper line to the hole—then, having fixed this in your mind, and settled on a little blade of grass or other mark just a little ahead of the ball, keep your eye on this as you move into position for hitting the ball. Put down your club behind the ball, directly facing this blade, and then have a look at the hole to again judge your strength, after you have got your position right. Then, bring your eye back to the blade over which you mean to putt, and so back to the ball again. Whatever you do, mind that your last look, as you strike, be at the ball. Do not be in too great a hurry to look away and see the ball going into the hole—there is no better way of keeping it out. In approach putting, you should give the greater part of your attention to the strength. The line will not be far wrong if the ball be so truly hit that the strength is pretty correct. Moreover, one seldom putts 25° off the line in a twenty-yard putt, as we all often do in a putt of a foot. The direction is an easier task, comparatively speaking, and if in our approach putts we apply too great attention to the line, instead of giving the greater share of it to the strength, we are apt to find that our next putt will come under the category again of 'approach putt,' instead of being so simple a 'holing putt' as to cause us no tremors. And as nine out of every ten approach shots are too short, bear in mind the eternal drone of the professional mentor—'Be up!'

(E) IN HAZARDS

The ideal golfer never goes off the course and never gets into a bunker. Mercifully, the ideal golfer has yet to be evolved. What a prig he would be! Hazards divide themselves, broadly, into bunkers and whins. On all seaside links—all real links—they are frequent (ubiquitous, a wild-driving grumbler would say). By 'bunker,' we should observe, we mean sand bunker.

What is to be done with the ball in a sand bunker depends upon two things—the nature of your lie in the bunker, and the

ELEMENTARY INSTRUCTION 145

height and nearness to your ball of the cliff of the bunker. And the nature of the lie is modified not only by its greater or less 'cuppiness,' but also by the consistency of the soil. We will consider a general, typical instance first. You are some four yards back from the cliff of the bunker and the bottom is neither

hard clay nor very loose sand, but something between the two. You are slightly cupped. What are you to do?

In the first place you are to take your niblick. You are not to go playing any tricks with your iron—you are too near the cliff of the bunker for that. (We are assuming the cliff to be of moderate height—say three feet.) You can but hope to get the ball out, and must endure the loss of a shot. If you attempt more, you will effect less. You should stand pretty much in the position to the ball which we have indicated for the three-quarter stroke, but with the ball rather more in front of you. You must grasp your club firmly with both hands, and you must aim to hit downwards into the sand, some two and a half inches behind the ball. To do this correctly you must not fix your eye on the ball, but on the exact spot on the sand which you have decided to be the place where your niblick-head should cleave it. It is a downward blow, and it is rather the concussion of the sand that explodes the ball up into the air than any actual contact of the club.

Now in these few words of instruction we give one piece of advice exceedingly difficult to follow, albeit its difficulty will very likely not be self-evident to the unsuspecting tiro. We have told him to keep his eye on a spot of sand just behind the ball. Now this is a very, very hard thing to do. Though the eye is so prone to take a glimpse away from the ball when it should not, it is now infinitely more prone to take a glance forward at the ball, when it should be rivetted on that little spot of sand behind it. It is nothing but an heroic effort of will that can enable the golfer to resist the temptation and be staunch and true to his speck of sand. But if he fail—if the eye wander to the ball— the niblick will wander there after it, the ball will be hit clean, or topped, and driven disastrously into the opposing cliff of the bunker. But if he gain the victory, and keep his eye on the proper spot, the club will yield due obedience, the sand will be spurted, and the ball will rise in the air and land—no great distance forward, maybe—but safe beyond the bunker's clutch.

The nearer the ball lies to the cliff of the bunker, the farther behind the ball must the niblick-head dig down into the ground, in order to accomplish the quicker rise of the ball. And the softer the sand, the farther behind is it possible to aim so as to convey impetus to the ball—that is to say, the softer the sand, the straighter may the ball be made to rise. In some of the hard clayey-bottomed bunkers of the St. Andrews links, on the other hand, it is necessary to hit very near the ball, for the soil is so stiff that if you hit at all far behind the impetus never reaches the ball at all. So much for this particular shot, then —an up and down stroke, with the eye kept, if possible, on the spot at which you judge that the niblick-head should cleave the sand. In this shot, no less than in others, accuracy is of infinitely more importance than power, and many defeat their own object by trying to hit too hard.

The bunkers on St. Andrews links are for the most part well defined, but on many of the very best links, Carnoustie, Prestwick, Westward Ho, Sandwich, there is a lot of loose ill-defined rubbish, the sandy out-blowings of bunkers, which is very hard indeed to play out of. In the first place, you are always irritated by a doubt whether you are allowed to put your club down before striking. If you do you are apt to think you are a cheat, if you do not you suspect yourself of being a fool—for you have little doubt that your adversary would put his down, in like circumstances. However, when in doubt, be honest is a good rule ; and you will probably play the stroke better from having a clear conscience. It is a bad one to play though, at its best. There is no especial rule. How it should be treated must depend upon its degree of embeddedness. If lying clean, you may take an easy full ordinary swing at it. If slightly cupped, you may address it in the terms of persuasion suggested in our remarks on the jerking stroke. If severely cupped, you can best hit into the sand behind and be content to send it a very modest distance with the niblick.

Out of a very hard-bottomed bunker we once saw a first-class player do a very ingenious trick. The ball lay quite clean, but on very hard-baked clay. There was a very high cliff in front—it looked an impossibility to surmount it ! But before the abrupt part of the cliff there was a moderate rise of the ground, and the soil of this rise was likewise clayey and hard. The player called for his driver, of all clubs in the world ! He took a full swing—the ball struck on to the hard rise, bounded into the air, and went on its way rejoicing over the green sward a tremendous distance. But this perhaps hardly comes within the proper province of 'Elementary Instruction.' Neither does, perhaps, the advice to carry in your set a left-handed club—if you be at all ambidextrous by nature—fall within this category ; but we remember once seeing Bob Kirk extricate himself from an apparently hopeless situation, and win an important match, by this expedient.

But perhaps the most treacherous balls of all are those which lie perfectly clean and smooth on soft sand. They look pleasant enough, but unless they are swept off perfectly clean the shot is utterly ruined. There is no special nostrum for their negotiation, except the general one to swing very easily, bearing in mind that the least inaccuracy is even more fatal here than elsewhere.

The chief hazard, other than sand, with which the golfer has to contend, is, as we have said, 'whin'-gorse. There is no especial rule as to what you should do when you get into it, except to get out again as soon as possible. It is much more yielding stuff than its appearance would lead one to suppose, and an accurate blow will take the ball a long way out of a very hopeless-looking whin-bush. The great thing in all these difficulties is to keep cool, to keep your head and your temper, and not to try to do too much. How many a medal has been lost by a man having a fair lie in a bunker trying to do a little bit extra with the ball, with his cleek or iron, instead of being humbly content to delve it out with the niblick ! It generally makes so very little difference whether you get fifty yards or seventy-five out of a bunker, but it makes a mighty difference whether you get out of it ever such a little way or leave your ball hopelessly stuck in under the ledge.

Bent grass is a common tribulation of the golfer. The ball has to be taken out with a coarse, clumsy stroke. If the whin is not quite so bad a trouble as its appearance would indicate, the bent grass is a great deal worse. It wraps round your club most irritatingly. There is the same tendency to 'pull' out of it as, in our remarks on playing through the green, we noticed there was out of the long wiry grass called windle-straws. Of this tendency, therefore, let the golfer be forewarned.

A CHAMPION IN DIFFICULTIES

The short rushes we encounter at Hoylake are very similar in effect to this bent grass; but Westward Ho has a peculiar kind of long rush, very sharp and stiff pointed, which we sincerely hope to be peculiar to itself. In these your ball is apt to get perched up—sometimes deep in the middle of them. Then it is the best course to take very careful aim with the point of your heavy iron, and with a short, stiff-arm, upward swing you are very likely to surprise yourself by smiting it out. We say an upward stroke, because it is only by following the general lie of the stiff reeds that either your ball or your club can come through them.

Though caution is doubtless usually the better part of valour, it is wonderful what shots can be made out of water if the ball be not too much submerged, by aiming well behind the ball, with the niblick, and keeping the eye on the spot at which the club-head is to splash the water—and open—as long as possible. We say, 'and open,' because the eye is very apt to shut involuntarily, in expectation of the coming splash.

The most ubiquitous hazard with which the golfer has to contend is wind. Low driving for against the wind, and high driving for down wind, are largely, of course, matters of low or high teeing. But the ball may be encouraged to an artificially low flight by swinging the club upon it with the hands well forward in front of the body. With a wind off the right side of the line of the drive a finished player will start the ball well up into the wind, to come round with a slight pull at the finish. He will thus get a longer drive than had his ball fought the wind all the way. But these are refinements that scarcely come within the curriculum of the teacher ; and we would never suggest to the learner to desert for them his natural formed swing.

CHAPTER V

ON STYLE---VARIOUS STYLES

BY H. G. HUTCHINSON

F the best writers upon golf, some — notably its able exponent, whether with club or pen, the author of the 'Art of Golf' himself —have the habit of writing with some contempt of 'Style.' They are a little fond of insinuating that, provided you hit the ball, the manner is of no importance, insomuch that a not inconsiderable portion of their writing seems occupied with a melancholy Von Hartmann-like denunciation of the folly of its own creation—for the manner, the form, as distinct from the substance, is all that writing can attempt to show for us. True it is that, provided the ball be correctly struck, the manner matters little; but then this is a large proviso, and before we can go so far as to say, without qualification, that the manner or style is of no importance, we have first to make up our minds that it is no easier to strike the ball in one manner than in another. This is the point that our slogging Philistine scribes seem a little to miss. It is true that Mr. J. E. Laidlay drives with his ball right away in front of him, while Mr. J. Ball drives with it nearly opposite his right toe. It is true that the former gentleman putts with his ball well in front of his left foot, while Mr. Macfie, in certain putting moods, putts with the ball behind his right foot: and these are all very fine players. It is true that Tom Morris until recently putted with his first finger down the shaft of the putter, and, save for an occasional aberration, was a very fine putter.

'Old Tom' one day missed a short putt, upon which the late Mr. Logan White, who was himself possessed of one of the most singular styles ever seen, remarked: 'If you were to have that finger amputated, Tom, you might be able to putt.' The phrase took Tom's fancy, and since that day, to avoid amputation, he has coiled his first finger round the shaft, like an ordinary human golfer.

The late Mr. John Blackwood, again, putted in a style which was contorted almost to anguish—facing the hole at which he was playing, with feet close together, the right heel raised from the ground, and the right knee bent forward. The ball was to the right of the right foot, and the putter was held away to the right side with vertical shaft, and only the extreme toe resting upon the ground. In this attitude of unspeakable discomfort he used to putt with a deadliness which was of world-wide renown.

Now, that all these fine players should play in so many varieties of style is perhaps remarkable, but it argues little against the importance of a good style. In the old days of cricket we are told of a much greater diversity of style than is now to be seen. We are all reduced so much to a stereotyped fashion that there is practically little difference between our batting and that of Mr. W. G. Grace—except that with us bat and ball do not meet! We may say, indeed, at cricket, that provided bat and ball do meet, and meet properly, the manner of the muscular adjustment matters little; but, nevertheless, we are not going to deny that with a certain 'style,' a certain recognised course of these muscular adjustments, it is far easier to make bat and ball meet frequently and properly. And it is not a whit less true of golf. Golf is at present in just the same position with regard to this matter of style as was cricket a certain large number of years ago, when some tutor, self-constituted, with all the confidence of genius, preached as a novel and striking truth the doctrine of keeping the left shoulder over the ball. Those who now tell us that style does not matter 'twopence'—that is the precise financial value at which they commonly estimate it—would then have said that it did not matter whether you kept your bat vertical or horizontal so long as you hit the ball—and they would have said so quite truly, in one sense—and a nice class of cricket we should see played to-day if such teachers as these had been the nation's accepted guides ! We should be still in the chaotic, catastrophic period of the game, as indeed we still are in the game of golf. It is probable that some fifty years hence we shall see less of that diversity of golf style which prevails at present, and that we shall see the royal and ancient game subjugated, much to its improvement, to the reign of more or less elastic law.

The law which to-day is mainly operative upon the style of golfers is the law of imitation. The golfer is as imitative as a monkey. With all ranks of the golfing faculty is this true, but the influence of imitation is mainly conspicuous, as might naturally be expected, in the plastic natures and muscles of youth. At St. Andrews there are so many fine players with fine swings that it is difficult to say on which particular model the rising player has formed himself; but you will, without fail, observe all the features of what we sometimes hear called—usually by those who have acquired it, and who therefore consider themselves entitled to look with some patronage on all others—'the St. Andrews swing.' On the other hand, North Berwick swarms with all sorts of editions of golfing Laidlays—Laidlays, not in name, but in style, and seldom in execution—bending forward over the left leg, reaching out for the ball far beyond it, and, with right leg drawn far, far back, exaggerating in the earnestness of that sincerest form of flattery the features of their master's style — following out with the utmost fidelity all its eccentricities, failing only to reproduce the genius.

Turn to Hoylake. There you see multitudes of more or

'THE ST. ANDREWS SWING'

less base copyists of Mr. John Ball, junior; the right leg, relatively, well advanced, the hands gripping resolutely round the club-handle, fingers uppermost.

And so, wherever you may go, you see the impress of the finest local player upon all the current coin that has more lately issued from the local mint—happy if it reproduce, along with the external semblance, some of the intrinsic worth of the original sterling.

Yet these styles of Mr. John Ball, junior, and of Mr. Laidlay are the styles of genius. Who that attempts imitation can hope to vie with their dash and *élan*? They are fascinating to the eye, indeed, but they are hardly the safest models upon which the young player—above all the player young in golf but old in years—should strive to form himself. Again, that loose slashing style known as 'the St. Andrews swing,' introduced probably by the genius of poor young Tommy Morris—who that has not breathed it into his growing frame with the sharp salt breezes of the east coast of Fife, shall hope, by taking thought, to reproduce it with success? There they are, lissome boys from the University, or the younger race of professional players, at about nine o'clock in the morning, driving off the edge of the last hole putting-green, under the suspicious eye of 'Old Tom,' who stands as sentinel to see that they trespass not with their drivers upon his beloved putting-green. Crack after crack rings cleanly as every ounce of their youthful muscle is thrown into the blow.

O duffer! ill will it fare with you if you strive to emulate their supple elasticity. This is but the fruit of a boyhood spent golf club in hand. Swing with their young insolent fearlessness—it is but a caricature!—for the confidence which with them is the crown of skill, with you will too likely be the curse of your incompetence.

Look rather at Mr. Alexander Stuart, a frequent medal winner of the Royal and Ancient. His is a free long supple swing, indeed, but formed upon quieter methods. There is more repose—less fascinating dash, maybe; but more apparent absence of effort. His is the safer style for your model. Or, again, look at Mr. Leslie Balfour. His is a style of almost laborious painfulness, yet the swing comes through free, and describing a perfectly true circuit; and, despite the apparent rigidity of leg and arm muscles, none have a better record upon the St. Andrews medal-winners' list than he—none, we may possibly say, so good.

Among the host of free slashing swingers it is perhaps invidious to mention names. The Blackwell and Goff families furnish brilliant examples among the amateurs—among the professionals, the Simpsons, Rolland, and many more. The mantle of talent of poor 'Young Tommy' has fallen perhaps more conspicuously, in the putting department of the game upon his younger brother Jamie Morris, for whom none, probably, are quite a match in this important detail.

In the quick movement of another famous professional, Willy Campbell, we see even more than the normal freedom of St. Andrews, and yet it is not quite the same style of swing as that of these others that Campbell has acquired upon the links of the Lothians.

Greatly to be admired, again, is the swing and style of Bob Fergusson, Willy Campbell's frequent opponent upon the links of Musselburgh—so square and solid he looks, his very stance expressive of the dogged resoluteness of his play, yet with great loose free-working shoulders swinging as true as if the backbone were a pivot! And that forward dig of his with the iron, which used to lay the balls up on the plateau-pitched holes of North Berwick as if by magic! His is a style which any golfer may with advantage study.

Then at Musselburgh too is seen a very fine player with a style in some respects very noteworthy—Brown by name, a slater, rather than golfer, by profession, yet who defeated all comers in the professional championship at Musselburgh a few years back. He stands with legs very far apart, and the swing back seems wild and irregular, but—this is the saving clause—he has developed a pause of quite unusual length at the height of his swing, a provision of nature, as it would seem, whereby he can correct the errors in aim contracted by his methodless upward stroke—a provision of nature excellent when truly nature's offspring, yet to him who would try to acquire the lengthened pause by study apt to prove a bitter delusion and a snare.

Still keeping to the ranks of professional players, we see a singularity of style exhibited by Willy Fernie, another ex-champion and one of our very finest players. He, as he addresses himself to the ball, turns his wrists right back and over, so that the club-head points straight out to the line in which the ball is to be driven. He knuckles over-forward, somewhat, as he thus points his club, and looks rather as if he fancied himself, lance in hand, about to transfix some imaginary foe. Yet, once these preliminaries over, no player has a more easy or perfect swing. Stay, there is one—Willy Park, descendant of a great golfing race, and champion in 1887 and again in 1889 —his swing, though very long, in ease and apparent simplicity bears off the palm from all. 'He makes a very easy game of it,' is the comment of the critic who watches the art with which Park conceals his art. Of all the professionals, moreover, and of amateurs also, there is none that drives a longer ball.

In ease and perfection of play he is perhaps equalled by Jamie Anderson with his careless little switch. The latter does not drive the length of Park, but the deadly accuracy of his iron approach shots, which he plays with scarce any dwelling on his aim, compensates him well for this deficiency.

Among the 'has beens' of the first flight of professional play, though still a young man, no golfer had a more beautiful or truer style than Jamie Allan. His arms used to be thrown away forward after the ball, almost like a windmill-sail revolving ; and he, like Mr. John Ball, junior, used to play with the ball comparatively near the right foot.

Then why, it may be asked, if this latter was a characterising feature of the play of two such very fine golfers, should it be protested against as an unwise method for the learner to strive to acquire? Well, these, to tell the truth, were in a measure instances of the errors of genius, of the errors which, to genius, may be pressed into such service as to be almost of advantage. For there is no question, provided the ball can thus be struck truly, that in this position it will be struck with greater power. But, again, this is a large proviso, and the difficulty which has been indicated as attendant upon this attitude— the difficulty, namely, of a free swing with the right shoulder so near over the ball—was only overcome by these two golfers by the exceeding suppleness and activity of their young anatomies. The error is easy enough to imitate ; the genius to turn it to good account is, unless of natural growth, well nigh impossible to cultivate. Even with these young players, to whom sometimes, though in less degree than most others, would occur occasional periods of aberration, the fatal tendency always latent in their style, the tendency, viz. to 'hook,' by bringing the arms round, instead of straight away, in the effort to overcome their self-imposed difficulty, would make itself painfully manifest. The cloven 'hook,' as we may say, would peep out, and the balls would go sailing away to whins and bunkers, instead of flying correctly down the course.

The very 'hook' or 'pull' itself is fraught with dangerous fascination, for the slightly hooked ball is the longest that can be driven. Many a fine driver, in the proud confidence of his best game, has been seduced by this alluring temptation. For a drive or two all goes well. The hooked balls, with due allowance made, return to the centre of the course, and go careering down it to the admiration of the gallery ; but then there is 'a hook too much and a hook too long,' to transmute Browning's 'Fireside' into golfing parlance, 'and life is never the same again.' For at the next drive, when the golfer, warned all too late, strives to revert to the old straight forward driving, he will too often find that the knack, or the inspiration, or whatever it be, has deserted him, that he has lost the true light of correct straight driving while following his will-o'-the-wisp down these rocky by-paths whose end is 'bunker.'

There are players, fine players—Captain W. Burn, late of the 14th Hussars, is one—who always play for a pull on their ball, and stand so as to make due allowance. It is a tempting of Providence; do not yield to its fascinations.

With the majority of our truest drivers the ball has a tendency upon most days of their golfing life to fly somewhat with a curve to the right. There are of course red-letter days when the ball flies perfectly straight off the club-face, turning neither to the right hand nor to the left; but red-letter days are the exception in this world of bunkers, and this ideal is perhaps but a one day a week or a one week a year game. For the greater majority of drives fly as if very slightly heeled.

Of players who stand dead square to their ball, as we may call it, whose club at the moment of meeting the ball is in a plane strictly at right angles with a line drawn from toe to toe, of these, two prominent instances present themselves : one, the late Captain Herbert Burn, 21st Hussars, a cousin of the last-named gentleman, and a player who with a quick short swing drove a beautiful low ball with great power from the fore-arm. A second instance bears a name of very great golfing renown, Mr. Gilbert Mitchell Innes ; but his is a quieter swing which, with a long powerful club, daintily picks up the ball from off the turf. Both these gentlemen are for the most part low drivers, with great run upon their balls. Mr. John Ball, junior, and Jamie Allan drive a class of ball which is doubtless, in both, the outcome of the similarity which has been noted in their styles. Their balls start low-flying from the club, then rise, as the initial velocity begins to diminish, and after making a great carry, drop to the ground comparatively dead. It is a peculiarly fascinating style of driving to watch, and is seen to marvellous effect in a long approach drive up to a hole on a plateau or just beyond a hazard.

Among golfers who play for a pull, it would be a great omission to fail to notice the style of Mr. Henry Lamb ; and yet his is hardly truly a pull, for it is not so much that the ball starts away in one direction, and then curves towards the left, as that Mr. Lamb swings so far out round with his arms before the club meets the ball, that the ball starts away somewhat in the direction of mid-on, to borrow a point from the cricketer's compass, and keeps this direction, when struck according to the intention, throughout its flight. It is thus, properly speaking, not a pull, though it has a tendency to develop itself into one, when Mr. Lamb is a little out of his best form, but a straightforward stroke, starting in an abnormal direction in relation to the position of the striker; and, considered from the point of view of this position, it has the effect of a pull. This was lately amusingly instanced at Eastbourne, where Mr. Lamb came for the first time to play golf. The 'caddie' at that time at Eastbourne was small and crude, but scarcely as immature as some of those tiros for whom he carried. He would at times venture upon a piece of well-timed admonition. When, therefore, Mr. Lamb's caddie saw his master taking up his position for his first drive in a manner which seemed to menace the windows of the new pavilion, he, in ignorance alike of Mr. Lamb's genius and its eccentricities, said hurriedly, 'You ought to stand more round to the left, sir.' Mr. Lamb thanked the boy gravely for the advice thus given to one who, in point of golfing experience, might have been his maternal grand-parent, and drove his ball some two hundred yards, straight down the course, to square-leg.

This matter of style is a deep mystery. Mr. Everard is a golfer whose style is markedly the reverse of elegant, yet his merits of execution are undeniable. What greater contrast can there be between Mr. Everard's style and the easy, true ellipse described by Mr. Macfie's driver? The latter is the straight player—*par excellence*—of the golfing fraternity, and we can well see the reason of it in the correct ease of his swing. Who but Mr. Macfie will take his driver when a full shot distant from that dreaded second last St. Andrews hole, perched up between the bunker and the road—between the devil and the deep sea— and land it right up on the green? We others all sneak up short to the right with a cleek; but Mr. Macfie lightheartedly lashes the ball home with the driver. It is a *tour de force*—one of those strokes of which we, who cannot emulate them, are apt to say, with a smile, that 'it is not golf.'

All these, whose swings we have as yet roughly dissected, drive with the full swing—that is to say, at a certain point in the upward swing the arms begin to bend, and the club goes round behind the head till its toe points at an angle towards the ground. There are, however, very many players who have but half swings ; their arms are but little bent, and the club does not rise greatly above the horizontal line, pointing to the right.

The best player who adopts this style of driving is, almost beyond question, Mr. Arthur Molesworth. The power of his stroke depends, in fact, little upon swing, but is obtained by lunging the weight of the body upon the ball, with tautened muscles of the fore-arm as the club descends. Another player of this order of swing, the Rev. R. A. Hull, has taken second honours on a St. Andrews medal day, but his swing, being more vertical than Mr. Molesworth's, frequently imparts a cut to the ball which acts detrimentally to its flight. For the most part, this half swing is characteristic of the golfer who has acquired the game comparatively late in life, after the muscles had lost the suppleness of youth, and the joints had become set.

And then, in addition to these more or less recognised styles, there are swings of diverse and wonderful grotesqueness. There is the 'Pig-tail' style, the 'Headsman' style, the 'Pendulum,' the 'Recoil,' the 'Hammer-hurling,' the 'Double-jointed,' the 'Surprise,' and the 'Disappointment.' Of each of these styles, which are real living styles, and no fictions, their respective names are in a measure an explanation. The 'Pig-tail' style is associated with the names of two very good golfers—Mr. John Ball, sen., and Colonel Stanley Scott. The latter of these players has not, of late years, kept up his game in full practice ; but the former has acquired such skill, with his eccentric methods, that he was a close 'runner-up' in the Amateur Championship in 1887, and was only defeated, in the semi-final heat, by one hole by the eventual winner. The peculiarity of the 'Pig-tail' style is this : that at the point in the upward swing whereat, with most players, the arms are bent to allow the club to reach back over the shoulders, behind the head, with these 'pig-tailers' the club is brought forward somewhat in front of the face, and describes evolutions roughly analogous in their curves to the tail of the animal from which they take their nickname.

The 'Headsman' style has no merits, whether abstract or concrete, to recommend it. It is opposed to all theories of perfection, and no golfer that ever adopted it has ever come to such fame as to plead its apology—as has been done by Mr. Everard for what he will perhaps forgive us for calling the 'Stuffed-Bird' style, in which he produces such astonishing results. The 'Headsman' style consists, as its name implies, in a straight up and down chop, as though the ball were the head of a mediæval rebel upon the block.

The 'Pendulum' style with the driver is a wearisome infliction, having little effect, whether for good or evil, upon the actual swing, since the penduluming is necessarily confined to addressing the ball; though, with the iron putter, as before noted, it is probably the most useful style that can be acquired. It consists in swinging the club monotonously to and fro over the ball, before striking, to the wearying of the eye both of striker and spectator.

The 'Recoil' is a style usually confined to very short drivers, and is exhibited, not in the actual swing, but in the immediately following movements. The player jumps backward, the instant the ball is struck, as though from the force of recoil, and follows this up by running a pace or two further back, whence he stands watching the ball in its flight. Whether the object of all this is to make the drive appear, by so much, longer, or whether the movements are entirely objectless, has not yet been determined.

The 'Hammer-hurling' heresy, as we may call it, is the result of a morbid exaggeration of the theory—within reasonable limits both truthful and useful—that the golf stroke should be all swing and no hit. With a driver of the same weight as a

THE 'HEADSMAN' STYLE

heavy hammer of the throwing sort, it would probably be the best style to adopt; but circumstances alter cases, and with a golf club other styles are better.

The 'Double-jointed' is a style which really does require this peculiar physical conformation for its exhibition in highest perfection. Some by no means despicable performers play more or less in the double-jointed method. Its individuality consists in a tremendously exaggerated length of back swing—so much so that Mr. W. T. Linskill, perhaps its chief exponent, is said to have sometimes knocked his ball from off the tee with the club-head as it swung round until it became quite vertical again behind his back. Such length of swing, combined with much knuckling in of the left knee and much turning on the left toe, brings the club-head down very near the ball.

The 'Surprise' is a style adopted by golfers who have laboriously endeavoured to infuse a quite unnatural degree of freedom into their address. In the abnormal wriggling incidental to this 'freedom falsely so called,' they so work their body round as almost to turn their back upon the ball, peering for it, as it were, over the left shoulder, out of the corner of their eye. After a little of this manœuvring, they seem to catch a sudden sight of the ball and to be in a hurry to flog it unawares before it has time to get away, and while it thinks they are taking no notice of it.

The style which we have termed 'Disappointment' is one which is commonly contracted by players who have taken up the game rather late in life. In addressing, they bring the club up well above the shoulder, so that you imagine that they are on the immediate point of striking it—instead of which, they arrest the club, with a jerk, just as its head comes down to the ball, and it is with a sense of disappointment that you realise that this manful effort was but a preliminary to the real stroke, which immediately follows. It is a style which is apt to be fatal to real freedom.

Thus have we briefly reviewed the chief varieties of the

golfing style, denoting the features in each which appear praiseworthy, and also certain grotesquenesses which are mainly worthy of attention as showing what to avoid. In doing this we have as yet confined ourselves almost exclusively to driving styles ; but there is no department of the game in which the style of professional players, and of those amateurs who have learnt the game professionally, so to speak, is so readily distinguished as in the manner of playing the iron approach shots. With right foot well forward and right fore-arm well down, almost on the hip, left elbow somewhat squared and body facing towards the hole, there is no mistaking the style of these finished artists. There is the free wrist play as the player looks up from the ball and measures his distance and assures himself of his direction. Then, as the club rests for a final moment behind the ball again, there is the characteristic knuckling over of the whole body and limbs towards the hole ; and then the club is raised with arms more confined near the body than in the driving stroke, and the flashing iron-head descends with a cross-cutting downward stroke, cutting out a little fid of turf, while the ball flies away— far too far as it appears to the unpractised spectator : but see ! the ball has pitched, and instead of running gaily forward over the putting-green it breaks to the right, with the spin imparted to it, gripping into the turf each time it touches it, and rests but a few yards further, though several yards more to the striker's right, than where it pitched. To the finished golfer the approach shot thus accurately judged, with fine allowance for the cut, and finely executed, gives perhaps an even more exquisite thrill of ecstasy than the fair full drive with which familiarity has bred a certain measure of contempt.

With equal ease and certainty can we recognise the professional and professionally modelled putter of the Scottish greens, with his ball by his right toe and the same characteristic knuckling over that we observed with the iron. And yet, outside this group of initiates, what a multitude of putting styles there are, and how many balls are putted straight and true in all of them ! Some hold the putter so low that a shaft seems almost a superfluity ; some pin their faith on the crook of their left elbow ; the key-note of others' creed is the right fore-arm steadied on the hip ; some putt with the ball well beyond the left foot, others with it actually behind the right. What is the *juste milieu*? It is hard to say. At least, the form of the question may suggest part of its answer, that extremes should be avoided. To combine the utmost mechanical regularity compatible with free liberty of muscle to co-operate in the instructions of eye seems to be the aim for our acceptance whether

AGRICULTURE

with putter, iron, or lordly driver ; and it would seem as if it were the preponderant development of what is in its nature and in moderation virtuous that leads us into vicious eccentricities.

And, besides styles of swing and posture, there are styles of feature, styles of dress, and above all styles of language, as numerous as the whole nation of golfers itself. A certain learned Scottish judge transfixes his ball, as he addresses it, with such a menacing *coup d'œil* as threatens five years' bunker servitude, at least. The same learned gentleman has the further singularity of address with his putter that he brandishes his weapon with equal vigour, before the stroke, for a putt of nine inches and a drive of some hundreds of yards. This has a most curious appearance. On one occasion J. O. F. Morris was standing, with his customary courtesy, flag in hand, at the last hole. The learned judge was some nine yards from the hole, and, brandishing his putter with his accustomed zeal, so terrified J. O. F. Morris—who, being unacquainted with the player's peculiar style, naturally supposed it the prelude of a full stroke—that he absolutely turned tail and bolted out of the line of fire.

In point of dress it is perhaps to be regretted that few good golfers in the North make a practice of wearing the red coat, the old golfing uniform. On some Southern greens it is held necessary as a kind of danger-signal to the non-golfing public. In the North it is deemed that a non-golfing public merits no consideration.

But in the matter of Norfolk jackets and knickerbockers, spats, and parti-coloured stockings, checks and stripes, the golfer is a bird of bright and varied plumage. 'No man can play with his eye continually caught by those confounded white spats,' is a complaint heard more than once from some sombre-suited crusty old golfer seeking excuse for a bad putt which has lost the hole to a smart young opponent. Yet you cannot tell the golfer by his plumage. Some of the dandies are no despicable opponents, though the veteran shooting-coat which has taken colour from all kinds of winds and weather, and clings adaptably in loving familiar wrinkles to the owner's frame, is the more common external sign of the workman within.

Of language, too, there is more difference in the form than in the substance. The 'Tut, tut, tut!' of the eminent divine —the accurate theologian, though the inaccurate golfer—is it not the expression of the same inward emotion as the more sulphurous exclamations of the vulgar tongue? But no matter what the style of exclamation he affects, let the golfer who is about to utter it bear in mind the excellent advice of Mr. Punch, and 'Don't.' On the links, no less than on the moors, is much sound of human voice to be deprecated. There will be much occasion for talk, which will not be neglected, on the incidents of the round when it is over; but when a weighty golf match is in progress, whatever be the proper style of play, of aspect, or of clothing, of golfing language there is but one style transcending every other, and that style's characteristic is its brevity.

CHAPTER VI

OUT OF FORM: A CHAPTER FOR ADEPTS

BY SIR WALTER SIMPSON, BT.

HARDLY any athletic sport survives our youth. From most sports a man begins to think of retiring almost before he has reached his full strength; but the golfer has not necessarily developed his best game till long after white hairs cease to be a novelty. There would be nothing phenomenal in winning one's first medal after tieing with a son. It does not happen to be the case at present, but two decades ago all the amateur medals were being carried off by what the cricketers and football-players of that day would have called old men. Again, many youngsters, no doubt, have won the professional championship: but there are well-known men—Morris, Ferguson, and Fernie, for example—who were past the first blush of youth when they began to beat all comers.

Although, then, there is no reasonable age at which improvement ceases to be possible or even probable, still, after a few years of play, whether we are to make further slight advances or not, most of us, 'for better, for worse,' reach a standard which is recognised as our game. We are sometimes 'off' this game, sometimes 'in' it. Besides this most golfers have an ideal game, the purified essence of their performances, the way in which they would play were it not for occasional missed balls. On this they base their calculations as to the number of shots they ought to take to the round. On this, with an allowance for mistakes indeed, but on the assumption that each of these will only cost one shot, they are handicapped and are entitled to win prizes. It is not with these occasional bad shots made by all, champions not excepted, that this chapter will deal. It has nothing to do with the fact that some players, and these not necessarily the best, are steadier than others; but with that common state of affairs in which a man decidedly and for some time continues to play a game which is below his average.

When a golfer goes off his game the reason of his doing so must either be due to some misconception or else to some fault in style; he either misguides or fails to control his club; he is, for the nonce, either stupid or clumsy. There are extremists who ignore style, who say that the only thing to do is to keep an eye on the ball, and to compel it to go. On the other hand, there are golfers entirely given over to analysis. Even before they have broken down, a few more than the number of mistakes which are inevitable by any man, and which ought to be taken no notice of, serve them as an excuse for trying to find out some error in stance, grip, or swing. But a little reflection must surely convince most people that their best game is not to be reached by play alone nor by thought alone. Evidently, wisdom lies between the extremes. The stylist ought to remember that confidence, concentration, patience, and accuracy are essential; whilst the man who knows nothing about his own mannerisms may suffer for forgetting that unless his club hits the ball in the right way his shots will not come off. Which has most to do with our game, style or sentiment, is of no practical importance. A correct idea of what we wish to do, and a correct way of doing it, are both essential. As it will be seen in the sequel that I consider it best in case of a break-down to seek first for a subjective cure, and only when that fails to search for a visible fault, it is natural to treat the subject in that order.

Prevention being better than cure, the first question which arises is, whether, having developed a good game, there is no way by which a man can make sure of continuing to play it. The thing is possible. If, after a player was master of a club, he ceased to dream of further improvement, thought no more of the matter, became neither more careless nor more careful, took no notice of his occasional bad shots, and (in driving) shut his eyes to the length of his carry, he might continue steady. Not only is this a possible case, but if not for a lifetime, at least for long periods, many thus become masters of their game. Assuming all could get it, is the steadiness so attained desirable? There is the risk of thus securing what is not the best game we are capable of. This is a sufficient reason for a negative answer, unless a man loves winning matches better than the game. Besides, it seems to be more than a risk. Although there are many whose each drive is a copy of the last, this deadly uniformity is not characteristic of our best golfers. The story of their rounds is a story of mistakes and recoveries, of better play and worse to an extent one would not *à priori* expect. Whether, therefore, it be a prudent thing or not to set our hearts on repeating our average shots rather than our best, to close our minds to all desires but that of flicking the ball cleanly, it is not a plan for getting over uncertainty in play, which one is justified in proposing. Quite properly the general run of golfers from the best to the worst have a less pawky feeling towards the game. They wish to lose no opportunity of improving, and from over-eagerness to do so they often break down. There is constant ebb and flow; but surely not necessarily to as great an extent as is usual. The history of a man's game is in most cases as follows. After a break-down he plays humbly, putting in practice all he knows as to the elementary necessaries of a good style, and one day to his surprise he finds himself playing his game. This is the critical moment. If he would let well alone, continue to play with the same care which restored his form, and look upon each shot as an isolated result not guaranteed by the last, nor guaranteeing the next, he might remain master of his game, and have it to fall back upon when, say, a few days of hitting harder, or of attempting a more fanciful mode of approach, had proved unsatisfactory. But the usual course of affairs is different. As soon as he becomes conscious that he is playing steadily, the player gets out of himself to take a look at all the good things he is doing, so that they may be put in practice should he (which at the time seems improbable) ever break down. Having made a mental note, he proceeds with confidence. He ceases to bestow all this bothersome attention on each shot. Should anything go wrong, are there not the notes to refer to? He hits with freedom, imitates A's swing or B's stance, takes any liberty, and yet hits well. In a few days there is a crash, and he cannot hit in any way. It seems to take more than a lifetime to teach some golfers that, as a train will run a long way without an engine, so their game keeps on without care. They know the train will finally stop, and that even should an engine be hooked on before it does, that it will not immediately be going full speed. Yet if after a few careless rounds their game slackens or stops, they do not see why it is so. Instead of attributing it to want of attention to individual shots, they look for some extraneous cause, hunt for it, lose patience, break down.

Without further illustration I wish emphatically to point out that many break-downs, if not most, are due to ourselves and not to our style, and that many of them might be very trifling, if we would but accept this fact. In most cases we will not. We want to do some harder thing than bathe in the waters of Jordan. We want to find some fault in style and correct it.

To be told to do anything so simple as thump patiently, carefully, ploddingly, is an insult to the ambitious golfer. He wishes to be the master of his game, not its slave.

Of course the break-down may be due to a fault in style. How are we to know whether there is or is not one needing correction? Should friends to whom we appeal assure us they see nothing to account for our ineptitude, we may be sure that style is not to blame. Should no two point out the same fault, we may with equal confidence abstain from analysing it. In short, except when there is little doubt as to the fault, or as to it and failure being cause and effect (a state of matters which will be considered in its proper place), we should proceed as if our minds only were to blame, and submit to what the doctors call a course of general treatment. Contrary to what might be true in illness, general treatment can do no harm, as it really consists in what more or less constantly we ought always to be doing. General treatment means putting away all but the first principles of golf, and approaching the ball like a beginner. Perhaps it would in most cases be a good thing for the player to read over the elementary didactic chapter of this volume, and come next day to the teeing ground prepared to verify his grip and stance carefully, and to swing as cautiously as if he had never swung a club before. I do not, of course, mean that he ought to try a new style; on the contrary, he ought to verify the pet foibles in which he secretly believes as much as the orthodox essentials. He ought to revise the whole subject, working out the problems in his own way—revise it rapidly, which he can do because he knows it pretty thoroughly.

It is of great importance to discriminate between peculiarities which it is sensible to retain and those which should be discarded. One kind may be called natural, the other artificial. A natural peculiarity is part of a man's scheme for hitting the ball. His may not be a neat way of arriving at good results; but it is not a wrong one, because it has brought out the right answer. Of natural peculiarities a golfer is only semi-conscious.

For instance, that which an onlooker would call a break in the swing is a feeling of slow back to the player ; a straddling of the legs is his plan for standing firm ; falling over the ball gets his shoulders to work. There scarcely exists a good golfer who could not tell you of something he supposes himself to do which you would not recognise from his description. Artificial peculiarities, on the other hand—that is to say, peculiarities which are copies of the natural ones of some good player, or 'open sesames' of our own invention—consciously adopted, can never be worth keeping. They help us for a round or two to play better because they give confidence, and then either fade out or are discarded. For instance, the amateur champion of 1889 has a naturally peculiar stance easily imitated. Artificial copies of it are at this moment ruining many a man's game. His imitators stand with the left foot very much nearer the ball than the other, because this is what their model does. Having heard about it so much, this brilliant golfer is no doubt now aware of what his position is, but a few years ago he was not; and, in answer to a question about it, he could only suggest that it was the means he had chanced upon to work out the problem of standing firm. That swaying of the body is precisely the fault this stance seems to engender in the swing of his imitators is a fact on which alone quite a chapter of instructive comment might be written.

When we have entirely broken down in our play it will be found in some cases beneficial to leave off the game entirely for a time. By doing so the bad tricks we have fallen into may be forgotten when we begin to take up the game once more. Being necessarily of recent growth these bad habits cannot be deeply rooted, and may wither whilst we are away from the green. But unless it happened to suit their plans in other respects, few men would care to take such an heroic course. A similar advantage is offered, however, by the long involuntary breaks in their opportunities of playing which are the lot of most men. These chances of inaugurating a better game ought always to be kept in view by the returning golfer.

By whatever means we arrive at the tee with unprejudiced minds—whether the immediate golfing past is put from us by an effort of will or obliterated by time and other distractions —there will be no benefit if we assume that there is nothing more to be done. In the case of undertaking a revision without leaving the green, that there is more to do is abundantly self-evident, and ought to be equally so in the other cases. Yet it is very usual for men not only to throw away the valuable opportunity absence from the links offers for recovery or improvement, but also to act in a way which insures their playing badly. Because from want of practice their best play is impossible, they indulge in a few careless rounds, instead of recognising that if there ever is a time when a golfer can afford to play loosely this certainly is not it.

We now come to the second part of our subject, the detection and cure of specific faults. This is a delicate matter, but not so difficult as some think it to be. In regard to faults in style, it is impossible to insist too strongly on the necessity of remembering that to find them out and avoid them is not all we have to do. As on the one hand it is unwise too readily to try a remedy, so on the other our game will suffer if without sufficient trial we discard the remedy we have applied. The following would be a sensible mode of procedure. Try the correction, and if it succeed you are a lucky man. If it does not, try another. If that too fails, it is midsummer madness to attempt more patching. Almost certainly the whole game is out of tone. Therefore, the thing to do is to go back to the first correction attempted, and keeping it and all the elements of good golf in view, to play a constrained cautious beginner's game, such as we have advised when the break-down is purely sentimental —a game which feels stiff, in which the swing feels short, which we are convinced cannot enable us to drive a ball; but which in reality can, because the hands are firm, the sweep unhesitating, and nothing is neglected. If this care be conscientiously taken for a round or less, the player to his surprise will suddenly discover that he is playing his game. The recovery will not be sudden, but the player's attention having been given entirely to hitting the ball, the knowledge that he is himself again will burst upon him in a moment. The odds in favour of this being the history of the case are so great that it is scarcely worth while adding that, if it is not, the player must go through it all again, giving some other fault a good share of attention. The reason why such a course is almost sure to effect a cure is that when a man is not grasping at every straw, but really trying to discover his fault, he is pretty sure to detect the true one. Even should he have failed to do so, the fault which can resist the care he has been taking must be very firmly rooted. With these cautions we proceed to examine the principal faults into which men drift.

Whether in the case of a beginner or an old player, the ball when driven has a great tendency to curve off to the right. There is perhaps nothing more difficult to get rid of than this form of bad driving; and why? Because it is assumed that when a ball curves to the right it does so always for the same reason, various terms for the fault notwithstanding. Now this is not the case. A ball will curve to the right if the club reaches it with the face laid back, or if the ball is sliced, from either of these causes singly or from both together. It is very evident that to enable him to correct the result the player must know what is its cause or combination of causes. He must also get rid of the common fallacy that hitting off the heel, which often accompanies slicing, is a cause of skid. There is nothing more hopeless and heart-breaking than to try to get rid of this without attending to the slice which causes it; nothing more important than to distinguish between this and heeling, which is caused by a faulty aim.

If a man is only heeling—that is, hitting the ball from the neck of the club—it will not go to the right. It will only be foundered. If by examining his club the player finds that he is always hitting off the heel, that he slices some balls, founders some, and, above all, if he hooks a few off the heel, heeling is the fault that has got a hold of him. He may ignore the other results. They are each more or less occasional, whereas the heeling is persistent. When this is the state of matters the cure ought to be easy. He has only to be careful about aiming. Heeling as an isolated fault is, however, very rare; but it should be attended to at once, lest there come the temptation unconsciously to add slicing, so that the ball may carry in one definite direction and not be foundered.

Laying back the club and slicing proper send the ball to the right for different reasons. The former does so because the face is not perpendicular to the line of fire, but at an obtuse angle to that line. The latter does so because, although the face itself is perpendicular to the line, the club is swung across it. The faults are different, but the result the same. They both put a right-hand spin on to the ball.

When spin is put on the ball by laying back the club, the grip is pretty sure to be wrong. The player has his left hand too far round, and its knuckles nearly or quite out of his sight. This disproportion in the way of holding may be noticed whilst he is addressing, or it may be arrived at during the swing. The man who cuts a ball because of the lie of his club will usually be found not only to be gripping wrongly with his left hand, but also to be holding too tightly with it, and too loosely with the right. Although some good players allow the club a little play in the right hand, it is not necessary to do so. A man who is cutting ought to be encouraged to allow it none. He ought to aim at gripping equally firmly with both hands, and with neither hand more round the club than the other.

By far the commonest cause of balls spinning off to the right is slicing. There is a certain class of bad players who, persisting in gripping in the wrong way, never hit the ball with a straight face, and consequently never drive straight; but as a temporary cause of balls flying to the right, slicing is by far the most common. We slice when, instead of sweeping along the line of fire, we draw the club towards ourselves across it. One

THE PICNIC ON THE PUTTING-GREEN—'JUST THE PLACE FOR IT'

OUT OF FORM

reason why we are so prone to do this is that straight up over the shoulder and down again across the body is by far the most comfortable way to swing a club. None but muscles adapted to swift motion are called upon. In the true swing the club-head goes back along the line of fire, and as near the ground as possible, by means of the arms, the rest of the swing (till the club is away round) being largely done by the trunk pivoting on the haunches. Now the muscles which do this latter part of the swing back are not adapted for swift work; when used together with the muscles of the arms they are like cart-horses yoked to 2.20 trotters, and act as a wholesome drag on this too straight and rapid swing. One sees an analogous thing in rowing. At twenty strokes to the minute any tiro willingly 'gets his back into it.' But at thirty-eight strokes or more he would fain do all the work with his arms.

There is a misconception of another kind, which is apt to make recovery from slicing more difficult than it need be. To use Mr. Galton's word, many golfers 'visualise' a swing as a scythe-like motion, not as a straight forward sweep. They make the mistake of picturing a club as striking the ball in the same way as the bat of a cricketer does who plays across the wicket. The feeling that the club-head describes a curve along the ground causes men instinctively and almost unconsciously to allow a little for this curve, and what they visualise as its result—a pull. I am inclined to think that this way of misconceiving a swing and its result is accountable for the fact that, compared with 'heeling,' pulling is a rare aberration. Whether this be so or not, let the golfer who has been accepting this mistaken theory get rid of it, and let out boldly. It is at least undeniable that a freely swung club has no tendency to pull the ball.

Having cleared the ground of some misconceptions about slicing, the next point is how to cure it. Evidently, the time-honoured imperative 'slow back' ought to be taken into consideration. What is too fast back every man must decide for himself. The child whose natural pace is a run, the youth who still trots for a mile or two without inconvenience, and the man who has golfed all his life, can each, in his degree, swing more swiftly than a late beginner. We are swinging too fast back when the pace is beyond what the slow body muscles can keep up to. To make these work, to make it easy for them to do so, is the chief part of the problem of curing slicing. If a man is using his loins, he need have no apprehension that he is swinging too fast. But if he finds that he can quicken, and is inclined to quicken to an unlimited extent without inconvenience, the arms only are swinging the club, which either spins the ball to the right, or, its taking that line being prevented in some way (*e.g.* turning in the face), drives it weakly.

By altering our position (position, not distance) towards the ball we facilitate the swing of the body, and cure slicing. As the alteration to be made depends upon the way a man has of standing whilst addressing the ball, a word must be said on that subject. One style is partly to face the direction in which the ball is to go, and to lean on the right leg. Another is rather to turn the back to it, and put most weight on the left. There is, of course, a third style possible—namely, to stand perfectly at right angles to the line of fire. This stance may be ignored as not existing in practice. A compass-needle swings on a point, but a human being inevitably emphasises his position on to one leg or the other. Which of these two classes is most prone to slice? There is little doubt that those who stand 'open,' and who have most of their weight on the right leg (the leg to which the other class must transfer it whilst swinging the club back), oftenest commit this fault. One can see why this is so. By exaggerating the position to absurdity, such a relation of man to ball can be arranged that nothing short of a half circle on the loins could get the club far enough back to do anything but slice. Whether or not to advise a player who stands 'open' to draw his right leg back and lean on the other is too revolutionary, it is, at any rate, the position from which slicing is most

'OH! WHAT A SURPRISE!'

easily cured. Some people think it has other advantages. In the days of feather ball, of light clubs, and narrow links little cut up by irons, neatness and accuracy were of more importance than power, and the open style therefore the best ; but with the heavier clubs and heavier balls of to-day, a style which is more effective to force out of a cup is by many authorities considered better. If the slicer of the old school is not prepared to change his stance entirely, all that he can be advised to do as to his feet is to plant his left more nearly in a straight line with the ball, and to be on his guard not to bear too lightly on that leg.

The player in the modern style has more resources of this sort against slicing. He ought to draw his right foot further back and further away from the ball in proportion to the amount of 'skid' there is on his ball. As the matter is usually (and, indeed, correctly) explained, this lets him 'get his shoulders into it.' Golfers will understand that this is practically what I have called using the loins. How the moving of the foot acts in cancelling the tendency to slice, if still misunderstood, will be brought home to the reader by that most convincing argument, a swing with a club.

To shorten the swing is often effective against slicing. As there is much prejudice against this, and as it would cure not slicing only but many other kinds of bad play were it not for the reluctance of golfers to submit to it, it is worth while to try to show how mistaken the prejudice is. Because it seems inevitable that they must shorten their driving, is the reason why men would do anything rather than cut off a segment of the circle they describe. Most golfers have proved at one time or another by experience that doing so has lengthened their carry. But they look upon this as an accidental result of something else (they do not quite know what), and are persuaded that, in the end, their drives must be shorter. It seems to them a very simple and incontrovertible piece of reasoning. There is a flaw in it, nevertheless. The flaw consists in regarding the completeness of the circle as the main thing, its size a secondary matter; whereas, within certain limits, the size of the circle, of which a segment is described, has far more to do with driving than the amount of segment. A consideration of the annexed diagrams will explain my meaning, and show why my statement is true.

The owner of swing No. 1 would call No. 2 a half swing, although measured it is longer than his, and as a rule he would

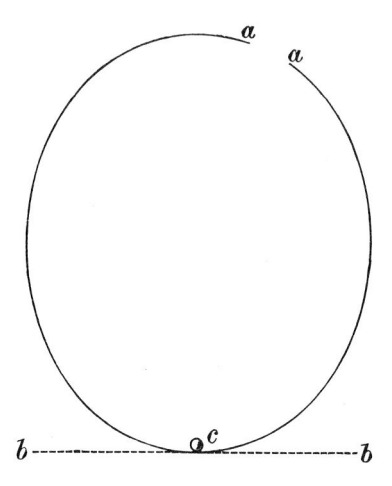

FIG. 1.—A '*small*,' but commonly called a '*full*,' swing.

a a, curve described by the club; *b b*, intended direction of driving; *c*, the ball.

This curve is classed as and called a '*full*' swing. If classed according to essential features, it would be called a '*small*' swing.

rather continue to slice than work his loins so as to allow his shoulders to describe No. 2, unless they were prepared to do the further work of completing the circle. Of course it is all the better if the club-head comes well round; but that is of no moment as compared with the size of the circle. As in so many other matters, it is the loose use of words which misleads. It would be well, in the interests of golf, if the terms 'full swing,' 'short swing,' 'half swing,' were boycotted, and words referring to the size of the sweep substituted, such as 'big swing,' 'little swing,' &c., or, better still, 'flat curve,' 'sharp curve,' &c. So long as descriptions of styles are based upon the comparatively unimportant fact of the amount of circle described, beginners and others will be misled, and energy wasted on what are, too often, meaningless gyrations.

At golf misfortunes seldom come singly, although we are taking them one by one. Whilst still in the miseries of slicing, or just as we are recovering, a fit of the costly vice of topping

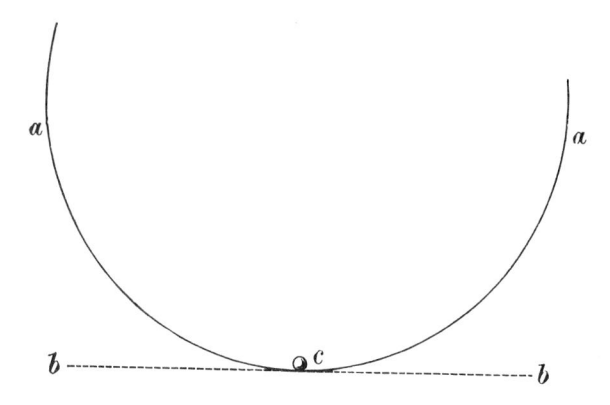

FIG. 2.—A '*big*,' but commonly called 'short,' or '*half*' swing.

a a, curve described by the club; *b b*, intended direction of driving ; *c*, the ball.

This curve is classed as and called a '*short*' or a '*half*' swing. If classed in reference to essential features, it would be called a '*big*' swing.'

may overtake us. Before a hole is played out, a new ball may be nothing but a rolling mass of black grinning mouths, disgusting except as evidences that at all events we can hit hard. A fit of topping in the days of feathers must have been positively ruinous. To remember at such a time that it is not the top of the ball we want to hit, but a part of it which we can scarcely see, to remember this always, is not a bad thing. But this alone will not cure us. Topping is apt to come with slicing. When we describe too small a circle, swing too much up and down, there is only a proportionally small part of our sweep during which club face and ball will meet, a part still smaller if we draw the club across the line of fire, which we have seen is almost inevitable with such a swing. Although, mathematically speaking, a tangent to a curve touches it at a point, in golf they are practically in contact for an inch or two when the sweep is large ; but if it is sharp this advantage is lost.

Topping, however, has other causes, causes which are independent of slicing. Men often find that for one reason or another they are driving higher than they like, and they try to prevent this by just a touch of top. If they would but think, it would be at once obvious that this is impossible. A ball is topped or it is not topped. There is no intermediate stroke. What! no such thing as a half-topped ball? is the incredulous cry at once hurled at me from the throats of several thousand readers. No! a ball hit to spout up cannot be made to rise the proper height by being also hit to 'dook,' except, perhaps, when it is hit from a tee as high as the club-face is broad. Skying, for this cause, may be passed by. It is cutting from above downwards which makes a series of shots to rise too high, just as cutting across the line causes them to go to the right of the desired direction. If a ball is hit so as to give it the spin which makes it rise too high, topping or half-topping cannot give it a lower trajectory. When the swing is true, no matter the size of the curve if the ball is at the point where the curve touches the ground, the shot will be perfect. If the curve is large and the ball is hit as the club descends, it will have a little upward spin ; if as the club ascends, a little downward spin ; but in neither case enough spin to be of material importance. When the curve is a small one, the effects are different. The ball, hit as the club descends, will rise too high ; as it ascends the ball will get so much downward spin as to prevent it (practically) rising at all. There is no time of hitting the ball as far as one can see at which half-topping would be effective. Therefore, get down to the ball always, and trust to a flatter swing to cure rocketing.

A consideration of the effect of cut upon a tennis ball will make my argument as to the futility of attempting to keep a golf ball down by half-topping, or, as some would say, hitting cleaner, still clearer. At tennis spin can be put on the ball by laying the racket back. Cut can be put on a golf ball in the same way. Bringing the racket down at an angle to the line of fire also spins the tennis ball. It is with this we have to do. That the only way not to put a spin on the tennis ball is to meet it squarely cannot be questioned. The analogy is perfect, and proves, as I submit, that the only way to make a golf ball fly true is to sweep it from the tee as squarely as the manner of a drive permits.

A fear of breaking a club, or of losing impetus by striking the ground, are two other reasons why golfers top. Of the latter it is enough to say that a swing which will dig the club into the ground so as to check it, is so up and down that it would not be of much use in any case. Experience teaches that an honest 'sclaff' has no bad effect except, perhaps, when the ground is frozen, and the game cannot be properly played at all. Besides digging when the swing is too sharp, there are other things which prevent men from learning that they may sclaff with impunity. Hitting off the toe, and hitting off the heel, and turning in the nose, are all apt to break clubs. When along with any of these a player also takes the ground, he is apt, very naturally, to blame the latter for the break. Taking the ground is, therefore, dreaded and avoided, with the result that topping is a constant trouble, till long experience has proved it to be not only harmless, but to some extent desirable.

Hooking is not nearly so common a fault as skidding to the right, because there is not the same temptation to push outwards across the line of fire as there is to draw the arms in. In fact, it is scarcely possible to do this much, unless when we intentionally force. As a rule, a hooked ball owes most of its spin to the club face being turned in. There are many golfers who have no occasion to guard against hooking. Those who have are, for the most part, persons unduly ambitious of long driving. Turning in the face keeps a ball down, and thus makes it go further. Standing far from it also lengthens the carry. Press ever so little when your club is turned in and yourself over-reached, and the hook is certain. Getting the right hand under the club, and gripping hard with it, helps a man to force, only at the imminent risk of the face getting turned in during the swing. To cure himself of hooking, a man has, as a rule, only to give up pressing. If that is not enough, it may be that stooping forward has become a habit he is not conscious of. The case of golfers who all their lives have had a wrong conception of the use of hands is more difficult. If you have begun golf and continued it with the idea that the right hand is a propeller and the left a fulcrum, you probably grip too hard with the former, and get it or both too much round under the handle. Hooking is never far away from such a style, but to induce those who have it to change is scarcely possible. In spite of its crampedness, it drives a long because a low ball, and anyone who has tried knows how hardly will a long driver be induced to give up his 'screamers,' no matter how occasional they are.

The style of driving with the left foot nearer the ball is credited with being more conducive to hooking (and to wildness generally for that matter) than the old style. It is useful to remember that it is not the style of address itself which betrays players into fits of hooking, but a fault which it allows to grow. A man who stands open is made aware that he has got too far from his work by losing his stability and 'falling in.' Not so with the other style. He can overcome the immediate bad effects of stooping by increasing the relative distance of his two feet from the ball almost indefinitely, and thus getting his left leg as a prop. For the moment it is much easier to use this correction than to stand up. Accordingly, stooping, and a tendency to be wild in consequence, is a common blemish on this style. It need not be; but one can easily see that it always will be. Knowledge of this tendency will, however, guide the player to the proper remedy when his hooking or other wildness becomes so serious as to demand energetic treatment.

A nasty and not uncommon form of break-down is what may be called general debility. We do not miss; we do not even seem to hit uncleanly. The ball rises to the proper height, and goes straight; but the distance is contemptible. For a cleek shot we need a driver. For a wrist iron shot a full one. When this occurs there is usually a sense of discomfort. We feel cramped and powerless. Our swing has neither beginning nor end, other than that we arbitrarily make for it. After a time we become accustomed to the discomfort, and do not feel it; but the golf continues as unsatisfactory as before. At this stage it is possible to detect that comfort has been obtained by giving a twitch after the ball is hit, instead of sweeping the arms away; and the player, if he observes this, sets to work to follow up the stroke. He finds that he cannot, and if he persists the discomfort returns. A follow up more vigorous and angry than usual may break a shaft over the left shoulder. He is a lucky man who grasps the meaning of this little mishap, viz. that he has gradually acquired the habit of standing too near his ball. I say gradually. Within a foot or so it is not of practical consequence how near or how far off the ball is. But if a man is continually at the nearer limit his style changes. Everything in his play, including the carry, becomes cramped and small. When the cause is understood, doing everything on a larger scale will soon effect a cure; not only that, it will develop a fine game; for to have persevered in hitting with the middle of the club through so much tribulation proves that the man's eye is in.

The player, without being too near the ball, may find his swing checked against the left shoulder if he is slicing badly, but the course the ball takes makes it easy to discriminate between these two cases.

There is a class of fault to which the beginner rather than the mature player is addicted; although the latter is by no means safe from it. Until—and this may be for years and may be for ever—a man is convinced that smooth swiftness and not violence make him master of the ball, he tries to get his body to assist him in wrong ways. Properly the body must remain stationary. It must swing round as does the compass in the binnacle, but not as the boom sways about in a calm. At different parts of the stroke the weight of the body is transferred from one leg to the other, as a natural consequence of swinging, but any removal of the body as well as of its weight is wrong. One sways (*i.e.* moves) away to the right as the club rises, from a feeling that this is swinging, and that hurling the body at the ball is hard hitting. In addition to this misapprehension there is, in the case of the tiro, also the real difficulty of not swaying, which would all the more quickly be overcome if it were not the custom to teach beginners to rise on the left toe, instead of leaving that to be the inevitable result of the body revolving in the proper way. A man who has fallen temporarily into this fault of swaying his body will find he is foundering his ball. He will be conscious of hitting uncomfortably hard, and will find, if he asks himself, that he is thinking of the ball as a heavy object. Let him reflect that drawing back and throwing himself forward would burst open a door, but would not send either a door or a ball more than a few yards. He will often be told that he is hitting too hard, and that there is a limit to the power which is effective in driving. There is no such limit if power is applied in the proper way, but there are certain ways of applying force which are harmful.

The experienced player is not likely to fall into this way of attempting to drive so grossly as that it shall be noticed, but he is very apt to be guilty of an invisible form of what is practically the same fault, very difficult to detect, because as far as I know it has never yet been clearly defined and pointed out. When a ball is foundered, or in some other respect badly hit, the player usually accuses himself of forcing, swinging too fast, or not using his shoulders. There are many who have golfed through life with this stone around their necks. A laboured, forcing style may be suspected of concealing it. Often there is no outward indication, and only the player himself can lay his hand upon it. He can do so by asking himself in what sense he interprets the maxim, 'Let your body into it.' Properly 'let' here means 'allow,' not 'put.' An illustrative case will best explain what is meant. Suppose the driver to be swung back to its limit, it is the fore-arm alone (we are exaggerating so as to make the point clear) which swings it forward again. The shoulders and body ought only to follow, neither dragged nor arresting. If at any moment the shoulders take the initiative the fault is committed. As a worm travelling looks as if a wave passed along it from head to tail, so the wave of muscular contraction for a golfing swing must pass from the extremities inwards. When the wave travels in the opposite direction, all the motions may seem correct, but the result will be unsatisfactory. Young Tom used to fall forward after a stroke. Many a bad player does so too ; but the one fall is the very antipodes of the other. Young Tom let his body go with the club : the other pushes the club instead of swinging it, and ends by throwing himself at the ball.

Driving through the green may be passed over as being the same thing as driving from a tee, except in regard to one form of break-down which can only originate in that part of the game, a break-down caused by going to a new links. It is a curious fact that, although golfers are at most times ready to blame anything rather than themselves, when a different kind of turf might fairly be credited with a falling off one seldom hears that excuse. No doubt the links we are accustomed to vary with the weather, but its effects are recognised and soon mastered. Natural and radical differences between green and green, however, are not clearly recognised as a difficulty, or much angry thumping and disappointment would be avoided. To give detailed hints on this subject would take up too much space, without perhaps being of more use than the simple advice to golfers to be on the look-out for them. If on changing ground a man finds himself unaccountably 'off,' the first thing to do is to attend to its quality and to master its peculiarities. For instance, many players find St. Andrews links exceedingly baffling. The hills and hollows force themselves on the attention, as also the fact that to get out of the bunkers demands a special kind of skill ; but that such beautiful turf is (probably from being much walked on) peculiarly hard is not at all manifest. Particularly if you have a 'sclaffy' style beware of the links of St. Rule. Taking turf there is apt to turn your club, or if by gripping hard you avoid this, there is a jar you cannot feel satisfied to endure. Being determined to get down to the ball, which is an essential element in your scheme of driving, you hit harder. The holes being long increases the temptation to 'let into them.' It is exactly the most unwise thing to do. What is required is to take the ball clean, which a more than usually easy swing helps one to do. But not taking turf, just as much as sclaffing on hard ground, inclines those accustomed to scrape along the ground to pull in the arms or else to sweep them round, to slice or to hook. These results we must avoid by taking more than usual care to follow up the blow with a correct sweep in addition to the careful aim. It is the quality of St. Andrews links which makes their professionals recognisable anywhere. They seem to pick the ball off the tee as a bird picks up a seed, and to fly away with it, instead of tearing it from its place, which many equally good players from softer greens seem to do.

Under the head of approaching is comprised every shot—not a putt—into which the sense of weight enters as an essential element. To notice all the ways in which men try to master the problem of getting near the hole would not only be endless but also unprofitable, because, in addition to the vagueness and profusion in the terms used to describe approach shots, such as three-quarters, half-quarter, wrist, &c., each player interprets these arbitrarily and according to a scheme understood only by himself and his caddie. I shall therefore only deal with the ordinary modes of approaching, however named, leaving fancy shots to those who trust in them.

Approaching differs from driving in that the club is not swung as far as possible, but drawn back in proportion to the distance to be covered. Accuracy in drawing back being the chief point, most men face the line of fire and play off the right leg, the position which best insures accuracy, because it enables them to support and guide the arms against the body. It is a modern fashion to play off the left leg instead, which no doubt also gives the necessary support, but not so well: so that one is inclined to think that it is adopted in order that driving and approaching may be on the same plan as much as for any real advantage. To attempt approaching without emphasising the stance in one way or the other, or to consider that it is fragments of a full swing which are required, is unsound.

When an adept's driving leaves him for a season, it does not do so entirely. His slicing, toeing, heeling are not as grossly manifest as at an earlier stage. It is otherwise with approaching. A medal winner unable to hit with any part except the socket of his iron is no uncommon phenomenon.

Slicing is the most common and dread disease of both approaching and driving. What is true of the latter applies here, except that (even when one plays off the left leg) it is not likely to be advisable to alter the distances of the feet from the ball, but only the angle at which it is between them; because, accuracy being of more moment than power, the position is pretty certain to be already as emphatic as it can be. In which direction the correction is needed can easily be determined for both slicing and pulling, if here again it be remembered that it is possible to place the ball so far back that one must come straight down on it, or so far forward that it can only be reached by clawing it round.

A cause of slicing which must be carefully watched is the taking back of the club. Instead of returning to the ball along the line it was withdrawn over, it describes a loop. This must evidently cut the ball. It is next to impossible to avoid making this loop or slightly wavering if our arms are free from the support of the body from the shoulder downwards, as they are when driving. The line can be kept if we draw the club back fast; but a quick swing instead of a steady withdrawal will make itself evident by general uncertainty in our shots. By one shot the ball is topped; at the next our club is pulled up dead, sticking in the turf. One shot goes high, another low. As for the cleanly hit balls, the distance they go is variable beyond conception. One intended to loft over thirty yards covers a hundred and lands in the sea. We know when this sort of thing is going on that our swing is too fast; but as soon as we succeed in withdrawing the club more slowly, every ball if not hit off the socket is sliced as badly as if it were. Why? Because to take the club back accurately, to control the distance it is withdrawn so that it shall be proportioned to the intended length of carry, we must have one arm at least down to the elbow rubbing against the body. To get this support it is not difficult to apprehend that we must play very decidedly off one leg or the other. The trouble is that often after this point is attended to the arms are still free, unless an elbow is wilfully tucked in, which has the effect of making us feel more like trussed fowls than golfers. This results because we are stooping too much over the work, instead of standing up, or because the hands are not pressed down, or perhaps are round under the club handle instead of over it. Even when these details are recognised it is often very difficult to shake into the correct position, the position in which we can withdraw the club and swing it down again firmly without waver and without effort to a distance completely under our control.

Another cause of slicing is a too free use of the wrist. When it is the intention to play an ordinary approach shot—a shot without spin and without cut—the left wrist cannot be too taut. There is a wrist shot proper to which we shall devote a paragraph presently. A hesitating mingling of these two can only produce varied and undesired results.

When approaching off the right leg it is quite exceptional for the golfer to pull, at least continuously. When control of the swing is lost we are of course occasionally erratic in this way as well as in others. But if pulling is the rule the player may feel confident that he is not drawing his club far enough back, and is making up for this by hard spasmodic hitting. Approaching off the left leg, he is liable to hook. Indeed, it is almost correct to say that the fault being the same we go off the line in the direction of the leg leant upon. This applies to many faults, but not to all. For instance, slicing is equally common to both styles. Hooking, again, is a certain proof of forcing, as we have just said, when the old style is adopted, but is not as regards the new one. Whatever the style, the temptation to force approaches is very great, and needs constantly to be guarded against. It is recognised by most golfers that distance is most accurately measured by the inches the club is withdrawn, not by the amount of effort put into the stroke. It is not usual to play as if the opposite were true, but a compromise which is, if anything, worse, is constantly being attempted. For some reason or other measuring distance in the proper way is not natural, and unless we are paying attention a slight degree of compromise slips into our game—so slight, perhaps, that the extent to which our approaches become less deadly is not noticed. By using a little more effort instead of swing, topping, getting under the ball, toeing, &c., appear, and, lastly, when the swing has disappeared altogether there is a steady series of hooked balls.

Speaking of forcing approaches, we are face to face not only with a cause of break-down when it becomes noticeable, but with the reason why on the whole approaching is such a weak point in most men's game. So strong is the inclination that it is exceptional for anyone to go a whole round without occasionally sparing a short shot or forcing a long one, although the practice is admitted to be wrong. The contempt in which that small class who deliberately use a full swing at all distances (regulating its pace) is held proves this. It would be well for golf if when we laugh at this style the lesson were taken to heart,

and it were appreciated that a single length of swing is foolish
for any two distances however nearly the same. Doubtless a
compromise with forcing arises sometimes from inability to
regulate swing, because from causes already discussed the arms
have no support against the body. But it is just as often
because the importance of this matter is not realised. In proportion to their skill in other departments it is unpardonable
that in the case of most players holing in three off the iron
without any exhausting display of good putting is not more the
rule than it is. A golfer who does not from thirty yards get
within ten of the hole considers he has made a bad shot. It
ought to be equally easy to get as near from any distance within
a hundred yards. It ought purely to be a question of inches
of swing to mark off which a man could surely soon learn by
practice.

To go out driving balls entails more walking than is
pleasant, besides (unless one has something definite in view)
being of doubtful advantage. But to practise approaching
might be made very amusing. At the very least, whilst waiting
for the adversary's arrival the time might thus be utilised instead of being wasted in aimless putting. A very conscious
style may cramp driving, and thus shorten it. But it is of no
consequence how far one can drive with a quarter shot. To
know one's distances is here the essential thing. Approaching
it is not possible to be too well aware of what one is doing.
The stroke is not natural. It is not played instinctively in
the proper way. In practising, after the player had seen that
his position was correct, the point needing attention would be,
the speed and length of swing back. This speed ought never
to vary, or, more correctly speaking (for the speed with which
the ball is reached of course varies with the length of swing),
the force used should be uniform for all distances. After
noting that the club is taken back and brought down again
straight along the line of fire, one should learn how much
swing is needed for different carries—learn this so accurately
that it should be almost possible for each golfer to draw up for

himself a comparative table of inches of his swing to yards of carry.

Approaching in the ordinary style there is one other point which requires constantly to be attended to—namely, the after swing. The length of this part of the stroke ought not, like the swing before the ball is reached, to be proportioned to the distance to be covered. Except perhaps for very short shots, which scarcely come under this head, the after swing must not be stinted in any way. Many of the best players make a point of following up the ball as much for all approaches as for a drive. You see them watching the result with the iron or cleek, as the case may be, still resting on the left shoulder. If it does not come naturally to a man to complete his swing so entirely, he need not do so ; but at any rate it ought never to be lost sight of that clipping the after swing with any idea of regulating distance is the same kind of fault as, and has similar bad effects to, doing so before impact. It keeps the ball back, but, as with jerking before the ball is reached, at the sacrifice of all precision. In short, the distance to which the club is withdrawn is the only thing which ought to vary. This alone is quite enough to make a man master of all distances between a drive and a putt, provided there is no abnormal difficulty in the player's and the hole's position.

It cannot, however, be overlooked that there are many other schemes for dividing approach distances, which it would be shirking my task to dub fanciful and ignore. Some players are less ambitious, being content to attempt, say, three distances, for each of which they have a definite plan. Others, whilst looking upon three or even two distances as practically enough, are ambitious in another direction. Instead of being satisfied with one uniform height of loft, they aim at controlling their shots in that respect, using one plan or another according to the nature of the ground. When the chances are in favour of a ball with a normal trajectory being well treated during its run, they play it simply ; when the ground is rough, they then try to make it fall as dead as possible. For short approaches, there are weighty authorities who assert that the distances are most easily controlled by loft and spin. They hold that what are occasionally called quarter shots ought all to be played from the wrist, with more or less spin, so as to fall more or less dead. Whichever scheme of lofting, or whichever of the endless compromises, a man adopts, there is no doubt that he will be constantly breaking down if he has not very definite ideas as to what he is attempting. For want of these there is no shot in all golf which men are more constantly losing and recovering than the lofted approach shot. Whether used occasionally or always, at certain distances, the lofted approach is not a fancy shot, although many players have to regard it in that light. They lose the knack, and not knowing what it is which lofts a ball, they have to give it up till by chance it comes back. The extent to which the heel of the club is pressed down, and the hands are over in the grip, is often relied on to make the difference between an ordinary and a high loft. Sometimes faith is placed in the amount of slice. The first of these (the heel down and the hands over) is a means by which the proper swing is facilitated, the latter is an inevitable result of swinging in the required style. Slicing does not raise the ball, but one cannot avoid slicing when delivering the lofting blow. Holding tight with the right hand, and many other points which will suggest themselves, are in like manner not causes of lofting, but results of adapting one's position to the problem of the right swing. To come to the point without further beating about, loft and back spin are the result of describing a small ellipse with the club, and not a large segment of circle. To do this the club is swung by the wrists. To let them work its heel must be down, and the hands over the grip. From the style of the shot, we must slice across to some extent; but it is not this slice, but the slice from above downwards, which causes both the high loft and the back spin with its dead fall. If this required proof, Parks's new patent lofting iron would prove it, as that club was devised solely to obtain this back spin.

Being off one's putting is not a subject about which there is much to be said. Once understood, there are few faults into which players can drift unwittingly. If a man is off his putting, pretty surely the cause is mental. Patience, confidence, and unflagging attention are always required. Putting is entirely a conscious act, no part of which can become a habit. Driving may be to a great extent mechanical; but the nearer the hole we get, the less becomes our freedom, and, consequently, the intrinsic pleasure of hitting. To name the commonest faults into which men allow themselves to drift is all that seems necessary. Of these, jerking instead of drawing the club far back enough to sweep it evenly away is a very bad one. All the advantages of really, although not technically, pushing the ball are thus lost. Getting into any of the attitudes discussed under 'approaching,' by which the player loses the support of his elbow against the body, puts him at a disadvantage. Standing at a proper angle to the ball is of great importance. Men are apt to allow themselves too much license in this respect, forgetting that in such a delicate operation it is not enough to be sure of hitting the ball clean.

No doubt some men are born better putters than others; but the very prevalent idea that for certain kinds of turf or for certain conditions of the putting-greens special faculties exist is one requiring a word of remonstrance. Till the strength required for a new kind of turf is understood, one may easily fail; but unless there is more required for successful putting than accurate hitting, to suppose oneself better suited for one green than another must be fancy. To get over being put off one's game by the nature of the ground, the thought of what it is like should be put away, and its keenness and tenacity alone studied. On the same groundless assumption of it being possible whilst putting to do something more than set the ball rolling at the proper pace and in the right direction, men seek to recover lost deadliness in the art by changing their club. Sentiment apart, this can but necessitate learning the use of each separately. To condemn the changing of clubs, it must be noted, is not to assert that there is only one proper club to putt with. Many good putters use cleeks, putting irons, &c. The fact that their cleek is better balanced, or their putting iron a better tool than their wooden putter, is a good reason for the adoption of one of the former. A badly balanced club is by no means to be overlooked as a real cause of going off in putting.

CHAPTER VII

HINTS TO CRICKETERS WHO ARE TAKING UP GOLF

By H. G. HUTCHINSON

GREAT number of English golfers are reformed and reforming cricketers — men who have scoffed at golf in the pride of their cricketing youth and are now toiling through the bunkers of repentance, greatly envying those who learnt the game when young. To these it were well to address some special words of advice, seeing that through the training of their muscles in the use of the cricket bat, they have special difficulties to overcome if they would avoid villainous misuse of the golf club. In penning the following remarks, addressed especially to the aforesaid class, the present writer is fortunate in being able to avail himself of suggestions from one who, having been in the very first class of cricketers, has worked his way up to very nearly first-class golf—Mr. R. A. H. Mitchell. These remarks are, in fact, substantially Mr. Mitchell's own.

First. The ball which the cricketer proposes to strike is a ball in motion. At the moment that bat and ball meet, it is probable that the cricketer is not looking at the ball at all. Whether or no it be possible for him to see the ball at the moment of striking, it is certain that in most cases his eye is carried forward, as if hopefully prospective of the delight of seeing the ball whizzing through the air. This is how it is with the cricketer, and this is how it should be. This is how it too often is with the golfer, and this is emphatically how it should not be. The cricketer has to judge, from his sight of the ball coming towards him from the bowler's hand, where his bat is likely to meet it, and plays accordingly. But he must not treat the golf ball with this disrespectful levity. He must keep his eye rivetted upon the ball. This, then, is the first and great temptation, common to all golfing flesh, but especially besetting the reforming cricketer.

Second. How often, in the Badminton Cricket Book, Mr. Lyttelton speaks with encomium of a 'quick-footed' batsman. There is little to be said in praise of a like quality in the golfer. In cricket, one foot or other (most often the left) is rightly moved. True, at the moment that bat meets ball the batsman ought to be firm on both legs ; but at golf, to move either foot, even while making your addresses to the ball, is an almost inevitable means of securing their rejection. It is such a dreadful habit, that it seems almost unnecessary to preach against it. But it is doubtless committed, and is a temptation which besets the path of the cricketer.

Third. 'A cricketer,' observes Mr. Mitchell, 'is naturally apt to swing too short and too quick, and the right hand is always predominant. Unless a man is swiping, he does not draw his bat far back, nor does he bring it far forward ; consequently he is trained for a cramped swing at golf.' The long and short of it is that the golf stroke is a swing, and the cricket stroke is a hit. The swing which the cricketer dare not

'ARRY. A SKETCH ON LONDON LINKS

indulge himself in, because of its tendency to send the ball into the air, is just what the golfer wants —just, or something like it. The cricketer stops his stroke in order to keep the ball along the ground. It is part of the training adopted for the very same purpose that makes the cricketing golfer apt to stand too much in front of the ball. If, at net-practice, a cricketer is knocking a ball back to the bowler, as it lies upon the ground, he will naturally have the ball close to his right toe, and will hit it with the power of the right arm. And this is just what he is apt to do—and just what he must try to get out of doing—with the golf ball.

The cricketer, too, does not swing his bat away back from the block-hole as he lifts it. No, he just lifts it, without any particular method. And he is apt to do the same with the golf club—to bring it too straight up : therefore, also, too straight down. Moreover, the habit of checking the arms, with the view of keeing the cricket-ball along the ground, makes it hard for the cricketer to learn to swing his arms away after the golf-ball is struck. He is apt to bring his arms round his body, close in. Now all these faults are mainly due to the predominance of right hand—which hand ought not only not to be predominant, but ought to be tenderly used, with light grip, while the left hand does the burden of the work.

Fourth. The next special difficulty may, perhaps, be best indicated by saying that the golfer plays, and ought to play, with a very crooked bat. At cricket the ball should be very near the batsman when he hits it, but at golf it should be far out, away from the player. It is a result of this difference that the cricketer can seldom play with flat clubs. Short and upright clubs will be almost universally found to suit the reforming cricketer best.

Fifth. A cricketer does not need to adjust the position of his feet so accurately, with reference to the direction in which he is going to hit the ball, as does the golfer. The cricketer will direct the ball a little more to the 'off' or the 'on' merely by the manner in which he wields the bat with his arms. And he has a great temptation to proceed on the same methods with a golf club. One has often heard a reforming cricketer, being coached by a golf professional, told to aim 'more to the right,' say. What does he do? He promptly turns out the face of the club, so as to make it face more to the right. If told to aim more to the left, he, conversely, turns in the face. Now this will not do. The cricketer must remember that in all cases (for present practical purposes) the face of the club is to be at right-angles with the line in which he is going to drive the ball. The direction of the drive is to be regulated by the position of the feet and body, which, with reference to the ball, should be constant (except in special cases of lie and wind). If the player try to modify, by any other means, the direction, slicing or pulling—in a word, failure—will be the inevitable result.

Sixth. The term 'wrist stroke,' though not, as we have before insisted, in our opinion misappropriate, is doubtless often misleading, and is apt to be especially so to the cricketer, whose tendency is to use his wrists as in cutting and in off driving. The fact is that in the golf stroke, though the wrists are greatly used—so much so that in some cases the whole stroke is made with them—nevertheless it is not a hit with the wrists, but a swing with the wrists: in this sense, that the club is swung down with an effort of the wrists, but there is no checking of it with the wrists, as the club hits the ball. The club swings through, and the wrists turn upward again, turning the hands towards the player's left, after the ball is struck.

Seventh. Though in the cricket hit the feet should be firmly grounded, nevertheless the legs do not take nearly the same active part in the stroke as in the golfing swing. The cricket stroke is more a hit from the upper part of the body. In the golf swing every part of the frame seems to share in the stroke, somewhat after the manner in which the steely spring of a good shaft works with gradually increasing power from handle to head throughout its length.

CHAPTER VIII

ON NERVE AND TRAINING

BY H. G. HUTCHINSON

OF all the games in which the soul of the Anglo-Saxon delights, there is perhaps none which is a severer test of that mysterious quality called 'nerve' than the game of golf. It is a game in which a very great deal is apt to depend upon a single stroke—indeed, upon each single stroke throughout the round—and it is at the same time a game which calls for delicately-measured strokes, and, consequently, for steadiness and control of hand.

'I cannot understand it at all,' a famous tiger-slayer was once heard to exclaim, in desperation. 'I have shot tigers in India, knowing that my life depended upon the steadiness of my aim, and could swear that the ball would go true through the heart; but here is a wretched little putt, a foot and a half long, and I miss it of very nervousness!'

Singularly enough, it is just these short little putts—those which there is no excuse for missing, and which, in practice, we should infallibly hole, almost without taking aim—that are the great trials of nerve in the big match. The somewhat longer putts are far less trying, and it is just because there is no excuse for missing that our too active imaginations picture to us how foolish we shall look if we fail, and thus suggest to us a sufficient cause for failure. It is very silly, but it is very human.

Is there any means, then, to be found by which we may cultivate confidence, and silence our morbid imaginings? In a great degree, confidence depends upon health, and upon the spontaneous, harmonious action of eye and hand. We all know how, on those black days when eye and hand are not working well together, purely imaginary difficulties are apt to present themselves upon the smoothest surface of the simplest putt. How rubs and depressions, which are invisible to every eye except our own, appear as insurmountable obstacles, though they have no existence outside of our fancy. Nevertheless, if we fancy our molehill a mountain, we shall need all sorts of scaling ladders and alpenstocks.

There have been golfers who have doctored themselves with such soothing drugs as opium and laudanum to lull their nervous excitability ; and no doubt, without recourse to such heroic remedies as these, we may do much for ourselves, according to our individual temperaments, by a clear understanding and discrimination of the uses and abuses of tobacco. But the great point is that we should not try to train ourselves ' too fine'—we should not be too healthful. When our liver is energetic, and our pulses are bounding through our veins : when we feel, in fact, that the Sphinx of Golf has yielded up her every secret, and we go forth over-confident to the ' tee '— then is the very time that it will be revealed to us that we are in a fool's paradise—that it is not this abnormal flow of healthfulness that will bring us success in the game ; but that it is our ordinary rather muddle-headed condition that is the most conducive to that stupid, dogged, persistence of hard work which only earns its well-deserved reward. The golfer who has started in the morning depressed, with a burning headache, has often fairly astonished himself by his performances, the secret lying in the benumbed condition of his nervous faculties, which do not conjure up for him non-existent difficulties.

Of medicinal treatment, therefore, or of dietary regimen let us have nothing beyond that which is generally necessary to the preservation of the *mens sana in corpore sano*. It is not good, indeed, to eat too much or to drink too much; but it is almost equally bad to let down the system, by over-carefulness,

THE LAST HOLE (ST. ANDREWS)

below its ordinary standard. Eat heartily, for you will find your nerve all gone if you try to play golf upon an empty stomach.

The best advice of all for nervous golfers is, that they should strive to concentrate all their attention upon the immediate stroke, banishing from their minds as much as possible all visions of its possible ultimate results.

It may be said to be almost a natural consequence of the above proposition, that one should not hang over a stroke for any abnormal length of time. In practice matches—that is to say, in unimportant matches—you should make it your habit to play as hard and as carefully as if the greatest issues hung upon the result. It is very difficult, but if you have formed a habit of considering the result of each stroke *before* playing it —not *while* you are addressing yourself to the ball—and of carefully making a study of each putt, you will not find yourself thrown off your mental balance when the exigencies of a great match imperatively demand all these elaborate precautions. If you do not cultivate this habit, you will find yourself thinking, when the great occasion comes, what an inordinately long time you are taking, and when you address yourself to the ball, your mind will be either bothered by these distracting considerations, or you will have hastened to play the stroke with what you feel to be undue haste. Either species of preoccupation is equally pernicious. Therefore, form a habit of playing carefully, whether in small matches or great, whether you be winning or losing, and so will your nerve not be unnecessarily tried when the solemn occasion comes.

Some golfers find it very difficult to refrain from 'pressing,' with all its attendant fatalities, when playing against a longer driver than themselves. This is a fault which you must zealously set yourself to eradicate; and the means of so doing is to put yourself continually in the way of being outdriven. Seek out the longest driver, professional or amateur, of your acquaintance, and after a course of being outdriven in unimportant 'half-crown' matches, you will grow to acquiesce in your inferiority in this department as a thing inevitable, against which it is useless to contend, and you will then be able to play up to the utmost limit of your capacity with the same unconcern as if your tee-shots were leading all the way. You must keep on repeating to yourself, too, that driving, after all, is but a very small part of the game. Success depends far more upon approaching and putting. This is, indeed, quite a commonplace, but the power of recognising it so fully as to be able to act upon its truth is given by nature to but few; and it is only by some such method as here indicated that it can be cultivated.

We have all heard how Goethe, when he found himself dizzy on a height, scorning this weakness of his flesh, made it a habit to go constantly to the height of a spire and look down below till he could bear the sight without flinching. So should the golfer school himself. It applies not to driving alone, for there are many who have acquired a certain moral golfing ascendency over others—have, as it is termed, 'established a funk' by the consistent deadliness of their putting and approaching. It seems hopeless to try to struggle against them. But in all such cases the chief hope of a remedy lies in accustoming yourself to the burden, in putting yourself in the way of the very antagonists whom you most dread: and after a while familiarity will breed contempt.

There is a certain courage of despair which is superior to all nervousness; it means, indeed, that in the absence of hope there is no spur to the imagination. Thus, when a man is some three holes down and five to play, he will sometimes suddenly come out with a game which he was not in the least capable of producing when it seemed as if it might have given him a chance for the match. He will then, maybe, pull off these three holes to his own advantage, in a manner that is a revelation even to himself. The match will then stand all square. Then it is that little fiend in his imagination will awake and get to work again, representing to him the enormous nature of the issues that hang upon these last two holes. It is a very common feature of golfing experience to see the golfer at this moment fall off from his game in the three preceding holes, and play with even more than his former nervousness, a relapse which is very mysterious to those who have not meditated upon its causes. This is the point of all others in the match at which it behoves the player to apply himself exclusively to the duty that lies nearest to him, to play the stroke he is engaged upon without a glance forward or back. Thus only can he still the suggestions of his too active imagination.

Practice ever makes perfect, or nearly so, and to those golfers who are in the constant habit of playing big matches the strain grows to be less. Of that there is no doubt. In the tough dogged fights, constantly carried to the very last hole, which are waged over the great centres of Scotch golf, the golfer grows case-hardened to bear the strain; but it is less so in the South, where such great contests are of rarer occurrence. Nevertheless such opportunities of familiarising himself with severe nerve tests should be eagerly sought by every golfer who aspires to make a mark in his chosen arena. The mere watching of important and exciting matches is of use. Indeed, many golfers can bear witness that they have felt their nerves more severely strained while watching a match of this nature than has ever happened to them while actively engaged in similar matches.

But there is an even more insidious danger than that of finding oneself on the occasion of a great match in insufficient general practice; and that is the danger of finding oneself 'stale,' as it is called, as a result of over-practice. This is the greater danger of the two, because its extent is so extremely likely to be under-estimated. It is in large degree a matter of temperament the amount of practice that a golfer may with best advantage permit himself, but it is certain that a continual grinding away, day after day, at the game has a wearisome effect upon a man's eye and muscle, and, above all, upon his keenness. True, you do not need to be too keen, and eager, and 'fit,' but it is quite possible to play oneself into such a state that it is absolutely a wearisome task to have to hit the ball, a condition in which the utmost power of your will cannot compel you to concentrate any tolerable amount of attention upon the game.

It is scarcely necessary to state that these remarks do not apply to a neophyte who is still in the educational stage, but have reference to the golfer who has arrived at years of discretion, whose 'game' is formed, and with whom it has almost ceased to be a question of improving his game, and who is rather

'KEEP YOUR EYE ON THE CAMERA'

desirous to learn how he may find himself in proper fettle to produce at the required moment the best specimen of the game of which he is capable. The same rule cannot be formulated for all men, nor for all circumstances. For instance, the man who has learned golf from his childhood, with whom it has become second nature, an act almost as spontaneous as walking, will be able to come into his best game with less practice than will one who has not been educated from early youth to the golf-ground. The game of the latter, being more a matter of calculation and regulation of muscle, will need longer time to get its mechanical muscular adjustments properly arranged. On the other hand, he is perhaps less likely than the former—the natural born golfer—to get stale ; for he depends less upon the freshness and keenness of his mood.

The conditions of the match in contemplation, for which all this practice, or refraining from practice, we are considering is but preparatory, must not be neglected in reviewing the position. There is a difference in the amount of immediately preceding practice which will enable a man to play best on one particular day, and the amount of practice which will best fit him for a tournament of, say, a week in duration.

A natural born golfer is never more likely to produce a really brilliant game than about the third day of his resuming play after a month or more of abstinence from golf. This is more especially likely to be the case if he have been exercising his muscles, and leading a healthy open-air life in the interim. He is then very likely to play in a way that will be a surprise, but if he be not very inexperienced, or very injudicious, he will be apt to look upon himself with suspicion. The ball always flies off without effort from the centre of the club-face, all the 'missable' putts go in—he is playing with great enjoyment in the game after his long abstention ; and he is playing with the confidence that the two preceding days of practice have given to his well-accustomed hand ; but he will know, by former unhappy experience, that it is but too likely not to last. It may be all very well for that third day, and the game may seem ridiculously simple. But on the fourth day he will be very apt to rediscover that he is human ; that it is possible to miss ; his confidence in himself will be shaken, he will not be in sufficiently good practice to discover and remedy the cause of failure, and all the old cycle of mistakes, struggles, and hard-won triumphs will have to be recommenced.

Thus it is that this surprising excellence after a long holiday is apt to be found a delusion and a snare. It is fascinating, but it is not likely to be very conducive to lasting success. It may do as a preparation for a single great day ; but it is not a good preface to a week or more of hard matches.

On the other hand, we may take a notable instance of the evil results of 'staleness' even from among the very highest of professional talent. At the professional championship meeting of 1887, held at Prestwick, the favourite, among a very large and strong field, was, unquestionably, W. Fernie. Of all the professionals who had gathered themselves together there, some days before the great event, he had been doing the best work—had been doing, in fact, almost perfect work. It may almost be said that for days before the competition he had not struck the ball off any part but the true centre of the club. He started for his competition round, followed by a large gallery. His first drive was struck off the heel of the play-club. It was almost a revelation to Fernie, as to the spectators, that he could do such a thing. But the second ball was likewise struck from the heel, and throughout the whole of that day he scarcely struck a ball off any other part of the club than the heel, and was practically nowhere in the competition! It is a remarkable and instructive page in golfing history that it should have been possible for so fine a player, in such fine form as he then was, to so completely 'over-golf' himself.

'But,' some are in the habit of answering, to reasoning such as this, ' but the professionals are in the habit of golfing continuously all the year through.'

The very simple reply is that, without certain limitations, which those who bring forward this statement do not apply to

ON NERVE AND TRAINING

it, it is absolutely untrue. The ordinary golf-professional is always busying himself in one way or another about golf, it is true; but a great many amateurs who consider themselves to play very little golf, play many more matches in the course of the year than the professional does. The latter is engaged in the shop, or is carrying clubs, or, if he be in the happy position of green-keeper, is occupied in that department of his business during four at least out of the six working days of the week. Sometimes he will, perhaps, go out after working hours, or after the master for whom he was carrying has finished playing, and will play a few holes out, and back again, with some others of his class. More ordinarily he will content himself with a few putts, or little iron shots, at the short holes, or maybe will have taken his preliminary golfing canter in the form of a few driving shots, from the tee to the first hole, in the morning. But a real match is for him an exception. If a match comes in his way at all, it is commonly in the form of running in double harness with an amateur yokefellow of very humble prowess—a match which does not excite his interest, or in the least degree try his nerve—practically, in fact, no match at all. But the measure of truth that underlies the remark of those who would have us think that the professional is for ever match-playing consists in this, that the professional, throughout the year, never for any length of time together is without a club in his hand. The club is never out of his hand long enough for it to become strange and unfamiliar to his grasp. Even in the shop he is ever handling and waggling a golf club; and this in itself is a species of practice.

And this is, in all probability, a key to a deal of the professional's success—that he never comes to the game with the club feeling like a new experience to him—that he is not away long enough to be *forgetting*, as the amateur is apt to be, at the call of business or other pleasures—that there is no need, with him, for laboriously re-acquiring the little secrets which he had before wooed from the coy keeping of the goddess of golf. It is this that enables him to continue, when the occasion arises, in a steady dogged manner of play which is the despair of most amateurs, and which carries him through a long series of encounters without perceptible change in his nerve or power.

It is this sort of practice, then, which is most helpful of all to the golfer. It is a mode of conducting golfing business which does not occur to many. The majority of amateurs are in the habit of golfing their hardest, in the most exciting matches which offer themselves, during every hour of daylight which, in the course of a brief holiday, is available for golfing purposes. Then, after this plethora of golfing exercise, they are in the habit of betaking themselves to quite other pursuits, probably never handling a club until the next course of match-playing—and then they launch out into lamentations because they 'cannot get into their game.'

Yet what can they expect? It is entirely and exclusively their own fault. Perhaps it may be given to few of them to have at their disposal a lawn or field wherein they can amuse and profit themselves by driving shots and iron strokes before going off into town in the morning. If these means are at their disposal, they have but themselves to blame if they do not return to the links just as ready to take their place among their compeers as when they left it six months ago. But, in the absence of such advantages as these, there are few, indeed, who dwell in so small a domicile as not to contain at least some one room in which they can find space to swing a golf-club; which really requires hardly greater scope than the swinging of the proverbial cat. And even this indoor handling and swinging of the club is most invaluable practice, failing opportunities for the safe driving of a ball. You will find that, instead of having again to 'get into your game,' as after former periods of abstention, you have forgotten nothing of the experience acquired before. The club will seem familiar to you, on the links, by reason of your practice in your bedroom ; and there is no exercise more healthful and refreshing than a few swings at an imaginary ball, after your morning bath. But even in these swings you ought not to let your muscles fly away with too undisciplined freedom. If the practice is to have its full value, you should make each of these swings with all the care of a stroke from the tee on a medal day; for it is possible to get into bad golfing tricks in your bedroom no less than upon the links.

But probably there will be but few who will find themselves precluded from all but this exclusively indoor practice. There will be few but will be able to find a little grass-plot suitable for practising short iron strokes and putting, and these, after all, are the strokes that need the greatest amount of practice. How confident the professionals all seem of their little iron strokes, and how timidly most amateurs address themselves to them! What is the cause? Simply this, that the professional is ever amusing himself, while he is waiting on the tee for his master, or in the many idle moments that his mode of life affords, in 'chipping' the ball up to a hole, real or imaginary, with his own or his master's lofting iron. These are, perhaps, the strokes in which practice will most repay you—they are now and again so essential, and lack of confidence in dealing with them is so fatal! And if the worst comes to the worst, it is possible to practise them with comparatively slight risk to life and property in the front hall.

Approach-putting is another department of the game in which you are not likely to injure your play by over-practice. When Jamie Anderson was at the best of his form—and it was the best golf then extant—he might have been seen any morning, before the ordinary amateur breakfast-hour, wending his way to the ladies' links with his putter and his little boy. Regularly, every morning, father and son would play two rounds of these short holes, and at that time, largely no doubt as a consequence of this preliminary practice, it was a fact to be made a note of if Jamie, in the course of a match, failed to hole in two from twenty yards.

Certain athletic people are in the habit of telling us that golf is 'an old man's game'; nevertheless a day's hard golf makes no inconsiderable call upon the physical powers. This will be very convincingly borne home to anyone who attempts to play after allowing his muscles to grow flabby by a period of inaction. It is therefore advisable to school oneself into some sort of muscular training, by means of walks or some kind of hard exercise. Especially should the grip of the left hand be exercised, for it will inevitably be found that this will tire first, with the fatal result of throwing the burden of the grip of the club upon the right hand, whence a chain of disastrous consequences will ensue.

Nor is it the muscles only of the hand that will suffer from the unaccustomed strain. The skin will be found to have grown soft, and will rise in painful blisters, unless you have been engaged on some work of the 'horny-handed' kind. If, however, you have been practising swings in your bedroom every morning, you will find that your hands will not have lost the hard epidermis with which your last golfing exploits furnished you. Vaseline, applied at night—not in the morning, or it will make it hard for you to have a firm grip of the club—is perhaps the best remedy. When the hands are soft, before they have developed actual blisters, powdered resin, well rubbed in, is a hardening, though dirty, application. Cracks, somewhat similar to sand cracks, are apt to appear in the callous skin after a hard course of golf, and are most unpleasant. For these, melted pitch run in, and covered with kid, which will stick to the pitch, is a rude style of treatment, but perhaps about the best.

Some golfers are greatly bothered in warm weather by perspiration in the palms of the hands, making it difficult to hold the club. The best remedy appears to be either the powdered resin recommended for soft hands, or powdered chalk. Of course if the golfer can tutor himself to play in gloves, he is superior to almost all such inconveniences ; but there are very few who are able to do themselves full justice with anything between the leather of the grip and the naked hand. To some it happens to cut the flesh of one finger with a nail of one of the other fingers. It is a very painful affair, against which the best protection is afforded by india-rubber finger-tips, similar to those used by photographers to preserve their skin from contact with the chemicals.

Above all, think of all these little requirements before you start on your round. Do not find yourself at a loss by being brought up half-way round by the discovery that your boots have not enough nails, or some one or other of the many indispensables (such as the canvas cover to keep the rain from your club-handles) is left at home.

There is one particular stroke which, it is to be hoped, will not often fall to your lot to play ; but of which it is most useful to have a mastery—the niblick shot out of sand with a bunker cliff in front. It peculiarly needs practice, for it differs from every other golfing stroke in that it requires that the eye of the striker should rest not on the ball, but just behind it. And since it is not likely to befall you to have to play the stroke on an average more than once in the round, it is one which it particularly behoves you to practise in an odd moment. It is not merely a matter of getting the ball out, but the strength may with practice be regulated to a great nicety, and since the occasion for it is apt to arise when close up to the hole, proficiency at this stroke is often very valuable.

Now, though we have said that a man ought not to play golf

too much, so as to make himself 'stale,' and have also advocated a constant handling of the club, so that it shall never become unfamiliar to him, we have nevertheless not indicated at all the *juste milieu* which is likely to be most conducive to success. This happy medium differs, as we have said, with different golfers, but we shall probably not go amiss in saying that, with any considerable prospect of golf before him, a man will be doing fully enough if he play four days' golf—two rounds of the length of St. Andrews links, a day—in the week. More than this is a weariness to the flesh ; two days a week is indeed, for purposes of practice, fully sufficient, but such moderation can scarcely be fairly demanded of the human golfer.

CHAPTER IX

HINTS ON MATCH AND MEDAL PLAY

By H. G. Hutchinson

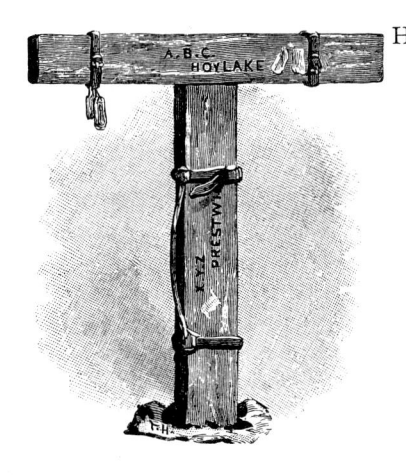

THE primary difference between match play and medal play is that, whereas under the former conditions the score is counted by the result of the holes, under the latter the result is estimated by the sum total of the strokes played at each of the holes. It thus not unfrequently happens that he who has won a match by holes has yet taken more strokes in the entire round than he whom, on the computation by holes, he has vanquished. Whereas in match play the score of any individual hole is not carried forward to affect the score of the succeeding one, in medal play the whole cruel sum forms a factor in the ultimate result. It therefore requires a somewhat different kind of golfing excellence to carry the competition to success in these different departments.

Match play, wherein one is pitted against one, or two

Charles Lees, R S A C. E. Wagstaffe, Engraver

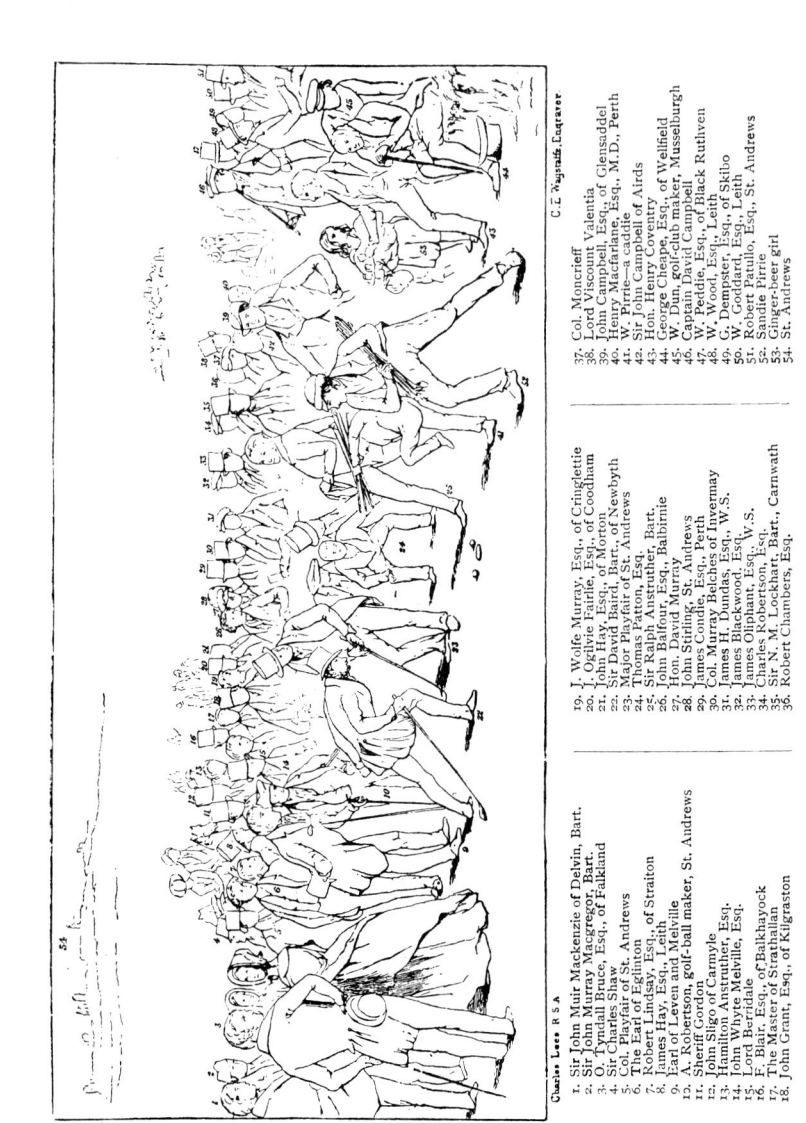

1. Sir John Muir Mackenzie of Delvin, Bart.
2. Sir John Murray Macgregor, Bart.
3. O. Tyndall Bruce, Esq., of Falkland
4. Sir Charles Shaw
5. Col. Playfair of St. Andrews
6. The Earl of Eglinton
7. Robert Lindsay, Esq., of Straiton
8. James Hay, Esq., Leith
9. Earl of Leven and Melville
10. A. Robertson, golf-ball maker, St. Andrews
11. Sheriff Gordon
12. John Sligo of Carmyle
13. Hamilton Anstruther, Esq.
14. John Whyte Melville, Esq.
15. Lord Bervidale
16. F. Blair, Esq., of Balkhayock
17. The Master of Strathallan
18. John Grant, Esq., of Kilgraston
19. J. Wolfe Murray, Esq., of Cringlettie
20. J. Ogilvie Fairlie, Esq., of Coodham
21. John Hay, Esq., of Morton
22. Sir David Baird, Bart., of Newbyth
23. Major Playfair of St. Andrews
24. Thomas Patton, Esq.
25. Sir Ralph Anstruther, Bart.
26. John Balfour, Esq., Balbirnie
27. Hon. David Murray
28. John Stirling, St. Andrews
29. James Condie, Esq., Perth
30. Col. Murray Belches of Invermay
31. James H. Dundas, Esq., W.S.
32. James Blackwood, Esq., W.S.
33. James Oliphant, Esq.
34. Charles Robertson, Esq.
35. Sir N. M. Lockhart, Bart., Carnwath
36. Robert Chambers, Esq.
37. Col. Moncrieff
38. Lord Viscount Valentia
39. John Campbell, Esq., of Glensaddel
40. Henry Macfarlane, Esq., M.D, Perth
41. W. Pirrie—a caddie
42. Sir John Campbell of Airds
43. Hon. Henry Coventry
44. George Cheape, Esq. of Wellfield
45. W. Dun, golf-club maker, Musselburgh
46. Captain David Campbell
47. W. Peddie, Esq., of Black Ruthven
48. W. Wood, Esq., Leith
49. G. Dempster, Esq., of Skibo
50. W. Goddard, Esq., Leith
51. Robert Patullo, Esq., St. Andrews
52. James Wilson
53. Sandie Pirrie
53. Ginger-beer girl
54. St. Andrews

FINISH OF A BIG MATCH
(From an old Picture)

against two, both on a side playing alternate strokes with the same ball, is the true primary form of the game. The other, the play by score, may be said to be merely a device for bringing a large number of competitors together so that their respective merits may be tested by the result of a single round, or, in rarer cases, two rounds.

But besides this main difference between match and medal play, which is at once obvious, there is another important feature of difference the results of which are more subtle. In the medal round any individual player pursues the more or less uneven tenor of his way in happy ignorance of the good or ill fortune that is attending upon the vast majority of his rivals. The partner with whom he plays his round is the only one of them all whose operations he is able to follow with any exactness. He may get a cursory glimpse of the performances of the parties immediately before or behind him, but for the more part he is entirely in the dark with regard to his prospects in the competition.

In match play the very reverse of this is the case. Each player watches his opponent's game, stroke for stroke, and in some measure modifies his own game as he perceives what is required of him.

Such being, then, the essential points of difference, let us first take for consideration the game under its primary conditions as played by holes.

What is the feature that will probably first strike one of the uninitiated on reading or hearing an account of a golf match? Without doubt its fluctuations. Golf matches mostly run, roughly speaking, in this wise. One side gets a hole or two up on the first few holes ; about half-way round, or thereabouts, the players find themselves about level ; then there is a hole or two of give and take ; one side gets one up and five to play ; and this is likely to be a crucial point in the match, and the leader at this stage will probably come in winner by some three up and two to play. Now all this in and out running may perhaps seem to the uninitiated very inexplicable. Why, it will be asked, if one side can win one hole, can it not equally win the next? There is no definite answer possible, except that it does not. The reason is to be sought partly in the irregularity of the working of human eye and muscle, and partly in the very subtle influence exerted by the varying conditions of the game upon the more or less sensitive human nerves. A brief analysis of these complex conditions may reveal to us some of the essential elements of success.

The fact noticed above, that one side generally assumes, early in the game, a slight lead which is ordinarily soon lost, is itself not without a meaning. It is fully recognised that many golfers may be heard to declare in all honesty that they dislike winning the first hole. They have so often proved it to be but a futile flash-in-the-pan that they have grown to look upon it with something more than suspicion. They regard it as a thing of ill omen.

Without going so far as to admit the justice of this view—indeed, there is every reason for strenuously opposing it—we may yet concede this much, that there must be some sort of basis for a paradox so unlikely to gratuitously suggest itself.

The basis of fact consists, shortly, in this : that the generality of golfers enter upon a match in a spirit of happy light-heartedness, with a carelessness, comparatively speaking, which is the result of the knowledge that the end is still eighteen holes distant, that in the course of these eighteen holes there are manifold chances ; in fact, that it is of very little consequence what happens in the first few holes. They do not frame this to themselves in words as they march off after their first drive, in spite of the paradox about the fate of the first hole which they may utter from an armchair, but the idea is latent in their minds and has its effect upon their play nevertheless. We will suppose that the first hole, thus played without any grave sense of responsibility, is not halved, but, as more often happens, falls to one side or the other. This has the exhilarating, bracing effect upon the loser of a douche of cold water unexpectedly sluiced upon his back. He suddenly wakes to the fact that he is engaged upon a serious business, and begins to apply himself in earnest to his task. On his opponent, on the other hand, the winning of this first hole has had a precisely contrary effect, tending to encourage and foster the lightness of heart with which he set out upon his round. Such being the respective mental attitude of the two competitors, it follows, almost of natural consequence, that the hole of vantage is soon wiped off, by which time both parties will be beginning to settle to their work with equal earnestness.

There is something very charming in this cheery careless way of setting forth upon a round, and it may be the best frame of mind of all for a very friendly match, one in which friendship is to have the first claim, and golf the second ; but it is not the frame of mind conducive to winning golf matches. In truth, the too genial golfer may with some justice be mistrusted as a partner. Of a noted professional we have heard it said, 'he is a dour player.' The phrase is excellent. The characteristic Scotch adjective most aptly describes the quality of dogged purpose which is most useful in the old Scotch game. The pleasantest man to play your round with is not the man whom you will find it most hard to beat. It is the silent fellow, who applies all his attention to business, that you will find the difficult nut to crack.

Let us look at another golfing dictum in which a famous old amateur player, who had taken out all the best professionals of his time and beaten them, one after another, summed up the secret of his victories. 'The way to beat a professional,' he said, 'is *never to let him get a hole up.*' It is, of course, a counsel of perfection : of too great perfection to be practical, as it appears on the first blush. Yet there is in it a kernel of sound common sense. Apply yourself to your work from the very commencement. Do not let a hole, or maybe two, slip away from you unawares. Be hard at work, from the very start, to avail yourself of your adversary's errors. That is the meaning of the almost absurd sounding dictum ; and it contains a world of truth. There is no harder thing in golf, nor one more conducive to success, than strict attention and striving to do your best—which does not imply painful study, but only honest work—from the very first stroke of the match to the last.

How many matches has not every golfer to look back upon wherein he sees, photographed with painful distinctness on his mind, the one careless stroke which was the turning point, to his disadvantage, of the entire match ! In well nigh every golf match which is at all a close one there is almost inevitably some one notable turning point, a crisis at which the golfing quality is put to its severest test. In the case of two golfers, evenly pitted, it is most interesting to watch. After the first few holes are over there will be a ding-dong, give-and-take contest, in which the luck of the green will give now one and now the other a quickly passing advantage. They fight on neck and neck, the match draws nearer its conclusion, and still the balance hangs even. The excitement grows constantly ; they are passing through the crucial test. Then one or the other, in the expressive golfing parlance, 'cracks.' He plays badly, just because it is the moment at which he most wants to play his best ; it has become a test of *morale*, rather than of mere eye and muscle. And the moment the one 'cracks' he is done for. The other gains confidence ; the intensity of the strain has passed for him, and it is scarcely in human nature that the golfer who has 'cracked' at the crucial moment can pull himself together, even if there were yet time.

This is the manner of the practical decision of almost every golf match ; the cases wherein they are fought out with equal 'dour' determination to the very end by both parties are exceedingly exceptional, and are efforts of genius for which no treatise can assume to suggest advice.

Now in this match we have been following, no scope has been allowed, after the very earliest holes, for any of those careless strokes which occasion the loss of the majority of matches. We have been following a match at high pressure. There has been but one crisis really, and that not determined in its results by a superiority of attention but by a superiority of nerve-mastery. But in most matches carelessness has been the cause of failure—carelessness which we may avoid in future by its full recognition, as a deadly thing, in the past. But even in this, our model high-pressure match, we see how the crisis, from the point of view of one player, might have been averted —how, if we may say so, the pinch might have been felt by but one player only. For had one of the opponents applied himself to the first few holes which he played with somewhat less concentration, with but a fraction of that intensity of purpose which he devoted to his game when the match grew to its fever-heat of excitement, he might early have acquired a substantial advantage which might have saved him altogether from this subsequent severe expenditure of nervous force. The nerve-power is a very exhaustible quantity, and not only is it advisable to husband it by all possible means in view of the match at the moment in hand, but it has to be remembered that where a series of severe matches have to be played it becomes increasingly difficult to concentrate oneself when the previous strain has been severe. Any golfer who has lived through a tournament extending over several days will bear witness, of his own experience, to the truth of this ; and we see here a further testimony to the necessity of losing no time in settling down to work early in the match, in order to miss no chance of avoiding the pressure of the crisis.

As we stand on the teeing ground awaiting our turn to strike off, there is commonly a little graceful strife of courtesy as to which party shall strike off first--in golfing parlance, 'take the honour.' Courtesy is ever commendable, but it is probably always a slight advantage to take the honour. The frailty of human nature has again to be put into the witness-box to give evidence to the justice of this view. When the opponent has led off with a fine rasping drive, the noble, but somewhat treacherous, spirit of emulation rises in the breast of the rival, and he is tempted to 'press'—ever so little, but just a little too much—in order to outdo his antagonist's effort. Disaster may not follow, but it is to be remembered that so long as the holes are halved, so long does the honour lie with him who took it at the start, and so many opportunities present themselves for the error which is born of the too emulous spirit. The first striker will lead off, on the other hand, with an open mind, without prejudice, so to speak. There will be no subtle influence to tempt him to depart from his usual natural swing. 'How will you like it,' is a query we once heard put to a staunch old golfer about to be partnered with a slashing long-driving young opponent—'how will you like it having to watch that young slasher drive off first?'

'Oh, I know how to treat those boys,' said he; 'I just stick my hands in my pockets and look the other way.'

There was a deal of sturdy, strong sense in this old golfer's implied confession of the weakness of his golfing flesh, and in the means he adopted of taking himself out of temptation's way. He would not even look at his opponent's drives, lest, in striving to go and do likewise, he should come to confusion. To turn your back when your opponent plays is a *tour de force* which could not always be adopted without a suspicion of discourtesy. It is a far simpler plan to take the honour, and, as long as you are able, to keep it.

It is not to be denied that there is something to be said on the other side, also —in favour of seeing what your opponent is going to do before determining upon your own course of action. You may gain a delightful confidence by seeing his erratic or feeble drive in the receptive bosom of a whin or bunker; but whereas fairly good tee shots are commoner than bad ones, the probability is rather the other way; and it is but on the rare occasions where a hazardous but feasible 'carry' presents itself, that the advantage of seeing your opponent go first is a substantial one.

Nor is it only from the tee that this very human spirit of vanity or emulation is a source of danger. Your opponent, we will imagine, is a strong cleek player. At some 140 or 150 yards from the hole he drives the ball upon the green with his cleek. You have a consciousness, which you will not admit to yourself, that it is a trifle beyond your own range with the cleek, but your ball is a yard or so nearer the hole than his was, and a demon of false pride suggests to you the possible comments and comparisons of the spectators if you now take a wooden club. Result: You take the cleek with a sense of your own folly—full of self-distrust and of the self-contempt of your better nature; you press, and do not do even *your* best with the inadequate weapon; you lose the hole, possibly the match, probably your temper; the chain of consequences depending on the act of almost idiotic vanity is infinite.

Again, your ball and your opponent's lie at about equal distance from the hole—some thirty yards. He neatly lofts it with his iron. It is now your turn. The iron is your *bête noire*. You are good at your putter approaches, but the former is the more artistic, 'golfy' weapon; and your opponent used the iron. You strive to emulate him. Result: As before.

Now all this sort of thing will not do at all. You must root this futile vanity out of your golfing system as you would the plague. Fight against it—it is an almost universally besetting sin.

Before starting out for an important match, it is very useful, if you know your opponent's style of game, to think over the points at which your emulous vanity is especially likely to be tickled by his prowess. Is he likely to out-drive you or to out-play you by his excellent iron approaches? Arm yourself with the *æs triplex* of an obstinate resolve to go on your own way unaffected thereby; and start out to play, like that celebrated professional, 'dourly.' It is an un-Christian counsel, but the mood for success in golf matches is a silent hatred—temporary only, be it observed—of your opponent. The genial golfer may be a pleasant fellow to walk round the links with, but his game is all too apt to bear the same resemblance to golf that 'bumble-puppy' bears to whist; and worse than that, it tends to produce a similar degeneracy in your own game. Do not, of course, be aggressively rude to an opponent, but do not bother your 'dour' mood to make yourself agreeable. All your powers of charming will be needed for your ball.

Try to treat your adversary as a nonentity. It is comparatively rarely that his game will have an influence upon yours. It is a paradox which it is most invaluable to recognise as a truism, that it is your adversary that wins you the match. Golf matches are not won by the transcendent prowess of the victor, but by the mistakes of the vanquished. All you have to do is to do as well as you can, and your adversary will soon win you the match by his errors—alway provided that yours are not greater or more numerous. This is the rule of true golfing wisdom ; but it is not without no less wise exceptions. With five up and four to play, the most common prudence will counsel you to accept no doubtful risks. Likewise, when you have a stroke in hand, you will play short of, or round a bunker, which, under reversed circumstances, it would be equally obvious wisdom to attempt to 'carry.' In accepting, when conditions are beginning to look desperate, or even merely anxious, a risk of this nature, it should be remembered that its successful accomplishment will exercise a certain moral effect on the opponent. Indeed, in all matches there is a deal to be made out of a study of this 'moral effect,' which is commonly far too much overlooked. Unfortunately, it is of little use in playing against professionals, for professionals have next to no morals—in the sense of susceptibilities.

Then there is a fatal error, which it would be hardly worth while to mention, but that its extent is scarcely ever realised— the error of underrating an opponent. The folly of so doing is a platitude of all games, but it is a folly which is even more egregious in the case of golf than in most others, inasmuch as golf excels all, other things being equal—a proviso which excepts cricket—in its glorious uncertainty. For at golf an ordinary player will one day play a game which would easily give a half to the game he plays the next day—that is to say (and this holds good of the very steadiest players), that his occasional game varies what we may call a 'quarter' on either side of his normal game. If, therefore, on a day on which he happens to be playing a quarter below his normal game, he be pitted against an opponent who, for his part, is playing a quarter *above* his normal game, the two may make a very even match of it, although the one may be generally able to give the other the very large odds of a half. It is thus shown to be possible that a man may be beaten on even terms by a player to whom he could commonly give a half—and that without supposing any exceptional carelessness on the part of the former. It needs no further demonstration to show the extreme folly of treating with contempt an opponent at a game where such differences of individual performance are possible. But there is a further point to be considered—a point which again involves a reference to the mysterious *morale*, or sensitive nerve of the golfing human being. The inferior player, playing on equal terms with his avowed superior, has nothing to lose, and all to win. All glory is his in the remote event of his victory : he feels no shame in his defeat. With the better player the case is precisely the reverse. He gains no glory from so insignificant a foe, but he is deeply humiliated if he is by chance overcome. So put your shoulder strenuously to the wheel no less when you feel confident of victory than when defeat seems inevitable. He who bears himself equal to either fortune, he it is who is the successful golfer.

Caddies and professional advisers generally are very fond of urging their masters to play to 'get inside' the opponent—that is, to play to get their ball nearer to the hole than the opponent's. This is, of course, desirable enough, but it is advice which the golfer should scorn to accept as a worthy ideal. Strive to get as near the hole as you possibly can—that is far better counsel. Do not be content with merely getting nearer than the opponent. Too many golfers in playing up to a hole are apt to take as their object to get their ball somewhere on the green, with at most but vague reference to the position on the green of that hole. This is really but slipshod work. Aim always to get *into* the hole. Speaking about the relative advantages of playing to lay the ball dead or of playing to hole it when on the putting-green, Jamie Anderson once waggishly observed, 'I always play to get into the hole as soon as I am in reach of it with any club.' That is the heroic purpose with which every golfer should take his club in hand, when the little flag is within the very extremest range of practical politics. It is a counsel which will save many and many a stroke if consistently borne in mind.

But have not many holes been thrown away, it may be asked, by a too liberal interpretation of the doctrine of the great St. Andrews maxim that 'the hole will not come to you'—by running out of holing in striving for a long putt? Yes, indeed, many have been thus lost, but they bear but a very small proportion to the holes that have been thrown away by weakness in putting. In watching the play throughout a match between even very high-class players, it will be frequently remarked that a ball which rests, after a long putt, some yard and a half short of the hole is regarded with some complacency, while one that travels about the same distance past is pursued by infinite nameless objurgations—and this, in spite of the copy-book maxims of 'always be up,' 'be past the hole,' with which the golfer's system is fairly saturated. The old Adam of being afraid of the hole is felt above all training. Of course with two for the hole it is folly to imperil your chances by striving to hole in one, but you should always play to be at least the length of the hole. There is a further seldom noticed reason why your endeavours should never fall short of this: your calculations of strength are always based upon the assumption that you are going to hit the ball clean—now, you cannot hit it cleaner than clean, but you may very possibly hit it less clean; every departure from strict accuracy of aim will therefore shorten the length of your stroke below your mental estimate—nothing is likely to make the stroke in excess of it. Therefore, harden your heart, and be up. This is no less necessary, but rather the more so, because its necessity is here less fully recognised, in approaching the hole than in actual putting. An approach stroke which passes the hole is, with some timid golfers, almost a phenomenon. These are invariably, almost, some ten to twenty yards short; and they rest content and take no shame to themselves for their shortcoming. It is very lamentable, but it seems ineradicable from human and golfing nature.

Then the golfer has also to steel himself not only against the effect of his opponent's prowess, but also of his eccentricities. There are few golfers without eccentricities, whether of temper, manner, or what not. Some summon spirits from the vasty deep to wreak upon their hapless ball the vengeance which their own clumsiness more justly deserves; some decline to recognise any merit in their opponent's game, ascribing his every success to fortune; some lag behind, at a pace suggesting a funeral; some start off as if engaged on a six days' go-as-you-please race; some are inveterate chatterers. Against all these distracting influences the golfer must bear a firm front, pursuing his own way, with calm nerves and smooth temper.

No man has a right to object to another's playing the game in his own fashion, provided he do not violate any of the rules of golf or of etiquette, and the golfer may choose his pace according to his own judgment. In the critical moments of a match it is a great mistake to hurry. The more anxious the situation becomes, the more inclination the player feels to hurry up to his ball and get it over, the more should he take himself by the head and compel himself to go slowly; otherwise he will inevitably arrive at the ball with fluttering nerves and uneven pulse, and the result will be disaster and yet further irritation.

An affectation of any of these named eccentricities assumed for the express purpose of putting the opponent off is a shift to which it is to be hoped no gentleman golfer would resort; but we have heard a professional whisper to his partner at the start of a match, 'Come along, Sir, let us walk fast; Mr. So-and-so '—naming one of the opponents—'cannot play if he is hurried.' Surely we need to harden our hearts if such diabolical devices are to beset our path.

Hitherto, in our remarks upon match play, we have dealt

solely with the golfer's duty towards himself; now let us look at him in another relation—in foursome play—and consider his duty towards his partner. All that we have said up to this point will apply not only equally, but even in greater measure, for he is now responsible to another as well as to himself. He has, above all, to prove himself trustworthy; he must less than ever dare to take a liberty or hazard a risk, except with his partner's express approval. Moreover, he must consider the style and power of the man who is his yokefellow. Thus, should he perceive that he is able to drive his ball within some sixty yards of the hole by going straight—whereby his partner will have a bunker between him and the hole for the next shot— and should he also perceive that by playing out to the right he will give his partner a longer shot, but free of any intervening obstacle, it will become his duty to say to himself, 'Is my partner a good iron player? Will he be likely to do better within sixty yards of the hole with a bunker between, or will it be advisable that I should put him farther from the hole, without this hazard confronting him?' He should take his partner into his counsels, since it is on the partner that the responsibility will fall; and he should be almost entirely guided by his partner's views. Of course his partner, if a man of ordinary modesty, will only put forward his views as a tentative suggestion if he happens to be much inferior in golfing knowledge. Nevertheless, the superior should be chary of his advice; each man can play his own game best. 'A man will generally make a better stroke with a club which he happens to fancy, even though it be palpably the wrong one, than with the right one which has been put into his hand at your suggestion.' You will, of course, give each other mutual counsel and encouragement, but it should be so managed that the player whose turn it is to play should feel that he is acting on his own initiative. The inferior player of the two should, especially, be humble, and accept no risks. A respectable mediocrity should be the utmost of his effort, leaving it to his more accomplished partner to force the game if a critical occasion should demand it. Nevertheless, as has been said, even the leader should play with stricter regard for caution in foursomes than when playing his single ball. He will sometimes need to throw dust in a measure in his partner's eyes, so as to cover the latter's weaknesses without making too apparent the extent of his appreciation of them.

At the long hole at St. Andrews, going out, the weaker player commonly strikes off. Some hundred and fifty yards from where his ball will probably rest there are, to the left of the course, some hummocky hills and hollows. Into these a shrewd professional will sometimes be seen to deliberately drive his unskilful partner's ball. Now why is this? It is so often seen that it can hardly be considered the result of accident. The professional's cunning motive is this. Some eighty yards from these hummocks is a cross bunker in the face of a hill, right across the course. If the professional had driven straight down the course, the amateur plodder would have had a chance of carrying this bunker. He could not, however, have possibly reached the hole. The risk of the carry would therefore have been greater than the resultant advantage ; and yet no professional, with an eye to the main chance of future employment, would have had the impudence to suggest to the plodder that he should putt up short of the bunker. Therefore it is that the professional plays the ball away to the left in order that from the bad lying ground the amateur shall not be tempted to their joint destruction, but shall contentedly play the ball up short of the bunker with his iron, leaving the professional to drive it home with his iron or cleek.

There can be no better example of the sort of study which a good foursome player should make of the chances of the game viewed in the light of the capabilities of his yokefellow. Think carefully over the task which your own shot will leave to your partner before you decide how to play it. Think before starting of the tee-shots at which superior length of driving will be of greatest advantage, and arrange your order of starting in accordance with the results of this calculation.

If there seems to be little room for choice in this respect, strive to arrange matters so that the better player shall get a majority of the approach shots, for it is in these that his superior skill will be most likely to make itself felt. If in these days of various golf balls—Silvertown, gutta-percha, and Eclipse—there be a difference of opinion as to the preferable ball, let the better player have the choice, and let that choice be adhered to throughout.

Foursomes are a very pleasant modification of the game of golf. The 'dourness' of attitude which we have indicated towards the opponent—a kind of grim Carlylean earnestness—is in no way the appropriate mutual manner between partners. There should be between them that sympathy and unity of purpose which are essential to the success of partnerships : and not the least enjoyable foursomes are those between a good and an inferior player against two others of similar relative merit —a style of match peculiarly productive of good-fellowship and pleasant variety.

Whether in foursomes or singles, the staunch Anglo-Saxon quality of dogged pluck is invaluable. Of golf even more than of other games is it true that the game is never lost till it is won. Struggle on to the bitter end—never say die. If the end is to be bitter, better to die fighting hard than to throw up the hands in a base surrender ; and in how many cases has not what seemed inevitable defeat turned to a glorious victory, a victory plucked out of the very jaws of defeat, and so much the greater triumph for its unexpectedness? That caddie went perhaps a trifle far who rushed forward, having a pecuniary interest in the match, as his master was speaking of giving up the hole, and intervened with a 'Gie up the hole, mon ! what are ye thinkin' of? Wha kens yon mon may no fall doon deed afore ever he comes to the hole?' When we arrive at the condition at which 'nothing can save us but a stroke of apoplexy,' then, and not till then, it perhaps becomes the part of courtesy to gracefully admit defeat.

Of match play there remains but one more species to consider—the three-ball match ; a little perhaps suggestive of the pawnbroker, but no more likely to lead us to that bunker of life than golf in any other form. These matches are of two kinds, that wherein each plays against each, and that wherein two are in combination against a third, though each play his individual ball. The score of whichever of the two does the hole in the fewer strokes counts against the score of the unsupported player. The latter plays against the best ball, as it is called, of the other two.

Of the first kind of these three-ball matches there is little to be said in addition to hints already given. The petty irritations and annoyances against which each has to steel his breast are multiplied twofold, in that he has two opponents in place of one ; but herein there are compensations, for while he may be losing to the one he may be winning from the other. With the exception of the last sentence, this remark holds equally good of the single-handed player in the second-named species of three-ball matches ; but the combination of the other two introduces some new features.

The players who are best able to avail themselves of the advantages of this combination are those of the brilliant flashy order—those who do one hole in three and the next in thirteen. It is clear that if they manage the disposition of their respective threes and thirteens judiciously the result will reduce the opponent to the profound depths of desperation. The general lines of policy which the partners should pursue are on this wise : the first player should accept any risk that presents itself, with all the confidence that is inspired by a consciousness of a second string in reserve which may recover his only too possible failure. When the balls lie on the putting-green there is often scope for the wisdom of the proverbial serpent. The one will play to lie dead, to secure the half of the hole, which done the other may play, with a free hand, for a ' gobble.' These tactics and their previous discussion are excessively trying to the nerves of the solitary third party ; and he almost requires to take to himself an extra plating of the *æs triplex*.

This style of the three-ball match is often very interesting ; but as a general rule three-ball matches are to be deprecated on an at all crowded green, for their progress is necessarily but slow.

Perhaps some apology is needed for the ungraceful attitude which we may seem to have recommended the golfer to assume towards his opponent. Unhappily it is inevitable. No golfer can really play to the utmost of his game who is discussing politics, the crops, the weather, and the grouse. Many excellent games have we all played wherein joke and friendly chat were the order of the day ; and these were perhaps the most enjoyable. But yet we knew that these were not golf. More pleasurable perhaps, but still not the game. Out of our high-pressure matches there is indeed little enough of pleasure to be got while they are in progress. It is too severe a strain. But the pleasure comes in the retrospect, in our triumph over the skill of our opponent, over the difficulties of the ground, over our own faltering nerve. It is no otherwise with other games which seem more genial. Is a cricket match at Lord's —All England *v.* Australia—true immediate pleasure to all who are engaged in it ? The pleasure on these great occasions is in the triumph, not in the actual play, or if triumph be not our portion, in a consciousness of a well-contested struggle. And the keener, the more serious, the crueller the struggle has been, so much the keener is the delight of the triumph. After all it is worth all the genial 'bumble-puppy' matches ever so many times over ; not as an every-day thing, perhaps—that would be too severe for human flesh and blood—but as an occasional experience—once or twice a year, not too many times in a lifetime. Even the great St. Andrews medal is not so great a test of nerve and 'staying power' as those tough matches in which each stroke of the opponent has its effect on your own *morale*.

Upon the medal day, when you play for score, it should be your aim to play without reference to your partner's performance. You have not, as in match-play, to now attempt a long carry in the hope of retrieving a well-nigh desperate hole, nor is there any wisdom in then playing with the studied caution which prudence dictates when a stroke to the good of an opponent in a match. Think of your opponent merely as one of the great crowd against whom you are contending. Do not be disconcerted if he seem to be drawing away from you. By playing quietly and serenely your own game, there is infinitely greater chance of his 'coming back to you' than if you strive by superhuman efforts to overhaul him. But let us take the game from its commencement, and see what should be your course even before you commence to play.

Before every game of golf it is advisable if possible to have a brief preliminary canter—not too severe. If you happen to be drawn late you will find the subsequent advantage of taking one or two practice strokes with each driving club. When in the course of the actual match you come to take any one of these weapons in your hand, you will feel that the previous stroke or two has made the weapon familiar to you, and you will handle it with confidence. But if you should be drawn early it will not be worth your while to rush forth, after a hasty breakfast, and play some hurried strokes. The hurry will pass itself on, in the form of irritation to your nerves at the very moment when they need to be most reposeful. Moreover, these hurried strokes are more than likely to be failures, and will therefore produce a result the very opposite of that confidence which it was their purpose to impart. Even if you are drawn to start late, you should practise these driving strokes some time before your turn is at hand, and should then take a rest until your time comes.

But, however pressed you should be, you may certainly manage to put in time to practise a few strokes with that most 'telling' yet most treacherous of all clubs, the lofting iron. Who does not know the feeling, to whomsoever St. Andrews is familiar, of the shiver that comes over the heart of the golfer as he takes the light iron into his hand at the very first hole to loft over—alas, how often is it not over!—that sluggish little burn that guards the hole like the never-sleeping serpent of the Hesperides? How familiar that iron had felt to his hand last night; how strange and uncomfortable it feels this morning! Whereas, had he taken but a practice shot or two before starting, he would have laughed at the little stream with a careless heart—with all the confidence which breeds success.

And should you, or should you not, practise 'putting'? Some players aver that the less you practise putting the better. This is true and it is false. It is undeniable that in 'holing out' —in short putts—the eye is apt to weary; and it is well to practise few if any of these. Approach putting, however, it is very valuable to practise, to get familiar with the strength of the greens and of the club; but this practice, again, requires discretion. A very great many golfers may be seen practising round the last hole green; which green, therefore, becomes considerably more keen than its fellows along the course. Practice upon this green, therefore, produces its natural result in a shortness in the approach putt at the other and slightly heavier greens. Since the original sin of golfers is doubtless to be short, it is desirable to practise approach putting upon some green rather heavier than the generality of those upon the course. This may seem a minor point, but it is one well worthy of grave attention and observance. Moreover, whatever the particular species of stroke you may be practising, never leave off after making a bad one. Keep on at it till you make a good one, and then leave off, with the good impression and the confidence in your skill strong in your mind. It is like the final glance which a beauty gives at the most becoming glass in her dressing-room, before descending to the triumphs of the evening—it gives her strength in the consciousness of her power.

But too much previous practice is a mistake, a weariness. The most really valuable practice is that which you should put in over-night. Go out with the few clubs of which you feel most doubtful the previous evening, and though in the first of the morning you will not feel the benefit, yet, after a stroke or two. you will find that the old familiar strength and accuracy that you have gained over-night is coming back to you. It is somewhat on the principle of the schoolboy who reads over, the last thing before going to bed, the piece which he has to repeat by rote in the morning. If there is any particular stroke or any particular club which you are conscious of being temporarily 'out of,' the day before the big match or medal day is the time to go out and insist upon a thorough explanation with that club. On the morrow it will not unlikely prove, perhaps even to your own surprise, the very club which you can handle with most confidence.

If you have still some time hanging upon your hands, after your practice and a subsequent quiet rest, it is by no means a bad plan to go and take a look at the exact position of such of the holes as are not too far away. It is usual to slightly alter the position of the holes on the morning of the competition. A sight of the flag, as you approach, will but give you a very general idea of the relative positions of hole and surrounding hazards, and any doubt upon this delicate point is quite incompatible with anything like confidence. It is not a very good thing to follow out the play of one of your chief competitors. If he is playing particularly well, it will discourage you ; if badly, there is sure to be some fiend ready with a constant whisper that he is but one out of all the crowd, and that any feeling of confidence inspired by the failure of one among so many must be a folly.

At all events, do not follow out any match so far that you will have to hurry back to be in time for your turn. Rather come back some half-hour or so, at least, before the time, and sit down in a quiet corner of the club-house and read a book. A 'shilling shocker' or, still better, a 'penny dreadful,' if procurable, is perhaps the best mental aliment on such occasions. Your critical faculty will not be very widely awake, you will hunger for crude sensations. These will distract you from the master sensation of the day, your medal play, and you will go forth calm and collected to the 'tee.'

Before starting, however, you should have taken a good

solid lunch, if you start thus late, for the nerves and muscles must be fed for the work before them ; otherwise there will ensue a dreadful sinking feeling before the end of the round. If you start some while after breakfast, yet too early for lunch, take out some sandwiches with you, and a pocket-flask.

Whatever you do, do not, in justice both to yourself and your partner, take out under your protection any genial non-golfing friend. It would seem almost absurd to dwell upon such counsel as this, yet have we all seen, often, such an atrocity committed, even by experienced golfers. It means misery to all concerned—to your friend, who, with the best possible intentions, yet cannot but feel that he is always in the way—to your partner, who is irritated both by the unwelcome presence and by your own lack of proper golfing intelligence—and finally, if you have any conscience at all, to yourself as deliberately responsible for the whole outrage. If your friend will consent to go and efface himself in the gallery, if you are fortunate enough to possess sufficient skill to attract one, very well and good. He will do no further harm. But there are comparatively few men who are capable of realising the possibility of circumstances under which their room may be preferable to their society. Your best plan, in most cases wherein you have once committed the first desperate *faux pas*, is to approach your amiable friend ostensibly with the motive of begging his sympathy for that you find yourself mated with a partner of such fidgetty petulance that he actually appears to deem his – your friend's—charming society an inconvenience ! Incredible as this will seem, your friend, in contemptuous pity of the frailty of golfing flesh, will probably so far defer to its weakness as to content himself in the future with hovering on the horizon. There are other far more heroic remedies, which will suggest themselves without naming, but the best of all of them is to tell your friend to stop at home and to come out to-morrow—when he will get just as much fun—to watch your half-crown match.

Now, just before you leave the club-house to go down to the tee, say to yourself these words in a tone of inward resolve :— 'I will not be short in a single approach shot to-day.' (This is of course not meant to exclude a mental reservation of those cases in which there is a bunker close beyond the hole.) If you can keep this brave resolution constantly at your heart, and boldly act on it, your score will not be much behind your previous best.

One other piece of advice, and we will at length get our first tee-shot struck. Not a few golfers are in the habit of husbanding up for the medal day some wonderful driver with which they were playing remarkably well about a fortnight before. 'Where's that club you were driving with the other day?' you ask one of these worthies. 'Oh,' he will answer, 'I'm saving it for the medal day;' and on the medal day, out comes the precious club—and ten chances to one he cannot hit a ball with it.

This is the height of folly. You cannot trust the caprice of the goddess of golf. When she has deigned to inspire a club with some of her wisdom, so that it charm the ball successfully, continue in constant play with that club. In a few days it will be no longer the magic wand: therefore use it while the mood and inspiration are upon it; in a brief space you will find all its potency in your hands transferred to another weapon.

There is an enormous deal in the club we, for the time being, fancy. Now the golfer should recognise this, and in a very great measure humour his fancy. As a general rule, most do so; but many are afraid to act, on a medal day, on the principles which at other times guide them. Thus we often see a man playing execrably with his wooden putter for a medal, confessing that he 'feels as if he could putt better with his iron putter,' but stultifying the promptings of this almost Divine instinct because, forsooth, 'he does not like to change on a medal day.' Was ever such folly heard? Yes—heard often: but let it never be heard again. 'You will play better with the club you happen to fancy, even though it will be palpably the wrong one,' than with any other.

The effect merely of a change of club is at times magical. Every golfer will tell you this. There are golfers who, if they have missed but one putt of which there was reasonable expectation of holing, early in a medal round, will at once condemn that club, without further hearing, as, for that day, and for them worthless. They will at the very next hole take another club, and not again trust themselves with one that has so betrayed their confidence. This is of course pushing the principle to an extreme, but it is madness that is not without method.

It is important throughout the entire game of golf to bear in mind that no stroke stands by itself. It has no isolated result. The object is not to outdrive or to outplay the opponent at any one stroke, but to play the stroke that shall put you in the best possible position for playing the next stroke. Each stroke must be calculated with a view to its effect upon the next stroke. And though this is universally true, and is commonly not considered nearly so much as it deserves, it is more true and important in medal play, where your strokes should be in no way affected by your partner's play, than in match play. Calculate each stroke with a deliberate look ahead and forethought for the stroke that is to come after. That is to say, think where it will be most desirable to place it in order that your next stroke may be most telling. And commence your foreseeing calculations from the very start.

It is very common to see medallist after medallist starting from the tee to the first hole, flustered by the surrounding spectators, and anxious to get the shot over rather than intelligently collected and thoughtful of its results. We may take an illustration from the first hole at St. Andrews. If the wind be at all in your favour—*i.e.* East, as, on that Eastern shore, it is very apt to be—it is no very impossible matter to spare yourself all the anxiety of that first iron shot over the burn, to which reference has been made before, by carrying the burn with your

THE DAWN OF GOLF

second drive. But this is commonly only possible off a well-struck tee-shot. Here, then, it is of paramount importance that the tee-shot be a good one : it will very probably spare you a whole stroke. Yet how many do we see expending less pains and care upon this tee-shot than upon almost any other on the round, partly because they are so anxious to get it over, and be away from the spectators, and partly because there is no bunker within range of practical politics to deservedly punish a badly struck ball. The start, moreover, is a very important epoch in the game, and likely to stamp its own characteristics upon the entire round. 'Well begun, half done,' is truer of a golfing medal round than of most things.

But this studying and calculation of the exact and far-reaching results of each stroke must be done—as all other studying and calculation over the game of golf—before you begin to address yourself to the ball. If you hover over the ball in a state of indecision, the condition of your mind will transmit its own quality into your stroke. It will be ineffective. Even with regard to so comparatively simple a matter as the choice of the club, this is true, and it is very much more so with regard to the choice of the main object of the stroke. Your mind should be made up when you address the ball, but it should not be made up without due deliberation. '*Nec temere, nec timide*,' should be a just description of the golfer's conduct. '*Festina lente*' is another classical paradox which the golfer may take to himself—excellently indicating the controlled *élan* which is the ideal mental attitude for golf.

Moreover, although previous to addressing yourself to the ball you should have made this careful study of the progression of results from each single stroke, your mind should be undivided in its attention while the stroke is being played, and should concentrate itself upon that stroke alone. The whole argument should run as follows :—'Such and such a spot is the best within my reach whence to play my next stroke. I can reach that spot with such and such a shot with such and such a club.' Take the club in your hand, and apply all your attention to playing correctly the stroke which your previous reasoning process has concluded to be the best possible.

Perhaps the most fatal beam of all that can float over your mental vision is the vision of a past hole badly played which you are filled with some insane notion of 'making up for.' The idea of 'making up,' by present extra exertions, for past deficiencies is one of the most deadly and besetting delusions that is prone to affect the golfing mind. Its results are *inevitably* ruinous. You must bear in mind that it is not your own performances that win you matches and medals, but the performances—the mistakes—of your opponents. Your utmost is to do your duty, so to speak. You can do no more. If a man could be invented who could play even a very moderate class of game without ever making a bad mistake, he would beat the world. Any such approximation to this mechanical accuracy as erring human nature is capable of has, besides its intrinsic merits, the virtue of partially paralysing an opponent. If you can imbue him with the idea that it is but by the merest accident that you will make a mistake, you have him already half-beaten. Invaluable above all is it to acquire a reputation of 'never giving in.' In playing for medals, in which class of competition it would especially seem that previous bad play must hopelessly cripple your ultimate chance, it is always worth while to struggle to the bitter end. On some days there seems to be a species of epidemic golfing paralysis in the air. With all conditions in favour of fine scoring a large field of crack players will sometimes, for some inscrutable reason, send in universally bad returns. How often do we hear it said, 'If only I had known that everyone was so bad, I believe I might have won ; but I thought I had no chance !' This is just what you had no business to think. It is your business to work honestly on to the end, and then, and not till then, you may begin to speculate on your chances. Even if unsuccessful, you will then have but little cause for self-reproach ; while there are few things in golf more mortifying than the reflection that a little more care and 'trying' would have won you a coveted distinction.

Concentrate all your attention upon the stroke and the hole which you are at the moment playing; it cannot be too often reiterated. Keep your mind religiously closed to all temptations to prematurely form estimates of the result. These will but render you morbidly anxious and nervous. You must control your springing imagination, and cultivate a professional callousness of mental fibre. Singularly enough, the effect of the perpetual backward glancing over results achieved is apt to be equally disastrous whether the retrospect be rosy or 'bunkery.' 'I played awful well going out, but then I began to get anxious,' is the epitaph over many a golfer's buried hopes. Men get 'terrified by their own score,' as it is called. Many an one is capable of playing heroically when imbued with the courage of despair who is totally unable to endure his prosperity with an equal mind. The secret is to shut our eyes, so far as possible, to prosperity and adversity alike: to go on in happy stupidity, intent only upon the duty that lies nearest to us—the immediate stroke before us. It is here that the majority of professionals have a great advantage over the more imaginative, more sensitive, more cultured amateur. If we could but develop a creature with the requisite muscular and visual organs, and with no nervous system whatever, what a magnificent golfer he would be ! And it must be our effort to annihilate our nervous system, so far as may be, if we are to meet with any great success in golf, above all in scoring play. It is almost an absurdity to ask a man who is anxious about the result not to count his score at all, as he goes along. He does so almost unconsciously, involuntarily, and inevitably. But he should dwell upon it as little as possible. Its every detail is too likely to be photographed upon his mental sensitive plate, so that it is but through its distorting, obscuring medium that he can view his ball at all. But he must put it behind him and out of sight as much as he possibly can.

Perhaps the greatest and most unintelligent piece of cruelty that can be inflicted upon a man who is making a good score, and has but one hole to play, is to come up to him, under the guise of sympathy, and whisper in his ear, 'If you do this hole in four, you will tie.' There are possibly some who prefer to know what they have to beat—to know the best score in— and there are certainly a few who *say* they prefer to know it. If there really are any at all of the former class, they are certainly most exceptional cases ; and for a golfer who knows anything of the game to come up with such unsolicited intelligence to another, and to impart it without previous diligent inquiry of the player's views upon this point, ought to be punishable as a crime.

To what extent it is advisable for a medal player to converse with friends who may be walking round with the match must greatly depend upon his individual temperament. This is of course supposing that these friends are themselves golfers, or are at least able to take an intelligent interest in the game. Non-golfing acquaintances should be studiously cold-shouldered upon a medal day. But from those who are capable of giving sympathy, whether in misfortune or prosperity, golfers of a certain temperament will probably derive some moral support. Conversation even upon the minor topics of life, such as politics and metaphysics, may in cases serve as a useful distraction from the all-absorbing business of the day. They may bring a beneficial relaxation. But these cases and these temperaments are in the minority. The vast majority will get along better if they treat the 'gallery' as practically non-existent ; going their own way in that mood of silence best described by the Scotch phrase 'dour.'

Of all others, however, it is the man with whom you are partnered from whom you best may seek the relaxation of a few occasional snatches of conversation. Opposed though your interests are, you will both be imbued with a similar sense of the exigencies of the situation, and you will meet in the same mood. From him you have a right to expect some measure of consolation, and he from you, likewise, in return. You have a fair right to expect this much, but you will be trespassing beyond your fair rights if you persist in obtruding your conversation upon him a moment after he has by the gentlest hint intimated that he would rather be without it. Prior to the debt of consolation, due from each to the other, is the claim to absence of annoyance. Silence was probably invented before speech; and the primary right of every golfer is to expect from his partner silence should he desire it.

There are very many to whom silence is impossible—even comparative silence. It is obviously, therefore, of importance to select a partner whose moods are likely to be agreeable to your own. To secure this end, and to decline without offence ineligible partners, demands often some skill in the stroke known as the 'white lie.' There is perhaps no case in which it is more pardonable.

In medal play even more than in match play you should endeavour to swing well 'within yourself,' in your driving shots. Swing 'easy.' You will never be put to any necessity for attempting anything beyond your ordinary drive; for here, even more than in ordinary matches, you must divest yourself of all idea of rivalling your opponent's efforts. Swing easy and walk slowly; for thus will your pulses be beating more quietly when you come to those delicate strokes upon the putting-green than after great muscular exertions, even if crowned with success. The importance of quiet movement, and its effect upon the nerves and pulses, is not nearly sufficiently appreciated by the majority of golfers. And the greater the tax is likely to be upon your nerve-power, the more studiously should you avoid every possible occasion of irritation. Go quietly, and the more anxious your situation becomes, the more you desire to get the crisis over and have done with it, the more quietly should you swing, and walk, and play. Any hurry is bound to defeat its own ends.

It is such a game to irritate you! As old Allan Robertson used to say: 'It's aye fechtin' against ye.' And it is not everyone who is blessed with the cheerful serenity and superiority to circumstance which distinguished that old worthy, and his compeer, and sometime rival, old Tom Morris—'born in the purple of equable temper and courtesy,' as we have seen that latter described in print. The generality of us need to treat our nerves with tenderness—to wrap them up in cotton wool, else will our evil tempers and petulances get the upper hand and bring us to confusion.

THE MAN TO BACK

To this end we must take to ourselves the classic motto, '*festina lente*.' To this end, to descend to grosser needs, should we keep our golfing machinery well supplied with food and drink.

If ever you see a man who has tied with another for a medal, toying in the luncheon interval with a biscuit and a lemon and soda, you may go out and bet your modest half-crown against that man with a light heart. But if you see him doctoring himself with a beaf steak and a bottle of beer, or, better still, a pint of champagne, you may go forth and back that man with as stout a heart as though you had yourself partaken of his luncheon. The golfer will not do good work unless he is fed. And it is real good hard work that he has to do—work that will need a stout heart to do it efficiently. For it is a game of hard rubs and annoyances, a game of which the exasperations no less than the fascinations were never better summarised than in these words of the grand old golfer : ' It's aye fechtin' against ye.'

CHAPTER X

ETIQUETTE AND BEHAVIOUR

By H. G. Hutchinson

IN connection with the game of golf there are certain points of etiquette which, though not of such a nature as to fall within the jurisdiction of written law, are pretty accurately defined by the sanction of custom. Breach of these observances is not punished by the loss of the hole or of a stroke, but rather by the loss of social status in the golfing world. You do not exact an immediate penalty from him who thus outrages *les convenances* ; but in your heart of hearts you propose to yourself the severest of all forms of punishment, viz. never to play with him again.

Of all delinquents against the unwritten code, the grossest offender is perhaps he who stands over you, with triumph spiced with derision, as you labour in a bunker, and aggressively counts your score aloud. The act of ostentatiously coming out of his own path to look at you is, of itself, almost on the boundary line between good and bad form. Apart from the indecent gloating over your misfortunes which such conduct on his part would seem to imply, it also contains the infinitely more offensive suggestion of a suspicion of your possible unfair dealing when shielded by the bunker's cliff from his espionage. But when he goes the length of audibly counting up your unhappy efforts, with undisguised satisfaction as the sum increases, you can scarcely look upon it otherwise than as an impugnment either of your arithmetic or of your honesty.

There are, indeed, certain circumstances which may almost, in a medal competition, justify such a proceeding; for in a medal competition, in the absence of markers, each player is responsible for the correctness of the score, as returned, of the other, and, setting the question of honesty—as it is to be hoped we may—on one side, there are medal-players whose arithmetic, as a matter of fact, is *not* above suspicion. It is, moreover, far more difficult than is generally recognised to keep exact account of the strokes at those unfortunate holes where the total approaches the two figures. It is scarcely possible for a man to be in honest doubt as to whether he has played four strokes or five; but it is a very different thing where a question arises as to whether he has played eight or nine. One among so many is a small item easily forgotten. Nevertheless, unless the player for whom one is scoring is known to be what is called a 'bad counter'—which not a few perfectly honourable gentlemen and golfers unquestionably are—there is no justification for the *audible* enumeration, one by one, of his strokes. One's duty to one's neighbour—in this case, to all the others engaged in the competition—can be adequately performed, without offence to the sufferer, by silently marking off on the card each stroke as it is played. Should the player think fit to contest the accuracy of this marking, each stroke may for the future be audibly impressed upon him, as it is played, without any regard to the sufferings which he will then have deservedly brought upon himself.

But all such espionage can only be justified by a sense of your responsibility to the other competitors. In a match there is no conceivable excuse for it. If it be a friendly match, to start with, it cannot long continue such if either subject the other to such indignities; and if it be a big match, there will be a sufficient number of onlookers to check any possible inaccuracy of scoring. If you have not faith in a man's scoring, do not play with him; and if you play with a man, do not act in such a way as to suggest that you are suspicious.

But there is a subtler crime than that of miscounting his score, of which a man may be, and of which many often are, guilty in a bunker; and it is a crime which again raises another delicate point of etiquette. He may be touching the sand with his iron. Every golfer knows the rule that you must not touch sand in a bunker, with the club, as you address yourself to the ball—that you must not rest the club-head behind the ball. Almost every golfer does so, however, accidentally, now and again, and some do it habitually. Etiquette has its word to say, not about the touching of the sand, which is a distinct breach of a hard-and-fast rule of the game, but about the tempering justice with mercy in bringing the criminal to account. Let us first see what the custom is, in regard to breach of this rule, and let us then see what the custom ought to be.

With the first class, of those who touch sand accidentally, occasionally, the custom certainly is to continue playing on, lightheartedly, as if they were all unconscious of the rule and of their breach of it. And no one thinks of claiming the stroke as a foul one. Why?—because it is the custom not to claim it, and in the presence of this custom the man who claimed his rights, under the rule, would be regarded as a sharp practitioner. There are, doubtless, also many cases in which the player is himself quite unconscious of having touched the sand; he will indignantly deny having done so, and in the absence of a referee the just claim results in nothing but mutual irritation.

Next, what is the custom with regard to the habitual touchers of the sand? The first two offences probably go unnoticed. At the third they are possibly cautioned. At the fourth a threat is made to claim the hole. Probably this is about as often as their opponent will have seen their bunker performances, and when the round is over they will tell all their friends what an ungentlemanly fellow their late opponent is, and will probably meet with a great amount of sympathy !

Even in a match with money depending on the result, it would be deemed a quite unheard-of thing to claim a hole for a first offence of this nature ; and yet it is an offence which may just give the culprit the match. Do not be deceived upon this point : it is not that by resting the club on the sand the lie of the ball is materially improved, but it is that by the faint impress a guide is given to the eye, if the sand be soft ; or if it be hard and caked, a guide is given to the hand, by the sense of touch, of the distance from hand to ball. And on the one stroke thus feloniously aided who shall say how many matches may have turned ? But if the difficulty were confined to match-playing alone, we might perhaps allow the custom, absurd as it is, to rest without reproach. A man has, there, but his own moral weakness to blame for allowing another to get the advantage of him by a breach of the rules. But where it becomes a question of medal play, where one of two partners is responsible to all the other competitors for the score of the other, how can it then consist with his duty to allow to go unnoticed direct breaches, each of which should be counted a stroke, of a rule written down in black and white ?

What the custom ought to be it seems almost absurd to need to state. The custom ought, of course, to be that the rule should be enforced, just as much as any other rule of the game of golf. A conscientious man, with a proper regard for the rules of the game, should as little think of not counting a stroke when he has inadvertently touched the sand in addressing his ball as he should when he has missed a short putt. By the rules of the game one is as much a stroke as the other, and either is as much a stroke as the longest shot ever driven from the tee. And if we do not play golf by the rules of golf, by what are we to be guided? Shall we not call anything a stroke with which the player of it is dissatisfied? That would make a pleasant game, possibly, but it would not be very much like golf.

Why all this immorality has crept into the game, especially with reference to the touching of sand, it is hard enough to say. If a man makes a foul shot by hitting the ball twice, and is conscious of it, he will ordinarily tell you so, and give up the hole without further parley. Or if he were himself unaware of it, and if you draw his attention to it, on the evidence of a disinterested spectator or of that little tell-tale mark of white paint which chips off the ball when struck in the air, he will generally yield the point without demur. Some of us are indeed rather sensitive about drawing attention to an error of this nature also, but we have fewer scruples than in pointing out that the sand has been touched—yet most inconsistently, for the double shot can be but an accident, and, moreover, an accident that is not in the interests of the player, while the sand touching is, with many, an habitual sin, and gives a distinct advantage.

Altogether there is no so-called petty infringement of the rules about which there is so much custom-sanctioned laxity as in the matter of touching sand, and we greatly need that some of our leading golfers should inaugurate a change in that particular. But there are certain other little points wherein a laxity of custom sometimes appears, wherein a rigid application of the rules of golf would make the game far pleasanter, and far less liable to those little roughnesses of temper which at times crop up in the course of matches.

For instance, it will sometimes happen that, in spite of a player's utmost carefulness in the removal of loose sticks and straws from the neighbourhood of his ball, the latter will roll ever so little from its place. This, by clearly expressed rules of the game, counts against him; but there are those who, with full knowledge of the rule, instead of manfully paying the penalty, will appeal to you with a question as to 'whether you want them to count that?'

This in itself is a distinct breach of etiquette, for it throws you who are innocent into a position in which a question of etiquette upon your side arises. Of course the proper and honest answer is 'Yes,' because that is the answer given by the rules of golf, and because, at the moment, you are supposed to be playing golf. But it is just this latter fact that your opponent does not seem to realise; and if you are too authoritative in pointing it out to him it is not impossible, in consequence of the laxity on these points introduced by custom, that he may, however absurdly, regard himself as rather hardly treated by your assertion of your rights. The very fact of his asking the question indeed is a suggestion that he will so regard it. What are you to say? Is the point at issue, and your respect for your own strength of mind, of sufficient value to compensate for the chance of losing your opponent's good opinion?

These are questions which each will answer according to his temperament; but our great point is that such questions ought never to arise. Nor would they ever arise but for the reprehensible laxity in the application of the rules of the game, which thus gives openings for those very unpleasantnesses which their lax interpretation was presumably intended to avert. Let the rules be applied in their proper strictness; let us play golf according to the rules of golf, and in the strict game we shall find freedom from all such annoyance.

An ingenious method has been suggested whereby, under stress of the question proposed above—as to whether the penalty imposed by the rules shall be exacted—a hypersensitive person may escape from the immediate difficulty and yet administer a rebuke to his opponent. Let him allow the breach of the rule to his opponent, without penalty; let him then, in his opponent's presence, himself commit a similar error, but on his opponent's requesting him not to count it (as he can scarcely fail to have the grace to do), let him reply with such emphasis as he is capable of that *he* always plays the game. This is true etiquette and courtesy; but it is poor golf, indeed; nor shall we ever get golf in its integrity and to our satisfaction until we play it according to the rules formulated for its guidance.

Now on many links, as at St. Andrews, it oftentimes happens that after a shower of rain there will be left what is termed 'casual water' on the links—puddles of rain-water not contemplated in the rules. It is very customary on such occasions for parties to make, before starting, a mutual arrangement, whereby it is agreed to take out of these pools of 'casual water' without penalty. This is, however, distinctly a matter of special arrangement. In the absence of any such arrangement, it is scarcely fair to ask your opponent, 'What are we to do about casual water?' as soon as you find your ball in one of these puddles. The strict rule is that you lose a stroke for taking it out, and no arrangement made on a previous occasion has any jurisdiction over this one. Any suggestion that such an arrangement was tacitly understood should be left to emanate from you—not from him, to whose advantage it will be ; and it is your part, in all etiquette, if there is reasonable cause for supposing any such tacit understanding, to suggest and insist upon it. And so it is in all cases of a possible doubt of this nature ; it is from the party to whose disadvantage it will be that the question and its answer should arise. The opponent should never be left in the position of plaintiff for his rights. If you make a double shot, if you touch sand, if you move your ball, give up the hole, or pay the penalty, whatever it may be, without question, and if a question of genuine etiquette arise, always endeavour to answer it in your opponent's favour ; for all you will lose in golf matches by thus dealing you will more than compensate in self-respect, which is nearly as important.

So far, then, the license introduced by custom has been somewhat of an offence. There is a point, which is chiefly seen in playing on the St. Andrews links, in which it makes matters smooth and easy. A ball lost in the burn is always treated, not as a lost ball, but as a ball in the burn, which involves, of course, more or less of an assumption. You are allowed to take another ball and drop it, with one stroke as penalty, just behind the burn. This concession has extended itself to other pieces of water upon other links. According to the strict rules, it is probably open to a vexatious objector to say that he does not believe the ball went into the burn, that it is lying in some hole on the green, and that, unless recovered, it must be treated as a lost ball. A purely vexatious appeal of this nature would assuredly be given against him by the committee of the club, who would certainly support the immemorial usage in preference to the letter of the law.

An amusing controversy of this kind occurred at Hoylake. A player's ball went down a rabbit-hole. It could be seen at the bottom of the hole, but all efforts to scoop it up with the iron were fruitless. The player was about to drop another ball behind the rabbit-hole, with the loss of one stroke, according to the rule for a ball found in a rabbit-hole. His opponent objected. 'You cannot do that,' he said. 'That is a lost ball.'

'Lost ball!' said the other. 'What do you mean by lost? Why, there it is!'

'Yes,' said the first, 'there it is, and you cannot get it from there. I say that a ball is lost, unless you can *gather* it.'

And the case was referred to the committee, who gave it against the player, who expressed his intention of never returning to play golf at Hoylake till he had trained a ferret to draw golf balls.

This was pressing the strictness of the law somewhat far; but there is another class of instances in which laxity of enforcement has led to considerable immorality—viz. with regard to the limits within which it is permissible to clear the putting-green of loose impediments. Twenty yards is the distance allowed by law; but we often see, in unimportant matches, players clearing the ground for a much larger radius. For the most part they do so thoughtlessly; though there are probably a certain number who sin with deliberation, salving their apologies for consciences by the thought that they are no worse than their neighbours. Now no one likes to be too severely critical about a yard or so, because it is the general custom not to be thus critical, and because he whom it especially behoves to be so—the player himself—is not careful. If it were but fully realised how great is the effect on the match of one long putt laid dead, which might not have been laid dead had the player taken his iron in hand to loft over the obstacle at twenty-one yards from the hole which he feloniously removed, there would not be this laxity of practice, and this sensitiveness about claiming the penalty for the rule transgressed. This rule, however, is not treated with the universal contempt, as if it were quite beneath the notice of a gentleman, which is evinced for the rule which refers to the touching of sand.

Broadly speaking, there is no breach of true etiquette in enforcing rules ; the breaches of etiquette consist, for the most part, in the breaches of the rules.

There are certainly a good many golfers who consider themselves grossly ill-treated if they are asked to hole out a short putt ; and, singularly enough, it is just those very golfers who most often justify the request, by missing the short putt, who are most indignant at it. You have a perfect right to ask a golfer to hole out every single putt ; and no golfer ought to take offence at your so asking him. There are, of course, putts which it is positively vexatious to ask the veriest duffer to hole. Common sense ought, and does, draw a fair line in the matter. Perhaps one of the most offensive of all breaches of etiquette is committed by him who, after missing one of these little putts, says to his opponent, airily, 'Oh, I thought you'd have given me that!' It is a remark one is very apt to make in the irritation of the moment, and it is a remark which it well becomes the opponent, in the magnanimity of his triumph, to forgive ; but we can only excuse it to ourselves in proportion as we feel a shameful repentance for it afterwards.

Sometimes the remark will take the yet more offensive, and usually mendacious, form of ' I thought you *had* given it to me.'

There is often a genuine misunderstanding about these

'APPROACHING THE LAST HOLE'

short putts. Players are in the habit of giving them to each other, and are apt to assume them given before such is really the case ; but in all these instances he who has missed should as cheerfully as possible, hold himself bound by the results of his own unwarranted. assumption, and not try to shame his opponent into weak-minded liberality, or an uncomfortable feeling that his action may be held open to the charge of sharp practice. Neither is it altogether the best of form to ask your opponent (if the putt be one that can, conceivably at all, be missed) whether or no he expects you to hole it out. It is hardly a fair question, as it may put him in a dilemma between conceding you a stroke which he does not consider an absolute certainty, or feeling that you may, perhaps, consider him a little severe upon you if he request you to play it. All these delicate questions would be avoided if it were established as a constant and universal custom that all putts should be holed in match play, as in medal play.

It is impossible to frame rules which shall cover every possible contingency, and there should be, between gentlemen, a certain amount of give and take, such as will smooth off the rough edges of injustice or absurdity which in exceptional circumstances appear under the strict letter of the law. In a match played a few years back, a dog seized the ball of one of the players, as it rolled over the putting-green, and bore it off into a carriage which was standing near. According to the written law it was incumbent on the player to play the ball out of the carriage, where the dog had deposited it. This, surely, was one of those exceptional cases wherein the courtesy of the opponent might have suggested a fairer alternative to the, in this case, unjust requirement of the generally fair rule.

In the amateur championship meeting of 1888, held at Prestwick, one of the competitors played his ball into a spectator's pocket. This was a 'lie' of which the rules took no special cognisance, and the only general rule applicable to the case, viz. that every ball shall be played where it lies, except as otherwise provided for, would have been strenuously contested by the spectator who owned the pocket. It was a case in which the mutual courtesy of the players had to step in to suggest some reasonable solution, which, in point of fact, was speedily forthcoming.

How such questions could have been determined had they arisen with respect to a scoring round, it is happily not for us to determine ; but the safest rule is to play the stroke according to each of any reasonable suggestions, and to leave to the committee of the club under whose auspices the competition is being held the task of deciding as to which solution is the right and fair one. These are points which, as they arise from time to time in match play, will probably, as we have said, be determined by the mutual courtesy of the players ; but in any case it should be remembered that in these points of etiquette it is more graceful to concede than to claim, and should mutual courtesy fail to suggest a satisfactory solution, it is better to play under protest—that is to say, subject to a subsequent appeal to the committee—than to persist in a protracted wrangle.

Discussion of these points opens another subject which is ruled rather by custom than by written law, viz. the respect to be paid to the feelings and wagers of ' outside bettors '—that is, of parties who have no active part in the match, but have made bets upon it. The outside bettor is rather in the habit of assuming very high ground, speaking as if the fact of his having wagered a sum varying from a shilling upwards upon the result had bought over into his service for the time being the player whom he has honoured with his confidence. He is apt to feel himself somewhat injured if the man he is backing yields a point of merest courtesy to the opponent, and he seems to consider that by the mere fact of having wagered an insignificant sum he has formed some subtle contract with the player so favoured, that he will play in accordance with his backer's fancy.

This way of looking at the case is so very absurd, that it is scarcely possible to state it in reasonable terms ; but it is a view which largely prevails in the golfing world, that a player engaged in a big match has to consider, besides his own interests, the interests of any number of people who, without taking him into their confidence, have seen fit to put their money on him. It is practically equivalent to saying that the player becomes, for the time being, the property of the public. The public, at all events, deems itself entitled to grumble very audibly if the favourite of its choice does not struggle, in the public interest, to the bitter end. The golfer is, in fact, treated as if he were a race-horse.

The sooner the outside bettor can dispel from his mind this idea of proprietorship, the better for all concerned—for the game generally, and therefore, so far, for the bettor himself, and infinitely better, certainly, for the player in big matches. It is not, of course, as if the bettor had come to the player before the match, and had said to him, 'I am going to back you, and I hope you will play up.' This may, indeed, savour of impertinence, if backer and player are not well acquainted; but if the player acquiesce in the backer's proposition, thus stated, it undoubtedly places the matter upon a somewhat different footing. But, apart from some such previous colloquy, the bettor has no conceivable claim upon him whom he is so apt to regard as his *protégé*. Should the *protégé* be four up and five to play, and should it then for inscrutable reasons please him to give up the match, his backer may indeed, and undoubtedly will, level curses upon his fortune; but he has no standpoint whatever from which to find fault with the player. He is nothing to the player, he has made no contract with him, tacit or express; he has chosen to back him, with all his caprices and foibles, not as a machine, not even as a race-horse, but as a free-volitioned man.

There is a further injury that this false 'respect for outside bettors' inflicts upon the golfing world; it is not unfrequently made the cloak of little meannesses which would not be attempted were not the player thus given the opportunity of shifting his responsibility upon an absent or fictitious scapegoat. Thus : A questionable point is at issue, and the cunning and mean golfer thus clothes himself in the garb of magnanimity—' Well, if it was only myself to be considered, I would give it to you; but there is outside money on this match, and so I feel that I ought to claim my full rights ; ' and his full rights, in the mouth of this man, are very apt to encroach a little beyond their province, and to become the opponent's wrongs. No, no ! let us put back the outside bettor into his proper place — that is to say, let us show him that he has no *locus standi* at all whence to dictate to the player he favours, but that he must consider his money to be laid out at his own peril—and thus will this one at least of the many occasions for petty meannesses be abolished.

Possibly next upon the little list of these delinquents against the unwritten code of golf etiquette comes he who complains outrageously of the good luck which falls to his opponent's share. We all know that there is a great deal of luck in the game; but we also know, in moments of sober reflection, that on the whole the balance of luck, good or bad, for us or against us, hangs very nearly even. Complaints of one's own bad luck are infinitely bad taste. But this class of offence is nothing compared with aggressive outcries against the good fortune of an opponent. If circumstances *can* aggravate a sin so intrinsically evil, it is even more criminal to complain of the good luck that befalls him with whom you are partnered in a scoring competition than your antagonist in a hand-to-hand match. Generally recognised etiquette goes so far as a kind sympathy and interest in the efforts of your partner for the medal round. A community of trials make you feel in a measure dependent upon each other like fellow knights errant in a world peopled with monsters in the shape of all the other competitors. Usually a man is generous enough to feel that, if he does not himself win, he would prefer the victory of his partner to that of any other ; and when his own fortunes have become desperate, he will lend that partner all the comfort of his sympathy and moral support. This is less the result of the prospect of any little reflected glory than of a genuine fellow-feeling for one passing through the same vale of bunkers as oneself.

Nevertheless you cannot expect your partner's grief for your unmerited misfortunes to be as poignant as your own. This would be pushing altruism to an excess incompatible with that degree of egoism which Mr. Herbert Spencer assures us to be indispensable in this world in its present state of imperfection. But there may, after all, lurk in this altruism, so far as it goes, a certain measure of intelligent egoism ; for our partner may reasonably expect sympathy from us, when he falls into misfortune, in just the proportion in which he has shown sympathy for us. It is a casting of bread upon the waters which will not fail to bear fruit in return.

You may, without suspicion of your kind motives, weep with a weeping partner on a medal round a measure of tears which, if shed over the sorrows of an antagonist in a match, would inevitably suggest the tears attributed to the crocodile. Nobody ever believes that you are genuinely sorry for the ill-luck of a man you are trying to beat. It is very seldom that you will be able to appreciate that any bad luck at all falls to his share. Nevertheless it is expected of you to make some half-hearted expressions of sympathy. The antagonist will have no real faith in them, but for the time being, and failing other sympathy, he will be fain to find some solace to his woes in what he knows to be the fool's paradise of your consolations ; and a certain show of this fictitious sorrow is imperatively demanded by all the kindly rules of etiquette.

It is no less necessary that you should put the utmost curb on yourself to restrain too loud and childish accusations of your own ill-luck. If you can but realise the fact noted above, that your adversary is not at all likely to be able, though with the best heart in the world, to appreciate the fact that your misfortunes are due to any other cause than lack of skill, your own self-respect will help you to restrain yourself. He cannot look upon your lamentations as otherwise than puerile, if he believes them causeless ; and you will become both a better golfer, and a pleasanter, if you bring yourself to regard your unkind treatment at fortune's hands with equanimity; for not only is irritation an annoyance to all who come within its sphere, but re-acts disastrously upon the *morale* and game of its unhappy subject.

Truth is great; but it is sometimes indispensable to be petty and untruthful, and no man can possibly expect to bring a foursome to a happy issue who conducts his relations with his partner on perfectly truthful principles. Etiquette is here at one with the most elementary principles of good policy. You must always, during the match, try to give your partner in a foursome an impression that you are more than pleased with him. This impression is usually a very false one. It is scarcely possible not to give a partner credit for more than his fair share of the misfortunes of the joint firm. It is seldom that we can fairly realise the extent of our own contributions to them. Nevertheless good form and good policy compel us to convey an impression the very opposite of this to our partner. We must lead him to think that we are enchanted with him, and he will then play with all the confidence of one enchanted with himself. One might as well try to make love as to play a foursome on perfectly truthful principles.

The laws of etiquette prescribe for us a certain line of conduct not only to our partner in a foursome, and to our antagonist in a single, but also to our other neighbours on the golf links. One of the first things that the young golfer has to learn is that the prime requisitions for good golf generally are silence and immobility. If he be not careful to preserve these conditions, he will render good golf an impossibility not only within the circle of his own match, but also for the moment with any other of the matches which his own may chance to meet. He who rushes noisily up to a match, demanding with loud geniality 'how you stand,' irrespective of whether anyone is playing a stroke at the moment, is a nuisance who ought to be abolished from the golf links. At least there is no law of etiquette which should restrain the terms in which such an one should be answered. It seems scarcely necessary to state so universally observed a maxim as that it is your duty to stand perfectly motionless and silent while another member of your match is playing. Any breach of this first law of golfing etiquette is, happily, of rare occurrence. Offenders are of that class with which we determine 'never to play again.' But scarcely less obnoxious than the talker or the walker is he who rushes on wildly after his own ball immediately he has struck it, partially obstructing our line of aim, and obviously only coming to a halt, at the moment at which we deliver our stroke, out of compulsory respect to the barest exigencies of golfing courtesy.

The proper course of proceeding is this : to drive off first, if it be your honour, and then to stand clear of the teeing ground, behind your adversary's back. Do not stand close enough to him to annoy him, wherever you stand, and do not stand 'behind his eye,' as it is called—that is, in a line which would be a prolongation, backward, of the line of flight of the ball he is about to drive. Find out where he prefers you to stand, if he be a nervous player ; but it is a safe rule to stand, motionless, behind his back. There are men in the golfing world—gentlemen, in some respects—who appear to be not above taking the petty advantage which annoyance to an opponent, caused by neglect of these little points, brings. It is not much use writing on points of etiquette for such as these ; but there are also a very large number of golfers who, blessed with prosaic nervous systems themselves, thoughtlessly do not appreciate that others can be affected by the trifles of their surroundings. It is to these that one may say a word which may be gratefully received. They should bear in mind that to be forced to make a complaint upon any one of these trifling conditions is no less trying to a man of finely strung nerves than is the very circumstance of which he complains. Seek, then, to avoid giving him reason for making the complaint.

If it be your opponent's honour, it is far better that you should allow him to drive off from the tee before you think of teeing your own ball. Most teeing places are rather circumscribed, and even if you do not absolutely put down your ball upon its little eminence before your opponent has played, you are very apt to bother him as you crawl about the ground looking for the most likely spot. Let him have his shot in peace, and you may fairly expect him to show you equal courtesy in the happy event of your regaining the honour.

After all, what is courtesy but unselfishness and consideration of others? How grossly then does not he offend against every dictate of courtesy who scalps up the turf with his heavy iron, and leaves the 'divot' lying, an unsightly clod of earth, upon the sward! What shall we do to such as he, as, playing after him, our ball finds its way into the poor dumb mouth of a wound which he has thus left gaping, to call down upon him the vengeance of gods and men? In vain we print upon our rules that 'it is the first duty of every golfer to replace, or see replaced, turf cut out in the act of playing'—in vain we post up the ever-forgotten truism that 'golf is not agriculture,' with or without the addendum suggested by some cynical landlord —'though both are games of chance.' No—in spite of all our efforts, the scalps and divots still lie unsightly on the links, and 'nobody seems one penny the worse,' though we curse with bell and book and niblick the sacrilegious villain who left the raw, gaping wound on the sacred soil. No golfer is worthy of the name who does not put back his divot. It is no trouble, and is indeed rather amusing, as we watch how, like a piece of a Chinese puzzle, the divot fits back accurately into the chasm from which it was carved. A divot well replaced is, in most conditions of the ground, as a divot that has never been cut.

There is a rule forbidding players to drive off their tee-shot before the parties in front shall have played off their second— containing the obvious corollary that they are permitted to do so as soon as ever those in front shall have played. But if this corollary be acted upon without the necessary limitations placed upon it by customary etiquette, the rates of life insurance for the short driving, obese school of golfers would be high indeed. Two slashing youngsters coming behind them would imperil the valuable lives of old gentlemen off every tee. In a crowded state of the green, where the parties in front, however slow they be, are well up with the players in front of them again, all etiquette and custom requires that those in front should be allowed to travel well out of range before the legitimate privilege of the players behind, to drive after them, be exercised. We say in a crowded state of the green, and when the parties in front are well up with those again in front of them; for when this is not the case, when a certain slow-going match has a free space of a hole's length, or more, before them, when they are retarding the progress of all behind, then etiquette does not prescribe any such forbearance. The requirements of etiquette then fall upon the slow-coaches—that they shall allow the faster-going singles or foursomes to pass them by. Otherwise they have no just ground for complaint if they find the tee-shots of those behind them whizzing past their ears, after they have played their seconds, in such wise that they will probably deem it the part of prudence, no less than of courtesy, to let their swifter pursuers go before them. Yet the pursuers should in this case reflect that this concession is an act of courtesy, and accept it with due thanks.

In no case and under no circumstances save where a ball is lost, and permission obtained, is it excusable to drive into a party along the green, on the putting-green, or before they have played their seconds. Where the parties behind have infringed this great commandment more than once during a round, any means combining an insistence upon your rights with adequate courtesy to the offenders is beyond our ingenuity to suggest; but it may perhaps be urged that players thus offending have forfeited all claim to courteous dealing.

There is a certain point in regard to match play which has been the cause of considerable exasperation, upon occasions. It occurs more often, perhaps, than elsewhere upon the links of St. Andrews, where caddies, greens, and winds are keen. There the canny caddie upon a windy day will station himself at the hole in such manner as to shield the wind off the ball of the master for whom he carries. Not content with that, he will shuffle after it as it is propelled by the wind and with feet close together coax it, so far as possible, to travel in the way it should go, with all the art of a curler. Should the ball be over-strongly putted, and the wind be opposed to its course, he will jump aside to allow the full current to blow against it. This can, of course, be only done by the caddie who is standing at the hole. There occurs often, therefore, some competition between the rival caddies as to which shall have this post. There results discussion, and some unpleasantness. Now the proper etiquette is that the caddie of him whose turn it is not to play should stand at the hole; for it is in the interest of the non-player that the caddie, who can move aside, stands at the hole in lieu of the flag-stick, which the player might gain an advantage by striking. If this rule then be adhered to, there can be no opportunity for the caddie thus 'favouring' the ball; for even the least scrupulous of them do not go the length of attempting to turn the wind to the disadvantage of the ball of their master's antagonist. And as for this shielding of the wind off the ball, we would say that it is altogether opposed to the true spirit of the game, which consists in the combining of skill of hand with calculation of just such conditions of wind, &c., as this virtually unfair conspiracy between master and caddie tends to modify. In the abstract we believe that all gentlemen condemn the practice, though in actual course of play, partly from a dislike to check the zeal shown by the caddie in their interests, they often permit it without rebuke.

The relations between partners in foursomes are governed entirely by a tacit code of etiquette. The better player should be on his guard against any show of patronage in his advice; the inferior partner should show proper contrition for his misdoings, but should not be in a continual state of apology as if a mistake was with him an exception. The amount of conversation between partners should be determined by the inclination of him who wishes to talk least. The prior claim is that of the negative blessing of silence; and this is true no less in

ETIQUETTE AND BEHAVIOUR

your partnership with another in a foursome than in regard to your relations with an opponent in a match.

More especially is it incumbent upon spectators to preserve silence and immobility, and it is in the worst taste for them to come forward and offer unsolicited and probably unwelcome conversation with any of the players in the intervals of the strokes. Spectators should always remember what is due to

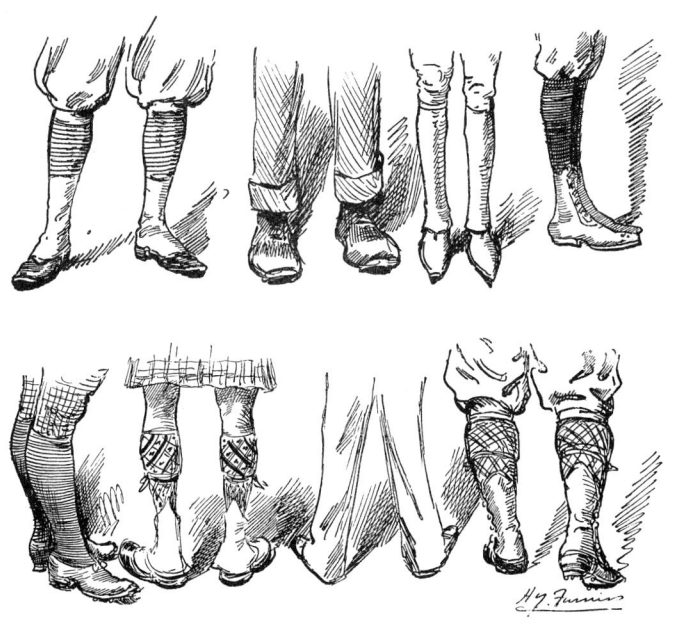

UNDERSTUDIES

those who are affording the spectacle; but it is no less true that a duty of courtesy is owed by the players to those who pay them the compliment of being interested in their performance. Moreover, golf links are commonly public places. The spectator has as good a right there as the most finished golfer, and the latter should not forget that if the former defer to the delicate requirements of his nervous system, it is but an act of courtesy, and should be received with the courteous acknowledgment due to such.

Modesty is a virtue, but the mock modesty, the pride which apes humility, was an occasion of much mirth to Satan ; and it is a breach, rather than an observance, of etiquette, and even of honesty, to so underrate your game as to gain an unfair advantage in arranging the conditions of a match. Do not tell a player whom you have defeated that he would be sure to beat you next time. He may think so, but he will not believe that you do, and the remark partakes of the nature of an insult to his understanding.

Finally, there are certain points of etiquette, such as those connected with dress, which differ, locally, and you should ever endeavour to conform yourself to the etiquette of the links on which you may be playing. Thus, on some links it is especially requested, as a means of warning the public of the approach of danger, that the golfers should wear red coats. It is but fair towards the local members of the club whose guest or visiting member you temporarily are that you should array yourself for the nonce in the uniform of the danger-signal. Otherwise, any damage inflicted on the unwary passer-by by your approach unheralded save by the hard flying golf-ball will be laid at the innocent door of the club, to the injury, in the opinion of the vulgar, of its local *habitués*.

CHAPTER XI

ON GIVING ODDS AND HANDICAPPING

BY H. G. HUTCHINSON

STONE BRIDGE, SWILCAN BURN

ONE of the best features in the game of golf is the ease and accuracy with which players of very different calibres can be put upon an equality by the giving and receiving of odds. In this respect it perhaps compares favourably with every other game. At cricket, odds are given by pitting sixteen or twenty-two against eleven; but this somewhat alters the normal conditions of the game for the givers of odds, who have to bat against twenty-two in the field. In billiards it is generally seen that the receiver of points wins by about the number given or is beaten by a like number; he is either so far ahead as to rob the game of all interest, or else is practically beaten when the game is but half-way through. At tennis, the receiver of points is crushed by having to play *against*, and against the result of, greater skill than his own. None of these drawbacks attach to a match between a tip-top player at golf and an indifferent player—for these two reasons : 1. Each man plays his own ball, without any interference from his antagonist ; 2. The game is played by instalments, so to speak ; by holes, on each of which, if need be, a stroke may be given, and the result of which is not carried on to affect the score of the next hole.

Thus the indifferent performer is not crushed beneath a sense of his own inferiority ; neither is the game of the skilful player at all directly affected by the incompetence of his opponent. Each goes his own way, and though the difference between them may be very great, it is very possible, so accurately can the relative strength of golfers be gauged, that the result of the whole match may hang upon the issue of the last putt.

Nevertheless, there is a certain point of uncertainty at which it becomes impossible so to handicap men as to bring about a good match. To be handicapped at all, a man must have some 'form.' And beginners, especially beginners of the young, lissome, slashing type, for a long time have no ascertainable 'form.' The Americans say of our English seasons that we have no climate, only 'samples' of weather. So, too, these youngsters have no 'game,' only samples of golf. With the best possible intentions, they play 'in and out' in the most suspicious way. The odds which will be a good handicap one day, will land them nine holes to the bad the next, and the third day they produce a game which a scratch player would have some trouble to defeat. They are as fickle as fortune ; there is no dependence on them.

Of course between bad players a stroke in a hole does not amount to near the same weight of odds as between two first-class players. With good players a large majority of the holes are halved, and it is quite the exception for one to win a hole from the other by more than one stroke. But with bad players —fourth or fifth class players—it is quite exceptional for them to come within a stroke, or even two, of each other, at a hole ; and for a hole to be halved is looked upon as a coincidence in which some are disposed to see the finger of Providence. There is thus, usually, a margin sufficient to cover an ordinary amount of odds, whose value is therefore reduced almost to a cipher. Indeed, players of very low calibre have been known to toss, before starting, to determine which should give the other a stroke a hole ; knowing well enough that this allowance, which is deemed perfectly overwhelming in the higher ranks of the golfing army, would be of little moment among such unfortunates as themselves.

Nevertheless, however badly a man may play, after he has been struggling for a year or so with all the infirmities of his eye and muscle, it will become gradually apparent to him that he has found his place. Hitherto he had been somewhat of a pariah. He was no one's child. The outer duffers would have none of him, fearing that he was too good ; the privileged classes would not open to him their exclusive ranks, for fear that he would spoil their matches. But at length he has found a resting-place ; no matter whether it be high or lowly, he has a *locus standi*—a recognised 'game.' It has become possible to make matches with him ; he has acquired a form which can be more or less relied upon, more or less accurately gauged. Sometimes he may play matches, say at odds of a stroke a hole, with a scratch player ; or sometimes, with a scratch player upon his side, he may engage in a foursome against another high-flyer, burdened with another slow-coach of humble prowess.

These are the matches that, if he be wise, he will cultivate ; occasionally putting his hand into his pocket, and giving the professionals a turn round. For it is but by playing with stronger players that the novice can hope to better his own game.

Golf is now spreading so widely, so many beginners are to be found in so many remote commons and heaths of the United Kingdom—including Ireland—that a most amusing ignorance of the real value of odds is very prevalent. Many of these, it is not too much to say, consider that a man who plays with a first-class player at odds of a stroke a hole, is scarcely, if at all removed from a first-class player himself. A stroke is such a small matter among the numbers which are recorded on *their* cards. What is one among so many? Thus they argue, forgetting that it is, perhaps, harder for the good player to save one stroke off his average number for a hole, than it is for them, out of the multitude of their sins, to redeem three or four from the average of their errors.

It will probably be a genuine surprise to these gentlemen to learn that the difference of 'a third'—one solitary stroke on each three holes of the round—is sufficient, fully sufficient, to place in different classes of the upper circles of golfing society him who is blessed in giving and him who reluctantly receives. In point of fact, the difference between first-class and second-class players scarcely amounts to this; for when we come to persons to whom is given 'a half,' we find ourselves already at the third class. Now, a third is six strokes, and a half is nine. If we are to be consistent at all, we must certainly admit a greater difference of odds betwixt third and second class players than we do betwixt first and second. We must, therefore, reduce the odds which may be held to mark a fair distinction between the two highest classes to four strokes in the round, and may arrange our table of merit somewhat in this way :—

First class: 'Scratch' players.

Second class: Those who receive four strokes in the round.

Third class: Those who receive a half, or nine strokes in the round.

Fourth class: Those who receive a stroke a hole, or eighteen in the round.

We are, of course, at present considering matches by holes, and eighteen-hole rounds. Handicapping by strokes, for competition rounds, we will consider later.

Now this table is a tentative, elastic endeavour to convey what golfers ordinarily mean when they speak of the different 'classes' of players. It must not be considered a hard-and-fast classification. Indeed, even among first-class players— who are so, mainly, by virtue of the steady evenness of their play—a man will one day play a game which could give a third, or a half, to the game he plays the next. On the other hand, the best professional taking out a novice for his first lesson, does but give him two strokes a hole ; and in point of fact, the novice will probably come a good deal nearer the professional, at these points, on their first encounter, than he will for some weeks afterwards. He will not yet have learned how easy it is to miss, and will play with all the confidence which is the fruit of ignorance.

Besides this mode of handicapping, by means of a half, a third, or four strokes, odds may be given in the form of bisques.

Under the former method the receiver of the odds has to state beforehand at which holes he will take his strokes, and is confined to a certain regular order ; he must take a stroke at every third hole, if he is in receipt of a third, or at every other hole, if in receipt of a half. If in receipt of four strokes, his choice is, at St. Andrews, even more restricted ; for the custom has become so hallowed, through long observance, of taking the four strokes at the two short holes and the two long ones, that its breach would seem little short of sacrilegious. But the bisque is a point which may be claimed at any moment. After the unhappy giver of odds has struggled manfully to gain a hole, the recipient will blandly turn upon him, and say, 'I take a bisque ; that makes it halved.' Nor is this all its effect ; for all through the round the giver of points will be playing with a paralysing consciousness of the bisque hanging, like a sword of Damocles, over his head. The sapient receiver of bisques will be sparing of their too speedy use. Rather will he keep them in reserve, playing, with much gusto, the game of cat and mouse with his formidable opponent.

Yet another means of handicapping for match play has been brought into general vogue by its use in the tournament for the Annual Challenge Calcutta Cup, at St. Andrews. This consists in the giving or receiving of so many holes up to start with.

Now, what proportion should the number of holes given

bear to the number of strokes given in a match by holes? To put it more concretely: suppose A, a first-class player, can give C, a third-class player, a half, that is, nine strokes, how many holes up ought A to give C so as to make a fair match of it? Generally speaking, about two-thirds, *i.e.* about six holes up.

But this rule, to become a useful guide, must be taken with its due limitations. It does not apply with equal force to all cases in which a half fairly marks the difference between the players. C, our typical third-class player, is a very steady-going old gentleman; and on a large number of matches he and young C′, a slashing but most uncertain player, are as nearly as possible equal. A, our first-class man, gives old Mr. C a half, and they play very equal; but whenever he gives the poor old gentleman six holes up instead, he always beats him out of the field. With young C′ also, A makes a very good match with a half; but when he comes to play the young man with six holes up, the scratch man finds himself quite unable to hold his own at all. Now why is this? The reason is not far to seek: old Mr. C goes steadily along, doing all the holes in about one stroke more than A will take for them, if he makes no mistake; but A does make a few mistakes, and C is always close at hand to take advantage of them, and also of all the strokes of his handicap allowance. But, without these strokes C is apt to find himself in, each time, in just one too many, so that his start of six holes is very soon swept off into limbo.

With young C′ it is quite different. One hole he will perhaps play quite as well as A himself can do. The next he will be bird's-nesting among the whins, after his erratic ball, and his stroke will not be of the slightest use to him. The hole before he very likely won without his stroke; so that altogether the odds of a half is not of nearly so much value to him as to old Mr. C. But with six holes up, to start with, it is quite different. Say that C′ does one hole in five and the next in twenty-seven, he is better off as against A, who has done them in five apiece, than is Mr. C, who has played each hole faultlessly, according to his lights, in six. But if C′ was in receipt of a half, and his stroke happened to come on his twenty-seven hole, he would but be equal to Mr. C in their respective relation to A. The steadier player has the better chance with strokes, the more brilliant and flashy player with holes—that is what it amounts to.

Another necessary limitation to our proposed proportion of holes to strokes, as two to three, may be best seen by a *reductio ad absurdum*. There are plenty of golfers, of quite well-recognised though lowly form, to whom a scratch player might well give 'a stroke and a half a hole,' that is, one stroke on one hole, and two strokes on the next, or twenty-seven in all. But there is no golfer in any world whose arithmetical arrangements are at all analogous to our own who could give, with any confident expectation of winning the match, two-thirds of twenty-seven in holes, or eighteen holes up !

Such are the stereotyped methods of handicapping in single or foursome matches. Other less recognised means have occasionally been tried. A gentleman at St. Andrews once made a match to play level with a brother golfer who was a far stronger player than himself, on the understanding only that he should be allowed to say 'Booh !' as his opponent was about to strike the ball, thrice during the match. History goes on to relate how, making the most of this concession, he continually stole up behind his opponent (open-mouthed, menacing him, as it were, with a 'booh !') with such disconcerting effect, that the receiver of the three 'boohs !' won the match, actually without having used any of his 'boohs !' at all.

On another occasion the same two gentlemen made a match on the following terms : that the stronger was to play with not less than eight clubs, and that the weaker was to have the advantage of naming, on each occasion, which of the eight the other was to use. Visions of compelling his opponent to take his driver on the stones and metal of the railway, and his iron niblick on the putting-green, enchanted the brain of the recipient of these strange odds. Judge of the disappointment and the fury of the poor duped golfer when his powerful antagonist appeared at the teeing ground equipped with eight clubs, indeed —nothing wrong about the number—but eight *cleeks*, each so like the other that their very maker could hardly have told them apart.

Many a match has been made, to the ensnaring of the unwary, between a scratch player confined to the use of a single club—sometimes a putter, even, or a niblick—and a third or fourth class player with all his set. These matches are all in favour of the better player. To one who has not seen it, the use a really good golfer can make for driving, and even for bunker play, of a putter, is almost inconceivable. To the first-class golfer himself it may be a revelation to find the very slight difference between his score with an unsupported putter and with all his armoury of tools. He begins to ask himself whether there be not, after all, something in the criticism of the uninitiated spectator :—' It must be all nonsense, having all those sticks ! ' So much, then, for handicapping in singles or foursomes.

In three-ball matches the best player of the three will sometimes be pitted against the other two, playing, as it is called, 'the best of their ball'—that is to say, that whichever of the two does the hole in the fewer number, his score shall count against the score of the single-handed player. Thus, if A be playing the best ball of C and C'—if A do a hole in 4, C in 5, and C' in 4, the hole is halved ; C and C' having, between them, managed to do the hole in the same number as A. Presuming that A can give each of them, separately, a half, he will probably have somewhat the better of this three-ball match. For the odds of the 'best ball' to have their true weight, it is necessary that the two players who are acting in combination should be of tolerably equal merit.

In arranging foursomes it has to be borne in mind that the combination—two on each side playing alternate strokes with the same ball—will not always be likely to turn out in exact accordance with the individual merits. For instance, taking A as the type of a first-class player, and C as the type of a steady going third-class player, and C' as a type of a third-class player of the slashing uncertain style, A and C will form a much stronger combination than A and C'. Some of the foursome rounds played by a first-class and a very inferior, but steady, player have been holed in very nearly as few strokes as the first-class player is capable of when playing his single ball. The inferior player will often play a little above his true form, in consequence of the confidence he derives from a knowledge of his partner's skill, and by dint of unenterprising and patient prudence will often avoid perils which might have brought down the long driver's arrogance in sorrow to the niblick. Therefore it is that a partnership of a scratch player with one to whom he would give a stroke a hole is commonly victorious over a combination of two players to each of whom the scratch man would allow a half.

Medal rounds, or competitions in which a large number of players take part, are usually decided by the sum of the scores taken by the respective players at each of the eighteen holes—eighteen being the normal number of holes in a competition round. The match is then said to be played 'by score' instead of by holes, as on the usual plan. It is, therefore, by strokes deducted from the total score, instead of by strokes deducted from the score of each hole, or certain holes, that odds have to be given. At first sight this mode of handicapping would appear to have few features of difference from the other—to present but few difficulties. 'If a man receives a stroke a hole—that is eighteen strokes in all—in match play, why, of course, eighteen strokes will be the number to be deducted from his total score for the round.' This is an instance of the truth of the paradox that there is nothing so misleading as facts, except figures. The man who receives a stroke a hole from a scratch player in match play will require probably somewhere about one half as many strokes more in score play. The reason is obvious. The better player is, almost always, by far more steady. It is very unlikely that he will exceed by more than one or two, at any hole in the round, the average fair number of strokes at which he might expect to do that hole. The inferior player, on the contrary, is equally unlikely to get through the round without exceeding his normal number at one or two holes by three, five, or even more strokes. In hole play, if he be ten strokes worse than his opponent, that does but involve the loss of a single hole ; but in playing for score the whole black balance of ten solid strokes has to form a factor in the ultimate sum total.

The receiver of a stroke a hole—or eighteen strokes—in match play will, it has been indicated, need one half more, or twenty-seven strokes in scoring play ; and this proportion would appear to hold good throughout—a third being a fair equivalent for nine strokes on a scoring round, and a half fairly represented by thirteen or fourteen.

Yet this general rule, again, must be accepted with its proper limitations ; it must be applied with discrimination and with a certain consideration of persons. The steady, old-fashioned, feeble golfer and his slashing, high and crooked-flying young opponent, are fairly matched, and, for hole play, rank in the same class; but in playing for score the 'pawky' old golfer will defeat the youngster nine times out of ten. The youngster may perhaps have an occasional four where the other has a six, but he will also have an occasional figure somewhere in the teens, while his opponent sticks to his uneventful sixes. The sapient handicapper will always bear in mind the effect of these individual idiosyncracies upon the due proportion between the odds in match play and in scoring rounds.

One of the standing difficulties of the handicapper's task lies in the difference in point of steadiness between the men with whom he has to deal. The better the player, the more often will he send in a score which fairly represents his 'game.' The majority of the cards sent in by long-handicapped players show scores far in excess of the figures which their fair 'game' should enable them to accomplish. It is only by striking an average of these wild scores that the handicapper could bring in these uncertain quantities to win as often as the steady scratch player. But the objection to handicapping upon this basis—upon an average of the scores returned, or likely to be returned—is that the long handicapped man will in that case sometimes return a card which, with his handicap allowance, will show an impossible score—a score with which the scratch player cannot hope to vie. And this is manifestly bad handicapping, for it is as if a runner in a hundred yards race were given a start which made his time nine seconds. And yet, as said before, handicapping on the basis of their true respective 'games' will result in a large proportion of victories for the better player.

Therefore, in this world of imperfections, where the relatively good, alone, is possible, it becomes the duty of the handicapper to do his best to strike a compromise—combining a minimum of wins at scores which are practically impossible for the scratch men with a minimum of the number of wins scored by the scratch men in excess of the wins of long handicap players.

'Taking one consideration with another,' in no case, even under the best possible auspices, is the handicapper's life an altogether happy one. To perform his office efficiently he will indeed need many of the qualities of the moralising policeman of Mr. Gilbert's opera. He will need the *robur et æs triplex* to preserve him from all the metaphorical niblick strokes of abuse with which he will be assailed. If, as is improbable, there be anyone who conceives himself kindly dealt with by the handicapper, he will be careful to keep this conviction to himself, with the judicious purpose of not injuring his own position in future handicaps. On the other hand, those who deem themselves ill used, whose name is certain to be legion, will be by no means reticent. Rather will they see fit to give exaggerated expression to their sense of harsh treatment, with a view to frightening the handicapper into awarding them more points in future. There is the man who gets querulous under a sense of what he is pleased to think an injustice ; there is the man who waxes abusive. With all such the handicapper must show himself inflexible ; sometimes he will find it necessary to be rude. It is recorded how a man once went to bed during a whole meeting, rather than play at what he considered insufficient odds. At the next meeting the handicap committee raised his points, and he swept the board. This is an example of what handicappers should not do. The handicapper must steel his heart alike against tears and execrations. Let him cultivate within himself a faculty for deriving the greatest possible satisfaction from a sense of having done his duty to the best of his natural ability; for, in sooth, after infinite trouble, he will find himself the most unthanked of all philanthropists. You do not need a man of very fine fibre for a handicapper; such are apt to be too sensitive; but you want a man of method, and a man quick at retort to crush complainants.

One of the besetting nuisances of the handicapper's life is the improving player. One month this man was perhaps at sixteen strokes. He failed to win the monthly medal, and yet he finds himself, the next month, down to fourteen. He thinks himself very hardly used, but, in point of fact, the handicapper was quite right. The handicapper knows that if the man had played anything approaching to his game he would have won the medal with sixteen. He also knows that the man has been practising, and has been upon the improving tack, during the four weeks intervening. If handicapping is to be anything but a sinecure, anything but a simple matter of arithmetic, such as subtracting two for a win; in fact, if the handicapper is to exercise any of the measure of golfing sense with which he may chance to be endowed, and in virtue of which, presumably, he was appointed to his office, then he was in every sense justified in reducing the improving player's odds; it was a just and reasonable reduction, and the only thing unreasonable about the whole matter is the player's grumbling. There is coming into general prevalence a stupid mechanical system of never cutting off men's handicaps except after a win; the consequence of which is that men grow unwilling to compete for the smaller club prizes for fear of having their odds cut down, as a penalty of success, at the big meetings. This is entirely the fault of

FIGHTING THEIR BATTLE OVER AGAIN

the wrongly based system of handicapping which has come into vogue. The essence of good handicapping is that everyone should have as near as possible an equal chance, quite irrespective of his wins in the past. There are certain prizes given for which previous prize-winners play under a penalty; these are on a different footing. The handicapper must take a general view of the rise and fall of the golfing barometer, accepting these recorded wins at their true worth, and no more —namely, as indexes, to be considered in conjunction with other indexes, of the height to which the mercury has reached.

On the other hand, the handicapper may find his difficulties in dealing with the improving player assume a quite opposite aspect. The improver, as we might call him, if the word were not already otherwise engaged—may win with his sixteen, and at the next meeting, though reduced to fourteen or lower, may win again. This will raise a terrible outcry against the handicapper; for everyone except the improver will deem himself hardly treated; and it will be in a measure a justifiable outcry, for it is probable from his having twice won that he was insufficiently reduced. It was an error of judgment on the part of the handicapper; and to exercise the requisite severity in pruning the odds of the rising player is one of the things that goes most to the heart of the humane handicapper, who will need to summon to his reinforcement the memory of such heroic examples of noble severity as the Iron Duke and the First Napoleon.

Certainly a handicapper will err greatly on the side of leniency if he give a man a point or two more because he 'has not played for so long.' Golf is indeed scarcely a thing which you can be said never to forget, like swimming, for it never becomes anything like so automatic; but it is a commonplace of golfing criticism that a man will often return to the game after weeks, months, or even years of abstinence, and at once fall, as if by magic, into his best game.

Again, we sometimes observe a grievous error in handicapping, some man winning with a considerable number of strokes in hand, and we are told the reason was that the handicappers did not know anything about him. So much the worse for the handicappers, is the answer : they ought to have made it their business to find out about him. But sometimes it happens that with the best will in the world it is not possible for the handicappers to arrive at any trustworthy 'line' about a stranger's play. In that case it becomes their duty to take care that he does not win ; and the stranger has nothing to complain of. If he honestly try to help the handicappers, it is almost impossible but that he should be able to indicate some player with whom they are familiar, and with whom he can place himself in some sort of golfing relation. But at all events it is obviously very hard upon all the players whose form is tolerably known that they should be put entirely out of the running because a stranger has come among them whose form is a mystery. Rather than run that risk, handicap the new comer out of it, and after a day or two's play he will soon settle down and his place will be found.

The despair of handicappers are those players who, from some paltry vanity or sort of delight at the satisfaction of seeing the scoring-card which has caused so much vexation floating in atoms down the breeze, habitually decline to record their score. Every instance of this immoral habit should be noted against them, together with every instance of their grumbling at their handicap, and a stroke deducted from their odds for each offence—at least, this is a useful menace to hold before their eyes. If put into literal execution, some pretty heavily handicapped gentlemen would soon find themselves in the position of scratch.

Each club should have a book, indexed and ruled in columns for names, dates, gross scores, handicap allowances, and nett scores, respectively, with a space for remarks on weather, disposition, and condition of the course, or what not. The index should contain, in alphabetical order, a list of the playing members of the club, and should refer to figures indicating the pages at which entries will be found of the performances of the player opposite whose name the figures stand. Thus, when a man's public form is wanted, for purposes of handicapping, it is merely necessary to look down the index for his name, turn up the pages indicated by the numbers standing opposite, and there you have 'the form at a glance.' The filling in of such a book will give but little trouble to the secretary or an assistant, and it will be a great aid, and a valuable means of saving wearisome researches, to the handicapping committee.

A handicap committee should be composed of as few members as possible, or they will talk endlessly instead of getting through their business; but it should include at least three different classes of players. These members, one from the highest, one from the lowest, and one from a medium class, will be probably quite sufficient, and in this comparatively small multitude of counsellors will be found a widespread wisdom of the ways and means of all sorts and conditions of golfers.

There is one last class of players which calls for the handicapper's especial attention—it is happily not a numerous class—those who are faulty as arithmeticians. Setting aside conscious fraud, which we may well hope to be very rare in competitions confined to amateurs, there can be no doubt that among the less gifted classes of golfers, whose figures to a hole are sometimes in the teens, there is a great scope for error. Some of the most single-minded of players—whose motives are above all suspicion—are notoriously faulty in addition; which, when it reaches double figures, is, indeed, no simple task. It is all very well to write at the back of the card that the strokes are to be marked as they are played. But the golfer is human, he is therefore careless; he often approaches the hole by a quite different route from his opponent whose score he is supposed to be recording—in fact, he often contents himself with taking his opponent's word for the figure, fraudulently filling in the 1, 2, 3, &c. after he has set down the total. Now it is not at all travelling out of their proper province for handicappers to dock off a point or two of the odds which their form would seem to justify in the case of notorious offenders of this order. But this must be done under pledge of most solemn secrecy ; for were the sufferer by the treatment to hear an inkling of its motive, he would either consider himself as a grossly insulted man or as for the future entirely freed from all responsibility with reference to the accuracy of his counting.

Taking one consideration with another, a handicapper's life is not a happy one.

CHAPTER XII

PROFESSIONALS AND CADDIES

BY H. G. HUTCHINSON

NE can divide into three classes those who derive a precarious subsistence from the game of golf : professional club-makers, professional players who eke out existence by work in the club-makers' shops, and professional caddies who would be professional players if they played well enough.

At most greens the hierarchy of the golfing profession is graded on this wise: The green-keeper, engaged by the club at a certain annual salary to look after the ground, arrange the tees, and read the Riot Act to small boys who play off the green with their irons, and generally to act as custodian. He will be the keeper of a club-maker's shop, in which he will probably do a certain amount of work himself at spare moments, and will usually have several men in his employ.

He will also be the overseer of one or more horny-handed sons of toil who, under his directions, roll, sweep and mow the greens and fill up iron-skelps and other wounds in the ground, at discretion. Besides this he will be open to engagements to play a round of the links when required, at a fixed fee, whether with skilled players or with tiros who need instruction.

Under him, in very indefinite control, which usually takes the form of a menace of reporting their misconduct to the club committee, will be ranged a number of professional players—a number varying in accordance with the demand—who mainly depend for their livelihood on engagements to play in foursomes with amateurs. The fees they derive from this source they supplement by job or time work in the club-maker's shop, on the one hand, or by carrying clubs, at a considerably lower wage than that which they receive for playing round, on the other. The ambition of the majority of these professional players is to one day rise to become keeper of the green at one or other of the many links now in existence in all parts of the United Kingdom.

The lowest stratum of professional golf consists, at most greens, of battalions of small boys, the caddies pure and simple, some of whom as they increase in stature will *develop through* the upper ranks of the profession, but the larger part, much to their profit, will at the proper age quit their somewhat capricious calling and be apprenticed to a trade. At well-organised clubs each caddie is invested with a badge as a species of good-conduct stripe, at the discretion of the green-keeper—with the secretary of the club as a judge of appeal—and it is a distinct breach of etiquette and of his duty towards other members of the club for a player to engage a boy who has temporarily forfeited this certificate of good conduct.

The High Priest of this hierarchy of professional golf is, beyond question, the custodian of the green for the Royal and Ancient Golf Club of St. Andrews—at the present time (and long may he continue to hold his office !) 'Old Tom' Morris. If not, possibly, the most lucrative, it is certainly the most distinguished position to which the golf professional proper can aspire.

We say the golf professional proper; for there are a certain number of club-makers, and smiths who forge iron heads with the skill of worthy descendants of Tubal Cain, who have never entered the lists with the professional players. There are others, again, who confine their business to the ball-making department. But all these artists, directly connected with and essential in the game of golf as their callings are, scarcely fall, nevertheless, within the ordinary conception of the term golf professionals.

From what has been said it will be sufficiently obvious that it is by no means every man, especially of those in that rank of life from which our professional players are drawn, that is able to adequately fulfil the manifold duties of custodian of the green at a popular golfing resort. He will need, in the first place, to be a man of not unpleasing manner, or strangers will naturally be disgusted at their reception ; for it is to him that they will probably first address themselves. He will need to have some knowledge of turf-cutting, and the technical knowledge generally necessary for keeping the turf on the putting-greens in fine order. He will need to be an observer of the growth of grasses. Thus Tom Morris has discovered that there is nothing like sand for links grass. If he sees an iron cut, he at once has it filled up level with sand, which experiment has convinced him encourages a growth of young grass. He will need to have a certain power of organisation and a moral influence over the forces—the caddies and professionals —who are more or less under his orders. And he will need to have a thorough knowledge of the theory and practice of the game of golf, so as to be able to tutor aright the young idea.

Again, he will need a business capacity for the proper management and development of his trade in clubs and balls. Points of difficulty anent golfing rules, and of delicacy anent golfing etiquette, will be often submitted to his arbitration, and he will need to decide these with both justice and judgment.

It needs scarcely to be added that the more general qualifications of sobriety, honesty, and industry are indispensable to his responsible situation. Finally, he must himself be a good club-maker, and be able to impart a fair measure of his own skill to his subordinates.

All these points considered, it is clear that it is a matter of no small difficulty to secure a really good green-keeper, and it is no less clear that a great measure of the comfort of the members of a club is dependent upon a good choice. A green-keeper's post is well paid, and there are now a great many openings, thus furnishing an inducement to steadiness, civility, and industry on the part of professionals, which were lacking in former years.

The professional, as we are now chiefly acquainted with him, is a 'feckless,' reckless, creature. In the golfing season, in Scotland, he makes his money all the day, and spends it all the night. His sole loves are golf and whisky. He works at odd times—job work or time work—in the shops ; but he only does it when reduced to an extremity. If he were but ordinarily thrifty, he could lay by in the autumn sufficient to carry him on through the season of his discontent, when no golf is. He can lightly earn seven and sixpence a day by playing two rounds of golf ; or, if he does not get an engagement, three and sixpence a day by carrying clubs. These are about the fees paid at St. Andrews and Musselburgh, which are the great manufactories of the professionals who go forth to many links as green-keepers. Many are engaged in a kind of body-service to their masters at a pound a week, which usually includes the advantage of a breakfast at their master's house, and the disadvantage of having to black his boots. In the medal weeks they pick up a little more, and an extra shilling or two comes into their pockets from bets which they make with little judgment, but which they seldom pay if they lose. They often sell with great advantage clubs to young players, who fondly imagine magical properties to dwell in the wand itself, rather than in the hands of the sorcerers who wield it. Occasionally they combine with golf-playing more general branches of industry, which they pursue in a spasmodic fashion. Thus, when we asked of one of them whether a brother professional had no other trade than that of golf, he replied, 'Ou aye ! he has that—he breaks stanes.'

For the most part, however, they are apt to be of that careless, not elevated character, which one could but expect of men who associate on terms of tolerable equality, but with far from equal means, with men who are spending money carelessly and rapidly, which they have made in scenes far remote from the professional's ken. The latter, therefore, concluding that the way to live life is to spend money as he sees his betters do, is reared in the midst of temptations. In the non-golfing time, his improvidence in the hours of plenty often brings him to very sore straits. But now that so many more openings are occurring for green-keepers, in the increase in the number of links all over England, we may hope to see these further inducements developing better habits in the professional class.

Yet they are by no means without their good qualities. The better ones amongst them are very loyal squires, and will support their master's interests, and, so far as possible, prowess, against all detractors. This does not interfere with the very freest criticism of his performances on their own part. The generality of them are superior to the amiable vice of flattery, and though Sir Walter Simpson states it as an essential quality in a good caddie that he should 'conceal his just contempt for your game,' you will be apt to find that insistence upon such a qualification will narrow your field of choice very severely. The Scottish caddie applies drastic treatment to your golfing diseases, as a rule—anæsthetics are not in his system, but very nasty tonics. 'Eh !' in a tone of deep disgust, 'yer eye was no within a foot of the ball.' They are very formidable critics, these grown-up professional caddies of the North ; and they are very useful 'coaches' of the unskilful golfer. Your caddie, if he be a good one, will speedily discover your besetting sin, and should be always ready to set you right when he sees you drifting into it. It is advisable, but not essential, that he should be a good player himself. Some of the best 'coaches' —the most skilful in the diagnosis of disease, in seeing 'what you are doing wrong'—are not, and never have been, in the first flight as players. The critical and the creative faculties are separable, though, as a rule, they coincide. But no caddie is a good one—worthy of the name, and of some three and sixpence a day—who does not give all his attention to setting you in the path of improvement. Want of keenness is the one great crime which we cannot forgive in these men-caddies. Such intelligence of appreciation is, of course, scarcely to be looked for from the little boys who carry clubs at sixpence a round or so on the Southern greens. But your higher scale of wages ought to buy you a human being bound body and soul to your interests. This is quite consistent with his passing the most candid, and even the rudest, remarks upon your game. Such may, indeed, be taken as an evidence of interest, and, as such, pardoned. You can hardly expect these hard, bitter gentry to appreciate the pain which they inflict on your cultured, sensitive cuticle, or the beneficial influence of a milder treatment. They have no nerves to speak of, and they do not see why you should. Their tonics, too, are often salutary. No, the crudest criticism is not to be feared so much as a withering indifference. The professional who carries your clubs like a machine, is the one who blights you like a upas tree. He who does not know where your ball is, does not even smile when you take the light iron where you ought to take the cleek ; does not know how many your opponent has played ; hardly knows, even, how the match stands—he is the man to be cashiered, and the rough, bitter, but interested critic to be taken to you and cherished in his stead.

Some caddies who for years have carried for the same master, seem to have taken the features of his game as factors in their own lives. They even tend to grow like their masters in face and carriage, and, without any regard to relative dimensions, are usually equipped in their master's cast-off clothes.

A CADDIE'S DUTIES

Once upon a time there was a caddie whose master's besetting sin was a snatching back of the club on the back swing. It had grown chronic, and chronic treatment was the only remedy. His caddie, therefore, was instructed, on each occasion of his master's addressing himself to the ball, to solemnly ejaculate, 'Slow back!' In course of time the master died, and the caddie was left survivor; but not without a heritage, for that inveterate habit of ejaculating 'Slow back!' refused to be eradicated. To the exasperation of many subsequent masters, by each of whom, in succession, he was forthwith incontinently dismissed, and to his own great mortification, he could not break himself of that croak of 'Slow back!' which prefaced, without respect of persons, each drive of each master. He lost all employment, and soon sank beneath the golfing horizon.

It is your caddie's business to find out how far you drive with each club; and since a life-long experience will have taught him the exact relative position to the hole of each blade of grass on the links, he ought to be always able to put into your hand the right club, almost without your asking for it. He will also know the idiosyncrasies of your play—to what extent he may allow you to 'greatly dare,' out of what lie you may be permitted to play with a brassy, and all such little niceties. Up to a certain point the best of them show very shrewd judgment; but their horizon is strictly limited. Exceptional instances, which have not come within their previous experience, are quite outside the scope of any but the very best. They work in a groove, but a groove that, so far as it goes, is very accurate; just as some men of very limited brain-power are very shrewd within their own narrow sphere of business. Their three great principles, on which they ring the changes, are, 'Don't press,' 'Keep your eye on the ball,' and, in approaching, 'Be up.' And these contain volumes of wisdom, always with the very large proviso that one be wise enough to interpret them aright.

But though it is legitimate and proper that a caddie thus

highly paid, as we are supposing, should supply upon these points his master's lack of experience, it is nevertheless pitiable to see the extent to which masters, many of whom really know better than the caddie, subordinate their volition to the latter's dictation. They do not seem to credit themselves with the intelligence of a tame rabbit; they do not even try to get away from the enervating influence; they are so much the creatures of their own paid servants, that if they lose their particular familiar they are helpless; they have lost all initiative; they do not know what club to take; they do not know how they ought to stand; they dare not trust their own judgment about 'the line' of an eighteen-inch putt; they are lost on the links like babes in a wood. Such subservience as this is lamentable; nevertheless, it is very common. Surely it is better to play one's own game, with reference to the subordinate only in a case of real difficulty, rather than to reverse the proper order of things, and transfer all the responsibility from the actual player to the paid assistant. There can scarcely, one would imagine, be any great satisfaction in holing a difficult putt when one of the chief points—the judgment of the line—has been referred to another. It seems almost like taking an unfair advantage over an opponent who may not be followed by an equally skilful adviser. This, however, is a point of etiquette, and custom, the queen of etiquette, has accorded it her august sanction.

Some of the very best players make their caddies indicate for them the line to the hole; but, apart from all other considerations, we would ask the golfer if he would not derive very greatly increased satisfaction from accepting upon his own broad back all the responsibilities which he should feel himself to have assumed when he struck from the tee the first ball of the match? It is scarcely conceivable that he could give any but an affirmative answer.

Activity is desirable in a caddie. He should be ever ready to run forward to the hole, to stand at it for your opponent, and thus prevent any possibility of his getting a good 'rub' by striking the staff of the flag. He should then be quickly at your side again, ready with your putter, and, if you persist in demanding it, his counsel. To have to hang over your ball, waiting for your caddie to come to you, is very irritating. Even more irritating, though happily less common, is it to see your opponent's ball strike the flag and lie dead, instead of going the length of its proper tether, some yards beyond the hole. Nevertheless some old men, whose age precludes any great speed of movements, are industrious, useful, hard-working caddies;

A GOOD CADDIE

and provided they are all this, are punctual at the start and have your clubs bright and clean, you cannot well expect much more.

But the caddie who ranges the links of the South is generally a very different being. He is commonly a small boy, escaped, or released, from attendance at Board School; and more inclined to revel in his freedom than to bestow any grave attention on your business. Alternate menaces and blandishments are generally necessary to stimulate his zeal to any tolerable pitch.

Yet he is very cheap ; and by talking to these little boys as if they were human beings, instead of treating them merely as little beasts of burden, they may be encouraged into very keen and intelligent partisanship. Of course they have not the technical skill of their more experienced brethren, but many a fine golfer could bear witness to good counsel occasionally received from the veriest *gamin*. These little boys ought always to be under the control of the green-keeper of the club. It should be at his discretion to issue to them badges entitling them to carry ; and if the rule be made that they are to be engaged only through him, the new-coming golfer will thereby be saved an infinity of annoyance from the pestering crowds that, at some links, surround him, all clamouring for employment.

For a good player, who is well acquainted with the green, it is very questionable whether boys are not preferable to men as caddies, apart from the matter of expense. As Sir Walter Simpson whimsically puts it, boys are 'more scoldable,' and their criticism is less formidable. A gaunt, disapproving man is a wet blanket to your efforts and spirits, but you go on your way unmindful of the best merited derision of a small boy. To instruct a beginner or to pilot a stranger round the course a grown golfing intelligence is a useful quality in the caddie ; but for the golfer who knows what he is about, has the pluck to play his own game, and is on his native heath, no species of caddie is so desirable as a bright active lad.

The metropolitan greens—Wimbledon and Blackheath—have developed a class of caddie peculiar to themselves. They, as a rule, unite the worst points of both the afore-mentioned classes. They are too big to scold, they are ignorant of golf, and they are expensive. But for the honour and glory of the thing, and the physical trouble, a man would do better to carry his own clubs. There are of course bright exceptions, but the typical instances are far from bright. The fact of the matter is that these are not really professional caddies. They may have no other profession, but if not they have no profession at all. For, as caddies, they are but loafers. The only condition under which the caddie's calling can be dignified by the name of a profession is that he should apply himself to it in the hope of rising. He must have ambition, or he will degenerate. And this is just what these metropolitan caddies are utterly without. They have no idea of handling a club efficiently, so that they can never achieve success as professional teachers or players ; and no one would ever dream of putting any one of the ordinary run of them into such a responsible position as the custodianship of a green.

The legitimate prizes of golf as a profession may be placed under three headings, though any two, or even all three, of these prizes are apt to fall into the same hands. First, in point of popular emulation, though not in point of emolument, is the achievement of notable success in playing the game ; which, combined with decency of manner and behaviour, implies fairly regular employment in the playing of matches, and the 'coaching' of neophytes. Second, the means of starting a club-making establishment, and of conducting it with success. And, third, appointment as custodian of a green.

For this latter appointment some at least of the qualifications essential to success in the two former departments are requisite; for no man, unless he be a good club-maker, or a good player —in all probability not unless he be both—can expect such an engagement. Club-making establishments, moreover, are seldom conducted except by the green-keeper, for few members of the golfing profession have sufficient capital or credit to set up for themselves without the pecuniary aid and assurance of patronage which this recognised position brings with it.

The great impetus which has of late years been given to the game of golf in England has opened up, as we have said, a far greater number of such opportunities than were formerly within the range of the practical politics of the profession. In another respect, however, the outlook is less bright than in former times. It is true that the competition of Eclipse golf balls and of the Silvertown Company has reduced the profits in this direction ;

but this is more than counterbalanced by the greatly increased demand for golfing material in all parts of the world. But it is in respect of the prizes for success in playing the game that the profession is suffering. Some years back, when poor 'Young Tommy' Morris and Davie Strath were at their prime, there used to be continual encounters between these two young heroes, stimulated by some small stake offered by an amateur who loved to see good golf. These were the chief opponents; but at all greens in the North there were constant professional matches on the *tapis*, in which various members of the profession would be engaged. Before them, again, when 'Old Tom' Morris was at his zenith, and Allan Robertson and the fathers of the present worthy generation of Dunns and Parks were at the height of their prowess, we hear of constant matches which thrilled the very marrow of the then discovered golfing world. But now such professional matches are but of occasional occurrence, and awaken but a lukewarm interest in our larger world. Why is this?

The reason is probably twofold. In the first place, a suspicion of foul play, a suspicion on the part of those who offered the prizes that they did not always get a genuine contest for their money, was no doubt a part of the reason. It need scarcely be said that no such accusation was ever laid at the door of any of those honourable professional players whom we have named; but in some cases a rumour was circulated, and this, combined with the growing tightness of money which contracted the purse-strings of former liberal patrons of the game, was not without its effect.

But probably a yet more potent factor in the conclusion was the great rise in the number, if not in the actual quality, of fine amateur golfers. In the increase of the quantity, it would be indeed strange if the quality also had not improved; and, hurling defiance upon all *laudatores temporis acti* who assert the contrary, we are prepared to affirm our conviction that it has—that the finest amateur talent of to-day is in advance of the finest amateur talent of the past. There are very many more players than formerly who devote a large share of the most athletic period of their life to the cultivation of the game of golf ; and this being so, it is but natural that out of this number there should arise some few who are competent to almost, if not quite, hold their own against the best professionals.

'Then why is it,' it will perhaps be asked, 'that no amateur has succeeded in winning the professional championship ?'

The professional championship, a 36-hole competition, is played over the greens of St. Andrews, Musselburgh, and Prestwick, in yearly rotation. It is the highest distinction of the golfing 'turf'—the *ne plus ultra*. And no amateur has ever won it.

The reason is undoubtedly this, that, though there have always perhaps been several amateurs capable of coping with the professionals on terms of fair equality, the supply of first-class professional talent is immensely larger. This will be readily seen by a glance at the list of competitors for the professional championships of many years past. The names of but three or four amateurs will be found in a field of some forty or fifty competitors ! It is not likely that in the presence of such odds an amateur would be found at the head of the poll.

Nevertheless it is probable that at any time the best professional is just a little bit the better of the best amateur. He has a staunch, dogged—almost brutal—perseverance. His lasting powers are so great. He lives more simply, despite temporary derangements in consequence of bad whisky ; his muscles are in hard-working order, and as for his nerves—where are they ? Well, they are there, but they are not upon the surface, as are the unfortunate sensibilities of the amateur.

Be all this as it may, however, it is probable that the rising interest which attaches to the play of amateurs has had an effect in diminishing the interest felt in professional matches and in proportionately diminishing the profits attached to professional play. There are money prizes in connexion with the professional championship, and to other tournaments open to professionals in various parts of the country ; but on the whole they are less than they used to be, and the majority live a precarious life, the soldiers of fortune, a capricious goddess who interferes greatly with the golfing sphere.

While the golfing talk of past days was mainly occupied with the achievements of the professional element, it is rather the names and doings of amateurs that are now the subject of discussion. This we may probably regard as a sign of good omen for the future of the game. Where a game falls too much within professional hands, it tends to lose that quality which is implied in the term 'sport.' We see this in the case of baseball in America, more conspicuously perhaps than in any other instance ; but we hear a similar complaint with respect to foot ball in the North of England, and it is certain that much of the active interest on the part of amateurs in the game of billiards is diverted into the passive rôle of playing spectators to the infinitely greater skill of professionals. It is ever a bad sign for the future of a game when the professional element becomes too predominant ; but that which is of good promise for the game of golf itself is not of good promise for the professor.

The profession offers prizes, as we have said, in the shape of engagements as keepers of golf greens, but otherwise its solid inducements are few and its temptations very many. Especially to be reprobated is the practice at some clubs of offering a 'drink' to a professional at the close of a round. If you leave him to himself there is no danger of his damaging his health by drinking too little. No golf professional is recorded to have died of thirst. On the other hand, the lives of many have been shortened and degraded by thirst too often satiated. Some of the clubs of the North would be greatly more pleasant places if a fixed price were authoritatively named for the recompense of professional caddies and players. There is a delightful uncertainty upon this point which more than the actual cost deters many from taking out a professional. The 'dour' silence in which he accepts your fee when you give him enough, and the sense of self-contempt for the moral weakness which prompts you to give him too much, are equally annoying with his open dissatisfaction and probable profanity if you give him too little.

On the whole, the professional is not a bad fellow. He has little morality ; but he has good, reckless spirits, a ready wit and humour which is only denied to the Scotch by those who do not know them, and he will show a zeal and loyalty in defending your performances behind your back—provided you overpay him sufficiently—very much at variance with the opinion which he expresses to your face. He is apt to be insolent in order to show you that he imagines himself to have some self-respect—which is a self-delusion—but if you can endure a certain measure of this, he is a good companion. Never, however, bet with him ; for so will it be best for him and best for you, as he is unlikely to pay you if he loses. This he is apt to do, for he is a bad judge of the merits of a golf match, a point which requires a delicacy of estimate usually beyond his powers.

So much for the rank and file of the profession. There are certain members of it whom every golfer calls to mind with esteem and even affection—Nature's gentlemen who never step out of their position, and yet never fail to make us feel that by right of courtesy they are equals with the best, men whose self-respect is no delusion. The beneficial influence upon the mass of the one or two of this type whom we find in the profession is almost inestimable, and it is our hope, and our expectation, that their example, combined with an increased wisdom in the method of treatment of the professional by his master, the amateur golfer, will in a few years lead to great improvement in the general morality and behaviour. It is, indeed, our belief that such an improvement is even now in progress.

It is singular, considering the proverbial thrift of the Scottish character, that, with every circumstance in his favour, the green-keeper so often fails to make any success of his club-making shop. It is purely from want of attention and business habits, from an importation of his breezy life upon the links into his little shop. He has been like the Homeric gods, who 'live easily,' but the Homeric gods would never have made a fortune in business. The professional club-maker must be better than they. Let him realise that a shop at a populous golf green may be made an important source of income, provided steady attention be paid to the work and to the workmen; but that, in order to make a good thing of it, it is of primary necessity to 'keep your eye on the ball.'

CHAPTER XIII

SOME CELEBRATED LINKS

BY H. G. HUTCHINSON

BELL ROCK LIGHTHOUSE

IN writing of some celebrated golf links, there is one point which is happily and incontestably settled for us—namely, with which we should commence. The links of St. Andrews —of the Royal and Ancient Golf Club of the East Neuk of Fife—holds premier place as indubitably as Lord's Ground in the kingdom of cricket. When two stranger golfers meet upon some neutral ground, one of the first questions that will pass from one to the other will most certainly be, 'Have you been to St. Andrews?'—and should the answer be in the negative, the questioner will immediately deem himself justified in assuming a tone of patronage which the other will feel he has no right to resent.

All the great mass of golfing history and tradition—principally, perhaps, the latter—clusters lovingly within sight of the grey towers of the old University town ; and, to most, the very name St. Andrews calls to mind not a saint nor a city, nor a castle nor a University, but a beautiful stretch of green links with a little burn, which traps golf balls, and bunkers artfully planted to try the golfer's soul.

This is the great excellence of St. Andrews links—the artful planting of the bunkers. Not, of course, that they were planted by any but Nature's hand; but planted by Nature, one would say, with an obvious artistic eye for the golfer's edification. Just around each hole they lie in wait for the unwary and unskilful ; and, along the course, just in such ambushes as to catch the ball that is not driven both far and sure. Kind Nature, too, has so laid out the ground that the holes can be, and are, placed at such distances from each other that every stroke tells—that is to say, that whereas at most links the majority of the holes are approachable with one or two full shots followed by an iron shot, at St. Andrews the majority of the holes are so disposed that they may be reached with two, or maybe three, real good drives. And the advantage of this, from the golfer's point of view, is that, whereas, in a hole at which an iron approach necessarily follows upon two good drives, the bungler who has foozled one of these drives may make up for it by taking a somewhat longer club for the approach shot than his opponent, and may be on the green in three, equally with the man who has played faultless golf; at St. Andrews, on the other hand, a weak or foozly drive means, in very many instances, a full shot lost—the two faultless drives will send the ball up on to the green, while the player who has foozled a shot will suffer his salutary and inevitable punishment in not being on the green in less than three.

The great point in which we are inclined to quarrel with St. Andrews as a golfing links is in the prevalence of banks and braes. Many of them one may avoid, but there are others so small, or so disposed, that it is the better wisdom to play to chance them, and it is very trying to the temper to see your adversary lying beautifully, a few yards back, while your own

THE WINDMILL, WIMBLEDON

somewhat better drive has finished up hard under a brae, hopeless for any other club than an iron. Yet it probably comes all right in the long run. At the end of the round luck has probably equalised itself. It is true that the St. Andrews links are much cut up by iron wounds. With the enormous amount of play which goes on during the autumn it is wonderful that they are not more so. Indeed a ground of more strictly golfing quality—*i.e.* of more sandy nature—would never stand the wear and tear to which St. Andrews is subjected; but after all to a really first-class golfer a cuppy lie is of very little consequence.

Some of the putting-greens are not what they should be—notably the 'heathery hole' and the end hole—but others, again, are things of beauty. The green of the 'hole o' cross' is probably the best in all the world of golf. The eleventh hole—the 'short hole coming in'—and 'the road hole'—the seventeenth hole—are two very crucial tests—the two points in the course where more chances of medals have been ruined than at any others. The short hole coming in is, we may say, on a calm day, but a cleek shot; but such a nervous one! There is the shelly bunker ten yards to the left of the hole—the Eden river fifteen yards beyond it—and that little round trap of a Strath's bunker not three yards nearer you and to the right of it, with all the ground breaking in toward the bunker! Many a stout-hearted golfer, if his score is good, will take his light iron and play a half shot to the left, and short, giving himself a clear run up for his next—and many more would have done better had they done so; but never, in a scoring round, play it how you will, will the stoutest-hearted fail to draw a breath of relief when that slantwise-lying little catchy hole is over. Then we may go on, sailing and slogging, till, steering along beside the railway, we have accomplished the 'corner of the Dyke,' and are coming to that dreaded seventeenth—so near the end, and so dangerous! For after we have piloted our way through, or round, or over the corner of the wall enclosing the Station-master's garden, and the little bunker on the left, and have turned up towards the right, with our seconds, then we see that little Garden of Eden—very different from the river so called—where the hole is, lying between Scylla and Charybdis (a dread vision such as may excuse any anachronism in our similes !), that horrid little round bunker to one side of it, and that hopeless hard road on the other. And the canny golfer we see approaching it in instalments, and the bold spirit, taking his fate in his hand, going for glory or the grave.

After that, the last hole is child's play. As long as we do not make an egregious top into the burn, or an equally egregious slice into a kitchen area of one of the houses on the links, we may go forward undeterred, and finish our medal round beneath the Club windows and the blessing of old Tom Morris, the guardian angel of the last hole.

And all the world is watching to see us do it ! Yes, call it folly, vanity, what you will, it is this that lends to golf at St. Andrews half its pleasure—the feeling that you are doing the right thing, the thing that has been the great absorbing interest of the whole atmosphere for years, the thing that is the great local interest of to-day. It makes a difference ; and St. Andrews is devoted to golf as no other place in the world is. The very houses and streets are called by names derived from the game. It is hard to believe but that the limbs of St. Andrew's cross have sprouted into golf clubs.

There has lately been a great upsetting of things at St. Andrews. A slashing young professional, Hugh Kirkcaldy by name, has done the round in seventy-four strokes, and the previous best was seventy-seven, by young Tommy Morris, after twice tieing. The world went on much as before, but St. Andrews felt that this was very stupid of the world. Really it is quite an epoch-making score, and it raises afresh the much-vexed question, ' Are the St. Andrews links getting easier ; and if so, how much ? ' They are undoubtedly getting very much easier —in a sense—and so are every other links in the kingdom. The whins have been, and are being, so trodden and hacked away that the course is very much broader. Therefore to a wild driver the course may be, on an average, a stroke a hole even easier. But the man who goes round St. Andrews links to-day in anything under eighty—much less in seventy-four—is not a wild driver. Whatever he may be on most days, on the exceptional day on which he does this extraordinary performance he never, we may say, drives a ball off the line. Perfect play— aided by luck—is a necessary condition of such a score ; and to perfect play it makes not the slightest difference that there may be the thirty or forty yards, or more, of clear ground on each side of the straight course. He has nothing to say to all that spare ground. It is as if it did not exist for him. Therefore, for these phenomenal scores we may say that this widening of the course makes practically no difference whatever. But, what it does is this—it multiplies very largely the number of *respectable* scores, of scores between eighty and a hundred, and upwards. In fact, Mr. Glennie's score of eighty-eight, which was for so long a record for the St. Andrews medal, was doubtless one which at that time was very much more than merely 'respectable,' under the conditions of greater accuracy then requisite. And the lower we go in the scale of play the greater the difference which this widening of the course will make.

In this we touch a weak point in the links of St. Andrews, more especially as a school for young players. The actual course is broad—very much broader than in old days—and the whins at the side of the course are in many cases very poor and patchy. It thus happens that there are many very tolerable lies off the course altogether, and all these facts (the broadness of the course, the chance of a good lie off the course, and the many chances of a bad lie on it) tend to encourage a slogging style, a style the great aim of which is distance with comparative indifference to direction. There is not a sufficient premium on keeping straight. Hence we see the golfing youth of modern St. Andrews sacrificing everything to length of driving, and developing a tremendous slashing style which is the direct consequence of the aforesaid conditions, but which is not a paying style over the links all through the country. We are not now contrasting St. Andrews with any particular links, but rather with the ideal links, to show in what details it falls short of absolute perfection and of its own approach to that perfection in the days before it was so much played over. On the other hand, it is not so greatly to be regretted, as many think, that the bad and cuppy lies along the course are numerous, for these tend to bring up the standard of golf by teaching golfers to force the ball away out of these lies.

There is also no links which so well teaches every kind of approach shot. Approaching with the putter and approaching with a lofting stroke from the iron are necessary at every links, but there is no links which so often calls into play the power of running the ball up with the iron. The reason of this is that many of the putting-greens are on a plateau with a steep grassy bank. Before this bank is reached the ground is generally too rough to admit of the use of the putter, and the ground of the putting-green being hard, it is often impossible to stop a pitched-up ball so dead that it will not run over the other side of the green. Then the running iron shot comes into play—the ball is skimmed over the rough ground, and sent running up the steep face on to the green. Bob Martin plays this stroke with great perfection with his cleek, but most prefer to use the iron.

Certainly the chief drawback to golf at St. Andrews is one which no true golfer can genuinely regret—namely, that there is too much of it. Not only do the links get congested from the number of matches, but the first few holes are complicated by shoals of schoolboys, all with cleeks and time-worn golf balls, all embryo medal winners, so that, at times, driving from the first tee is scarcely less dangerous to life and limb than driving through Threadneedle Street. Nevertheless, no golfer can deem himself fairly worthy of the name until he has paid at least one visit to St. Andrews. At that great head-quarters he will imbibe all that is best in the spirit of the game ; will see it there, in a degree which no other place can match, the pastime which is dear to the hearts of the people.

Yet nearer to the smoke of Auld Reekie, on the links of Musselburgh, we may see the game received with scarcely less interest by the great mass of the populace. That was a great occasion there when Bob Fergusson had to do each of the last three holes in three a-piece to tie for the championship—and did it! It was growing quite dusk, and from one side to the other the course was lined with a dense mass of spectators, gentlemen of learning, and top-hatted, from Edinburgh, the modern Athens, shoulder to shoulder with grimy miners, who had climbed from the bowels of the earth to see the play.

And it is a good links, too, although so narrow, calling out all the best qualities of the golfer. A links, too, which is sanctified by the memory of many a fine match of old days, when Allan Robertson, and the Parks and Dunns of a previous generation, and old Tom Morris were the heroes of their time. It is there that, besides many other noteworthy clubs, the Honourable Company of Edinburgh Golfers have their club-house, and play their 'dinner matches'—matches to which zest is added by stakes large enough to promote interest, yet not large enough to cause ill feeling, wagered over their wine at their dinners in Edinburgh. And it is a links which is a fine test of golfing prowess—though there be but nine holes. Yet the first three call for long strong driving, following, roughly, the course of the road, which forms the hazard upon the one side, while on the other are bunkers and whins which, alas! are fast going the way of all whins, so that they need the driving to be sure and straight, as well as far. Then, when we have reached 'Mrs. Forman's,' the third hole, with perhaps a visit to 'Lord Shand's bunker' by the way, we turn to our left, seawards, and leaving the clayey ground of the nature of the first five holes at St. Andrews, we come up along truer links turf, close beside—too close occasionally, if we heel our ball—the sea.

There is this parallel, in the change in the nature of the soil, after the first few holes, between Musselburgh and St. Andrews—nor need our parallel stop here. Whereas at

St. Andrews, at the fifth hole, we find ourselves in danger of that parlously-named bunker, 'Hell' (wherein we may observe the said bunker was much maligned at its presumably fiery baptism, since it affords often a fair good lie), at Musselburgh, shortly after turning seawards, we have trouble to avoid a bunker named 'Pandemonium.' Nor is Lord Shand the only eponymous hero of the golfing world; for have we not at St. Andrews, besides the before-mentioned 'Strath's bunker,' 'Tam's Coo,' 'The Principal's Nose,' 'Walkinshaw's Grave,' and others? Which St. Andrews bunkers, we may add, are nearly ideals of what bunkers should be; for whereas a good player can almost always get out of them in one, it will almost always cost him a full stroke to do so.

So, after 'Pandy' we go up to a fairly long stretchy hole beside the sea, and then come to the last three which Bob Fergusson holed, on that memorable occasion, in three a-piece, but which the best of us can scarce hope to achieve in like number; for, though we may reach the last and the third last in one a-piece, the second last, by the gasworks, will need a full drive and an iron shot, and we shall not do amiss if we hole it in four, and if our total for the nine is somewhere near forty. The record for the smallest score on Musselburgh, of amateurs or professionals, is held by Mr. Walter de Zoete, singularly enough, because he has played there but little, and has thus added another piece of testimony to the glorious uncertainty of the game.

Almost in the heart of Edinburgh, in these days of its extension, is Bruntsfield links, once the scene of much fine golf, but where few matches are now played, and those few much to the peril of the populace.

Almost equally accessible from Edinburgh, with Musselburgh, are the sporting little links of North Berwick. North Berwick itself can scarcely quarrel with us for calling them little, although there are the full eighteen holes (which, following the St. Andrews initiative, is commonly held the proper complement). But many of the holes are such very little ones.

Little as they are, however, they are wonderfully full of incident. There is the first, 'Point Garry,' high up above you, with every prospect, unless almost perfectly played, of your ball rolling down a steep place into the sea. Then at the next hole you are most apt to find yourself by the sad sea waves, if you heel at all ; or if you pull, to be under the garden wall of St. Anne's house. Then comes a hole on a little plateau most exasperatingly difficult to stay on—after which a hole, which is just a comfortable drive, in a little triangle formed by a wall and two bunkers. Then we play a cleek shot into an angle of a wall, for our next hole, and then a full iron shot over two walls and the corner of a fir-wood. This brings us to the 'Shipka Pass' hole—a very narrow course between the wall which skirts the wood and the sandhills which line the sea-shore. It is only a cleek shot, but any error in line or distance is fraught with disaster. Then, another little hole—just an iron shot in the angle of the wood and a fence of a field. So that, altogether we have in succession five holes which on a calm day may be easily reached in a stroke a-piece, and we begin to forget what our driver feels like. The last two holes out are rather uninteresting, though there is a chance of getting into a quarry in one of them and into a burn in the other—and so we have finished the ten holes out and start upon the eight of the home-coming. The second in gives a pretty little pitch for the second shot, just over a wall, with sandhills beyond, and then we come to what to the stranger is one of the most sensational shots in golf. The high sandhills in front curtailing your horizon, you have to harden your heart to drive, as it seems, into the midst of the German Ocean ; but instead, if you have played on the line laid down for you, you will find that you have carried a little corner of the beach, which bays in, and are lying on the putting-green of a hole protected by sandhills from the waves which are splashing on the other side of them. If your heart fails you and you drive to what looks something more like *terra firma*, to the right, you will find yourself wedged up somewhat too firmly against the too solid masonry of the wall of the wood—for we are again now passing through the 'Shipka.'

Then comes a cleek or iron shot which must pitch just over another wall, so far and no further—and then a full drive or brassy shot to carry you just over a bunker escarpment not inaptly called 'the Redan.' Two more holes—of respectable length, these—bring us again on the height of 'Point Garry,' thence to drive off into space, gravitating in 'the season' into crowds of children and nursemaids, for the home hole beside the Club. The putting-greens are very good and true, though small, the soil being of the proper sandy quality. The lies through the green are execrable—but then there practically is no 'through the green.' The second, sixteenth and seventeenth holes are the only ones at which it makes a scrap of difference whether you are able to use a wooden club for your second. All other holes may be reached in one and an iron, or one. In fact, the course is practically all hazards except the putting greens; but there are degrees of perdition in these hazards, a sandy, benty lie being preferable to being wedged in under a wall; and as the putting-greens are generally within reach of the tee, it does not much matter what sort of turf the course is made of. And it is in the shortness of its holes and the little pitch shots over its walls that the beauty of North Berwick, as a golf links, consists; as well as its weakness. There is no better school for 'approaching' in the world. In fact, you are always 'approaching'—even off the tee. Accordingly we see that North Berwick has developed probably the best approacher, with the pitching shot off a mashy, in the golfing world— namely Mr. J. E. Laidlay, who is in fact quite unsurpassable by any with all iron clubs.

But if North Berwick is the best place for approaching, it is one of the very worst for driving. You might just as well leave your driver at home. If you are an even medium driver, it is scarcely ever in your hand.

Another natural consequence of the shortness of the holes is that North Berwick links gets much blocked. It is a

THE SEA HOLE, ELIE

favourite watering-place, and also the scene of the golfing recreation of a large number of the Edinburgh bar and men of learning and business. And the waiting becomes often tedious. But there is a beautiful view to amuse one—a blue sea with dotted islets here and there, steamers passing up the Forth, and, opposite, the shores of Fife. A happy contrast is it, in this respect, to both St. Andrews and Musselburgh, from whose links we see but a dour grey sea unrelieved by islands, and an uninteresting surrounding scenery. Scenery is not, of course, golf; but golf is a pleasanter recreation when played in the midst of pleasant scenery.

Then, from North Berwick, you may make excursions to the links of Gullane and Luffness, within an easy drive. The last named are very fine golf, and the chances are that you have them to yourself, save for the rabbits and the plovers, and the solitude is an agreeable change from the crowd at North Berwick.

But going along those shores of Fife which we see from North Berwick, and long before we come to the Royal and Ancient links of the East Neuk, we come to the links of Elie, not greatly celebrated in golfing history, but deserving of fame both for their intrinsic excellence and for the many sterling good golfers of which they have been the nursery. For, not to mention others, it is the home green of the Simpsons, a very prominent name in the annals of professional golf of to-day, and of Douglas Rolland, who is perhaps the longest driver of the day. One, if not more, of the Simpsons has emigrated to Carnoustie, a links which the eye can just make out, on a clear day, across the Firth of Tay, from St. Andrews. It is a fine links, this—where the men of Dundee do the chief part of their golfing—of true sandy quality of turf, with high, menacing sandhills, and a burn twisting and turning about, over which you have to play many times in each round.

Northward again, upon the East coast, are the links of Montrose, a notable golfing course, good but narrow; and, northward again, Aberdeen, Dornoch, up even into the Orkneys, has the game won its way into local affections. All the Scottish coast is begirt by links, of more or less celebrity. There is no space to even name them all.

Upon the Mull of Kintyre, near Campbeltown, the glories of the links of Macrihanish are sung by all who have been so far afield to visit them. Nor should we omit mention of the King James VI. Golf Club, which plays upon the North Inch of Perth. But, descending upon the Ayrshire coast, we come to a links of more widely known fame—Prestwick, to wit.

For years Prestwick was celebrated as a twelve-hole course. It went dodging in and out among lofty sandhills. The holes were, for the most part, out of sight when one took the iron in hand for the approach; for they lay in deep dells among these sandhills, and you lofted over the intervening mountain of sand, and there was all the fascinating excitement, as you climbed to the top of it, of seeing how near to the hole your ball might have happened to roll. There is still a measure of this pleasurable uncertainty—there are still several holes thus disposed in hollows; but now that the course has taken unto itself the full-blown dignity of eighteen holes, comprising a deal of ground newly taken in, there is less of the backwards and forwards and cross work among the sandhills. It was inevitable that there should have been many, when the new ground was first taken in, who loudly proclaimed that 'Prestwick was ruined,' that 'the new holes were not golf' (which, probably, was quite true), and that 'they never would be golf' (which has since proved itself remarkably untrue). The third hole at Prestwick is perhaps the most noteworthy. A full tee shot brings you within some thirty yards of that famous bunker, with great shored-up, bluff face, the Cardinal's Nob. You will find youself with a good lie, and a fine drive will take you well on towards the hole; but if you happen to foozle, woe betide you. You will be ploughing in the sands, or playing a species of golf which seems to have been crossed with racquets against the great beams which prop up His Holiness' sandy nob. Or if you play a weak heeled shot to the low ground on the right, you will find your ball—or, more probably, lose it—in the rapid running waters of a burn. But if you have boldly and skilfully flown the face, a little iron shot will take you up to the hole, close up to the wall, over which you drive off, from the tee for the next hole, on to this much spoken of 'new ground.' You go along flat ground, with a burn to your right and bents to your left, for the distance of some two full shots (on the return journey this hole is enlivened by the putting-green being just over the wall you have just now

THE HIMALAYAS, PRESTWICK

driven over). And now, teeing on the brink of the burn, your next shot is over—let us hope over !—the mighty Himalayas. Such is the name not inappropriately given to these lofty sandhills. The hole is but the distance of a full cleek shot; and when you have climbed to the top of the sandhills, having crossed the burn by a wooden foot bridge, you may hope to see your ball lying comfortably on the putting-green of the hole. Five flattish holes of maybe somewhat doubtful interest, yet each a fair and sound test of golf, bring us to almost the same spot again, where we tee to again send our ball on its return journey soaring over the Himalayas. A full shot this time—no cleeks or half-measures, for beyond, at the far foot of the sand mountains, we remember that there runs that deep rushing burn. So we send our caddies forward—to the mountain top—and if we have struck a good long ball they will shout back the joyful news of 'over!' and with a full iron shot we may reach home to the hole. And then we travel back betwixt bents and burn, back to the hole just over the wall—and on to the old ground again.

And, we may ask, are not these flatter holes, which we have said to be of somewhat doubtful interest, on the far side of the Himalayas, almost a truer test of golf than those which lie in the dells of the sandhills? For, after all, the greater part of the fascination in these holes is in the uncertainty. We hurry up, all eagerness, to see which of the two similarly played shots —say to the seventeenth hole, for instance, which, more than any other, is typical of the old class of Prestwick holes—will have rolled down nearer to the hole. There is excitement and there is fascination in this—in the very uncertainty of it; but though uncertainty is the salt of golf, such a degree of uncertainty as this is not conducive to bringing to a fine test relative golfing merit. Nevertheless whatever we may say with respect to the comparison between the eighteen-hole Prestwick of to-day with the twelve-hole Prestwick of days gone by, it is certain that Prestwick need not fear the result of comparison with any links now extant. The putting-greens are mostly very good, and the lies through the green very fair. The course is full of incident and variety, and the scenery, with Arran, Ailsa Craig, the Heads of Ayr, and all the famed beauties of the estuary of the Clyde in the distance, is unsurpassable. Finally, it has the great advantage of being the property of the club, whose members and their friends have the exclusive right of playing upon it. The greater number of links both in Scotland and England are common ground where the populace have an equal right with the devotees of golf.

Only about half a mile from the end hole at Prestwick is the end hole of the Troon links, which have come into prominence chiefly by the liberal encouragement given by the Troon Club to professional golf competitions.

St. Andrews, Musselburgh, and Prestwick take it in annual succession to be the arena for the contest for the professional championship. The amateur championship is a far more recent institution, and has been played, so far, at St. Andrews, Prestwick, and at one English links, viz. Hoylake. It is on the Hoylake links that the members of the Royal Liverpool Golf Club pursue the royal and ancient game, and they are the scene of much good golf. For, in addition to the purely local talent, which is represented principally by the prowess of Mr. John Ball, Junior, Hoylake, close to Liverpool, though on the Cheshire side of the Mersey, is excellently situated as a halfway house for the meeting ground of Scottish golfers who venture so far southward, and of English golfers and the many Scotsmen whose head-quarters are in London.

And the links of Hoylake are associated, in the mind of every golfer who has played upon them, with the most perfect putting-greens in all the world. Though in summer of a glassy keenness, they are so beautifully true that more long putts, well judged in point of strength and direction, are held at Hoylake than on any other links. The features of Hoylake links are these putting-greens, the hedges which bound the course, and the little cops, or low banks, just over which two of the holes are placed. Playing to the first hole at Hoylake the great point of difficulty is to pitch, either with your second drive or with a short iron shot as your third stroke, over a sandy ditch, and not to run over the putting-green on the far side. Thence onward, you are mainly occupied with trying to keep out of fields which, with their hedges, bound the course on one or both sides; the other side, in the former case, being defended by sandy ground much honeycombed with rabbit-holes. Nine holes, thus accomplished, bring you within a short shot of the first house of the watering-place of West Kirby, and thence you return, betwixt the fields and the rabbit-holes, to the home hole in front of the hotel and club-house at Hoylake.

This general description has not been without a suggestion that it is very essential, for the successful negotiation of the Hoylake course, that you should drive straight. And this, in point of fact, is the main requisite for a good score at Hoylake. It matters less that you should drive far than that you should not meander off the course, for this will almost inevitably land you in serious trouble. You may even, at most holes, top your ball from the tee with perfect impunity, except, of course, for the loss of distance. And this is likewise noticeably the case at St. Andrews. Although distance is there so all-important, still a topped ball in most instances fails to meet with its deserved measure of punishment. Herein these courses show a marked contrast to the links of Prestwick and North Berwick, and to the English links which we shall shortly mention, of Westward Ho, Sandwich, and, in most cases, Wimbledon. And here, too, we see the reason of a great divergence in opinion with regard to the relative difficulty of the species of links thus compared. For we often hear it said, by unskilful players, that the St. Andrews course is infinitely easier than many a course—say, for example, Westward Ho—for which the lowest score on record is considerably lower than the lowest on record at St. Andrews. And the reason for this is, that at Westward Ho, which we are taking as an illustration, many a topped ball meets with dreadful punishment which, at St. Andrews, would go unscathed. But the good player, who rarely tops his ball, knows that by reason of the comparative shortness of the Westward Ho course (we are speaking of it rather as it was before its recent alterations) it is possible to hole it in an appreciably less number of strokes than the lengthy though less hazardous course of St. Andrews.

Also near Liverpool, upon the Lancashire side, are the links of Blundellsands, whose fame is quite eclipsed by that of their Cheshire rival.

Hoylake we have indicated to be somewhat similar, in respect of its comparative flatness, to St. Andrews and to Musselburgh ; but when we go South in England, to the links of the Royal North Devon Golf Club, at Westward Ho, we find a course which recalls the broken, and, in parts, mountainous nature of Prestwick, Carnoustie, and North Berwick. True, we do now but play over the lower lying spurs of that great ridge of sandhills known as the 'Alps,' over whose summits we used to drive in days long past. Yet the Westward Ho course is probably better golf to-day, in consequence of recent changes, than it ever was. The first three holes occupying some ground in old days unutilised, have enabled the course to be elongated, and stretched, and straightened out of its somewhat too complicated, criss-cross mazes. The new holes, though flattish, are fine golf, and the fourth hole brings us into the country of great sand bunkers, with precipitous bluff sandy faces, and of the strong sharp rushes, which have been the features from of old of the Westward Ho course—a course very full of hazard and of incident, where the most condign punishment visits the ball which is not perfectly played, both in point of distance and direction. This we may say is to-day the main characteristic of Westward Ho—that whereas on most links it is sufficient to keep straight (there being a certain course up the whole length of which it is safe to play), at Westward Ho, on the contrary, it is general necessary to pick out a certain *spot*—not merely a certain *line*—to which to drive the ball. And, the ball once driven there, what a blessed reward is ours! For the lies throughout the green at Westward Ho are better than those at any links in England or Scotland. On the other hand, it is but just to say, having ventured upon a comparison, that there is a weakness about Westward Ho in that the outlines of the bunkers are not sufficiently defined. Though precipitous on certain sides, these bunkers have usually as many wide mouths, belching forth wind-swept sand upon the green, as there are points to the compass. Hence, a ball which has fairly carried the bunker itself will often be found in an even worse lie, in this blown sand, than the ball that has been bungled into the heart of the bunker. Nevertheless, as a general rule, the ball that has been well struck from the tee will be rewarded with a very perfect lie, while that which has been topped will suffer a cruel fate. There is at almost every hole a carry from the tee—and the finish to the home hole, just over the burn and in front of the Club House, is probably the prettiest in all golf. Moreover, the alteration in the course which has brought the home hole across the burn has brought the commencement of the links and the Club House itself within half a mile or less of the lodging-houses at Westward Ho—a vast improvement over the old tedious walk, or jolty drive of a mile or more, alongside the famous Pebble Ridge.

It was at Westward Ho that golf took its fresh start in England, after dragging on for years and years a somewhat precarious existence under the auspices of the antique club at Blackheath. Indeed its success, in the struggling days of its infancy, was not a little due to the support it received from members of the Blackheath Club, under the leadership of their moving spirit, the late Mr. George Glennie, sometime captain of the Royal and Ancient Golf Club of St. Andrews.

The new life of English golf thus started at Westward Ho received its next development at Hoylake, which was followed by golf over Wimbledon Common under the auspices, originally, of the London Scottish Volunteers. Hence arose the London Scottish Golf Club, which so grew and prospered, with the support of the many Scotchmen in London, that its needs developed a demand for free action which it found in the secession of a large body of its members from the original society to form another club called the Royal Wimbledon at the other end of the common. The two now carry on a mutual struggle for existence, though the new club has taken decidedly premier position.

Wimbledon Common, familiar to very many as the scene of the annual rifle shooting competition (for which a new site is now in requisition), is of a wonderfully wild aspect when it is considered how near it is to the metropolis. In places the

THE POND, WIMBLEDON

golf course runs—no broader than a highway—through a wilderness of 'whins' more than breast-high. Then, again, you drive over great ravines full of alders and birches and jungle, like a Highland glen. Then there is a large pond to drive over; out of which, when drained, it is reported that a quite impossible number of golf balls are salvaged. The most English feature in the scenery is a windmill, a very salient point in your driving directions.

And on Wimbledon Common, on the three days a week on which golf is permitted, a very great deal of it is played, and of very good quality—by the many good golfers whose business or pleasure makes the metropolis their home. But the ground is very far from perfect. It is so hard and clayey, it is so cut up and kicky, the putting-greens are so uneven and pitty, it is even flinty and stone-roady. In fact, it is almost an insult to the game to dignify it by the name of golf. Rather may we call it a wonderful substitute for the game within so short a distance of Charing Cross.

Now Hoylake, Westward Ho, and Wimbledon are all eighteen-hole courses; but even within shorter radius of Charing Cross than the latter lie the Blackheath links, the scene of the play of the oldest known golf club in the kingdom, of no more than seven holes. But in the course of these seven holes is one which we may safely say to be the longest hole that the genius of the golfer has conceived. When we say that it is scarcely possible to reach it in three full drives, that it is most exceptional to be able to take anything but an iron to more than one shot, at most, after the tee shot, and when it is said that this hole, at its fullest length, has once been holed in three strokes, it will be seen that beside this feat all the recorded wonders of short holes holed in one fade into insignificance. Long powerful driving, and strength in jerking from heavy lies, are the main requisites for success at Blackheath, of which, as of Wimbledon, it may be said that it is a wonderful substitute for golf so near to London, and so surrounded by houses. At Blackheath, the historic, flinty links, you are allowed to play every day of the week ; but golf is practically given over on Saturday afternoons in favour of the winter footballers and summer cricketers. Blackheath, moreover, is the only links on which you habitually play with a fore-caddy, who runs ahead with a red flag, as if you were a traction engine, to scare away the nursemaids and to see that your ball is not stolen by a boys' school. In addition to these living hazards, the chief obstacles are lamp-posts, wooden seats, and roads, and footpaths. The club contracts for a sovereign a year for wear and tear of gas lamps broken by golf balls, and the agreement is probably in the club's favour. Inside the glass of a gas lamp is a lie about which we have not presumed to offer instruction. At neither Wimbledon nor Blackheath is there any sand—that is to say, the soil is not of a sandy nature, as is true links soil—therefore there are no bunkers, properly so called. This may indeed be said of all inland links—such as Malvern, Worcester, and even Eastbourne, which, though so near the sea, is on down turf, with a chalky subsoil.

But there is turf of the true golfing quality on the course of the Royal Isle of Wight Golf Club, at Bembridge—only, unfortunately, there is rather too little of it. Bembridge is a nine-hole course, and these nine holes are so full of crossing that but a small number of players can be accommodated with comfort. But the turf is good, the bunkers are good, and the putting-greens are good. The holes are shortish, but sufficient for the delectation of all but the most slashing of the young school of golfers ; and when there are not too many players the golf at Bembridge is hard to beat.

Further along the coast, within eight miles of Ramsgate, are the links of Sandwich, the latest discovery, of any note, of the golfing pioneer. Their discovery was hailed with great blowing of trumpets by all who had a share therein ; but, in justice, we must say that they fulfil the first condition of advertisement—viz. that the article advertised should be good. The first five holes at Sandwich are so good that, in our opinion, they are nowhere excelled ; and, throughout, they show a capacity for length—for calling into requisition strong

THE MAIDEN, SANDWICH

driving and long carrying power—such as no other links save St. Andrews rivals. There is, moreover, far severer punishment for devious driving and for topped shots than at St. Andrews. But unfortunately the later holes, with the exception of the last two, are by no means of equal excellence to the first five. For all the seaward portion of the links is of a mossy nature of soil, and cuts up greatly, affording soft lies and crumbly putting-greens. The feature of Sandwich links we may perhaps say to be the fifth hole—a drive, or brassy shot over the mountainous sandhill known as the Maiden. If you happily soar over this, you may find your ball lying in a little hollow close beside the hole; but should you top or foozle, there commences, indeed, the battle of Bunker's Hill—none can say in how many the finest player can hope to extricate himself.

Brief as is the history of the Sandwich links, and the St. George's Golf Club, it includes—thanks to the liberal prize-giving of its members—certainly as representative a gathering of professional talent as has ever been seen in the whole of golfing history; and far superior in both numbers and quality to anything ever before seen South of the Tweed. This took place in the autumn of 1888, when, in spite of cold, stormy weather, the professors were nearly unanimous in a favourable verdict on the new links.

Also of less or greater favour with metropolitan golfers are the links of Felixstowe and of Great Yarmouth, both good golfing courses—but chiefly happy after the manner of those societies whose 'annals are dull.' And, further northward, almost back to the home of the royal and ancient game, in Northumberland, we may especially name the links of Alnmouth, where is no mean local talent, and where, besides, has taken place many a notable professional competition.

We should not close this chapter without a word of apology to those many links, both in Scotland and England, of greater or less celebrity which our space precludes our mentioning, but which do good service nevertheless in fostering the game and bringing up good golfers to do it honour.

CHAPTER XIV

SOME CELEBRATED GOLFERS

By H. S. C. Everard

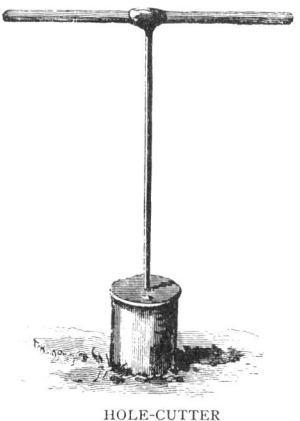

HOLE-CUTTER

THE history of golf shows that the game has been played for at least four hundred years ; but even if any records survived of doughty champions of the middle ages—and, so far as the writer knows, they do not—their performances would probably be regarded with less interest than those of latter-day players, who are known either personally or by reputation to the present generation; to these, therefore, we may confine our attention. It may be convenient to divide our celebrities into the two classes, Professionals and Amateurs, dealing with them in the order named. In looking back, then, some sixty years or so, the foremost figure that strikes the eye is undoubtedly the celebrated Allan Robertson: not that there were no fine players before his day—far from it, but probably it may be said, without prejudice to their memory, that none of them were so successful as he was in purely scientific execution ; indeed, there are not wanting some who declare that in this respect he stands alone even up to the present day, holding as unique a position in the annals of golf as does Roberts in those of billiards, and that, could he rise up now in the pride of his strength, he would still be the superior of any living player. Whilst rendering every justice to Allan, however, it may be remarked that those who claim for him this pre-eminent position are usually found to have a tendency, in comparing his skill with that of other noted players, to say, 'Oh, if the links were as difficult now as they were then, no one would come near him;' thus leaving rather unexpressed their opinion as to what the result might be if, given the links not only of St. Andrews, but in other places in their now existing state, Allan *redivivus* were pitted against other redoubtable cracks. That he was in advance of his age there can be no manner of question, as was young Tom some years later, and the marvellously accurate play of the former enabled him to do wonderful performances at a time when the St. Andrews Green was very much more difficult than at present, when it was more beset with heart-breaking whins, thick bents, and other visible and only too tangible signs of the 'abomination of desolation,' which would have entrapped the occasional loose shot of the very long driver, and then woe betide him! Lucky for him if he lost his ball outright, for the punishment would probably be less; the first loss the lighter if he submitted to the lost ball penalty, instead of belabouring the whins, unyielding as fate, in the bootless endeavour to return to the narrow course.

Whilst Allan was undoubtedly a most formidable player, he does not seem to incur any danger of having his merits underestimated by his admirers; rather indeed the contrary; and he is sometimes spoken of as never having been beaten. This, however, is not, strictly speaking, the fact. Comparisons are proverbially odious, but in connexion with the subject of Allan's play may be mentioned a remark made to the writer by Tom Morris. 'I could cope wi' Allan mysel',' he said, 'but never wi' Tommy' (alluding to his own son), thus showing, at any rate, his opinion of their relative merits. But perhaps the natural feelings of parental pride may in some degree discount the value of the now aged progenitor's opinion. That the 'Veteran,' however, has good grounds for his assertion that he 'could cope wi' Allan' is evidenced by the fact that he actually did play him, and beat him too, and that on two occasions. The first of these was for a small sum of money presented by Mr. William Hamilton, of Cairnhill, Ayrshire. The match was one round of the Green, and Tom was victorious by three and two to play. On a second occasion they played for a red coat presented by Mr. Wolfe Murray of Cringletie, Peeblesshire, and here again Tom emerged a triumphant winner of the dyed garment, which, it is understood, is preserved as a memento of the occasion even to the present day. The two never met in a really big match. On one occasion it was intimated to Allan that Tom was prepared to play him for 100*l.* a side, but the former, for whatever reason, made no response.

All are agreed that Allan's style of play was an easy and graceful one ; he played with long and light clubs, of each and every one of which he was the most thorough master. Time after time could he be trusted to land a full-play club or spoon shot as close to the hole as he would have done had he pitched it with an iron thirty or forty yards. If a hole was distant two full drives and an iron, it was a matter of perfect indifference to him in what order he played the shots. He could play the hole just as well if he took his iron for either first, second, or third shot. Nay more, such control had he over his clubs, that he would sometimes pretend to be putting an extra little bit of power into a shot, whilst in reality he was sparing it, so that it would land just short of a distant hazard, leading his enemy to suppose that, if he (Allan) could not reach it, no one else could ; then, acting on his mistaken assumption, he would very likely land himself with a well-hit ball, flop in the bottom of the bunker he thought he could not reach. These and such-like wiles are recorded of Allan ; and it is said that he could and did intentionally heel balls, or pull them, with the object of getting at a hole round a hazard, which to carry would have been inconvenient. As an instance of his playing with his head, it may be mentioned that it was frequently his practice to play from the incoming sixth to the fifth hole at St. Andrews with three short spoon shots, thus avoiding every difficulty, and making a sure five of the hole. But, as compared with the best modern play, it is difficult to see where the advantage of these tactics comes in ; for long drivers now frequently carry the whole lot of bunkers which can catch a tee shot, and get easily home in two, thus saving a stroke ; whilst if they fail to get over they are in no worse plight, for they can generally get out, and then home at the third shot. To Allan was due in a great measure the introduction of irons and cleeks for the approach to the hole, these shots having been previously played with baffy spoons. This new departure was not perhaps to be regarded as an unmixed benefit, for it naturally led to his having hosts of imitators of varying degrees of ineptitude, and their well-meant but ill-regulated efforts wrought in the aggregate much ruin on the hitherto virgin sward, and the resultant bad liers sorely taxed the patience of their successors.

Allan's most brilliant performance was the holing of St. Andrews links in 79. It is thus noticed in a local paper :

A noticeable event in the annals of golfing occurred on the 15th inst. (September 1858), when Allan, the champion, in a round with Mr. Bethune of Blebo, holed the links at 79, which has never been done before, and will not likely be soon done again. We subjoin the holes and strokes for the information of our readers : $1 = 4$; $2 = 4$; $3 = 4$; $4 = 5$; $5 = 5$; $6 = 6$; $7 = 4$; $8 = 4$; $9 = 4$; in all 40 going out ; coming in, $1 = 4$; $2 = 3$; $3 = 5$; $4 = 6$; $5 = 4$; $6 = 5$; $7 = 5$; $8 = 4$; $9 = 3$; in all 39. In a round immediately previous, with the same opponent, Allan holed at 87, which is likewise beautiful play.

Perhaps among the most important of his matches may be mentioned one of twenty rounds, or 360 holes, against Willie Dunn of Musselburgh, which he played in 1843, being then twenty-eight years old. This he won by two rounds and one to play. In 1849 a match for 400*l.* was played between

Allan and Tom Morris against the brothers Dunn of Musselburgh, over the last-named green, St. Andrews and North Berwick. Over their own green the brothers made a terrible example of the St. Andrews couple, winning by 13 and 12 to play; the latter, however, by a narrow majority, reversed the result at St. Andrews, leaving the final battle to be fought at North Berwick—for matches then were not decided as at present by the aggregate number of holes, and it was in consequence of this match that the then existing system was abandoned. It would be difficult to find in the whole annals of golf a more perfect illustration of the advantages of pluck and perseverance. The winners, as they unexpectedly turned out to be, halved the first round at North Berwick, lost the second by four, and halved the third; at the fourth hole of the last round were still further astern, being no less than five down, and their position became worse when four down and eight to play was announced. Odds of twenty to one were freely laid on the Dunns; but here began a most extraordinary run of surprises, for Allan and Tom won the first hole, then the second, halved the third, won the fourth, halved the fifth, and won the sixth, all square and two to play. Amid breathless excitement, Tom played a fine tee shot, which, however, was not well followed up by his partner; the brothers, however, by pulling their second shot off the course, landed under a large boulder, and thus lost the hole; so Tom and his partner, retaining their advantage, pulled this remarkable match out of the fire, and landed the 400*l.*, to say nothing of the twenty to one odds which had been laid when their condition appeared hopeless.

In 1852, at North Berwick, Mr. (afterwards Sir Robert) Hay announced to Mr. James Blackwood, the younger brother of the well-known editor, that he was prepared to take Willie Dunn, and play any two St. Andrews professionals, conditionally on the backers of the latter conceding the odds of two to one in the betting. Mr. Blackwood came to Tom Morris, and asked him if he would be willing to play, and, if so, whom he would select as his partner. Tom cheerfully agreed to do his

ALLAN ROBERTSON AND TOM MORRIS

share; but, as to Allan, it happened just then that he was rather off his game, or at any rate he himself thought he was, and many were of opinion that Tom would do better to take one Bob Anderson, who, though not so well known to fame as the two invincibles, was in reality just about as good as either of them, being a much longer driver, without a weak point in his game. Tom, however, determined not to desert his old ally, and his confidence, as the event proved, was not misplaced. The match was arranged for thirty-six holes over St. Andrews, the backers of the professionals laying 100*l.* to 50*l.* During the first round fortune was anything but favourable to the supporters of the honour of the home green, as they were no less than four down and five to play on the first round; but, as in their match against the Dunns, this acted only as an incentive to renewed exertions, and so successful were they in their efforts, that in the second round they not only made up their leeway, but by the time they had arrived at the fifth hole from home had actually won the match by six and five to play. In justice to the amateur, it should be stated that the loss of the match was in no degree attributable to him.

Another match may be mentioned which was regarded, so to speak, as a standing dish at Prestwick and St. Andrews. Allan and Sir Thomas Moncrieffe at every meeting used to tackle Captain Fairlie and Tom Morris. The two amateurs were as evenly matched as it was possible to be, and though the tussle used to be continued three and four days on end, neither party could claim the slightest advantage over the other.

In 1859 Allan developed an attack of jaundice, from which he never recovered, and in September of that year passed away, regretted by all who knew him. Apart from his excellent play, he is described as a charming partner and an equally generous opponent; no amount of 'cross accidents' could disturb his equable temper, and when steering an indifferent partner with consummate skill through the varying fortunes of the game, no irritable word or gesture was ever known to escape him, however valueless, not to say destructive, the endeavour of his *protégé* happened to be.

We have taken Allan Robertson as an outstanding figure, a convenient point of departure; but before he attained to his dominating position, allusion may be made to Tom Alexander, a ball-maker at Musselburgh, Tom Geddes, from the same place, and the brothers Tom Pirie and Alexander Pirie at St. Andrews. The two latter were weavers by trade. In those days— about 1820—and for some years later, professionalism in golf was not nearly so well defined as it has since become, owing partly to the more restricted means of intercommunication, greater paucity of links, and other causes.

The good old custom then obtained that every caddie was brought up to a trade independently of golf, and the two principal of those then in vogue were weaving and shoemaking. Thus, those with special aptitude for play passed their mornings in the town at work, and came down to the links about ten or eleven o'clock; if they were engaged to play or carry clubs, then so much the better for them: they had some four or five hours' pleasant recreation, for which they were well paid, and subsequently returned to their work.

The two Piries were fine players, but never engaged in any big matches, being chiefly taken out by amateurs in ordinary foursome play. Tom Alexander, however, played a match with Allan Robertson at St. Andrews; but the latter proved too formidable for him, and won by four holes from the Musselburgh man.

Bob Anderson has been referred to above. He on one occasion, with Tom Morris as his partner, played against Allan Robertson and Willie Dunn for a considerable sum in an eighteen-hole match at St. Andrews. He was, as has been remarked, an exceedingly long driver, being in this respect very evenly matched with Dunn; so his partner, arguing that their chances of success might be seriously jeopardised by Bob's continued endeavours to outshine his brilliant rival, with considerable generalship induced him to strike against Allan, whom he could easily distance; the success of these tactics was apparent, as they won the match, after very good play, by one hole. Subsequently he gave up golf, and worked at the mason's trade, but died at a comparatively early age of consumption.

As will have been already seen in our account of their matches against Allan Robertson and Tom Morris, the brothers William and James Dunn were in the first rank of players, and on their native green of Musselburgh were well-nigh invincible. They were twins, club and ball makers by trade, and remained a long time at home, but subsequently removed to Blackheath. Willie Dunn in particular was distinguished for a beautiful, easy style, standing straight up to his ball, and was, as we have remarked above, an exceedingly long driver. In support of this statement, it may be said that he once played a shot from the medal tee on the Hole o' Cross Green at St. Andrews, coming in to the fourth hole, and the ball was found in the little crescent-shaped bunker at the end of the Elysian Fields; this hazard in commemoration of the shot was christened 'Dunny,' a name which it retains to this day. The distance, as measured on the map, is 250 yards, and although by no means standing as a record for length (indeed the writer has frequently seen longer shots driven), yet it will probably be admitted that anyone who could make such a shot (and in this instance the circumstances of wind and condition of ground were not exceptionally favourable) must be credited with driving powers above the average. After he had been at Blackheath some years, a match was arranged between him and Willie Park, to be played at Prestwick. Dunn was tutored by Tom Morris, who put him through his facings every day for a week; he, however, was then past his best, and never won a single round against his mentor during the whole time. The result of the coming encounter was thus clearly foreshadowed, and in the end he was severely beaten.

James Dunn was also a very fine player, though not so long a driver by ten or fifteen yards as his brother; consequently it fell to the latter to uphold the family honour in single matches of importance, whilst the former took his share in foursome play, and could be relied upon as a steady, trustworthy colleague. He died unmarried ; but his brother was married and left a family, one of whom is the popular and highly efficient Tom Dunn, the well-known custodian of North Berwick, formerly green-keeper at Wimbledon. He and his brother Willie maintain the family honour, both being fine players.

As cricket runs in families, so does golf in perhaps even a greater degree ; and to mention the name of Park is to call up a host of brilliant reminiscences, records of championships won by one or other of the representatives of that name, and generally such deeds of derring-do as every golfer would fain aspire to. The first of the family who made himself famous was Willie Park, sen., who is still alive ; but, though by no means a very old man, he has altogether given up play. A Musselburgh caddie, he first began to make a name for himself somewhere about 1853, and, so strong a player had he then become, that money in abundance was forthcoming to back him against Allan Robertson ; but the latter could not be induced to play the match. However, though he declined, a foeman was found for him worthy of his steel in the person of Tom Morris, who took up the gauntlet nothing loth. But the backers of Park knew pretty well what they were about, and the result of the first match, and indeed of a second also, each of them over four greens for 100*l.* a side, was the infliction of such a decisive and thorough drubbing on the acceptor of the challenge, that, in the remembrance of it, *surgit amari aliquid* even to this day.

These matches brought Park more prominently into notice than ever, and he was now the rising, or rather quite the risen, sun. But unbroken success at golf is seldom or never attained, and a partial obnubilation of his rays was in store for him ; for, nothing daunted by his previous unpleasant experiences of this Tartar, Tom, with commendable assurance, issued a challenge in his turn, this time completely turning the tables on his rival and emerging a triumphant victor. These matches were the precursors of others, and, the ball having been literally and metaphorically set rolling, a number of matches were played between the two, at least six of which were for 100*l.* a side ; the net result of the whole was that honours were about evenly divided, at least neither gained a decided advantage. In one of their big matches—the fifth of the series— the finish was at Musselburgh, and the situation had become eminently interesting, as the match was all square, and but few remaining holes to play. The crowd, anxious for their favourite, the local man, to win, transgressed all rules of fair play, and repeatedly injured the position of Tom Morris's ball, to such an extent that the latter declined to continue the match, and, on appeal, the referee stopped the play, and directed that stakes should be drawn. About this period these two players may be regarded as the most successful exponents of the game ; not but what others might be named, and several of them, who ran them pretty close—Willie Dow, for instance, of Musselburgh, and Bob Andrew of Perth, known usually under the *sobriquet* of 'the Rook,' a player celebrated for his exceedingly pretty style ; still, take it altogether, the chief interest in big events centred round Willie Park and his rival. In 1860 the first competition for the champion belt was inaugurated. Thirty-six holes over Prestwick were played, and the issue decided by strokes. Here again Park was successful, and carried off first honours with a score of 174, being, however, only one stroke in front of Tom Morris. On two subsequent occasions he repeated his triumph, in 1863 and 1866, with scores of 168 and 169 respectively ; whilst in October 1861 he ran second, his failure to win on this occasion also being attributable, in the words of the 'Ayrshire Express,' to 'a daring attempt to cross the Alps in two, which brought his ball into one of the worst hazards of the green, and cost him three strokes ; by no means the first occasion on which he has been seriously punished for similar avarice and temerity.' This hole was then the second in the old twelve-hole round ; since the enlargement of the course it is now the seventeenth. In 1864 he again came to the front in three rounds of the North Inch at Perth ; this time his 168 was bracketed equal with Tom Morris ; the latter, however, was victorious in the two rounds played to decide the tie, and scored 110 as against 124 by Park. In 1875 we find him again to the front with a score of 166 at Prestwick, where he carried off the championship, this being the fourth occasion on which he had done so. Enough has perhaps been said to make it clear that this grand player was one of those who 'make history' in the golfing world. His style (though upon this point differences of opinion appear almost always to exist) was generally held to be most graceful; his swing was easy, with a pause at the end of it, and his balls travelled well; but perhaps, if any point of his game is to be particularised, it should be his putting. There he was deadly; fully conscious of his power to hole out almost every putt within a radius of six or seven feet from the hole, he played his approach putts, not merely to lay them dead, but to hole them outright, and so straight was he on the line, and so invariably was he up the length of the hole, that the percentage of long ones he got in was extraordinary; once arrived on the green, his opponent might prepare himself for the worst. This accuracy with his putter he retained to the last, and when his driving had become latterly enfeebled and short, and he lacked the necessary staying power, yet even then he was a player by no means to be despised. His last public appearance was in the championship at Musselburgh in 1886, when, though a mere shadow of his former self, he managed to play one very good round out of the four.

David Park, brother of Willie, was a very fine player, and in foursome play the two together, as in the case of the Dunn brothers, were a most formidable couple, especially, of course, over their own Musselburgh green; his iron approaches were particularly good. He ran very well up in many competitions, but never managed to pull off championship honours, nor was his name so prominently before the public in single encounters of importance. Of much shorter stature than Willie, he yet drove a long ball, the length of his arms in proportion to his body probably assisting him materially in this respect.

A third brother, Mungo Park, was successful in winning the championship at Musselburgh in 1874, with a score of 159. Owing perhaps to his having spent several years of his life at sea, he had not previously to this been much known as a golfer; but on this occasion he certainly upheld the family honours, and made his mark in the golfing world. He, like his brother Willie, was most dexterous in the use of the putter, long shots with which unpretentious club he would run up to the hole in the style so successfully adopted by the Musselburgh School of Instruction, a method of play which, when accurately controlled, produces, as on this occasion, valuable results. This victory in 1874 was all the more creditable, not to say unexpected, when we reflect upon the fact that among the defeated candidates was young Tommy Morris, then at the very zenith of his brilliant career. Subsequently to this, Mungo became professional and green-keeper to the Alnmouth Club—a position he still occupies. Of late years he has not been much seen in public.

The abundant honours reaped by the family are in no immediate danger of being forgotten; on the contrary, there appears to be every prospect of a considerable accretion to the pile; for the exploits of Willie Park, sen., are likely to be reproduced, if not excelled, by his son, who is already entitled to write 'ex-champion' after his name. Born at Musselburgh in 1864, and brought up in all the traditions of the game, he early evinced an aptitude for it which gave promise of great things to come in the future. At the age of sixteen he was engaged as green-keeper and professional by the Ryton Golf Club, where he stayed four years, at the end of which time he returned to his native town and started in business as a club and ball maker. His first public performance of note was a success at Alnmouth at the age of seventeen, when he carried off first honours in a field representative of the best modern talent. The year 1886 saw him again to the front at Troon, a charming green adjacent to Prestwick, just then beginning to be known. Here again all the leading talent of the day was assembled, and young Willie, one of the last to come in, produced an admirable card of 148, his figures showing 74 for each round. In 1887 he entered for the open championship at Prestwick, and won it in 161, thus improving on the position he had taken there three years previously, when Jack Simpson, D. Rolland, and W. Fernie finished in front of him. Later on, in 1887, he went to Alnmouth, and, being then in splendid trim, played havoc with the existing records of that green, holing one circuit of nine holes in thirty-six, and the four rounds in 156, these figures being quite unprecedented. Needless to say, this was also good enough for first honours. In connexion with this score may be mentioned the noteworthy fact, that in the entire day's play not a single hole ever cost him more than five strokes—a striking testimony to the steadiness and brilliancy of his play. The Northumberland green would appear to be rather a happy hunting-ground for young Willie, for on another occasion he emerged from the throng at the right end of the list, being this time bracketed equal with Willie Fernie; on playing off, however, the latter won. The night previous to this he accomplished a remarkable feat : at Musselburgh, in a private set-to with Archie Simpson, he holed the nine holes in thirty-three, establishing thereby a record. The match was followed with interest by about 150 people, and the details of the play were published in the 'Scotsman' the following day. Curiously enough, on no fewer than four different occasions has he occupied fourth place in the open championship. The number of minor events he has won is of course great, and on the whole he appears to be an excellent scorer ; but somehow the same good fortune does not so conspicuously attend him when it comes to a trial of strength with his brother-professionals. After he won the championship, Archie Simpson offered to play him a home and home match over Musselburgh and Carnoustie, and so brilliantly did the challenger play over the first-named green that he acquired a lead of some ten holes on the day ; but, curiously enough, he was not seen to the same advantage on his own green, and Park played there much the better of the two; but the stern chase was too long, and, though fully holding his own, he was unable to reduce the odds against him to any appreciable extent, and was beaten eight holes from home in the last round. A similar or indeed worse defeat he had previously sustained at the hands of Willie Campbell, over Musselburgh and North Berwick. Perhaps of all players young Willie is the most imperturbable: he appears encased in a triple armour of philosophical composure, against which the 'slings and arrows of outrageous fortune' hurl themselves in vain. Does he miss a short putt? (and who among mortals could be held blameless in this respect?) not a gesture of disgust is perceptible; does he foozle a favourite and particularly important shot? not a cloud appears on his brow: nor yet again, when carrying all before him, is it easy to detect any vestige of smug satisfaction, of that αὐτάρκεια, or self-sufficiency so characteristic of many golfers when being borne on the tide of success. His style of play, too, is deliberate in the extreme; he drives a beautiful long carry, his iron play is powerful and accurate, and his putting good; nor is he apparently yet converted to the modern style of putting almost entirely with a cleek. There is one shot, however, which has always caused him considerable trouble, and that is to make a ball lift and lie off an iron; so to weather this rock he has set his wits to work and evolved an implement which appears to give him every satisfaction. Without being either a lifting iron or a mashie, it partakes of the nature and characteristics of both; its shape brings the upper part of the blade, which is very concave, nearer to the ball, and so, whilst less turf is taken, a very considerable back spin is put upon the ball, which is sent very high in the air, and falls almost without any roll. Several good golfers, including Mr. J. E. Laidlay, present amateur champion, and Mr. A. M. Ross, the crack Edinburgh Burgess amateur, speak well of this invention. Park devotes a deal of attention to his business, and has made sundry experiments with a view to improving the various implements connected with the game. As a professional he is most civil, courteous, and obliging, and in every way a young fellow in whose hands the interests of the game will be safe.[1]

In fitting juxtaposition to the name of Park may be placed that òf Morris—Tom Morris to wit ; a name known, it may be said without contradiction, in each of the four continents of the globe. His name is so interwoven with the game that, as will have been already noted, it is impossible to go far afield without introducing him to the acquaintance of the reader, so to speak, by a side wind. That being so, the present historian merely proposes to effect a slightly more formal introduction, giving such additional details and incidents of his life as may conceivably prove of interest. These, it may be stated, have been taken down at first hand from his own lips, and in one or two particulars may be found to vary slightly from accounts which have already been published. The subject of our sketch, then, was born in North Street, St. Andrews, in 1821. His father was a letter-carrier, but at a later period abandoned this occupation for the weightier one of carrying clubs. At the age of ten or twelve Tom began to knock balls about, and, curiously enough, began to drive with his left hand below his right—a mode of play adopted by only two players in the writer's experience. It was by a mere accident that Tom became a golfer at all, for his career was marked out for him, and arrangements all but completed, under which he was to have been apprenticed to a carpenter ; but a casual question of old Sandy Herd, as to why he did not get apprenticed to Allan Robertson as a club-maker, put the idea into his head. Allan considered the matter, the upshot of which was that he agreed to take Tom, who served under him four years as apprentice and five as journeyman, and from that period began his golfing life. Possessing naturally a keen, good eye, he began before long to 'play a game,' which year by year developed until, in

---

[1] Since the above was written Park has added the championship of 1889 to his record ; a tie with Andrew Kirkaldy, in the lowest recorded score of 155 at Musselburgh, was composed of three thirty-nines and a thirty-eight. On playing off, Park won by five strokes.

measuring himself against Allan Robertson, the latter found himself obliged gradually to decrease the odds of a half to a third, thence to four strokes, until at last, if the 'old man' was not exactly 'beaten by the boy,' still the boy, or rather lad of twenty-two or thereabouts, rendered such an exceedingly good account of himself that the odds he was allowed were represented by zero. Here, then, was a fact. He could play the greatest living master of the game and hold his own ; but their interests were not divided, and it was rather as partners that they took the golfing world by storm. It was during Tom's period of service with Allan that their great match was played against the Dunns for 400*l.* ; indeed this was Tom's first appearance in public in a match of importance, and certainly it was a sufficiently trying ordeal for a youngster to be called upon to go through. How he acquitted himself, and the result of the match, having been already noticed, need not be here recapitulated. On the expiration of his time with Allan Robertson, he started business on his own account as club and ball maker, and continued at it for about three years ; at the end of which time, about 1851, chiefly through the instrumentality of Colonel Fairlie of Coodham, for whom he had carried clubs, he was appointed custodian of Prestwick Links, just then newly established as a golf course. In this capacity he remained fourteen years. During the last four years of this period he was subjected to incessant entreaties to return to his native city : for this length of time he held out, preferring the old twelve-hole course at Prestwick to St. Andrews ; but in the end his defences were broken down, and he returned to the old grey city, which he has never since quitted.

Tom, 'old Tom,' is a character, an institution, a subject on which a most interesting monograph might be written. Wherever golf is played his name is a password ; interviewers have interviewed him, journalists made copy out of him ; photographers photographed him (including in this latter connexion at least one very skilful lady amateur, who confesses to an absorbing admiration for him) ; artists have sketched him, with sometimes astonishingly happy results ; and, truth to tell, he, as he is known to us now, lends himself somewhat readily to artistic effort—his characteristic attitudes, his hands always in his pockets, except when engaged in the congenial occupation of grasping a club or filling afresh a pipe (which, by the same token, is oddly enough always a bran-new clay for choice), his grey beard, all these and sundry other points go to form an individuality as striking as it is unique. The writer recently came across a remark which he noticed with some attention ; it was that in writing, for any good results to be produced, the mind must be red hot behind the pen. As to the results here produced, the readers of this chapter will of course be judges ; but there is one particular as to which the writer's mind is as red hot in its conviction as the most ardent scribe could desire : this point is, that never could there be met with a more perfect specimen of what is called 'Nature's gentleman' than old Tom. Nobility of character is writ on his handsome sunburnt face in letters clear as day, and withal there is an admixture of naïve unsophisticated simplicity which is charming to the last degree. An illustration of what is intended to be conveyed may be given in the following anecdote. Many years ago, at the High hole at St. Andrews, Tom was working away in difficulties to the extent of three more or thereabouts, and still a very long way from the hole. Captain Broughton happening to pass by, remarked, 'Oh, pick up your ball, Tom, it's no use.' 'Na, na,' said he, 'I might hole it.' 'If you do I'll give you 50*l*.' 'Done,' said Tom, and had another whack, and by some million to one chance the ball actually did go into the hole. 'That will make a nice nest-egg for me to put in the bank,' he remarked, and, further to give the *ipsissima verba*, 'the Captain he pit on a gey sarous (serious) face, nae doot o' that, and passed on.' Within a few days the Captain honourably appeared with the 50*l*., of which, however, Tom resolutely refused to touch one farthing, remarking that the whole thing was a joke, and 'he wisna raly meaning it.' From all parts of the country communications reach him on recondite legal questions connected with the game ; as an arbiter his authority is acknowledged beyond dispute, in virtue of his vast stores of knowledge, of tradition, of golfing lore, of his years, and consequent wisdom. A veritable Nestor he ; gifted, moreover, he is with the faculty of harmonising the most hopelessly discordant elements. Is there a pull devil, pull baker sort of squabble on the teeing ground as to who should start first, about fifty balls teed in a row, and their respective owners all swearing at one another, down comes Tom, oil-bag in hand, lets out a few drops, and the raging waves acknowledge the soothing influence and subside at once into the ripple of a summer sea. But space forbids a longer expatiation on his merits ; he is a man of whom it is impossible to conceive that he could ever have had an enemy in the world. Most sincere, though unobtrusive, in his religious convictions, no amount of persuasion was ever known to be successful in tempting him to play golf on a Fast Day ; so long as these existed, 'he had never dune it a' his life, and wisna gaun to begin noo,' was the formula with which he usually confronted the would-be charmer, and all honour to him for acting up to his belief. Turn we now to his golfing capabilities. As to that, there is no doubt he was, when in his prime— we may add is still—a very fine player, though perhaps there has been a tendency in some quarters to withhold from him that recognition of his merit which is undoubtedly his due, and to make use of such phrases as 'respectable mediocrity' when referring to him ; and indeed, as a recent writer has well remarked, one really is perhaps apt to forget how good a player he was, owing to the fact of his fame in a great measure being overshadowed by that of his son, young Tom, with whom he freely admits he never could cope. Then, too, the standard of play has reached a height never approached in Tom's younger days : so many men, professionals and amateurs alike, are so very good, that his best performances are equalled and excelled every day ; this, too, tends to the belittling of his deeds of fame. But it is to be borne in mind that four championships have fallen to Tom's share—viz. in 1861, 1862, 1864, and 1867, with scores of 163, 163, 160, and 170 respectively over Prestwick, and that he was at least the equal of any man living for a great number of years. True it is that but for one peculiarity he would have been better still : one weakish place there was in his armour, and not a golfer but will know to what we refer. Those short putts ! Put him twelve feet from the hole, and not a better holer out could be named ; but with eighteen inches or two feet as the measure to be negotiated—but it were kinder to allow the figure of aposiopesis to come to the rescue. Candour, however, compels the admission that of late years he has evinced an enormous improvement in this latter respect. In his own words, ' I never miss they noo,' but it is improbable that he will ever live down his shady reputation regarding them ; and if he were to hole five thousand consecutively, but miss the five thousand and first, it is a moral certainty that the taunts of the tonguesters would be levelled at him as of yore. One day, many years ago, he had a most successful encounter with a putt of some six or seven inches, not with his putter, which he habitually used, but with his iron, and for many a long day afterwards, being convinced he was now at last happy in the possession of the magic secret, he toiled on valiantly with his weapon, with varying, but on the whole tolerable, success. His one theory is (and here few golfers will be prepared to question it), that whatever the club used, 'the ball *maun* be hit ' ; but the trouble is, or rather was, with him, that he couldn't hit it. ' Gin the hole was aye a yaird nearer till him, my fawther wad be a gude putter,' young Tom used to say of him with a touch of unfilial satire ; and Mr. Wolfe Murray once went so far as to address a letter to 'The Misser of Short Putts, Prestwick,' which missive the postman took straight to the champion. A running shot up to the hole with his iron is a part of the game at which he excels ; but the most remarkable thing about him is his retention of first-class all-round capabilities for long years after passing sixty. Before reaching that age, however, a spell of the most utter bad play, lasting four or five years, took possession of him ; and this was the more provoking, inasmuch as it occurred when his son Tommy was at the very zenith of his powers, and father and son were in the habit of playing other professionals. Never but on one occasion at North Berwick was old Tom much better than a drag upon his son, and it is the literal truth to say that at that time he did not play a game within a third to half one of his subsequent usual form from sixty years old till now. After passing that age he took a new lease of play, and won two professional competitions—one at Wemyss, the other at Hoylake ; and on his sixty-fourth birthday, June 17, 1885, he accomplished the remarkable feat of holing St. Andrews Links in the grand score of 81, whilst playing with Mr. Charles Hutchings, his figures being, out 5 5 5 5 5 4 4 3 4 ; home, 4 4 4 5 5 5 5 5 4. It will be observed that not a figure above a five occurs, and what is the more extraordinary, he had until that day never succeeded in going round without a six somewhere in his score. His driving is to the full as long as it ever was in his life, and when he gets what he calls 'ane of ma very best,' the longest drivers of the present day would have their work cut out to gain any very material advantage over him. For this wonderful game he is able to play when close upon seventy years old, he has no doubt to thank the strictly temperate life he has always led ; and it would be well indeed if some of the younger generation of professionals had the strength of mind to follow his example in this respect. Space forbids any copious account of the many interesting matches he has played during his long career ; his tussles with Park are the chief ones to be noticed, but he has encountered at one time or another almost every golfer of note. In a match with Willie Dunn in May 1851, the latter being dormy one, the finish is thus described : 'The last hole was in a very peculiar place at the top of a hill, and Tom's ball rolled first down the east side, and the next putt sent it over again on the west. Seeing that he could not halve the match, Tom gave his ball a kick in disgust, while Dunn took a snuff, and smiled satisfactorily, having the credit of taking the match by two holes.' An interesting match was played in 1857 over St. Andrews by Tom against Captain Maitland-Dougall, the former holing in 82, 39 out, 43 home, the lowest the links had then been done in. Captain Maitland-Dougall was only three strokes behind. In 1865 a most successful partnership was established between Tom and Bob Kirk, who tackled and vanquished all the best players of the day, including Willie and David Park, whom they beat by two, with a score of 86 at St. Andrews; W. Park and Andrew Strath at Prestwick, and on the same green Willie Park and Dow, by four holes. Then again he and Andrew Strath challenged any two for 100*l.*, but nobody had the courage to respond. One fact in his latter-day experience he is much impressed with, and that is his first battle with Mr. Horace G. Hutchinson. He played that gentleman at St. Andrews and got round in 82, but could only secure half of the match, whilst in a subsequent round, with a score of 83, he was defeated.

Finally, we may regard Tom Morris as a golfing celebrity of the first water; without the slightest reflection on his professional brethren, we may point to him as a model of what a professional ought to be—respectful and courteous he is to all alike, as much at ease in the presence of Royalty when piloting a Prince of the Blood round the links as when playing a match with his own particular crony. Nor has his popularity amongst every class ever caused him to outstep in the very slightest degree the limits of that position to which he has been called, and to which he is such a distinguished ornament.

Of the incomparable Young Tom, the veteran's eldest son, it is difficult to write without a keen feeling of regret at the early close of his brilliant and all too brief career. As applied to his golfing life, the motto *capite et supereminet omnes* had been a not inappropriate one in a metaphorical sense, and on his coat of arms the familiar heraldic device of balls and crossed clubs. A golfer is not made any more than Rome was built in a day, but it is probable that Tommy attained a rare pitch of excellence at as early an age as any golfer on record. On reaching sixteen he had already become a factor to be reckoned with, one certain to make his mark in any competition he engaged in. Born in 1851, the first we hear of him outside the family circle was in a match at Perth, in April 1864, when a sum of about five pounds was subscribed by some gentlemen there, during a tournament, to be played for by him and a boy of the same age named Greig. It may be of interest to quote a contemporary report of it :—

Perhaps the most interesting match of the day was between Master Morris, son of the redoubtable 'Tom,' and Master William Greig, of, as it seems, Perth juvenile golfing celebrity. They are really wonderful players, for their years, both of them. We had no idea that very-young-Perth could produce so proficient a golfer as Master Greig. He played with astonishing neatness and precision, but the honours of the day were in store for his competitor. Master Morris seems to have been both born and bred to golf. He has been cast in the very mould of a golfer, and plays with all the steadiness and certainty in embryo of his father. The juvenile competition was extremely interesting, and although the young Prestwicker gained the day, Perth has the very opposite of any reason to be ashamed of her youthful champion. It was very funny to see the boys followed by hundreds of deeply interested and anxious spectators.

Three years later, at the age of sixteen, came his first win of importance at Carnoustie, in September 1867. Prizes to the value of twenty pounds were competed for and sixteen couples entered ; three rounds or thirty holes were played, the result of which was a triple tie between young Tommy, Bob Andrew of Perth, and Willie Park, score 140. Bob Fergusson was next, 144 ; and Jamie Anderson, Bob Kirk, and Willie Dow tied at 145. On the tie for first being played off, Tommy won by a stroke or two, Andrew being second. It will be admitted that it was no small triumph for a lad of sixteen to distance a field wherein such leading exponents of the game as those above mentioned were arrayed against him. His father was also playing, but did not back him for the tie, as he thought him 'ower young' : events, however, proved he might well have done so, for in the matter of nerve and determination, as was afterwards abundantly shown, he was unrivalled. In the open championship of this year he occupied the good position of fourth, with 175, his father winning with 170, Willie Park second, 172, and Andrew Strath third, 174. The succeeding year saw him to the front at Leven, with a score of 170 for 36 holes, being one stroke better than Bob Kirk, and seven in front of Davie Strath, who in his turn was seven better than the fourth prizeman, Bob Andrew. This same year (1868) also saw him champion at Prestwick, and that too with the then unexampled score of 154, no less than six strokes better than it had ever been won at previously, his father in 1864 holding the next lowest record with 160—the sire on this occasion running second to his son with 157; Bob Andrew third, 159, and Willie Park fourth, with 162. The following year (1869) he absolutely spread-eagled the field, winning with 157 at Prestwick, no less than eleven strokes better than Bob Kirk, 168, and twelve better than David Strath, 169. Not content with these laurels, he added another and crowning victory in 1870, eclipsing his own brilliant play by a still more extraordinary score of 149, this last performance entitling him to the absolute custody of the champion belt, which he had thus secured three times in succession. The trophy so brilliantly won remains an heirloom in his father's family. It is worthy of remark that in this last championship one of his rounds was holed in the phenomenally low figure of 47, an average of under four a hole— a feat never before accomplished, the nearest approach being 49, done by himself and Andrew Strath. An interval of 12 strokes separated the winning score from the second best on this occasion, Bob Kirk and David Strath tieing at 161; and perhaps no more eloquent testimony as to Young Tom's superiority can be laid before the reader than the mere statement, for purposes of comparison, of the first and second scores when he won the championship. Taking these three years 1868, 1869, and 1870, we find Tommy's score in the aggregate to be 460, while the next best is 486, or an average of nearly 9 strokes better than any other competitor. Bearing in mind that the winner of this annual contest generally only succeeds in securing his position, often by the narrow margin of one stroke, or perhaps two, the inference to be drawn is plain.

This youthful hero, having thus effectually swept the board, matters came rather to a deadlock, and for a year there was an interregnum, during which no championship meeting was held; but in 1872 it was resuscitated under somewhat different conditions. A cup was subscribed for, and the contest was to take place over the three greens of Prestwick, St. Andrews and Musselburgh successively, in connexion with the respective autumn meeting of these clubs. The year 1872 saw the inauguration of the new *régime*, and again this extraordinary player came out as champion for the fourth year in succession over Prestwick, as a scorer of 166 ; the weather on this occasion being very adverse to low scoring. In this year also he had won a professional tournament at Hoylake, the first one of importance held over an English green : 85 and 82, gave him an aggregate of 167, Davie Strath being 168, and Bob Andrew 171. Sixteen professionals entered for this event. The narration of these exploits may be held to warrant the assertion that Young Tom was a golfer of unapproachable excellence, but there may be added also the further statement that he was the first legitimately to break the record of 79 established by Allan Robertson for St. Andrews links. The latter did his far-famed score in a private match, but Tommy's score was made in a scoring competition for prizes, in which, after twice tieing with Bob Fergusson at 87, he in the third round came away with such play as had never been seen. The details of this score, which stood unchallenged till October 1888, are as follows :

Out : 444564433 = 37.   In : 334654555 = 40.

The only professional who really ran him close was his friend Davie Strath, and with him he played some wonderfully good and close matches, but in the long run, and especially in competitions of importance, he appeared to have the inside turn. This was due, probably, to his extraordinary skill as a putter and holer out ; any sort of putt appeared to be dead to him, and of the short ones he missed fewer than any player the writer has ever seen. This may be attributable in part to the great pains he invariably took : if asked to hole out from a foot and a half, if he did by some rare accident happen to fail, it was not due to any lack of painstaking on his part, but rather to the unaccountable fatuity which appears on occasions to bewitch the very best of men. He invariably used a putter ; and had his right foot so close to the ball that it appeared sometimes as if the putter-head must strike his foot in being drawn back. Curiously enough, he was quite unable to use a cleek for a bad-lying put ; these he negotiated with his iron, which was very straight in the face. He was a very strong driver, with a rather forcing style, not with quite so full an all-round swing as some of his brother professionals, but every ounce of strength went into the stroke, and as for a bad lie, he seemed to positively revel in it. There was one particularly disagreeable ball, his control over which never failed to fill the writer with admiration, and that was when the position of the ball was so very much below the level of the ground on which the striker had to take his stance that he could with difficulty reach it at all, and that only by almost sitting on the ground ; this sort of ball he could, and generally did, drive with a wooden club as far as his best shots from the tee. In a gale of wind he was particularly good, as the height of ball he generally drove was eminently adapted to travelling well in the teeth of it ; his iron play was magnificent, and he also made frequent use of the iron niblick in approaching out of bad places. His power with this rather prosy and unpromising sort of instrument was also remarkable ; his father states that never will he forget a shot he saw him drive up to the gas hole at Musselburgh, out of a hole, with this club. In length it was about equal to a very fine long spoon shot, and quite straight up to the hole. As a partner to any beginner or abominably bad player, of what-ever golfing age, he was a tower of strength ; he always accepted the situation *à merveille*, whilst, if his ally could play at all, it was astonishing how strong the opponents had to be, if amateurs, in order to make a match of it. With men who would now be handicapped at from fourteen to eighteen strokes, he was never afraid to play combinations, any, or all of them, good enough to win the St. Andrews or any other medal. The recovering shots he used to make were sometimes deadly ; he appeared to have the gift of putting in just another half-ounce of pith where something extra was required ; so until the hole was actually won, or with less than about three shots in hand, the enemy were never safe with him. When playing his own ball, his performances were, as may be imagined, remarkable. On one occasion he proved the master of Davie Strath and Jamie Anderson, who played the best of their balls against him ; while at another time it is handed down as a tradition that for a whole week he played nothing but singles every day, backing himself each round for 83, at St. Andrews, winning every time ; and the last round of all, to give the others a chance, he took 81 and finished in 80. The last important foursome in which he was engaged took place in September 1875, when, in conjunction with his father, he played Willie and Mungo Park over North Berwick for 25*l.* a side. This was a return match to one played the previous year, in which the last-named couple had proved victorious by 3 and 2 to play ; but on this occasion the Morrises won a very close tussle, amidst considerable excitement, by one hole at the last. The match, however, does not seem to have been remarkable for any superlative excellence of play. In connexion with this match a sad incident occurred : when the last hole had been played out, a telegram was handed to young Tom, requesting him to return home at once as his wife was dangerously ill. No train being then available, Tommy and his father started off in a yacht which had been kindly placed at their disposal by a resident. They had barely cleared the harbour, when another message arrived, announcing that young Mrs. Morris and her new-born baby were both dead. But though the yacht was within easy hailing distance, it was judged expedient not to communicate the sad message to those on board, lest the shock should prove too great. There can be no doubt that the young champion never recovered from this blow; for he was devotedly attached to his wife, to whom he had only been married about a year. One more important match he played before his death. Mr. A. Molesworth of Westward Ho had announced that, on receipt of a third, he was prepared to play any professional; and this challenge Tommy was induced to accept. Two rounds a day for three days over St. Andrews were quite sufficient to prove Tommy's great superiority even at the odds conceded, and by the decisive majority of nine up and seven to play he defeated the southern representative. During a great portion of the match the links were covered with snow, and, indeed, the umpire gave it as his opinion that it should be postponed, but to this Mr. Molesworth would not consent. The putting-greens having been swept, therefore, they ploughed their way along as best they could, with the result above stated. Very shortly after this, on Christmas Day 1875, at the age of twenty-four, this grand golfer passed away lamented by all who knew him. A memorial, to the erection of which no fewer than sixty golfing societies contributed, marks his last resting-place in the cathedral burying-ground, and the inscription written by the late Principal Tulloch may be here quoted:

Deeply regretted by numerous friends and all golfers, he thrice in succession won the champion belt, and held it without rivalry, and yet without envy, his many amiable qualities being no less acknowledged than his golfing achievements.

As a match player, old Tom's youngest son, J. O. F. Morris, has had a fair measure of success. On one or two occasions championship honours seemed to be within his grasp; but notably in the year 1876 a fatal penultimate hole, the crucial 17th, at St. Andrews in the second round shattered his hopes and robbed him of victory. On this occasion he had two sixes to win, but in lieu thereof a 9 and a 6 had to be chronicled.

On two consecutive occasions he played his own ball against

the best of two and the best of three amateurs' balls respectively, accomplishing the round at St. Andrews in the very fine totals of 78 and 77, a remarkable feature of the case being that every single half round was below 40, viz. 39 and 39 = 38 and 39. The strongest point in his game is beyond question his putting, in which department (and the most important it is too) he is a player of outstanding merit, and, unlike his brother Tommy, he can putt indifferently well with any sort of instrument which the wit of man has devised for the purpose. His pluck is undeniable, another great point in his favour, and he has been known to pull off matches which for sheer audacity in undertaking them at all have excited a feeling almost akin to derision. He was born in 1856, and should thus be now (1890) in the prime of his game.

As a triple winner of the championship, and that too in consecutive years, the claims of Jamie Anderson to rank as a first-class professional are indisputable. Born in 1842, the son of David Anderson, or 'Old Daw,' a caddy at St. Andrews (who, by the way, is also rather a character, and familiar enough to generations of golfers), Jamie began golf when about ten years old, and, after the manner of his kind, developed into a fine player. We are not concerned to trace his upward career farther than in mere outline, and it may be sufficient to state that he first reached the wished-for goal in 1877, when at Musselburgh he won the championship with 160, an average of 40 per round, R. Pringle being second. In 1878, by means of a really wonderful finish, he again headed the field at Prestwick. A score of 161 had already been handed in by J. O. F. Morris, just in front of him. To tie with this he required to do the last four holes in 17, which was considered the proper number for faultless play—computed as follows, 5, 4, 3, 5. On this number he saved actually an average of a stroke a hole, and did them in 3, 4, 1, 5, which made him 157. Even with this, as it turned out, he only just won, for a formidable foe in the person of Bob Kirk came in behind him and had one putt to tie. This putt hit the hole, but did not remain in, and in disgust he missed the next, a short one, and thus totalled 159, the second best score. In 1879, over St. Andrews, Jamie again asserted himself with 170; the runners-up being Andrew Kirkaldy and Jamie Allan, who tied for second; and having thus proved his superiority over the three respective greens, it may be supposed he was well content to rest upon his laurels. When Young Tom was at his best, some very interesting foursomes were played between Jamie Anderson and Davie Strath, against Mr. Gilbert Mitchell Innes and Young Tom. About this time also the last-named player and Jamie challenged any two players, and offered to lay 100*l.* to 80*l.*, but there were no takers. One single-round match was, however, played; but for a small stake only. The two challengers were tackled by Davie Strath and Bob Kirk, who so far asserted their competence as to arrive at the comfortable position of two up and three to play, but lost all the last three holes, and the match by one. It is interesting to note that the scores were 80 and 81—magnificent play. Jamie had four big matches at different times with Bob Fergusson, honours being divided, the field of action being St. Andrews, Aberdeen, North Berwick, and Musselburgh; and it is probable that there was not much to choose between them.

In playing golf, Jamie's guiding principle appeared to be never to make a bad shot—a theory easy enough of enunciation, but one which some players find themselves wholly unable to reduce satisfactorily to practice. Not so with him, however: he was the very embodiment of machine-like accuracy, and when properly in his game, and in the real swing of the thing, he, as it were, conquered his opponents by tiring them out. No matter if they went away with a flourish of trumpets, they generally came back to him: one half-missed shot at rare intervals was his opportunity, always profited by.

In the writer's hearing he one day let fall the remark that he had played 90 consecutive holes without one bad shot or one stroke made otherwise than as he had intended, and it was this dead level of steadiness which brought him conspicuously to the front. Without being gifted with any extraordinary driving power —nothing indeed to compare with what is seen nowadays— he was nevertheless always straight and a fair length; and as a putter, and in the use of the iron in especial, his skill was, and is, proverbial. It was sometimes quite extraordinary to see

OLD DAW

with what judgment he would pitch a ball up to within a few feet of the hole half a dozen times in succession, and then hole his putt. In bad weather, too, he was a most trustworthy player, as he never appeared to be inconvenienced by cold; whilst as for wet or wind, or both combined, they operated most probably in his favour, inasmuch as while he was, or appeared to be, imper-

JAMIE ANDERSON

vious to climatic influences, the enemy, if he had a temper set at all near the edge, might conceivably be reduced to the verge of distraction by abortive struggles with rude blasts, and thus go off the game that was in him.

As a partner Jamie is charming to play with, his whole attention concentrated on the matter in hand, and a more thorough *judge* of the game does not exist. The half-instructed golfer is heard with painful frequency to go into raptures over a shot badly played by a good player, the shot nevertheless turning out well, lying dead perhaps. Not so our admirable critic : 'My ! but yon was a lucky yin, bad played, didna desairve it,' would be most likely his comment on such a performance. A capital club-maker, for many years he worked at St. Andrews on his own account ; thence he went to Ardeer, then to Perth ; and has now returned again to the Fife town. He does not play much now, but has as good a game in him still as he ever has played, and with practice would, no doubt, become as tough a customer as ever.

Incidental reference has been made to David Strath. This grand player, though never fortunate enough to win the blue riband, was nevertheless about as fine a player as St. Andrews has ever produced. He lives chiefly in the recollection of golfers as the determined opponent of Young Tom, and there are not wanting many who declare (and the writer is not indisposed to share this opinion) that for brilliant and steady play, combined with absence of mistakes, the golf that these two exhibited day after day has never been surpassed.

On one occasion they played twelve consecutive rounds, and, if the writer's recollection serves him, not one round by either player amounted to 88, and the great majority of them ruled about 80, or very little over. His style was the very poetry of swing, the most perfectly graceful and easy that can be imagined. If there was any one point in which he could not quite come up to Tommy, it was at the short game ; though Davie was a truly excellent putter, yet his rival was on occasions phenomenal. It is to be regretted that consumption deprived the golfing world of this brilliant player ere he had reached thirty years.

An elder brother of Davie Strath, Andrew by name, though perhaps hardly reaching the pitch of excellence attained afterwards by the younger scion, yet had the good fortune to win the championship in 1865 with 162 at Prestwick. It is remarkable that from 1860 until 1873 he was the only professional who managed to get his name interpolated as a winner between Park and the Morrises, who amongst them monopolised the trophy during the whole of that period. Like his brother, he also fell an early prey to consumption.

The next to break the chain was Tom Kidd, a St. Andrews caddy, a fine driver who won in 1873 at St. Andrews with the not particularly brilliant total of 179. Why the scoring generally should have ruled so high on that day is inexplicable, for more perfect weather for the purpose never was seen.

Bob Kirk is also a name well known on the links, no less than three generations of this dynasty being represented by identical appellations. The subject of this notice was the son of a St. Andrews professional (who is still alive), famous too, in his time, as a fine steady player, a contemporary of Allan Robertson. Young Bob early took to the game, and, albeit short in stature, was a tough, wiry sort of player, who drove a very fine ball, which he followed up with accurate and pretty putting. About the year 1867 he was in magnificent form, winning on May 3 the first professional prize with a grandly played 80, over his native green, 40 each way ; the next to him being David Park, 89. He defeated 'old Tom' by twelve in a 36-hole match, his first round being 83. Young Tom also succumbed to him by 3 holes, while in October the same year he again won a first prize with 85. Next year he repeated his victory over Young Tom in a 36-hole match, coming in 6 ahead and 4 to play ; while in a tournament at Leven he was only beaten by him by one stroke, 170—171 being the two best scores. For some years he was in the employment of the Blackheath Club as professional and club-maker, whence he returned home, but died at an early age. He left two sons, who, though still young, give every promise of carving out a successful golfing career for themselves.

In common with Young Tom Morris and Jamie Anderson, Bob Fergusson of Musselburgh holds the proud position of winner of the championship three years in succession, viz. in 1880, 1881, and 1882, his scores being over Musselburgh 162, Prestwick 170, and St. Andrews 171 ; whilst in 1883 he tied with W. Fernie at 159, and suffered defeat on playing off by only one stroke ; and then, too, he was a stroke ahead, and the last hole only to play, which his opponent negotiated by a brilliantly played 2 as against Bob's 4. It may be supposed that a player of this strength has had at least his share of success in other contests ; thus his first win was in 1867, when twenty-three years old, at Leith ; next, from 1879–1883, he won at Alnmouth three times, at Hoylake about that period three victories fell to him, and at North Berwick also, in 1879, he was first. In many other competitions too numerous to mention he occupied good positions when he did not win outright. A few of his most interesting matches may be noted. In 1868 and in 1869 he played old Tom Morris six matches over Musselburgh and Luffness, and administered the most exemplary castigation, for he won the whole series and each of them by a pretty substantial majority. In the next St. Andrews representative he found a harder nut to crack, for this was the redoubtable Tommy, and it was to the last degree unfortunate that the untimely death of the latter removed him from the scene before Bob Fergusson had quite reached the height of his fame. After twice suffering defeat at St. Andrews in 1868, Bob, the next year at Musselburgh, after most determined play, halved the match, and in a deciding round managed to win by one ; but Tommy was amply revenged later on at Luffness by winning 8 up and 7 to play. Splendid golf was the characteristic of a 36-hole match on a subsequent occasion at Musselburgh, in which Tommy was victor by one hole after being 3 down and 9 to play. Although Bob holed the last round in 40, he was four strokes behind his rival; later on they played for two days over the same green, Bob losing by 4 the first day, but winning on the second by 3 holes.

With Davie Strath he had several matches, in one of which, for 50*l.* a side, each player, curiously enough, won by four holes over his opponent's green, that match ending of course square.

With Willie Park, sen., he had several matches, the two principal ones being for 25*l.* a side, over Musselburgh, each winning one. In foursomes, Bob has taken a leading part in many a stiff encounter, perhaps the finest one ever played being that at North Berwick, wherein, with Willie Park, sen., as his partner, and Young Tom and Davie Strath as opponents, the Musselburgh men managed to win by three holes. With Davie Park in place of Willie, the Musselburgh men were defeated at St. Andrews by the narrow majority of one hole. Although winning the championship does not necessarily imply a decided superiority over all contemporary players, yet by general consensus of opinion Bob Fergusson, when in mid-career, was held to be the best golfer: when anything had to be done, there was a most invaluable ingredient in his composition— sheer downright tenacity of purpose and determination; indeed, the whole appearance of the man was such as might have suggested even to a stranger that such was his leading characteristic. Many fine players continually used to bring in wonderful scores (no doubt fully authenticated); but somehow, in anything worth winning, Bob was pretty sure to be in front, even if he did not 'lose' them altogether. To see him address his ball was in itself a study; broad-backed and sturdy, it appeared as if nothing short of a volcanic upheaval or a dynamite cartridge would have power to make him budge till the stroke was finished. His game was accurate and scientific at every point, whilst his physical power made him a most efficient wielder of the cleek and iron. With the first-named club, indeed, he played a match against Young Tom similarly armed at Prestwick, and beat him by four holes. He was never troubled with 'nerves,' and under disadvantageous circumstances, such as bad light wind, or bad weather, he played the game probably as well as it possibly could be played.

He accepted the post of greenkeeper at Musselburgh, and now, unfortunately, does not appear as a player, as all his time is devoted to the discharge—and the most effective discharge—of his new duties.

Although somewhat unaccountably, Willie Campbell, formerly of Musselburgh, then of Prestwick, has as yet failed to carry off the championship, yet it must be admitted that he is in every way a most apt pupil of his quondam instructor, Bob Fergusson, to whom he is indebted for much of the teaching which has made him so successful. Reviewing his career up to the present time, it would appear that match play rather than scoring is his great *forte* ; and further, it is unquestionably due to his initiative that a constantly increasing interest is being taken in professional matches—an interest, indeed, which was widespread among golfers in the days of Tommy Morris and Strath; but whether owing to the fact that other players suffered by comparison with these two luminaries, or that certain disagreeable incidents occurred in connexion with professional golf, certain it is that for a considerable lapse of years matches of this description came to be viewed with obvious disfavour. All honour to Campbell, therefore, for proving, with the help of his co-professionals of to-day, that the brotherhood are able to play as good golf now as was shown then, and to play it, moreover, in a manner to which no exception can be taken. A tall, strapping young fellow, he is admirably adapted for coping with every difficulty presented by the yawning bunker and tenacious whin; without being a sensational driver, he is yet long and very straight. But it is with the mashy that he does the most brilliant execution; he uses it for almost every kind of shot for which it can be used, sometimes even putts with it, and as for the last-named part of his game, whilst always steady, it now and again verges on the miraculous. The rapidity of his swing is such as to excite wonder among those who cling with affectionate superstition to the time-crusted maxim of 'slow back' and aphorisms of similar import.

WILLIE CAMPBELL

Still, he does not appear to lose power thereby, and most certainly there is no perceptible sacrifice of steadiness. In *sangfroid* and coolness he shows to great advantage, and is never more in his glory than when playing a big match before hundreds of spectators. His more important encounters may be briefly referred to.

About three years ago he began to rise into prominence, and one of his first antagonists was J. O. F. Morris, whom he played for 25*l*. a side home and home; the end of this being that Jamie pulled the match out of the fire, and won, after an exciting finish, by one hole. Not satisfied to rest under the stigma of defeat, Campbell, a few months later, had a return match with him, and this time amply revenged himself by winning 7 up and 5 to play. He later on, in the year 1886, took young Willie Park in hand, and played him over North Berwick and Musselburgh for 25*l*. a side. The result of this match was never in doubt, and Campbell ultimately won by 14 up and 13 to play, having in the course of the proceedings holed the four rounds at Musselburgh in the wonderful total of 152—5 strokes lower than the championship had ever been won there. He next turned his attention to David Brown, who had recently won the championship at Musselburgh in the lowest score then made—viz. 157—Willie on that occasion occupying second position, after a tough fight, in which, however, Brown had at one time much the best of it. The match was halved; but a return four months later ended in Willie's favour by 13 up and 12 to play. After again defeating Willie Park, and that too when the latter had risen superior to all competitors in the championship, with a victory too over Bob Martin and Willie Fernie to his credit (though in justice to the latter it should be stated that he was not at the time in form to undertake such a match), we find a sort of standing challenge of Willie's to play anyone for 100*l*. a side taken up by the brilliant young player Archie Simpson of Carnoustie. This match excited from the first the liveliest interest, opinions being about equally divided as to their respective merits; but, as the event proved, Archie on this occasion was unable to get within even measurable distance of the challenger. Carnoustie, St. Andrews, Musselburgh, and Prestwick were the four greens selected for play in the order named, and over all four was magnificent golf shown. April 12, 1889, was the opening day over Archie's home green, and the spectators were treated to an interpretation of the game in every way worthy of the men's reputation; the astonishing putting of Campbell being in especial a notable feature. No less than 9 putts of from 30 to 15 yards did he actually hole, whilst in no instance did he miss one in the whole day's play which he could be reasonably expected to get down. The end of this was that, though Archie Simpson played an admirable game, he was 3 down on the day. Three days later, at St. Andrews, in bitter cold weather, which acted prejudicially on Simpson's play, but did not affect Campbell in the least, the latter added 5 more holes, all won in the first round : he was thus 8 ahead, having played over St. Andrews in 84 and 85, as against 90 and 85 by Simpson. On the 16th, at Musselburgh, he forged still further ahead, scoring 159 to 163, and standing at the conclusion of the third day 11 up and 36 holes to play over Prestwick. On the last green he added still more to this advantage, and won easily in the second round by 16 up on the whole match. So ended this memorable battle, in connexion with which it may be stated that never for years, if at all, was such a huge crowd seen as turned out at Musselburgh to witness the play. Frequently did the men have to drive down a living avenue of human beings, extending from hole to hole, the spectators being packed ten to twelve deep on each side; and the wonder was how play could be carried on at all under such conditions. As has been remarked above, Campbell in the championship has been singularly unlucky; generally one exceedingly bad hole provokingly near the end of a very fine day's play has done the damage. But there can be little doubt that his turn will come, and no one will deserve it better. His reputation at Prestwick is monumental, he having holed the round there in the marvellous score of 71; he also had previously cut the record with 77, and that too in the championship.

In J. E. Douglas Stewart Rolland the little Fife village of

Earlsferry has produced a golfer of whom it may well be proud. Born in 1860, from the age of thirteen he worked for several years as a stonemason, to which fact he is probably indebted for much of the tremendous driving power with which he is gifted ; for there can be little question that the habitual use of the mason's mall is eminently adapted to the development of those muscles of the fore-arm and wrist which are of especial service in the long game. His physique is admirable, the very type of an athlete ; a model in whom a sculptor would rejoice —six feet in his stockings, erect as a dart, he measures $41\frac{1}{2}$ inches round the chest and $12\frac{1}{2}$ round the right fore-arm, his weight being 12 st. 12 lbs. Before joining the ranks of professionals he first came prominently into notice as the acceptor of a challenge thrown down by Mr. John Ball, tertius, the far-famed Hoylake amateur, to play a home and home match. This gentleman was, especially over the Southern green, generally looked upon as invincible ; but in this match Rolland, over the Earlsferry course, came in no less than 9 ahead, an advantage he retained, and indeed supplemented by additional holes during the second half of the match at Hoylake. A second encounter next day resulted in another win for Rolland, who, however, was 5 down and 6 to play, but won all the remaining holes. On a subsequent occasion, however, Ball won a match from him. While still an amateur he tied for second at Prestwick with W. Fernie at 164 for the championship, Jack Simpson winning with 160. He first competed as a professional at Hoylake in 1884, and in 1887 accepted the charge of the Malvern green. At the tournament played in connexion with the opening of the Sandwich green, he ran through to the final, in which, however, he was vanquished by Archie Simpson by the narrow margin of one putt, the driving in this match on both sides being something to be remembered. He was successful, however, in winning the prize for the aggregate score. In the professional tournament at Westward Ho in June 1889 he was singularly successful, winning over 30*l.* in virtue of a double victory, one being a competition by holes and the other an aggregate score of two rounds. These two rounds he holed in 83 and 85, total of 168, being one stroke in front of Sayers. His power of driving, and especially against the wind, is almost phenomenal, and it is not an uncommon occurrence to see him 40 or 50 yards in front of a shot which would in ordinary circumstances be considered an excellent one ; and he can probably drive as far with his cleek as the majority of long drivers can with a play club. In the short game, however, he is often not seen to such advantage, and he sometimes fails to hole out short putts with precision. Looking at his play as a whole, it was remarked by a not wholly incompetent critic that 'the strongest part of his game is his temper,' and there is considerable justice in the observation. It is a great pity that his duties at Malvern do not appear to admit of his measuring his strength in the annual championship held over the three Northern greens, as there can be little doubt that before long he would render a good account of himself. He is most highly spoken of by his present employers, as civil in demeanour, steady, unassuming, and a general favourite.

Lissom, active, and wiry, about 5 feet 9 in height, Archie Simpson is in the very prime of his youth : born at Earlsferry in 1866, he has already placed many fine performances to his credit. When only fourteen, as an amateur, he won a second prize at Elie in 56 for 12 holes, and a year later made the best score of the day, 85, in a club match at St. Andrews. His first professional success was at Leven, when with 80, the best first round played, and 85 he was second to his brother Jack, who scored 86 and 78. He was second at a tournament at Carnoustie in 1885, and the same year at St. Andrews only lost the championship by a single putt, scoring 172, as against 171 by Bob Martin. Here again his first round was 83, the lowest of the day. In other competitions he has taken a prominent place, and at Sandwich he scored his first really important win after a tie with D. Rolland. In professional matches he has suffered severe defeat at the hands of Campbell, but with W. Park, jun., he was successful, and also easily defeated

J. O. F. Morris by 12 holes in a home and home match for 25*l*.

A record of 74 over Carnoustie, where he is resident professional and club-maker, stands in his name, and it is not easy to see how this can be beaten. Always a long driver—with a wind following and slightly from the right—he drives at times a truly astonishing swipe, due probably to the fact that, while endowed with great wrist-power and a very long swing, he plays sometimes rather for a 'draw,' and gets his back, shoulders, and hips into the stroke in a way which must be seen to be understood. One of these shots at St. Andrews was from the medal tee, going out from the fifth to the sixth hole, and he practically compassed the distance in that one shot, having to play but a short run up to the hole with a putter for his second. The distance from hole to hole is marked as 359 yards. In his match with Campbell he showed himself to be fully the equal of that player, if not indeed his superior, from the tee, through the green, and in approaching; but his putting left much to be desired. Not that as a rule he is a bad putter—quite the contrary—for his success at Sandwich was due to his accuracy in this department; but somehow he too frequently 'lost' himself on the green in this particular duel, with the result which has been already chronicled. He is the youngest of six brothers, all of them fine players; Jack, an ex-champion, and Robert being the best known in golfing circles. It may safely be predicted that Archie will add many more laurels to those he has already won.

The neophyte when yearning for instruction, or, for that matter, the accomplished player when for the moment unfortunately a little 'off colour,' could not do better than put himself into the hands of Bernard Sayers of North Berwick, who combines in an unusual degree natural aptitude and thorough knowledge of the game with facility of imparting instruction in it. His early training was of a description probably unique in golfing annals, inasmuch as he was a professional acrobat, a calling he did not abandon until he had reached his sixteenth year, when he began golf and picked it up in a very short time, so quickly, indeed, that in two years he occupied fourth position in a professional competition at Glasgow, and now, at the age of twenty-nine, his performances over his own green at North Berwick are unsurpassed. He holds the lowest record for that course, viz. 68; whilst in a recent match with Mr. J. E. Laidlay he holed 5 consecutive rounds in 73, 72, 70, 71, 74, defeating the amateur champion in every match, and averaging 72 for these five rounds. With the help of D. Grant, a local professional of merit, he demolished his own record of 68, the two, in playing H. Kirkaldy and A. Herd of St. Andrews, holing out in 67 as follows :

$$
\begin{aligned}
& 4\,5\,3\,4\,3\,4\,3\,2\,4\,4 \quad . \quad . \quad . \quad 36 \\
& 4\,4\,2\,3\,3\,5\,6\,4 \quad\quad\;\; . \quad . \quad . \quad 31 \\
& \hphantom{4\,4\,2\,3\,3\,5\,6\,4 \quad\quad\;\; . \quad . \quad . \quad }\overline{67}
\end{aligned}
$$

In competitions he has won first prizes at North Berwick, Glasgow, Dunbar, Archerfield, Dirleton, Kinghorn, and Hoylake, while in 1888 the championship just escaped his grasp by one stroke, he being third to Jack Burns at St. Andrews with 172, beating D. Anderson, jun., after a tie. If genius be truly defined as 'an unlimited capacity for taking pains,' then indeed there is no one among professionals who can claim to be his equal. His putting is very exceptionally good, with either cleek or putter, and an article of his creed is that, 'if a man can putt, he can play anybody.' Certainly at Westward Ho, in June 1889, this maxim proved not far wide of the truth ; for Rolland, notwithstanding his prodigious driving, found Sayers one of the very toughest of nuts. Not only did the latter halve his round with him, necessitating an extra three holes for decision, in one of which a marvellous putt by the little one was followed by a similar one by his opponent— a good four hole being thus halved in three—but in the aggregate scoring rounds Sayers was again only one stroke behind, scoring 87 82, as against 83 85, gaining the prize for the best single round played ; whilst, in addition, the spectators organised a collection in special admiration of his admirable pluck when pitted against his powerful adversary, the contrast in physique between the two being such as to remind one of the giant and the dwarf; for to Rolland's stalwart form Sayers could only oppose 5 ft. 3 in. in height and 9 st. 7 lb. in weight; nevertheless, in the purely scientific part of the game, he showed to fully as great advantage.

In such single matches as he has played against Campbell and other professionals he has well held his own. To use his own phraseology, he 'can always come up to time when the bell rings;' and in any scoring competition over any green, but especially over North Berwick, no one would be entitled to say that a victory by Bernard Sayers was a fluke, for he is a consistently steady scientific player, and one certain to be pretty well placed.[1]

For a style of easy grace and entire absence of apparent effort, the champion of 1883, William Fernie, stands conspicuous. He is indeed a most deceptive player to watch, for he hardly appears to hit much at the ball, and yet he is one of the very longest drivers, and altogether in the very forefront of scientific and powerful players.

Born in 1857, he did not lose much time in beginning golf, for at five years old he was hard at it, and at fifteen won a professional prize after a tie with D. Strath, at 88, at St. Andrews. From sixteen to twenty-three he won the St. Andrews Mechanics' Club medal six times, included amongst which was an 81, a record for that club: successes at Earlsferry and Alnmouth followed, his score at the latter place being 164. A splendid 83 at St. Andrews, in a gale of wind, secured him a first professional prize, and after being second to Bob Fergusson in the 1882 championship, and tieing with him for first the following year, he succeeded in wresting a most brilliant victory from his formidable opponent by one stroke; all the more creditable as Bob had one in hand, and the last hole only remained to be played:

[1] Since the above was written Sayers has again lowered the North Berwick record to 66—38 out, 28 home.

but a long putt secured Fernie a 2 as against Fergusson's 4. This victory was at Musselburgh, and the score 159—an ex-

WILLIE FERNIE

traordinary incident being his taking no less than 10 to one hole, and winning in spite of of it. Next year at Prestwick he tied for second with Rolland at 164, when Jack Simpson won

the championship, and in the three following years was first at
Alnmouth, at North Berwick—after a tie with Archie Simpson,
at 156—at Montrose with a fine 74, and at Littlestone.

In match play he has encountered Willie Campbell three
times, and defeated him twice, by 7 and 6 to play, and by 2 and
1 to play ; but sustained one heavy defeat by 12. In 1882 he
played W. Park, jun., over St. Andrews and Alnmouth, and
won over both greens.

In physique he is powerful and well set, but at the same
time supple and active. His height, 5 ft. 9 in.; $40\frac{1}{2}$ in. round
the chest; a strong fore-arm of 12 in.; weight, 13 st. 2 lb. As
greenkeeper at Troon he has done much to improve that links
and exemplify in his own play the beauties of really first-rate
professional golf for the benefit of the young players of the
West. Several times he has done that green with the record of
73, and either there or elsewhere he is fully capable of holding
his own against any challenger who might throw down the
gauntlet. He is a most excellent club-maker, and spares no
trouble in carrying out any instructions given him.

Twice a winner of the championship over his native green
of St. Andrews, in the years 1876 and 1885, with scores
respectively of 176 and 171, Bob Martin may always prove a
dangerous opponent. The most noticeable characteristic of
his game when he happens to be in form is the perfect and
unique manner in which he runs up long half-cleek shots to
the hole. He invariably uses this club for every distance of
approach ; for, strangely enough, he is quite unable to do any
execution with an iron, and when he is perforce compelled to
loft and lie, he finds in the iron niblick—or in one of the many
modifications of it—a ready substitute, with which he is really
deadly. Being, moreover, a good putter and straight driver,
though not gifted with the great power of the more modern
school, his two great successes are easily accounted for.

The remaining ex-champions to be noticed are Jack
Simpson in 1884, at Prestwick, score 160; David Brown at
Musselburgh, in 1886, with 157 ; and John Burns, at St.

Andrews, in 1888, with 171 The first-named is the eldest of the six brothers of whom Archie is now the best known. Jack, when he first appeared in public, lost no time in making his mark; the tournament at Leven in 1884 gave him his opportunity, and with 86 and 78 he took first prize. It may be mentioned as an illustration of the brilliant game he was at that time capable of showing, that, with the last nine holes of the day to play, he required an average of four a hole to overtake and pass his brother, and he proved himself equal to the occasion, and won by a stroke. The family in this competition both beat the existing record for that green, Willie Campbell taking third place with 86 and 84. Jack's driving capabilities were of the very finest order, and some of the carries he frequently made were such as to elicit a sort of half-smothered groan of astonishment from any spectators who happened to witness them. His cleek driving also was tremendous, and so hard did he hit with this club that he could rarely get a head to last him for any length of time, for the 'blows and knocks' which this apostle of golf administered were such as to batter the heads into a sort of hoop—a reversed 'bulger,' so to speak—prussiate of potash and all similar hardening treatment notwithstanding. His magnificent swing, though rapid, was under complete control, combining extreme freedom with elasticity and power. For such a grand player the mistakes he made were numerous; but his power of recovery generally stood him in good stead, and, could he have played the more prosaic short game in a manner at all commensurate with his driving and approaching, he would have been well-nigh invincible. In scoring he almost invariably began with a terribly bad hole early in the day, a nine or ten in the first three holes being no uncommon occurrence for him; but even with this handicap he was generally well up at the finish. After leaving Carnoustie he migrated to the South, and took charge of a green in Derbyshire.

David Brown, a slater by trade, has, on the whole, played consistently well since the victory at Musselburgh which first brought him into notice. This performance was all the more meritorious when we consider that he had not the advantage of habitual practice, as while working at his trade he played only at irregular intervals. He scored a win at Selkirk in 1885 with 153, D. Grant and W. Campbell being second and third. At the opening of the Sandwich green he in practice made a record there of 78, and has taken prizes at Westward Ho and at other places. He is a very painstaking player, brimful of confidence, a long, powerful driver, and an exceedingly dexterous wielder of Park's patent 'Lofter.' Being only twenty-eight, he should have a fine career before him.

Like Brown, Jack Burns could hardly be regarded as a regular professional before he won the championship, though he has since abandoned his trade, that of plasterer, and accepted the position of greenkeeper at Warwick.

On his day he is a fine slashing driver, and, though his victory savoured somewhat of the unexpected, it could not be said to be a fluke, inasmuch as he had been well in the front rank in other competitions, and indeed was within four strokes of the winner in 1888, securing fourth prize on that occasion. His performance in 1888 was one of sterling merit, as there was a very strong breeze blowing from the north, a wind which appears to render it particularly difficult to perform the outward half of the journey in creditable figures. It is true that he had perhaps less of this adverse element to contend with than the earlier starters; but, look at it as we may, his score, even on a calm day, would be difficult to beat, and hence is all the more meritorious. He has not played in any important matches away from his native green; but at Warwick he has earned golden opinions as greenkeeper and instructor, no less by his civil demeanour than by the trouble he takes to bring forward young players who are desirous of improving their game.

Thus far the writer has dealt principally with those players who have singled themselves out from among their contemporaries by reason of a more than average degree of merit; there still remain some, however, who might with justice claim a more extended notice than the space at disposal permits. For instance, there is David Ayton, well known at St. Andrews as a fine player, with a graceful, easy, and very full swing, a frequent prize-winner on that green; the brothers John, James, and Matthew Allan, chiefly identified with golf at Westward Ho; Peter Paxton, formerly of Musselburgh, now greenkeeper at Eastbourne, whither he went after nine years' service at Malvern in a similar capacity, a first-prize winner three years in succession at Hoylake, first also at Littlestone (a new green); Alexander Herd, a really grand player, who won the St. Andrews Mechanics' Medal on New Year's Day 1889 with 78, a record for that club; David Grant of North Berwick; J. Kay of Seaton Carew; and Peter Fernie, a powerful player, well known at St. Andrews, Wimbledon, and some Southern greens. We may fitly close our notice of professional golfers by a reference to the Kirkaldys of St. Andrews (Andrew, John, and Hugh), all very powerful players, and more particularly does this remark apply to the eldest, Andrew, whose driving is a treat to see. He, in a handicap competition recently promoted by the visitors to St. Andrews, won the first prize from scratch, after tying with a grandly played 78 with Jamie Anderson, to whom he allowed four strokes. In 1888, also, in a similar contest, but by holes in a tournament, he beat every competitor. He has never played in any big match, but there can be little doubt that with practice in this department he could fully hold his own with any living player, for not only is he an exceptionally long driver, but his short game also is crisp, plucky, and accurate. He enlisted in the 74th in 1881, and was present at Tel-el-Kebir; but, his time having expired, he returned to his native green, where he had already reaped a certain amount of honour in 1879 when he tied for second with Jamie Allan at 172 in the championship, and won the deciding round.[1]

[1] Andrew Kirkaldy has still further improved his position by tying for the 1889 championship with W. Park, jun., at the unprecedented score of 155 at Musselburgh. On playing off he lost by 5 strokes.

In this iconoclastic age the destruction of records proceeds apace, and in this connexion the youngest brother, Hugh, a lad of twenty, has made himself famous.

For many years Young Tom's 77 at St. Andrews defied all and sundry assaults upon it, though on close analysis of his figures it was clear that a stroke or two could have been saved here and there. Every good round played over the green served only to accentuate the exceptional merit of his figures. But in October 1888 Hugh Kirkaldy fairly beat this 77. It is difficult in this age of progress to say what may or may not happen, but it would hardly be rash to assert that his outward half-round, at any rate, will never even be equalled again; this was as follows: $4 4 4 4 4 4 3 2 4 = 33$. To this he added 41 for the return journey, as follows: $4 3 4 4 6 4 5 6 5 = 41$. 74 in all.

Extraordinary and improbable as it may seem, within nine months of this date he actually beat this score; his second record being

$4 5 4 3 5 5 3 3 3$ . . . 35 out.
$3 3 4 4 5 5 5 4 5$ . . . 38 home.

In the first record he was playing against Bernard Sayers, and in his second against A. Herd and D. Leitch in a three-ball match, and on both occasions the round was the usual medal course. For purposes of comparison it may be stated that the lowest figure at which the Royal and Ancient medal has been gained is 83 (on two occasions), though in practice some five or six amateurs have succeeded in beating 80. Hugh Kirkaldy has a particularly long swing, and appears to great advantage when playing down wind; he holds his right hand a good deal round the club, and grasps very tightly with it. He is a capital holer-out, a long driver with his iron, and with a few years' experience will probably gain somewhat in consistency, when his game will become, so to speak, more consolidated than at present.

AMATEURS.

Having thus completed a survey of such professionals, past and present, as appeared worthy of mention, the writer turns—with considerable diffidence it is true—to the task of selecting a list of amateurs which shall be in some degree representative ; for any notice, however brief, of the many fine players now scattered through the length and breadth of the land (to say nothing of any retrospective allusions) would render it impossible to confine his remarks within the prescribed compass. A bare list of the names of medal-winners of the Royal and Ancient and other clubs would, of course, indicate tolerably clearly many who have risen to eminence ; but, on the other hand, such fare would be meagre, jejune, and lacking somewhat in interest.

Looking back, therefore, to the year 1840 or thereabouts, a time when the tall hat and swallow-tail coat were held to be adjuncts to the game no less indispensable and necessary than the feather ball and baffy ; looking back these fifty years or so, we find Sir David Baird of Newbyth, R. Oliphant, James Condie, the brothers Wood, Mr. W. M. Goddard, the brothers Playfair, Sir Hope Grant mentioned as in the forefront of every golfing battle. St. Andrews was the venue chosen to try conclusions ; here they would all assemble, if not every year at least biennially, and many interesting matches would be fought out on a links abounding with difficulties sufficient to try the mettle and nerve of the most skilful player.

At that time, too, to speak colloquially, golf was golf. Like marriage, it was not to be enterprised or taken in hand lightly, but with all befitting solemnity; and it may have been thought by these performers of old that the majestic garments in which they arrayed themselves withal were in a way emblematic, and represented, as it were, in concrete shape the momentous nature of the issues involved. And, truth to tell, those issues frequently *were* very considerable : 5*l.* a hole and 100*l.* a round were

MR. PAT ALEXANDER

MR. JAMES CONDIE

MR. SUTHERLAND

sums often played for, to say nothing of larger stakes, and the modern half-crown or even sovereign a round dwindles into insignificance when compared with such sums as those just mentioned.

Little need we wonder, then, at the sobriety of demeanour which was such a characteristic of the game; and the stern rebuke, now become historic, which was made by one of the old school, 'There's too much levity about this match!' acquires an added significance easily understood if we consider the conditions which frequently obtained. Of the players above named, two—viz. Sir D. Baird and Mr. W. M. Goddard—were in the habit of playing together with a remarkable degree of success, and held their own as an almost invincible combination. They were entirely typical of the old school. Sir D. Baird was a good driver, while Mr. Goddard, though lacking brilliancy in this respect, was nevertheless steady and safe. There were, however, two players of a younger generation who in the estimation of qualified judges were in every way equal, if not superior, to the undefeated couple. These were Mr. (afterwards Sir Robert) Hay and George Condie. By general consent the former was considered one of the very prettiest players who ever handled hickory. He stood very close to his ball, using therefore a very upright club ; he drove a long ball, and was particularly accurate with the baffy—a club to which he affectionately clung long after iron play had been introduced ; indeed, he never looked upon this latter substitute with much favour, nor used it at all if he could possibly avoid doing so. George Condie was a splendidly built man, and his style irreproachable, with a full swing of great power ; also an admirable baffy player, and accurate with all his clubs. He and his partner that was to be were probably as evenly matched as two men could be, but they never met in single combat till 1859, when, in a tournament at St. Andrews, Condie won by 6 holes in the final round of the competition. Such, then, were the two men who were to represent the young school against the old. That any two youngsters should have the audacity to venture upon such a match was sufficient to fill many of their opponents' supporters with amazement ; but, be that as it may, the match took place, a large amount of money depending on the result. And most interesting the match proved. Condie had never till then played before a gallery, and the fact of being the observed of some hundreds of people affected his driving very prejudicially, though, curiously enough, his approaches and putting were throughout all that could be desired. At one time the elder players held a distinct advantage of three holes, which appeared likely to be increased owing to Condie topping his tee shot from the high hole coming in ; but his partner with a magnificent drive put him on the green, and they won the hole, a turning-point in the match. Eventually fortune declared itself in their favour by one hole, a good putt having to be holed at the finish to secure the victory, and, as an instance of the scientific interest shown by golfers then as now, we may put on record the remark made by Mr. James Condie to his son : 'Ah, George, you should never have left your partner a downhill putt to finish the match!' Unquestionably the best men won, and if George Condie had not broken down in his driving, no doubt the match would not have proved such a close one as it did.

All the players in the above match appear in the lists of medal winners at St. Andrews. Sir D. Baird in 1841, 1849, and 1850—scores 100, 100, 107; Mr. Goddard in 1843 and 1849, with 103, 105; Sir R. Hay in 1848, 1851, 1852, 1872, with 101, 110, 99, 94; and G. Condie in 1848, and twice in 1850, with 104, 96, and 100. These scores appear very high when compared with first-class play of the present time; but two things have to be borne in mind: first, the altered condition of the links, and, secondly, the enormous increase of golfers who are to be ranked as first class; and whereas formerly first honours could perhaps have been gained by some half-dozen men or so at the outside, now it would be nearer the mark to say that in every field some twenty-five or thirty players are to be found, any one of whom might assert his capability. One result of the great foursome we have described was the bringing into special prominence of Mr. (afterwards Sir Robert) Hay, and his merits as compared with those of Mr. Goddard were freely discussed. In the end, a match was played for 100*l*., which the younger player easily won, and from that time till within a few years of his death he was acknowledged to be one of the very finest amateur golfers. Reference has been made in these pages to Colonel J. O. Fairlie of Coodham, who,

SIR ROBERT HAY, BART.

although he did not begin golf at quite the orthodox age, yet attained a very marked degree of proficiency; so much so, indeed, that the Golfers' Year Book for 1866 is dedicated to him as 'deservedly designated by the Earl of Dalhousie, the champion amateur of Scotland, as having held the Prestwick, St. Andrews, and North Berwick medals during the same season.' Twice winner of the King William the Fourth medal, at the autumn meeting of St. Andrews, he three times secured first honours in the spring, and also twice won the Bombay medal, his best score being 95. In 1853 the spring meeting was rendered noteworthy by an extraordinary and, so far as the writer is aware, unparalleled circumstance in the annals of medal playing. It became necessary on this occasion to play no less than four rounds before it could be decided whether Colonel Fairlie or Mr. Jelf Sharp was to be returned as winner of the first prize. A tie at 96 was the result of the first round on the Wednesday; two rounds on the Thursday resulted similarly, both players scoring 105 each round, and not until the end of a fourth trial on the Friday did victory declare itself in favour of Mr. Sharp by two strokes with 104. That Mr. Sharp, who was then but seventeen years old, played a plucky game against his more seasoned opponent no one could deny; the latter player had at various stages of the battle had considerably the best of it, being at one time 7 strokes up and 8 holes to play; but a series of reverses in the bunkers, then known more euphemistically than at present as the 'Devil's pot,' so diminished his spare capital as to leave him with but one stroke to the good, and the last hole to play; and this advantage was neutralised by a half-topped tee shot which only just cleared the burn. At St. Andrews and Prestwick Colonel Fairlie's reputation is worthily maintained by his sons, Messrs. F. A. and J. O. Fairlie in especial being golfers of first-class form.

The autumn meeting of this year (1853) was made famous by Lieut. James Campbell Stewart, 72nd Highlanders, holing the round in 90, this being 9 strokes better than this medal had hitherto been taken at. So fine a player was this gentleman that he was able to play Allan Robertson on even terms, and, on one occasion certainly, to hold his own, though probably in the long run the professional would have proved too heavy for him, as evidenced by odds of 2 to 1 laid on the latter.

In the golfing world few names are more familiar than that of George Glennie. At Blackheath, at St. Andrews, and Westward Ho, wherever he played he commanded admiration no less for the excellence of his play than for the qualities which rendered him such a charming partner or opponent. He began the game early in life, and speedily made his mark. In a competition among students they decided to handicap him by allowing him only one club to play with, and that one he was to have no voice in the selection of. A very battered and disreputable-looking middle spoon, which had seen better days, was given him; but this unpromising implement proved as effective in his hands as did the jawbone in those of Samson, and despite this novel handicap he proved too good for his field. His play was characterised by extraordinary precision rather than commanding power, and this it was which enabled him to make the celebrated score of 88 for the St. Andrews medal, with which his name is chiefly identified—this, too, at a time when a single badly played shot was certain to bring the direst disaster in its train. This score, made in 1855 for King William the Fourth's medal, was unbeaten until 1884, when Mr. Horace Hutchinson succeeded in scoring 87; but in 1879, in the spring meeting, Mr. W. J. Mure (whose graceful, easy swing is now seen all too seldom at head-quarters) scored 86, and that in a very strong northerly wind. Glennie's whole heart and soul were in the game even to the end of his days. As a judge and critic his words were words of wisdom, and his opinion few would have the hardihood to gainsay. As an illustration of his inexorable purism may be given the following anecdote. He was partnered one day by the eminent golfer who has contributed to the illustration of these pages. As ill-luck would have it, Mr. Glennie put the latter into the Swilcan Burn;

however, when the party arrived the ball was seen to be a
'floater,' and was gaily pursuing its career seawards on the
'drumlie' current. The artist remarked that he thought he could
manage to play it, so, recking little in his enthusiasm of such

MR. GEORGE GLENNIE

trifles as wet boots and stockings, down he marched into the
bed of the burn at a spot where he could intercept the ball
and, so to speak, take it on the wing.

The daring idea was crowned with success. Splash went the
niblick, away went the ball, and finished dead at the hole,

which was by this stroke placed to their credit. Far from volunteering any remark eulogistic of this exceptionally bold and successful movement, Mr. Glennie preserved unyielding silence. To ascertain the opinion of the sage his partner asked him, 'Well, what about that stroke?' The answer was unexpected. 'No gowf at a';' then, in a soliloquy, as he advanced to the teeing ground—'just monkey's tricks.' In commemoration of this justly celebrated player the 'George Glennie Medal' was instituted in 1881, and was presented by the Blackheath Club to the Royal and Ancient Golf Club. It is held by the player making the lowest aggregate score at the spring and autumn meetings.

In the clever 'Letter from the Rhine' descriptive of medal day at St. Andrews occur the lines—

> And next come the flyers to show them the way ;
> There's Innes, and Boothby, and lithe Robbie Hay.

The description is not amiss ; adding some few other names such as Mr. Robert Clark, Captain (now Admiral) Maitland Dougall, Mr. W. C. Thomson of Broughty Ferry, Dr. Argyle Robertson, the great oculist, the famous brothers Henry and David I. Lamb, and Mr. Charles Anderson ; taking these players together, it would not have been very rash to predict that the honours on any given Medal Day would have been divided between some two to be found in this list.

Mr. Gilbert Mitchell Innes was a notable example of a late beginner rising to the very top of the tree. Till the age of twenty-three or twenty-four he was innocent of the enjoyment this game affords, and not until a decade later did he begin to turn his attention to what was called by the late Mr. John Blackwood 'serious golf.' Yet another ten years elapsed ere he arrived at the culminating point in his career ; and about that time he played a series of matches, of which unfortunately he has preserved no record—matches, however, which for absorbing interest have probably never been surpassed. Partnered by young Tommy Morris, he played Davie Strath and Jamie Anderson some 600 holes, at the end of which the two professionals were two matches ahead but 8 holes behind, this anomaly being accounted for by the fact that in one match of 36 holes Mr. Innes and partner won by 11 ; one of their rounds being the then record—viz. 79. To his habitual practice against the finest professional talent Mr. Innes attributes the rare game he then played ; but whilst enthusiastic in his golfing, other forms of sport had also attractions for him, amongst them that of deer-stalking ; and on one occasion his desertion of the links for the heather-clad hills of the North drew from the redoubtable Tommy the remark, 'I can *not* understand Mr. Innes, when he's playing as fine a game as ony mortal man ever played, leaving gowf to rin efter a wheen stinking beasts and then comin' back, no able to hit a ba'.' Mr. Innes was a frequent medallist on the four principal Scotch greens, being either first or second on twenty-two occasions. At one of these gatherings at Musselburgh his score of 75 for the 16 holes as then played constituted a record for the spring medal.

MR. ROBERT CLARK

To Mr. Robert Clark is due the merit of evolving the interesting 'best ball' matches, wherein one stronger player plays his single ball against two or more opponents who at every hole count only the ball that has been holed in the least number of strokes. The first match of the sort was between old Tom Morris and Messrs. Clark and Gilbert Innes, the allies winning by a single putt, and much money changing hands over the result. Mr. Clark was a successful medallist : he played with exceedingly heavy clubs, which he wielded with a half swing, and was always seen to especial advantage in a gale of wind on a narrow course. Another late beginner who has made his mark at Montrose, Perth, and at St. Andrews is the ever-popular founder and president of the Warwick Golf Club, Colonel R. T. Boothby. Like Mr. Innes, he was over twenty ere he took to the game ; but once started he soon made up for lost time, and within about three years actually won the medal at St. Andrews in the then very good score of 94. This was by no means his only success, for other medals, first and second, have fallen to his share ; and also in a tournament at Perth in 1864 he was victorious, beating amongst others the famous George Condie. Perhaps his most interesting matches were played with the Rev. J. G. Macpherson as partner. This gentleman at one time was one of the very finest amateurs, being hardly, if at all, inferior to the best of the professionals ; indeed, he was continually in the habit of making scores of from 80 to 85 at St. Andrews, and when the two played together their rounds were usually phenomenally low. Whilst Mr. Macpherson was a magnificent driver, his partner was no less deadly in his cleek approaches and putting ; and the two in combination were, it may almost be said, more than a match for any two other amateurs, and but little behind the best professional talent.

For many years in every medal Colonel Boothby used to be partnered by Mr. Thomas Hodge, with whom, besides, he was in the habit of playing a large number of single matches, the very great majority of which were surprisingly close.

The last-named gentleman was one of those versatile and gifted individuals who are able to do anything they undertake very much better than the great majority of their less-favoured fellow-mortals ; thus, in his younger days, at wrestling, boxing, and single-stick he was almost unmatched. A splendid eye ensured supremacy at rackets and billiards, in which branches of sport he was nearly on a par with professional exponents ; in the cricket-field he was a successful bowler and very quick field ; whilst in sprinting, and generally as an all-round athlete, he was much above the average. Being gifted, besides, with great abilities, he started a school at St. Andrews, which for many years was about the most successful in Scotland ; here it was that his connexion with golf began, and numerous are the fine players he turned out ; indeed, with such an example before their eyes, it would have been odd if his boys had not taken to the game *con amore*, and to say of anyone that he was or had been at Hodge's was about tantamont to a declaration that he was an able golfer. The natural qualities which ensured Mr. Hodge's exceptional success in other branches of sport also stood him in good stead when he began to play golf, which was not until he had reached the age of thirty. Some four years afterwards he was elected a member of the Royal and Ancient Golf Club, and the next day won the medal with a score of 92. Three times in four years he secured first honours, the best of his scores being 89. These successes were doubtless due in part to the very careful way in which he practised score-playing as distinct from match-play; but as in other exploits so in his golf did nerve and determination do their work. The writer has by no means exhausted the list of his accomplishments—far from it. At the Scotch national game of curling, for instance, and at Wimbledon with the rifle, he made his mark, whilst as a trout-fisher his successes in difficult streams were a byword. Of his skill with brush and pencil the illustrations in these pages afford proof, and this talent he has during many years turned to such good account that a collection of his many sketches would afford an interesting history of golf so long as he has been acquainted with it.

Of the many fine players who are at present in the prime of their powers we may mention Mr. Alex. Stuart and Mr. John Ernest Laidlay, who share between them the honour of record score for the St. Andrews medal, viz. 83. This performance by the first-named gentleman in 1883 was all the more remarkable, inasmuch as before he started Mr. Leslie Balfour had already returned an 85, a score which usually enables its fortunate compiler to regard with complacent serenity the efforts of his rivals to eclipse it. Mr. Stuart is recognised as a very powerful player—always dangerous ; and at Musselburgh, Prestwick, North Berwick, and Hoylake, as well as at St. Andrews, he has repeatedly distinguished himself. Over the last-named green, indeed, the average of six occasions on which he appears as first or second is the very low one of $87\frac{5}{6}$. The Glennie Cup has also fallen to him. Mr. J. E. Laidlay is at present the holder of the title of 'amateur champion for 1889,' a position he right well deserves, for on him fell the brunt of the fighting at St. Andrews ere he could win it, and few who saw the finish between him and Mr. John Ball, jun., will ever forget it. The round was halved, and according to the conditions they had to play on till one or other won a hole. The nineteenth hole was halved, though here Mr. Laidlay appeared to have his opponent at his mercy, and at the next hole splendid drives by each player were followed by very long cleek shots to the green. That of Mr. Ball indeed was too long, and overran the table into a bunker beyond—a hazard, it may be said, scarcely ever reached under three shots. This bit of hard fortune enabled Mr. Laidlay with a brilliantly played 4 to win the match. As a boy at Loretto he was early fascinated by the game, for which physically he is eminently adapted, being wiry, active, and well-knit. At school he was the only boy who could draw himself up on a horizontal bar by the use of one hand alone. At the age of sixteen he performed a remarkable golfing feat at Musselburgh, holing the round in 36, each hole being done in 4, and from that time to this his golfing career has been on the whole a triumphal march from one victory to another. On every green he has visited he has done something more or less phenomenal ; whilst to detail in order the medals and prizes he has won would need more space than lies at the writer's disposal. To take the year 1887 alone, Mr. Laidlay in the course of it won eleven first medals and two second, three of these being won with record scores for the respective competitions. St. Andrews, Hoylake, North Berwick, Musselburgh, and Prestwick were the greens played over, and the scores included 83 at St. Andrews, 72 at North Berwick, and 79 at Musselburgh. In the more trying ordeals of tournaments also he has gone through to the finish, his final round at Carnoustie in 1885 being in especial a brilliant exposition of golf. On that occasion, in the course of the play, Mr. John Ball, jun., had made a remarkably good round of 79, which, however, was eclipsed by Mr. Laidlay's 77, which remained a record for some time. A year later he won a tournament at North Berwick, after playing off the tie with Mr. Horace Hutchinson ; several successes followed, until in 1889 he worthily crowned the edifice by winning the amateur championship. The capabilities of Mr. Laidlay are such, and his prowess is so well established, that it is not probable that any potential feat of his would now excite much surprise ; still, it may be worth while to indicate two out of many great performances which in his own estimation surpass anything else he has done. The first of these was the holing of the first ten holes at North Berwick in 33, a quite unprecedented score. For purposes of comparison it may be well to give his figures and those of Sayers, when the latter made the lowest recorded round of 66 :

$$\text{Laidlay, } 3\ 3\ 3\ 2\ 3\ 4\ 3\ 3\ 4\ 5\ \cdot\ \cdot\ \cdot\ 33$$
$$\text{Sayers, } 5\ 5\ 3\ 4\ 3\ 3\ 4\ 3\ 4\ 4\ \cdot\ \cdot\ \cdot\ 38$$

The second performance was the holing of two rounds at Musselburgh in 72, whilst playing the best ball of Sir Walter Simpson and Colonel Briggs. The first of these rounds was— 5 5 5 3 4 3 3 3 3 = 34. To these may be added a round played at Luffness in August 1889 with Mr. Horace Hutchinson, when both gentlemen lowered the record of the green, which stood at 75 ; Mr. Hutchinson doing 74 and Mr. Laidlay 69— 38 out and 31 home—this score comprising six threes. Enough has been said to show the manner of man Mr. Laidlay is ; his style is powerful if, perhaps, not exactly orthodox. There is indeed a story current to the effect that some admirer of his many successes, who had, however, never seen him play, journeyed down to North Berwick with that express object in view. As a result of patient and anxious scrutiny, at the end of the round he declared that Mr. Laidlay had every known fault at golf that he, the witness, had ever been taught to avoid. Genius, however, refuses to be trammelled by such minor considerations as grips, stances, right and left thumbs, and the other thirty-nine articles of belief which make the plodding golfer's life a burden to him; and the present amateur champion, faults or no faults, has not only gone on his own way rejoicing, but may be said to have introduced a golfing cult of his own. So sincere is the adulation paid to success! 'His miserable imitators swarm on every green in the Lothians,' says a well-known writer, and the words are true. Mr. Laidlay is also a photographer of great skill, and some of his expeditions to the Bass Rock with his camera have resulted in admirable photographs of fluffy young gannets and other seafowl which frequent its storm-beaten crags. He is addicted, besides, to nautical pursuits, and is often to be found catching lobsters in lobster-pots—an amusement which, he declares, is of the greatest assistance to him in his golf, inasmuch as he can drive much further with every club after the spell of severe manual labour involved in persuading the passive crustaceans to forsake their native element.

It is often averred that the two games of golf and cricket, if not exactly mutually destructive, yet react prejudicially on each other. Without entering into any polemical discussion on the matter, the conjecture may perhaps be hazarded—granting the fact to be as above stated—that if a child begins to knock about with a toy club as soon as it can walk, continues the process, and takes to cricket a good deal later, the disturbing influence of the latter will be imperceptible. In support of this theory Mr. Leslie Melville Balfour may be cited. He is in the very front rank of gentlemen cricketers in Scotland, whilst as a golfer his name is one to conjure with. He is not nearly so cosmopolitan in his play as Mr. Laidlay however, for whilst the present champion has won prizes on nearly every green in Scotland, and was also fortunate enough to establish a record at Cairo, Mr. Balfour's exploits have been for the most part confined to St. Andrews. True, he joined the Honourable Company in 1881, and won over Musselburgh three first medals in spring, and tied for a fourth; won the winter medal three times, his best score for that green being 81, and also carried off twice in succession a silver medal given as second prize in 1887. This is an undeniably good record; but taking into consideration the severer rivalry at St. Andrews, his red-letter days there are probably more deeply imprinted in his memory. *Bon chien chasse de race*, and Mr. Balfour is the son of an expert golfer, to wit Mr. James Balfour, whose name appears as a medal winner three times in the Royal and Ancient lists. On both sides of the house Mr. Balfour inherits very great strength of grasp and wrist power, which cannot fail to be of service to him in his cricket and golf. He is a very strong driver, and a particularly good scorer in rough weather; indeed, many of his medals have been won on very bad days, in scores which would defy criticism under the most favourable meteorological conditions.

Engrossed heart and soul in the game, he is not one who lets a chance slip if any care on his part can avoid it, and, besides being—apart from his skill—a right good partner, he has the enviable gift of being able to play up 'all he knows' whether Fortune smiles or frowns; nor, when matters wear their rosiest aspect, does he ever allow himself to drop his game and run the common risk of being unable to take it up again, thus imperilling, or even losing after all, a match to all intents and purposes practically won. The conditions under which alone prophecy may be safely indulged in are well known; but, looking at all the leading amateurs, Mr. Balfour strikes one as being one of the most likely to carry his fine play late into life—to be, in fact, a counterpart in the amateur section to the veteran Tom Morris among professionals. From the year 1874 until now, Mr. Balfour has carried off at intervals every medal played for over his native green, with the one exception of the silver cross contested in the spring; but it is a curious fact that the best medal score he has ever made—viz. 85—was compiled when playing for it in 1883, and it was certainly hard fortune that a lowest on record should have been made against him on that occasion. The family, however, is not unrepresented even here ; for in 1881 fraternal ability came to the rescue in the person of Mr. Elliott S. Balfour, who won the silver cross with a good score of 88. Five times winner in the autumn, four times second medallist, and five times winner of the Bombay medal, Mr. Balfour has also four times secured the George Glennie cup for the best aggregate scores at both meetings ; one of these—viz. 173—being so far the lowest score made for it. Such steadiness speaks for itself, and undoubtedly he is one of the finest golfers the ancient city has ever produced.

The name of Mr. Allan Fullarton Macfie at once suggests itself as being an indispensable addition to any gallery of golfing celebrities. This gentleman in many respects is a most remarkable player. Whilst unable to lay claim to the vigorous thews and sinews possessed by the great majority of his rivals, and being indeed constitutionally far from robust, he nevertheless makes such excellent use of the advantages with which he has been endowed that he is, most decidedly, one of the leading amateurs of the day. He perhaps more than any of his compeers approximates golf to an exact science. Never by any chance deluded into trying for more than he can do, content to let the club fall with an easy full swing, he makes accuracy the be-all and end-all of his aim. Perhaps the two players with whom he might best be compared are Allan Robertson and Jamie Anderson, in both of whom deadly steadiness was conspicuous in combination with thoughtful consideration, where the ball was to be placed in order that the next succeeding shot might be played to the best advantage. Hence, if the links at St. Andrews were suddenly to resume the aspect they presented some thirty years ago, it is very probable that this gentleman would then be a good deal more difficult to beat than he is even now. Of every kind of artistic shot which is to be found in the finished golfer's storehouse he is a past-master ; like a conjurer, he is continually, so to speak, juggling with the balls, and all sorts of niblicks, mashies, and quaint hybrids evolved from his own workshop have in his accomplished hands their multifarious uses. To no player does the fact of being outdriven make so little difference ; for, though a good driver, there are some terrific 'swipers' who have a slight pull of him in this one respect. But so long as he can reach the green in the same number of strokes as his opponent, he is certain to lay a long drive home, at least as close to the hole as an iron approach, if not indeed closer, and, as he is in addition a most beautiful putter, his successes are easily accounted for. A veritable Cœur de Lion, in almost every competition he plays well, and the harder the task the better he braces himself up to its performance; and in any tough match it is a most interesting sight to witness the serene infallibility with which he plays every shot all the way round, leaving the opponent to do as he chooses. Then, if once the latter makes a bad shot and fails to retrieve it, he most likely becomes, in the classic phraseology of the caddies, ' a waster.'

Mr. Macfie played about a dozen times as a boy at North Berwick and Bruntsfield Links, and not till 1879 at Hoylake did he begin to devote any attention to it, a few intermittent efforts a year or two previously being excepted. The year 1880 saw him a medal-winner for the first time, and thenceforth competitions on the greens of Hoylake, Blundellsands, Bembridge, Westward Ho, and St. Andrews have made it manifest that he is a golfer of quite first-class attainments. In 1885 he was successful in the final round of the Amateur Championship Tournament at Hoylake, defeating Mr. Horace Hutchinson ; the next year from scratch he won the Calcutta Cup Handicap Tournament at St. Andrews : whilst in 1889 the Spring Medal at St. Andrews, Queen Victoria Jubilee Vase (a handicap tournament), and three first medals at Westward Ho (one of them for the best aggregate score), fell to his share. When it is remembered that in some of his victories he has finished in front of such players as Mr. Horace Hutchinson, Mr. John

Ball, jun., and Mr. Laidlay, little more need be said as to his well-merited renown.

By example no less than precept has Mr. Horace G. Hutchinson done his utmost in the way of popularising golf on both sides of the Tweed. It is, moreover, worthy of consideration whether the general improvement perceptible in first-class amateur play is not, perhaps, traceable to this gentleman's influence, and to that of Mr. John Ball, jun.—both of them Englishmen born and bred. The standard of play which was considered and indeed was good enough to hold its own some dozen years or so ago, became altogether too low when these two ex-champions came to buckle on their armour. Mr. Hutchinson began as a boy at Westward Ho, his principal antagonist there being Mr. Arthur H. Molesworth, a very powerful player, whose name appears thirty-nine times on the list of prize-winners on the Devon green; whilst in addition he has carried off scratch medals at Wimbledon, where he now usually plays, no less than fourteen times, and has won the Club Championship once. In his early days Mr. Hutchinson began habitually to get in more long putts than anybody else, and as his strength increased so did his driving power, whilst in the course of time he developed a mastery over the iron in all its gradations that was almost irresistible. Thus it is not surprising that the medals he has won at Westward Ho alone would go far to stock a jeweller's shop. As a prize-winner on that green his name appears forty-four times. He has now won the Prince of Wales's Medal—a first prize—no less than eight years in succession, the gold medal six years out of seven, and the Lindsay-Bennet Medal for aggregate score seven years in succession.

When some years ago he began in a double sense to break new ground, it was apparent wherever he went that his mastery was complete, not only over his clubs, but over most people who found themselves in antagonism with him. On his first visit to St. Andrews, where, if anywhere, competent judges may be supposed to exist, his play was day after day keenly watched, and was of a nature calculated to arouse feelings well-nigh reverential in their intensity. On this green in 1886 he won the Amateur Championship, playing the final with Mr. Henry A. Lamb, who had just previously administered a severe defeat to Mr. John Ball, jun. The next year Mr. Hutchinson won this coveted trophy again, this time at Hoylake, where he played the final with Mr. J. Ball, jun., winning at the last hole. In this tournament, before the conclusion was reached he encountered an amount of opposition as stubborn as it was perhaps unlooked-for; for first of all Mr. John Ball, sen. (a strong player on his own green), playing up with surprising vigour and success, and, secondly, Mr. Gregor McGregor, of the Edinburgh Burgess Society, were all but instrumental in effecting his overthrow. The latter gentleman indeed halved his match, and only succumbed at the nineteenth hole, where the luck was against him; whilst Mr. Ball, sen., was with difficulty disposed of by the narrow margin of a hole. The final was productive of some magnificent golf, and might have been even closer than it was had not young Mr. Ball had the very hard luck to break his favourite brassy two holes from home. It will be seen that Mr. Hutchinson played in the final for three years in succession—viz. 1885, when Mr. Macfie won, in 1886 and 1887. Before succumbing in 1885 he had played a truly splendid game with Mr. John Ball, jun., each of them going round in about 80; but two extraordinary recoveries from difficulties enabled Mr. Hutchinson to win one of the most stubborn contests ever seen. At St. Andrews his name appears as medallist six times, 84 and 85 being his two lowest scores, and he carried off the Glennie Cup in 1884. Three points call for special mention in his play—his long and extraordinarily straight driving against a head wind, his great power of driving with an iron, and, most important of all, the marvellous and to his opponent wearisome accuracy of his holing out at distances from three or four club lengths and under. He has played over many greens, and has been largely instrumental in introducing golf at Eastbourne, which now, thanks to his exertions, boasts a flourishing club.

It is a matter of regret that Mr. John Ball, jun., the Hoylake champion, is not seen on the Northern greens more frequently. Beyond all question he is one of the grandest players who ever wielded a club, and in every way capable of winning the Open Championship in a professional field, for which competition, however, he unfortunately never enters, contenting himself for the most part with his home avocations and the attractions of the Cheshire green. Wiry and active, his sinews are like whipcord. Through the medium of an attractive and graceful style he exhibits great power, more especially with his cleek, with which club he drives sometimes the most astonishing shots; indeed, so strong is he with it, that it is but seldom necessary for him to take a wooden club through the green; this, a brassy for tee shots, and an iron, appear to constitute the greater part of his stock-in-trade. Though he has had, now and again, to acknowledge defeat on his own green, yet few will deny that for the most part he is as nearly as may be invincible. The following marvellous record stands in his name:—Thirty-six times he has won first medals; his best round is 77; his worst, 88; and (with the exception of 78) he has made every score comprised within these limits, the average of all his winning rounds being $83\frac{1}{18}$. Now, when it is remembered that Hoylake is afflicted very frequently with winds of exasperating intensity, that these winds are prone to select for their advent the special days when medals are to be played for, and that owing to the conformation of the course a player encounters them at ever-varying angles, it is difficult to see how such a record could be equalled, let alone surpassed. After being in the main rather unfortunate in his first endeavours to win the Amateur Championship, he in 1888 made good his claim to this distinction—a success which no one begrudged him, for unquestionably during the week at Prestwick he played consistently the steadiest golf. His most stubborn opponent on this occasion was the late Mr. James Mansfield, whose sudden death not long afterwards from the effects of an accident cast a gloom over the golfing world. To defeat this gentleman, Mr. Ball had to play his very best, and with a well-

MR. JOHN BALL

played 80 won the match by 2. He met Mr. Laidlay in the final, and won by 5 and 4 to play. To crown his achievements for the year, he went to Sandwich, where he won the Grand Challenge Trophy, worth 400*l*. This competition is decided by score ; and notwithstanding the fact that a bitterly cold gale of wind was blowing, of strength sufficient sometimes to send a high ball back towards the striker, he managed in one of his rounds to score 86—a figure untouched by a single professional, the whole army of whom were engaged at the same time in a contest on their own account. In 1889 he revisited the scene, and again returned triumphant ; this time an 82 for one of his rounds is at present the lowest score yet made by an amateur. The tolerably wide interval of 10 strokes separated him from his nearest opponent. It might be thought that a player of such a stamp would find it unnecessary to include in his orisons the well-known supplication for 'a guid conceit o' hissel' ; ' it is not so, however ; on the contrary, his garb is that of humility, and with meekness is he girded withal. In fact, so reluctant is he to be led into any discussion as to his own merits as compared with those of any great professional, that he will cheerfully announce his opinion that he would have no chance whatever if a match were played.

Mr. S. Mure Fergusson, one of the strongest players of the day, has had little cause to complain of want of success. Endowed with an admirable measure of self-reliance—a quality which in golf, as in other affairs, is as a panoply of steel to its possessor— the idea of defeat is to him, subjectively speaking, a probability unworthy of consideration. With a very long, powerful, deliberate swing, he gets over the ground with tremendous carries ; whilst in the *finesse* of the game, in his manipulation of delicate shots, and generally in all his quarter game, which he plays very prettily, he evinces the greatest discrimination. Putting entirely with his cleek, he rarely misses a putt which should be holed, and consequently, when he is in his best game, no more dangerous player can be named.

He has been very successful in winning medals at St. Andrews, his name appearing six times in the annals of the Club, on two occasions with the very fine scores of 84 and 85.

He was also the first holder of the Glennie Cup. Whilst occasionally playing at Wimbledon, the green in the South where he usually plays is Felixstowe, where he has, as might have been expected, added to the laurels he has gained in the Northern metropolis.

Of the brothers Henry A. and David I. Lamb, both first-class players of many years' standing, whilst the latter is equal to almost any effort of exceptional brilliance and power, the former is none the less renowned as a player of commanding capabilities and a consummate judge of the game, in every detail. A fourfold medallist at St. Andrews, he is perhaps even better known in the South as the efficient secretary of the Royal Wimbledon Golf Club, and latterly as one of the moving spirits in the formation of the new St George's Club, Sandwich. Prizes of every description have fallen to his share since his connexion with Wimbledon, which began in 1869. Sixteen scratch medals there tell their own tale, whilst more recently at Sandwich his star shone out with much additional brilliancy and lustre. As inventor of the 'bulger,' his name stinks in the nostrils of all who see a thing of beauty in the delicate curves of a real thoroughbred head ; but as a countervailing statement, it may be asserted that not a man could play in a match, with or against him, without being struck by the generous appreciation he displays for any merit in his adversary's game, by the philosophical composure and imperturbable good temper which are emphatically characteristic of Mr. Henry A. Lamb.

In making mention of the Royal Wimbledon Club, the names of Mr. Norman R. Foster and Dr. W. Laidlaw Purvis must not be omitted. Both of these gentlemen have earned distinction as first-class players. Having had during boyhood a common playground—the word is used in no disparaging sense—in the now disused Bruntsfield Links, the former continued his practice intermittently at Elie, whilst the latter, after residence in many parts of the globe, at one period so far north as 77°, resumed the game of his boyhood on joining the London Scottish Volunteers. Since then Dr. Purvis has devoted much time and attention to golfing matters, has won scratch medals and other prizes at Wimbledon, and was amongst the very first pioneers who made known the potentialities of Sandwich. At the opening tournament he holed that difficult course in the very fine score of 84, which has only recently been surpassed by Mr. John Ball, jun., in his amateur record of 82. Mr. Foster has won the Club Championship at Wimbledon once, and carried off four scratch medals and other prizes. Many names occur to the writer as being deserving of more extended notice than space will permit. There is, for instance, Mr. A. M. Ross, who for many years appeared to be invincible in the Edinburgh Burgess competitions at Musselburgh, where his scores of 40 and under were thick as blackberries. He, like the two gentlemen just noticed, also learned the game at Bruntsfield. Then there is Mr. James Cunningham, jun., whose graceful style and brilliant execution have ensured for him many a victory on the Forfarshire greens; Mr. C. E. S. Chambers, well known at St. Andrews and in the North Berwick district; and, finally, the brothers Blackwell of St. Andrews, one of whom is probably the longest driver ever seen upon that green, but who is now resident abroad.

It only remains to mention a name which every player who knew him holds in affectionate remembrance, an excellent portrait of whom by Sir Francis Grant adorns the parlour of the Royal and Ancient Club—Mr. John Whyte Melville of Bennochy and Strathkinness. For sixty-seven long years his figure was as well known on the green as his presence was welcome, and, though never attaining to a high degree of skill in his favourite pastime, yet his enthusiasm for it knew no bounds. From a hygienic point of view, indeed, he held it to be absolutely unrivalled, and was frequently heard to declare his conviction that for keeping the doctor from the door the game was a specific. His matches, once they were made, had to be gone through with the most rigid inflexibility, and few indeed were the eventualities which in his eyes could justify any attempt at evasion. On one occasion a foursome had been made up some two or three days in advance ; but when the day arrived it brought with it such a gale of wind and snow that the rest of the party imagined, not unreasonably, that it was altogether unfitted for play. One of them, therefore, having watched with speculative interest a bank of snow drifting up inside and under his front door, betook himself to his smoking-room, together with such comforts as were at his disposal ; the second made preparations for wiping off arrears of business ; whilst it is supposed the third stayed in bed altogether. But they reckoned without their host, for in due course in came the dogcart from Mount Melville, carrying its owner with his accustomed cigar. Not finding a living soul in the club, he drove round to the residences of each of the absentees, and haled them one and all ignominiously to the tee, though even he found it impossible after they did start to get further than the first hole. This is but one illustration which could be paralleled times without number ; indeed, his enthusiasm was a standing reproof to many armchair golfers not a third of his age, who, if a drop of rain might be expected to fall or a puff of wind to blow, were apt to plead indisposition or any flimsy excuse, rather than venture out in weather that was not altogether to their mind. The matches he used to enjoy the most were those in which he was partnered by a first-class player against two of second-rate merit. On such occasions, if a distance of some 200 yards separated him from the hole, and his shot did not diminish the interval by more than about ten paces, he would almost invariably remark, with touching faith in the infallibility of his coadjutor, 'It's all right ; I've made yon, I think,' being evidently under the impression that nothing much better could have been required of him. The same characteristic—a sort of artless simplicity—was apparent in a conversation he once had with the writer, in the course of which he asked the latter to state what he considered his bill for repairs to clubs had amounted to for the year just passed. Thirty shillings or so was the amount hazarded, being perhaps half or a third of what is usual. The answer given with triumphant satisfaction was, 'half a crown.' On returning from his matches he would ensconce himself in an arm-chair with a bottle of 'Golden Hop' and a biscuit as his frugal luncheon, as faithfully represented in these pages by the artist's brush. Though his best efforts failed to send a ball more than seventy or eighty yards, he was nevertheless a good partner, and subordinated his game to that of the stronger player with much judg-

ment; nor did he often lose a hole by putting his partner into difficulties, while on the green he frequently used his putter with telling effect. He was elected captain of the club in 1823, and in 1883 was nominated a second time, but, his death occurring in that year, the office was left vacant. It does not fall within the writer's province to follow Mr. Whyte Melville into other branches of sport; but as a devotee of golf he was most conspicuous — a central figure in his environment. At his hospitable table every golfer found a hearty and genial welcome, and there was a blank indeed when his place knew him no more. From the severe blow he sustained by the death of his talented son, Major George Whyte Melville, he never seemed to recover : when once the well-known cheery red coat was permanently replaced by one of black, the beginning of the end was in sight, and in 1883, at the age of eighty-six, he passed away, mourned by all with whom he had been brought in contact, as a true Christian gentleman, and valued personal friend.

NOTE.—No gallery of celebrated golfers can be at all complete which does not include Mr. H. S. C. Everard, the writer of the above chapter. A good cricketer and tennis-player, Mr. Everard early forsook these for golf, which he has since pursued with perseverance and success. A resident at St. Andrews, he has made a great mark in first-class golf. The second medal has fallen to him, though he has never won first honours on his home green. But at Carnoustie, and elsewhere, he has been more fortunate — most notably at Montrose, where he won the first prize in the open Amateur Tournament. No man in England or Scotland, probably, has more all-round knowledge of the game than Mr. Everard, and none is more devoted to it.—ED.

CHAPTER XV

THE HUMOURS OF GOLF

BY THE RIGHT HON. A. J. BALFOUR, M.P.

BASS ROCK

GRADUALLY round all the greater games there collects a body of sentiment and tradition unknown to or despised by a profane public, but dear to their votaries, and forming a common bond of union among those who practise their rites. This tradition relates partly to memorable contests and the deeds of bygone heroes, partly to the changes which time brings about in the most ancient sports not less than in the most memorable institutions. But it does not disdain to concern itself with less important matters. Even games are not to be regarded as wholly serious: they have their lighter side, and he must be unhappily constituted who cannot relieve the graver labours in which his favourite pursuit involves him by watching the humours and comparing notes on the proceedings of others who are similarly occupied.

Now golf gives unrivalled opportunities for investigations of this description. There is more to observe in it than in other games, and there are more opportunities for observing. This is so because the conditions under which golf is played differ fundamentally from those of almost any other form of out-door exercises, and every difference lends itself naturally to the promotion of an infinite variety of characteristic humours.

Consider, for instance, the fact that while the performers at other games are restricted within comparatively narrow limits of age, golf is out of relation with no one of the seven ages of man. Round the links may be seen in endless procession not only players of every degree of skill and of every social condition, but also of every degree of maturity and immaturity. There is no reason, in the nature of things, why golf should not be begun as soon as you can walk, and continued as long as you can walk ; while, as a matter of fact, it frequently is so begun, and always is so continued. What an excellent variety does not this give to the game, as a subject of observation, and how humorously is that variety heightened and flavoured by the fact that age and dexterity are so frequently bestowed in inverse proportion ! You may see at one teeing ground a boy of ten driving his ball with a swing which no professional would despise, and at the next a gentleman of sixty, recently infected with the pleasing madness, patiently 'topping' his ball through the green under the long-suffering superintendence of a professional adviser.

No greater proof, indeed, can be imagined of the fascinations of the game than the fact that so many of us are willing to learn it—and, what is more, to learn it in public—at a period of life when even competitive examinations have ceased to trouble ? Lord Chancellor Campbell, we are told, took dancing lessons at the mature age of thirty-four ; in order, as he said, to 'qualify him for joining the most polite assemblies.' But he took them in privacy, under an assumed name, and with every precaution that might ensure his maintaining his incognito. Would even Lord Chancellor Campbell have taken dancing lessons if the scene of his tuition had been a public golf link ? If the *chassés* and *coupés* of which he speaks had to be attempted before a miscellaneous and highly critical public ? If his first ineffectual efforts at 'figuring on the light fantastic toe' (I still quote the noble and learned lord) had been displayed to a mixed assemblage of professional and amateur dancers ? I trow not. Rather, a thousand times rather, would he have remained deficient in any graces lighter than those required for special pleading, and renounced for ever the hope of shining in 'the most polite assemblies' ! Yet, after all, no ordeal less than this has been gone through by those of us who have first become golfers in mature life. We have seen ourselves, often at an age when other people are leaving off the games they learned in their youth, laboriously endeavouring to acquire a game which certainly not less than any other punishes with eternal mediocrity those who too long defer devoting themselves to its service. We have been humiliated in the eyes of our opponent, in the eyes of our caddie, in the eyes of our opponent's caddie, and in our own eyes by the perpetration of blunders which would seem almost incredible in narration. We have endeavoured time after time to go through the same apparently simple and elementary set of evolutions. Time after time we have failed. We have, if playing in a foursome, apologised to our partner until we were sick of making excuses and he was sick of listening to them. Yet who has ever been repelled by this ordeal from continuing his efforts until age or sickness incapacitate him ? Who, having once begun, has been found to turn back ? It might indeed be supposed that, if before beginning all that had to be gone through were fully realised, our greens would be emptier than they are. But a splendid confidence, born of impenetrable ignorance, veils his future from the eyes of the beginner. It is narrated of one intending golfer that he wrote home to a friend, saying that all his arrangements for playing were nearly completed : he had purchased the necessary implements ; he had been elected at the club, and he had *hired a bunker for his own exclusive use !*

MAY AND DECEMBER

Ingenious commentators aver that for *bunker* in this passage should be read *locker*. But, however this may be, what delicious ignorance is there not displayed in these observations ! What blissful unconsciousness of miseries yet to come ! The writer little knew that in the case of this particular kind of real estate no process of hiring is by golfing law required ; that exclusive possession, though it carries few privileges, brings with it no envy ; that he might cultivate it with his niblick and the sweat of his brow till the crack of doom, and no man would be found to suggest that what Providence intended for the people should not be monopolised by the individual !

Strange legends are current as to the fate which has overtaken beginners wrestling with the horrors of a really bad bunker. I have been told of a game in which, when one of the players finally emerged from one of those yawning sandpits, a controversy arose between the caddies as to whether he had played *forty-five* or *sixty-five* before getting out ; and so hotly did the contest rage, and so convinced were the combatants, not merely of the righteousness but of the importance of their cause, that in the end it was only found possible to settle the point by the ordeal of battle ! On another occasion it is said that a player of resolute character disappeared from view down one of these abysses, and only made his presence known to the rest of the world by the clouds of sand driven up from time to time by the niblick. On returning to upper air he was politely asked by his opponent (who must have been at least as remarkable for patience as the other was for perseverance) how many he had played. 'I went into that place,' was the reply, 'at a quarter-past twelve. It is now a quarter to one. You are at liberty to form your own estimate !'

Very marvellous are the expedients sometimes adopted in order to enable the mature learner to acquire some stammering knowledge of a language which might have been acquired so easily and so perfectly during youth. In one case an enthusiastic beginner pinned a copy of the most important golfing maxims in a conspicuous place in his dressing-room, and in the intervals of his ablutions devoted his mind to their perusal during those early moments of the day when it is thought that new ideas most easily and permanently imprint themselves on the awakening soul.

Another wrote his saving formula, 'Slow back, keep your eye on the ball,' &c. on his shirt-sleeve; and before each stroke rend it solemnly in muttered tones to himself. A third, still more original, waited till he had got himself into the exact position recommended by the learned in driving off from the tee; and then, in order to embody in substantial form this evanescent moment of inspiration, sent for the carpenter, and, so to speak, had himself *built in* to a kind of wooden framework, into which he could always again be fitted when the occasion required it. It is said that his caddie was expected to carry this 'mould of form' round the course, so that whenever its inventor had to drive he might be certain, if he missed his shot, at least of missing it 'according to rule!'

Since golf, when it has been once begun, exercises this fatal fascination upon its votaries, it is perhaps fortunate that of all games it appears to the uninitiated to be the most meaningless. A *mêlée* at football may appear to involve a perfectly unnecessary expenditure of energy and a foolish risk of life and limb. But even the most ignorant can see what it is all about. Rackets and tennis, again, at once strike the beholder as being games which require great quickness of eye and great dexterity of hand. But there appears to be something singularly inane and foolish about a game of golf. Two middle-aged gentlemen strolling across a links followed by two boys staggering under the burden of a dozen queer-shaped implements, each player hitting along his own ball for no apparent object, in no obvious rivalry, and exercising in the process no obvious skill, do not make up a specially impressive picture to those who see it for the first time; and many are the curious theories advanced by the ignorant to explain the motives and actions of the players

Two Englishmen, it is said, visited St. Andrews in the

course of a Scotch tour. Looking out of the window of the train at the point where the railway runs along the links, they took their first survey of the game. The weather had been very wet, and at the bottom of some bunkers water was lying. 'These are the places,' said A to B, with ready ingenuity, 'where the Scotch play curling in winter.' 'No,' said B to A, 'these are the holes they use for golf, and the object of the player is to get out of one into another as quickly as he can manage it.' Armed with this superior knowledge, A proceeds down to the links, and finds an old gentleman struggling with destiny at the bottom of a bad bunker. At last the player succeeds in getting out his ball, but only with the result of sending it into the next bunker a few yards farther on. This is not an agreeable incident under any circumstances at golf; but conceive, if you can, the irritation of the player when he finds himself being loudly, and, as he no doubt thought, ironically congratulated by a spectator on the results of his stroke, and the well-merited success with which it had been rewarded! I do not know whether this story be apocryphal or not, but in any case the ignorance which it displays is not likely to be long continued in the southern portion of the island. There will soon be more greens in England than in Scotland, and more players of English extraction than of Scotch. 'Do you have much play here?' said someone to the keeper of a racket court in the neighbourhood of an English golf links. 'We used to, sir,' said the man; 'but ever since this d——d Scotch croquet has come into fashion, no one comes into the court.'

It is hard that a game which seems to those who do not play it to be so meaningless should be to those who do play it not only the most absorbing of existing games, but occasionally in the highest degree irritating to the nerves and to the temper. The fact itself will, I apprehend, hardly be denied, and the reason I suppose to be this, that as in most games action is rapid and more or less unpremeditated, failure seems less humiliating in itself, and there is less time to brood over it. In most games—*e.g.* cricket, tennis, football—effort succeeds effort in such quick succession that the memory of particular blunders is immediately effaced or deadened. There is leisure neither for self-examination nor for repentance. Even good resolutions scarce have time to form themselves, and as soon as one difficulty is surmounted, mind and body have to brace themselves to meet the next. In the case of golf it is far otherwise. The player approaches his ball with every circumstance of mature deliberation. He meditates, or may meditate, for as long as he pleases on the precise object he wishes to accomplish and the precise method by which it may best be accomplished. No difficulties are made for him by his opponent; he has no obstacles to overcome but those which are material and inanimate. Is there not, then, some natural cause for irritation when, after every precaution has been taken to insure a drive of 150 or 180 yards, the unfortunate player sees his ball roll gently into the bottom of a bunker some twenty yards in front of the teeing ground and settle itself with every appearance of deliberate forethought at the bottom of the most inaccessible heel-mark therein? Such an event brings with it not merely disaster, but humiliation; and, as a last aggravation, the luckless performer has ample leisure to meditate over his mishap, to analyse its causes, to calculate the precise effects which it will have on the general fortunes of the day, and to divine the secret satisfaction with which his opponent has observed the difficulties in which he has so gratuitously involved himself. No wonder that persons of irritable nerves are occasionally goaded to fury. No wonder that the fury occasionally exhibits itself in violent and eccentric forms. Not, however, that the opponent is usually the object or victim of their wrath. He is too obviously guiltless of contributing to a 'foozle' to permit even an angry man to drag him into his quarrel with the laws of dynamics. It is true that he may have the most extraordinary and unmerited luck. According to my experience, opponents who are winning usually have. But still he can hardly be blamed because the man he is playing with 'tops' his ball or is 'short' with his putts. Let him only

THE WORST OF SEASIDE BUNKERS IN THE SEASON

assume an aspect of colourless indifference or hypocritical sympathy, and the storm will in all probability not break over *him*.

Expletives more or less vigorous directed against himself, the ball, the club, the wind, the bunker, and the game, are therefore the most usual safety-valve for the fury of the disappointed golfer. But bad language is fortunately much gone out of use ; and in any case the resources of profanity are not inexhaustible. Deeds, not words, are required in extreme cases to meet the exigencies of the situation ; and, as justice, prudence, and politeness all conspire to shield his opponent from physical violence, it is on the clubs that under these circumstances vengeance most commonly descends. Most players content themselves with simply breaking the offending weapon against the ground. But some persons there are whose thirst for revenge cannot be satisfied by any such rapid or simple process. I have been told of one gentleman who threw the offending club upon the ground, and then with his niblick proceeded to punish it with piecemeal destruction, breaking its shaft into small pieces very much as criminals used to be broken upon the wheel. Even this procedure seemed inadequate to one infuriated golfer of whom I have heard. A shaft, be it broken into ever so many fragments, can be replaced and the implement be as good as new. Nothing less than destroying both head and shaft can insure its final disappearance from the world of golf. The club must not merely be broken, but must be destroyed, and from its hated remnants no new race must be permitted to arise for the torment and discomfiture of succeeding generations of golfers. This perfect consummation can, it is said, be attained by holding the club upright, the head resting on the ground, then placing one foot upon it and kicking it with the other, just at the point where head and shaft are bound together. By this simple expedient (which I respectfully commend to the attention of all short-tempered golfers) a 'root and branch' policy may be effectually carried out by destroying at one stroke both the essential parts of the club.

If there are any who hold the opinion that measures such as this can never be justified by any series of golfing disasters, however aggravating, I would reply in the language of a gentleman who, when remonstrated with for using his clubs in one of the methods above described, responded with unanswerable logic, 'Is it not better to smash your dashed clubs than to lose your dashed temper?'

While, on the whole, playing through the green is the part of the game most trying to the temper, putting is that most trying to the nerves. There is always hope that a bad drive may be redeemed by a fine approach shot, or that a 'foozle' with the brassy may be balanced by some brilliant performance with the iron. But when the stage of putting-out has been reached no further illusions are possible—no place for repentance remains : to succeed in such a case is to win the hole ; to fail, is to lose it. Moreover, it constantly happens that the decisive stroke has to be made precisely at a distance from the hole such that, while success is neither certain nor glorious, failure is not only disastrous but ignominious. A putt of a club's length which is to determine not merely the hole but the match will try the calmness even of an experienced performer, and many there are who have played golf all their lives whose pulse beats quicker when they have to play the stroke. No slave ever scanned the expression of a tyrannical master with half the miserable anxiety with which the performer surveys the ground over which the hole is to be approached. He looks at the hole from the ball, and he looks at the ball from the hole. No blade of grass, no scarcely perceptible inclination of the surface, escapes his critical inspection. He puts off the decisive moment as long, and perhaps longer, than he decently can. If he be a man who dreads responsibility, he asks the advice of his caddie, of his partner, and of his partner's caddie, so that the particular method in which he proposes to approach the hole represents not so much his own individual policy as the policy of a Cabinet. At last the stroke is made, and immediately all tongues are loosened. The slowly advancing ball is addressed in tones of menace or entreaty by the surrounding players. It is requested to go on or stop; to turn this way or that, as the respective interests of each party require. Nor is there anything more entertaining than seeing half a dozen faces

'HE LOOKS AT THE HOLE FROM THE BALL.'

bending over this little bit of moving gutta-percha which so remorselessly obeys the laws of dynamics, and pouring out on it threatenings and supplications not to be surpassed in apparent fervour by the devotions of any fetish worshippers in existence.

The peculiar feeling of nervousness which accompanies 'putting' is of course the explanation of the familiar experience that, when nothing depends upon it, it is quite easy to 'hole' your ball from a distance which makes success too often impossible when the fortunes of the game are at stake. 'How is it, dad?' said a little girl who was accompanying her father round the course—'how is it that when they tell you that you have *two* to win, you always do it in *one*, and that when they say you have *one* to win you always do it in *two*?' In that observation lies compressed the whole philosophy of putting.

It might be thought that among the 'differentia' of golf the conscientious annalist would have to enumerate the facilities for fraud which the conditions under which the game is played would seem to afford. The whole difficulty of a stroke depending as it so often does entirely upon the 'lie' of the ball, which may be altered by an almost imperceptible change in its position, it might appear that there was large scope for the ingenious player to improve his chances of victory by methods not recognised in the rules of the game. As a matter of fact, however, this is not so. In the first place this is no doubt because golfers are an exceptionally honest race of men. In the next place, if there are any persons of dubious morals among them, they probably reflect that, as they are accompanied by caddies, it would be hardly possible to play any tricks except by the connivance of that severe but friendly critic. It is not probable that the connivance would be obtained, and it is quite certain that in the long run secrecy would not be observed by the confidant. Honesty under these circumstances is so obviously the best policy, that the least scrupulous do not venture to offend.

Strange legends, indeed, I have heard of matches played and won by very singular contrivances. A contest is told of one couple who went (without caddies) to play a match that was finally to determine their respective merits. But after a long and rather wild drive, player A lost his ball in the middle of some long bents. A prolonged search ensued, in which both players joined. Suddenly player B espied his opponent's ball, and, wisely reflecting that no simpler or more certain method of winning the hole could be found than that of compelling his opponent to give it up, quietly picked up the ball and secreted it in his pocket. In the meanwhile player A began to be anxious lest that very evil should befall him through natural causes which player B had been endeavouring artificially to produce. His ball was nowhere to be seen, the limit of time was nearly reached, so he bethought him that *his* best course would probably be to take another ball out of his pocket, to drop it in some convenient spot, and to proceed with his play. The plan was no sooner determined on than it was executed, and with a shout of satisfaction he called his opponent's attention to the fact that he had found his ball. 'No, no,' said player B, 'that cannot be it; this is your ball' (producing it from his pocket); 'I picked it up myself awhile ago!'

Another anecdote is told of two players not less well matched than the gentlemen whose performances I have just narrated. They determined to play a match by moonlight. The antagonists were in every respect worthy of each other, and as the match proceeded fortune did not appear to incline to either side. At last they came to a long hole, say 400 yards or so, and to each it occurred at the same time that a critical moment had been reached, and that it was necessary to adopt heroic measures. They drove off two long balls which, to the eyes of the ordinary spectators, appeared to vanish into the night far beyond all human powers of vision to follow. But each of the combatants declared that he saw perfectly where his ball had gone, and they walked off with unfaltering steps in the direction of the hole. When they had gone about 180 yards, each began to be rather surprised that the other showed no signs of indicating that he had reached the place where he expected to find his ball. But no! Both went on with unhesitating stride. Two hundred yards, 250 yards, 300 yards distance from the teeing-ground were successively reached and passed; at last, when they got to the putting-green, some hundred yards or so beyond the longest recorded drive, both balls were found lying within a club's length of the hole, the fact being that each player had arranged to be able to drop a ball through a hole in his trousers pocket when he should reach some point conveniently situated beyond that to which the other should have been able to drive. The plan was undeniably a good one, its only defect being that it must necessarily break down if adopted by both players at the same time.

But what account of the points in which golf differs fundamentally from other games, what study of its peculiar humours would be complete which did not give a place of honour to the institution of *caddies*? Wherever golf exists there must the caddie be found; but not in all places is he a credit to the great cause which he subserves. There are greens in England—none, I rejoice to think, in Scotland—where, either because golf has been too recently imported or because it suits not the genius of the population, many of the caddies are not only totally ignorant of the game, which is bad, but are wholly uninterested in it, which is far worse. They regard it as a form of lunacy, harmless to the principals who pay, and not otherwise than beneficial to the assistants who plenteously receive, but in itself wearisome and unprofitable. Such caddies go far to spoil the sport. For my own part I can gladly endure severe or even contemptuous criticism from the ministering attendant. I can bear to have it pointed out to me that all my misfortunes are the direct and inevitable result my own folly; I can listen with equanimity when failure is prophesied of some stroke I am attempting, and can note unmoved the self-satisfied smile with which the fulfilment of the prophecy is accentuated; but ignorant and stupid indifference is intolerable. A caddie is not and ought not to be regarded as a machine for carrying clubs at the rate of a shilling a round. He occupies or ought to occupy the position of competent adviser or interested spectator. He should be as anxious for the success of his side as if he were one of the players, and should watch each move in the game with benevolent if critical interest, always ready with the appropriate club, and, if need be, with the appropriate comment.

It need not be said that a golfer, too prone to seek for sympathy from his caddie, not unfrequently puts himself in the position of hearing the truth against him instead. 'I went out yesterday,' said a friend of mine to his caddie, 'in forty-five.' 'You'll never do that again,' was the unsatisfactory if truthful rejoinder. 'I beat Mr. So-and-so at half a stroke yesterday,' said another. 'If I were you,' was the reply, 'I would take care never to play him again.' Even encouragement is occasionally given in a form probably not wholly agreeable to the recipient. I have heard of a youth at Westward Ho who was carrying for a distinguished general, more eminent no doubt upon the field of battle than on the golfing green. The play of the veteran was more than usually indifferent. He topped his ball with unvarying success from bunker to bunker. At last the boy lost all patience and exclaimed, 'Come! come! old gentleman, this will never do.'

As I have had occasion to mention Scotch caddies and English caddies, let me repeat a story I have heard about a French caddie at Pau, which would seem to indicate that the sympathetic criticism of the caddie abroad is no whit behind that of his insular brother, hampered though he may be by the difficulties of a foreign tongue. An English player who knew no French made a fine approach shot with his iron and succeeded in laying his ball dead. He turned round to his French attendant for applause. The latter saw what was expected of him and did his best to rise to the occasion. He described the shot in the only English words which he had heard habitually associated with any remarkably successful stroke in the game. Looking full in his employer's face, and with his most winning and sympathetic smile, he uttered the words, 'Beastly fluke!'

No doubt the French youth conceived himself to be conveying the most agreeable of compliments to his employer, but I would not have it supposed that if players in Scotland are resolved on hearing from their caddies nothing but what is pleasant they cannot be accommodated if they set to work in the right spirit. It is told of a caddie at one time very well known at St. Andrews under the name of 'Long Willie,' that he was in the habit of carrying for a player so ill-endowed by nature for the game, that though his driving was of the shortest, he never could see where his ball went to. He seldom played matches, probably because he seldom could find anybody who cared to play with him. But he used to get hold of Long Willie and make him tee a lot of balls for him, and would strike them off, under Long Willie's directions, one after the other. Long Willie used generally to lead him up close to the Martyrs' Memorial. The present club-house was not then built, and the gentlemen used to drive off one little 'shottie' after another to some such accompaniment as this from Long Willie : ' Eh, Mr. So-and-so, but that's a maist awfu' drive.' ' Guid save us, saw a body iron the like o' that.' Long Willie used to send a boy on ahead, who used to gather the balls and carry them on down towards the burn—some two hundred yards or more, so when the balls were all driven Long Willie used to toddle away down with his short-sighted master further than mortal man had ever driven before, and there they would come on the balls, where the boy had put them. Then they would go back and begin again. And after a few turns of this Long Willie would say, ' Eh, well, Maister So-and-so, I think we've may be done enough for the day. It's nae a guid thing to over-gowf yersel', ye ken.' And so Long Willie would get his half-crown, and the short-sighted gentleman would go home and say that Long Willie was a most invaluable caddie, that he could drive ever so much further when he had Long Willie to carry for him.

After all, however, the humours of golf can be but very imperfectly exhibited in description or illustrated by anecdote ; nor has it been my intention in these few pages to add one to the many excellent collections of golfing stories which the piety of golfers in successive generations has given to the world. It is only on the links that these humours can be studied ; it is only by those who are familiar with the game that they can be appreciated. To such there is infinite entertainment to be derived from watching the different methods of play, numerous as the multitude of players. 'Some golfers,' explained a novice to his friend, 'when they hit the ball, swing their caddie (*sic*) only a little way, others swing their caddie right round their head.' This gentleman's knowledge of technical terms was doubtless imperfect, but he had the root of the matter in him. No two men use their clubs alike; no two men deal in the same way or in the same temper with the varying changes or chances of the game. And this is one, though doubtless only one, among the many causes which make golf the most uniformly amusing amusement which the wit of man has yet devised.

A tolerable day, a tolerable green, a tolerable opponent, supply, or ought to supply, all that any reasonably constituted human being should require in the way of entertainment. With a fine sea view, and a clear course in front of him, the golfer should find no difficulty in dismissing all worries from his mind, and regarding golf, even it may be very indifferent golf, as the true and adequate end of man's existence. Care may sit behind the horseman, she never presumes to walk with the caddie. No inconvenient reminiscences of the ordinary work-aday world, no intervals of weariness or monotony interrupt the pleasures of the game. And of what other recreation can this be said? Does a man trust to conversation to occupy his leisure moments? He is at the mercy of fools and bores. Does he put his trust in shooting, hunting, or cricket? Even if he be so fortunately circumstanced as to obtain them in perfection, it will hardly be denied that such moments of pleasure as they can afford are separated by not infrequent intervals of tedium. The ten-mile walk through the rain after missing a stag; a long ride home after a blank day; fielding out while your opponents score 400, cannot be described by the most enthusiastic deer-stalker, fox-hunter, or cricketer, as otherwise than wearisome episodes in delightful pursuits. Lawn-tennis, again, is not so much a game as an exercise, while in real tennis or in rackets something approaching to equality of skill between the players would seem to be almost necessary for enjoyment. These more violent exercises, again, cannot be played with profit for more than one or two hours in the day. And while this may be too long for a man very hard worked in other ways, it is too short for a man who wishes to spend a complete holiday as much as possible in the open air.

Moreover, all these games have the demerit of being adapted principally to the season of youth. Long before middle life is reached, rowing, rackets, fielding at cricket, are a weariness to those who once excelled at them. At thirty-five, when strength and endurance may be at their maximum, the particular elasticity required for these exercises is seriously diminished. The man who has gloried in them as the most precious of his acquirements begins, so far as they are concerned, to grow old ; and growing old is not commonly supposed to be so agreeable an operation in itself as to make it advisable to indulge in it more often in a single lifetime than is absolutely necessary. The golfer, on the other hand, is never old until he is decrepit. So long as Providence allows him the use of two legs active enough to carry him round the green, and of two arms supple enough to take a 'half swing,' there is no reason why his enjoyment in the game need be seriously diminished. Decay no doubt there is ; long driving has gone for ever ; and something less of firmness and accuracy may be noted even in the short game. But the decay has come by such slow gradations, it has delayed so long and spared so much, that it is robbed of half its bitterness.

I do not know that I can do much better than close this desultory chapter with a brief autobiography, taken down from his own lips, of perhaps the most distinguished professional of the century—a man known by name to all golfers, even to those who have never visited St. Andrews—old Tom Morris.

This transcript of a conversation held on New Year's Day, 1886, is not only interesting in itself, but contains much sound

OLD TOM TELLING HIS STORY

golfing philosophy. I give it to the reader precisely in the shape in which it has been given to me:

'A gude new year t'ye, Maister Alexander, an' mony o' them ! An' it's come weel in, the year has ; for it's just a braw day for a mautch. Lod, sir, it aye seems to me the years, as they rise, skelp fester the tane after t'ither ; they'll sune be makin' auld men o've a'. Hoo auld am I, d'ye ask, sir? Weel I was born June 16, 1821 ; and ye can calc'late that for yoursel'. Aye ! as ye say, sir, born and bred in St. Awndrews, an' a gowffer a' ma days. The vera first time, I think, I hae mind o' mysel' I was toddlin' aboot at the short holes, wi' a putter uneath ma bit oxter.

'I was made 'prentice to Allan as a ba'-macker at eighteen, and wrocht wi' him eliven years. We played, Allan and me thegither, some geyan big mautches—ane in parteecler wi' the twa Dunns, Willie and Jamie, graund players baith, nane better— over fower greens. It was a' through a braw fecht atweens— green an green—but we snoddit 'em bonnie ere the end o't. I canna ca' to mind Allan an me was iver sae sair teckled as that time ; though a wheen richt gude pair o' them did their best to pit oor twa noses oot o' joint. But it was na to be dune wi' Allan an' me. An awfu' player, puir Allan ! the cunningest bit body o' a player, I dae think, that iver haun'led cleek an' putter. An' a kindly body tae, as it weel fits me to say, sir, an' wi' a walth o' slee pawky fun aboot him.

'I left Allan to keep the Green at Prestwick, and was there fourteen years. Three years efter Allan deed I cam to keep the Green here ; an' here I hae been sin syne. Na ! sir, I niver weary o' the gemm ; an' I'm as ready noo to play any gentleman as I was in ma best days. I think I can play aboot as weel yet as I did in ma prime. No, may be, drive *jist* sae lang a ba' ; but there's no muckle odds e'en in that yet. Jist the day I was sixty-four, I gaed roon' in a single wi' Mr. H. in 81. No that ill for the " Auld Horse " as they ca' me—it'll tak' the best of the young ones, I reckon, to be mony shots better than *that*.

'An it had na been for gowff, I'm no sure that at this day, sir, I wad hae been a leevin' man. I've had ma troubles an' ma trials, like the lave ; an', whiles, I thocht they wad hae clean wauved me, sae that to "lay me doun an' dee"—as the song says—lookit aboot a' that was left in life for puir Tam. It was like as if ma vera sowle was a' thegither gane oot o' me. But there's naething like a ticht gude-gowing mautch to soop yer brain clear o' that kin' o' thing ; and wi' the help o' ma God an' o' gowff, I've aye gotten warsled through somehow or ither. The tae thing ta'en wi' the tither, I hae na had an ill time o't. I dinna mind that iver I had an unpleasant ward frae ony o' the many gentlemen I've played wi'. I've aye tried —as ma business was, sir—to mak masel' pleesant to them ; an' they've aye been awfu' pleesant to me.

'An' noo, sir, to end a long and, maybe, a silly crack—bein' maistly about masel'—ye'll jist come wi' me, an ye'll hae a glass o' gude brandy, and I'll have ma pint o' black strap, an' we'll drink a gude New Year to ane anither, an' the like to a' gude gowffers.'

CHAPTER XVI

THE RULES

UNFORTUNATELY the game of golf has no body whose legislative functions are so fully and formally recognised as those of the Committee of the Marylebone Cricket Club in respect to things pertaining to cricket. Nevertheless it is from the 'Rules of the Game of Golf as played on the Links of St. Andrews' that almost every golf club has derived its rules, either directly or indirectly. But there have been certain little divergencies; at one links here, at another there, a little difference in penalties has perhaps crept in unnoticed, all of which have tended to make difficulties in playing the game over the great number of courses upon which the golfer of to-day may take his recreation.

There was always this difficulty, that though a man might be playing in strict accordance with the rules to which he was most accustomed, he might be directly transgressing the local code. The inconvenience of this was manifest. Then began letters to the 'Field,' pointing out the trouble, pointing out certain faults, of loose statement chiefly, in the St. Andrews code, suggesting, sometimes (such revolutionary spirits are there, even among such a conservative body as golfers!) that an 'Association' should be formed to draw up a body of rules to 'supersede' the St. Andrews ones.

Yet still the cry went up, 'We do not so much care what the code is, but we want some code that can be universal.'

The answer was, 'St. Andrews is the original fountain-head of all the codes, St. Andrews is the acknowledged interpreter of all the unwritten rules. All moot points are subjected to the arbitrament of the committee of her royal and ancient club. Why not, all of you, adopt the St. Andrews rules, *en masse*?'

And then the answer was, 'St. Andrews rules deal with the Eden, the railway, the station-master's garden, and so forth. We do not possess these advantages on our links, it would be folly to embody such rules in our code. Therefore it is impossible for us to adopt, *en masse*, St. Andrews rules.'

In 1888 St. Andrews herself awoke to a recognition of this fact, and of the responsibilities of her high position. She eliminated from the main body of her rules those which deal exclusively with local features, putting these in a separate department under the head of 'Local Rules for St. Andrews Links,' while she headed her main body of rules with the bold title 'Rules of Golf.'

By this action on her part, St. Andrews has cleared the way of obstacles to the adoption of a practically universal code, approved by the best wisdom of the golfing ages. These rules, like the British Constitution, are a growth. It is not to be denied that hard cases may be put which these rules do not meet; but experience amply shows them to be sufficient for the proper conduct of the game of golf by all those who are willing to play it, and to interpret the rules in a fair just spirit, not attempting to show the ingenuity of their cavilling, but being humbly grateful for the guidance thus afforded.

We have already expressed an opinion that the game would

THE RULES

be more pleasant if played somewhat more strictly. Nevertheless we may here point to an instance of a rule which, by the courtesy of custom, is never in certain conditions enforced, and which we should never wish so to see enforced. Rule 9 provides that 'no player shall play his teed ball till the party in front have played their second strokes, nor play on to the putting-green till the party in front of him has holed out.' No penalty being laid down for the infringement of this rule, it follows from rule 45 that the loss of the hole is, strictly, the result. This rule 45 is, however, *never* applied to this condition, and it may be doubted if the committee of any club would not decide that the rule of custom, so well recognised, was, in this instance, to be held to supersede the letter of the law.

A code of rules which shall cover every conceivable case is scarcely possible to frame, and would certainly be most voluminous ; and the St. Andrews rules combine, better than any of the modifications of them which have come under our notice, the essential qualities of reasonable brevity and generally adequate protection against unfair play.

These St. Andrews rules, then, we append to this chapter *in toto*: the Rules of Golf, for the guidance of players (we would indeed like to pass an Act of Parliament making it compulsory for every golfer to go through an examination in the rules before taking part in a prize competition), the local St. Andrews rules, and the table showing at what holes handicap strokes, according to their number, shall be taken, to guide young clubs in the drawing up of their local by-laws.

RULES FOR THE GAME OF GOLF.

I. *Mode and Order of playing the Game.*

1. THE Game of Golf is generally played by two sides. Each side may consist either of one person or of two, who play alternately. It may also be played by three or more sides, each playing its own ball.

2. The game commences by each side playing off a ball from a place called the *teeing ground* for the first hole. In a match with two on a side, the partners shall strike off alternately from the tee ; and the players opposed to each other shall be named at starting, and shall continue in the same order during the match. The player entitled to play off first shall be named by the parties themselves, and his side shall continue to lead off, till they lose a hole ; and although the courtesy of starting is generally granted to captains of the club and old members, it may be settled by lot, or toss of a coin.

3. The hole is won by the side holing at fewest strokes ; and the reckoning of the strokes is made by the terms *odds* and *like, two more, three more, one off two,* &c.

4. The side gaining a hole shall lead at the next (except at the commencement of a new match, in which case the winner of the previous match is to lead), and is entitled to claim his privilege and recall his opponent's stroke should he play out of order. This privilege is called the *honour*.

5. One round of the links is reckoned a match, unless otherwise stipulated. The match is won by the side which wins one or more holes in excess of the number of holes remaining to be played.

6. If, in a double match, a player shall play when his partner should have done so, his side loses the hole.

II. *Place of Teeing and Playing through the Green.*

7. The ball must be teed within the marks laid down by the conservator of the links, which shall be considered the 'Teeing Ground.' The balls shall not be teed in advance of such marks nor more than two club lengths behind them.

THE RULES

8. A ball played in contravention of this rule may be recalled by the opposite side.

9. After the balls are struck off, the ball furthest from the hole to which the parties are playing must be played first. No player shall play his teed ball till the party in front have played their second strokes ; nor play on to the putting-green till the party in front of him has holed out.

NOTE.—9 (*a*). It is requested that when a party is waiting to approach the hole, the party that has 'holed out' will not cause delay by trying their putts over again.

III. *Changing the Balls.*

10. The balls struck off from the tee must not be changed, touched, or moved, before the hole is played out (except in striking, and the cases provided for by Rules 4, 5, 7, 8, 9, 13, and 16) ; and if the sides are at a loss to know one ball from the other, neither shall be touched without the consent of both.

IV. *Lifting of Break Clubs.*

11. All loose impediments within a club length of the ball may be removed, unless the ball lies within a bunker, on sand, on a molehill, on a road, or other hazard, or touching a growing whin. (Rules 6, 9, and 12.)

12. When a ball lies in a bunker, sand, or any other hazard, there shall be no impression made by the club whilst addressing the ball, nor sand nor other obstacle removed 'before striking at the ball.'

13. A ball lying on sand sprinkled on grass on the course for the preservation of the links, shall be treated as if it lay on grass.

14. On no occasion is it allowable to press down any irregularities of surface, to improve the lie of the ball.

15. When a ball lies near a washing-tub, or implements used in the up-keep of the links, they may be removed, and when on clothes, the ball may be lifted and dropped behind them, without a penalty.

V. *Entitled to see the Ball.*

16. When a ball is completely covered with fog, bent, whins, &c., only so much thereof shall be set aside as that the player shall have a view of his ball before he plays, whether in a line with the hole or otherwise.

17. Nothing that is growing may be bent, broken, nor removed, except in the act of striking at the ball, or in the special occasion provided for in par. 16.

18. A ball stuck fast in wet ground or sand may be taken out and replaced loosely in the hole it has made.

VI. *Clearing the Putting-Green.*

19. All loose impediments, except the opponent's ball, may be lifted on the putting-green.

20. The term 'putting-green' shall be considered to mean those portions of the links devoid of hazards within twenty yards of a hole.

NOTE.—20 (*a*). When ice or snow lies on the putting-greens, parties are recommended to make their own arrangements as to its removal or not, before commencing their match.

VII. *Lifting Balls.*

21. When the balls lie within six inches of each other, in any situation, the ball nearer the hole to which the parties are playing must be lifted till the other is played, and then placed as nearly as possible in its original position. Should the ball furthest from the hole be accidentally moved in so doing, it must be replaced without a penalty. The six inches to be measured from the nearest surfaces of the balls.

22. In a three or more ball match a ball in any degree lying between the player and the hole must be lifted as above, or, if on the putting-green, holed out.

VIII. *Ball in Water.*

23. If the ball lie in water, the player may take it out, change it if he pleases, drop it, and play from behind the hazard, losing a stroke.

IX. *Rubs of the Green and Penalties.*

24. Whatever happens to a ball by accident, such as being moved or stopped by any person not engaged in the match, or by the fore caddie, must be reckoned a 'Rub on the Green,' and submitted to.

25. If, however, the player's ball strike his opponent or his

opponent's caddie or club, or is moved by them, the opponent loses the hole.

26. If the ball strike himself or his partner, or either of their caddies or clubs, or is stopped by them, or if, while in the act of playing, he strikes the ball twice, the player loses the hole.

27. If the player, or his partner, touch their ball with the foot or any part of the body (except as provided for in Rules 4, 5, 7, and 8), or with anything except the club, his side loses a stroke.

28. If the player, whilst addressing himself to the ball on any occasion, except at the tee, touch it so as to cause it to move, or if his hand, foot, or club, touch a bent stick, or anything which causes the ball to move, or if the player's caddie move the ball, he loses a stroke.

29. A ball is considered to have been moved if it leaves its original position in the least degree, and stops in another; but if a player touches his ball so as to make it merely oscillate and not leave its original position, it is not considered to have been moved.

30. If a player or his caddie strike the opponent's ball in any manner, that side loses the hole; but if he plays it inadvertently, thinking it is his own, and the opponent also plays the wrong ball, it is then too late to claim the penalty, and the hole must be played out with the balls thus changed. If, however, the mistake occurs from wrong information given by one party to the other, the penalty cannot be claimed, and the mistake, if discovered before the other party has played, must be rectified by replacing the ball as nearly as possible where it lay.

31. If a player's ball be played away by mistake, or be lifted by any agency outside the match, then the player must drop it, or another ball, as near the spot as possible without any penalty. Should this occur on the putting-green the ball may be replaced by hand.

X. *Ball Lost.*

32. In match playing, a ball lost entails the loss of the hole. Should the ball not be found within ten minutes, the opposite side can claim the hole.

XI. *Club Breaking.*

33. If, in striking, the club breaks, it is nevertheless to be counted a stroke, if the part of the club remaining in the player's hand either strike the ground or pass the ball.

XII. *Holing out the Ball*

34. In holing, no mark shall be placed, or line drawn, to indicate the line to the hole ; the ball must be played fairly and honestly for the hole, and not on the opponent's ball, not being in the way to the hole ; nor, although lying in the way to the hole, is the player entitled to play with any strength upon it that might injure his opponent's position, or greater than is necessary honestly to send his own ball the distance of the hole.

35. Either player, when it is his turn to play, may remove, but not press down, sand, or worm heaps, lying around the hole, or on the line of his 'putt ;' but this must be done lightly by the player or his caddie, with the hand only. Except as above mentioned, or when the player is in the act of addressing himself to his ball, the putting line must not be touched by club, hand, nor foot. If the player desires the 'line to the hole,' it may be pointed out by a club shaft only.

36. If, in holing out, the ball rest upon the flag-stick in the hole, the player shall be entitled to have the stick removed, and if the ball fall in, it shall be considered as holed out ; but either party is entitled to have the flag-stick removed when approaching the hole. When a player's ball rests on the lip of the hole, his opponent, after holing in the 'odd' or the 'like,' shall be entitled to strike away the ball which is at the lip of the hole, claiming the hole if he shall have holed in the 'like ;' and the 'half' if he shall have holed in the 'odd.' But no player shall be entitled to play until his opponent's ball shall have ceased rolling.

XIII. *Unplayable Balls.*

37. In *Match* playing every ball must be played, wherever it lies, or the hole be given up, excepting where otherwise provided for (Rules 4 and 8).

38. If a ball lies in any of the holes made for golfing, or on ground under repair by the conservator of the links, it may be lifted, dropped behind the hazard, and played without losing a stroke.

39. In all cases where a ball is to be dropped, the party doing so shall front the hole to which he is playing, standing behind the hazard, and dropping the ball behind him from his head.

THE RULES

XIV. *Asking Advice.*

40. A player must not ask advice about the game, by word, look, or gesture, from any one except his own caddie, his partner's caddie, or his partner.

XV. *Parties passing each other.*

41. Any party having lost a ball, and incurring delay by seeking for it, may be passed by any other party coming up.

42. On all occasions a *two-ball* match may pass a party playing three or more balls.

43. Parties turning before going the whole round must let any two-ball match that has done so pass them.

XVI. *Balls Splitting.*

44. If a ball splits into two or more pieces, a fresh ball should be put down where the largest portion of the ball lies; and if a ball is cracked the player may change it on intimating his intention of doing so to his opponent.

XVII. *Breach of Rules.*

45. Where no penalty for the infringement of a rule is specially mentioned, the loss of the hole shall be understood to be the penalty.

SPECIAL RULES FOR MEDAL PLAY.

1. If the lowest score should be made by two or more, the ties will be decided by the parties playing another round, either that day or the following, as the captain, or, in his absence, the secretary, may direct.

2. On the morning of the medal day new holes will be made, and any member playing at them before he competes will be disqualified.

3. Before starting each competitor must obtain from the secre-

tary a scoring card, and in the absence of a special marker the players will note each other's score. They must satisfy themselves, at the finish of each hole, that their strokes have been accurately marked; and on completion of the round hand the card to the secretary, or his deputy.

4. All balls must be holed out, and when on the putting-green, the flag must be removed, and the player whose ball is nearest the hole has the option of holing out first. Either player can have another player's ball lifted if he finds that it interferes with his stroke. The ball that has been lifted must be carefully replaced.

5. If a ball be lost, the player returns to the spot, as near as possible where the ball was struck, tees another ball, and loses a stroke. If the lost ball be found before he has struck the other ball, the first shall continue the one to be played.

6. A player striking his caddie, or himself, or his clubs, with his ball, or who, in the act of playing, strikes the ball twice, shall lose one stroke only as the penalty.

7. A ball may, under a penalty of two strokes, be lifted out of a difficulty of any description, and teed behind the same.

8. No competitor may play with a professional.

9. The ordinary Rules of Golf, so far as they are not at variance with these special rules, shall also be applicable on medal days.

LOCAL RULES FOR ST. ANDREWS LINKS.

Starting—Telegraph Board.

1. When the telegraph board is placed at the first teeing ground, a person will be in charge of it, to note the order of starting.

Ball in Water.

2. If the ball lie in any position in the Swilcan Burn, whether in water or not, the player may take it out, drop it on the line where it entered the burn, on the opposite side to the hole to which he is playing, and lose a stroke, or he may play it where it lies without a penalty.

3. Should a ball be driven into the water of the Eden at the high hole, or into the sea at the first hole, the ball shall be teed a club length in front of either river or sea, the player or side losing a stroke.

Ball Lost.

4. A ball getting into the enclosed ground (between the Road and Dyke holes) called the Station-Master's Garden, shall be treated as a lost ball.

5. Parties having caddies may pass those carrying their own clubs.

Medal Play.

6. All competitions for the medals of the Club will be decided by playing one round of the links of 18 holes [1]—the competitor doing it in fewest strokes shall be the winner.

7. The order of starting will be balloted for the previous evening.[2] Any couple not at the teeing ground when their number is called must go to the bottom of the list. A party starting from the first tee must allow the party in front of them to cross the burn before striking off.

8. A ball driven into the water of the Eden, or sea, may be treated as a lost ball.

9. All private matches must be delayed till the last competitors have finished the first hole.

Disputes.

10. Any dispute respecting the play shall be determined by the green committee, with power to add to their number.

Bye-Law.

If a ball lies within two yards of a seat at the high hole, it may be lifted and dropped two yards to the side of the seat farthest from the hole.

[1] Excepting the 'Glennie Medal,' which is awarded to the player whose combined scores, at the Spring and Autumn competitions of the Club, are the lowest. The Medal to be presented at the Autumn meetings.

[2] Intending competitors must give in their names to the Secretary *not later than Five o'clock p.m.*

Table showing at what Holes Strokes are to be taken.

Strokes																		
1	8																	
2	5	11																
3	2	8	14															
4	3	7	11	15														
5	2	5	8	12	16													
6	2	5	8	11	14	17												
7	2	5	8	11	13	16	18											
8	2	4	6	8	11	13	15	17										
9	2	4	6	8	10	12	14	16	18									
10	1	3	5	7	9	10	11	13	15	17								
11	1	3	4	6	7	9	10	12	14	15	17							
12	1	3	4	6	7	9	10	12	13	15	16	18						
13	1	2	4	6	8	9	11	12	14	15	16	17	18					
14	1	2	3	5	6	8	9	10	11	13	14	16	17	18				
15	1	2	3	5	6	7	8	9	10	11	13	14	16	17	18			
16	1	2	3	5	6	7	8	9	10	11	12	13	14	16	17	18		
17	1	2	3	4	5	6	7	8	9	10	11	13	14	15	16	17	18

CHAPTER XVII

GLOSSARY OF TECHNICAL TERMS EMPLOYED IN THE GAME OF GOLF

Addressing the ball.—Putting oneself in position to strike the ball.

Approach.—When a player is sufficiently near the hole to be able to drive the ball to the putting-green, his stroke is called the 'approach shot.'

Baff.—To strike the ground with the 'sole' of the club-head in playing, and so send ball in air.

Baffy.—A wooden club to play lofting shots.

Bone.—See *Horn*.

Brassy.—A wooden club with a brass sole.

Break-club.—An obstacle lying near a ball of such a nature as might break the club when striking at the ball.

Bulger.—A wooden club with a convex face.

Bunker.—A term originally confined, almost exclusively, to a sand-pit. Its use is now extended to almost any kind of hazard. See *Hazard*.

Bye.—The holes remaining after the long match is finished.

Caddie.—A person who carries the golfer's clubs.

Carry.—The distance from the place where the ball is struck to the place where it pitches. Hence a *long carry*, and a *short carry*.

Cleek.—An iron-headed club used for driving, and sometimes for putting.

Club.—The implement with which the ball is struck. The heads are of three kinds—wood, wood with a brass sole, and iron only.

Course.—That portion of the Links on which the game ought to be played, generally bounded on either side by rough ground or other hazard.

Cup.—A small hole in the course, usually one made by the stroke of some previous player.

Dead.—A ball is said to be 'dead' when it lies so near the hole that the 'putt' is a *dead* certainty. A ball is said to fall 'dead' when it does not run after alighting.

Divot.—Piece of turf cut out by an iron club, which should always be carefully replaced.

Dormy.—One side is said to be 'dormy' when it is as many holes ahead as there remain holes to play. (This word is probably derived from the French, like many Scottish terms.)

Draw.—To drive widely to the left hand. Identical in its effect with Hook and Pull.

Driver.—See *Play Club*.

Face.—1st, the slope of a bunker or hillock; 2nd, the part of the club head which strikes the ball.

Flat.—A club is said to be 'flat' when its head is at a very obtuse angle to the shaft.

Fog.—Moss, rank grass.

Foozle.—A bad, bungling stroke.

Fore!—A warning cry to any person in the way of the stroke.

Foursome.—A match in which two play on each side; those on a side playing alternate strokes with the same ball.

Gobble.—A rapid straight 'putt' into the hole, such that, had the ball not gone in, it would have gone some distance beyond.

Golf ball.—Made of gutta-percha, or some composition into which gutta-percha largely enters, strongly compressed in a mould. They are numbered by the makers—26, 27, $27\frac{1}{2}$, 28, 29—according to the number of drachms (Avoirdupois) they weigh. A $27\frac{1}{2}$ gutta-percha is $1\frac{13}{16}$ inch in diameter.

Grassed.—Said of a club whose face is slightly 'spooned' or sloped backward.

Green.—1st, the whole links; 2nd, the putting-ground around the different holes.

Grip.—1st, the part of the handle covered with leather by which the club is grasped; 2nd, the grasp itself.

Gutty.—An euphemistic term for a gutta-percha ball.

Half one.—A handicap of a stroke deducted every *second* hole.

Half shot.—Less than a full swing.

Halved.—A hole is said to be 'halved' when each side takes the same number of strokes. A 'halved match' is a 'drawn game;' *i.e.* the players have proved to be equal.

GLOSSARY

Hanging.—A 'hanging' ball is one which lies on a downward slope.

Hazard.—A general term for bunker, long grass, road, water, whin, molehill, or other bad ground.

Head.—This word is a striking specimen of incongruity and mixed metaphor. A head is the *lowest* part of a club, and possesses, among other mysterious characteristics, a *sole*, a *heel*, a *toe*, or *nose*, a *neck*, and a *face!*

Heel.—1st, the part of the head nearest the shaft; 2nd, to hit from this part, and send ball to the right hand.

Hole.—1st, the four-inch hole lined with iron. The holes going out are generally marked with white, and those coming in, with red flags; 2nd, the whole space between any two of these.

Honour.—The right to play off first from the tee.

Hook.—See *Draw*.

Horn.—A piece of that substance inserted in the sole of the club to prevent it splitting.

Hose.—The socket, in iron-headed clubs, into which the shaft fits.

Iron.—A club made of the material its name implies, with the head more or less laid back to loft a ball.

Jerk.—In 'jerking' the club should strike the ball with a downward stroke, and *stop* on reaching the ground.

Lie.—1st, the inclination of a club when held on the ground in the natural position for striking; 2nd, the situation of a ball—good or bad.

Lift.—To lift a ball is to take it out of a hazard and drop or tee it behind.

Like.—See under *Odd*.

Like-as-we-lie.—When both sides have played the same number of strokes.

Links.—The open downs or heath on which golf is played.

Loft.—To elevate the ball.

Made.—A player, or his ball, is said to be 'made' when his ball is sufficiently near the hole to be played on to the putting-green next shot.

Mashy.—A straight-faced niblick.

Match.—1st, the sides playing against each other; 2nd, the game itself.

Match play.—Reckoning the score by holes.

Medal play.—Reckoning the score by strokes.

Miss the globe.—To fail to strike the ball, either by swinging right over the top of it, or by hitting the ground behind. It is counted a stroke.

Neck.—The crook of the head where it joins the shaft.

Niblick.—A small narrow-headed heavy iron club, used when the ball lies in bad places, as ruts or whins, &c.

Nose.—The point, or front portion, of the club-head.

Odd.—1st, 'An odd,' 'two odds,' &c., per hole, means the handicap given to a weak opponent by deducting one, two, &c., strokes from his total every hole. 2nd, to have played 'the odd' is to have played one stroke more than your adversary. Some other terms used in counting the game will be most easily explained here all together :—If your opponent has played one stroke more than you—*i.e.* 'the odd,' your next stroke will be 'the like ;' if two strokes more—*i.e.* 'the two more,' your next stroke will be 'the one off two ;' if 'three more'—'the one off three ;' and so on.

One off two, One off three, &c.—See under *Odd.*

Play club.—A wooden-headed club, with a full-length shaft, more or less supple,—with it the ball can be driven to the greatest distance. It is used when the ball lies well.

Press.—To strive to hit harder than you can, with adequate accuracy of aim.

Putt.—To play the delicate game close to the hole. (Pronounce *u* as in *but*).

Putter.—An upright, stiff-shafted, wooden-headed club (some use iron heads), used when the ball is on the putting-green.

Putting-green.—The prepared ground round the hole.

Putty.—Eclipse ball—so called from its comparative softness, and to rhyme with *Gutty.*

Rub on the green.—A favourable or unfavourable knock to the ball, for which no penalty is imposed, and which must be submitted to.

Run.—To run a ball along the ground in approaching hole instead of lofting it.

Scare.—The narrow part of the club-head by which it is glued to the handle.

Sclaff.—Almost synonymous with *Baff,* which see. The distinction is so subtle as almost to defy definition.

Scratch player.—One who receives no allowance in a handicap.

Screw.—See *Draw.*

Set.—A full complement of clubs.

Shaft.—The stick or handle of the club.

Sole.—The flat bottom of the club-head.

Spoons.—Wooden-headed clubs of three lengths—long, middle, and short—the head is scooped so as to loft the ball.

Spring.—The degree of suppleness in the shaft.

Square.—When the game stands evenly balanced, neither side being any holes ahead.

Stance.—The position of the player's feet when addressing himself to the ball.

Steal.—To hole an unlikely 'putt' from a distance, by a stroke which sends the ball, stealthily, only just the distance of the hole.

Stroke.—The act of hitting the ball with the club, or the attempt to do so.

Stroke hole.—The hole or holes at which, in handicapping, a stroke is given.

Stymie.—When your opponent's ball lies in the line of your 'putt' —from an old Scotch word, meaning 'the faintest form of anything.' *Vide* 'Jamieson.'

Swing.—The sweep of the club in driving.

Tee.—The pat of sand on which the ball is placed for the first stroke each hole.

Teeing ground.—A space marked out, within the limits of which the ball *must* be teed.

Third.—A handicap of a stroke deducted every *third* hole.

Toe.—Another name for the nose of the club.

Top.—To hit the ball above its centre.

Two-more, Three-more, &c.—See under *Odd*.

Upright.—A club is said to be 'upright' when its head is not at a very obtuse angle to the shaft. The converse of *Flat*.

Whins.—Furze or gorse.

Whipping.—The pitched twine uniting the head and handle.

Wrist shot.—Less than a half shot, generally played with an iron club.

INDEX

ADD

Addressing the ball, 445
After swing, the, 199
Alexander, Tom, 340
Allan, Jamie, 86, 103, 138, 157, 159, 362, 381
Allan, John, 381
Allan, Matthew, 381
Amateur championship, the, 325
Amateurs contrasted with professionals, 307, 383–409
American description of golf, 7
Anderson, Bob, characteristics of his play, 339, 340
Anderson, Charles, 390
Anderson, David (Old Daw), 361, 363
Anderson, D., jun., 375
Anderson, James, his style, record and portrait, 124, 134, 157, 222, 236, 355, 359, 361–364, 381, 390, 398
Andrew, Bob, 343, 355, 356, 357
Annual Challenge Calcutta Cup, St. Andrews, 281
Approach, the, 38, 61, 166, 197, 222, 224, 445
Approaching, 110–135, 194, 195
Aston, 19
Ayton, David, 381

BLA

Badges of caddies, 294, 304
Baff, 445
Baffy, the, 59, 103, 335, 445
Baird, Sir David, 383, 384
Balance, how to preserve, 33
Balance in putters, 62
Balfour, Elliott S., 398
Balfour, James, 397
Balfour, Leslie Melville, 98, 393, 396–398
Ball, John, jun., 66, 154, 155, 157, 159, 325, 372, 394, 395, 400, 401, 402–404, 406
Ball, John, sen., 152, 161, 401
Ball, inertia of the, 32 ; advice to keep the eye on the, 33, 87, 134 ; other references, 6, 11, 14–16, 19–21, 27, 28, 68, 74, 104–109, 204, 240, 436–446
Behaviour. *See under* 'Etiquette.
Belgian game of chole, 2, 4–6
Bethune of Blebo, 335
Betting, 17, 49
Bettors, 266
Biggar, 19
Bisques, 281
Black, Parson, 18
Black spoon, the, 40

BLA

Blackheath Golf Club, 26, 27, 328, 390
Blackheath Links, characteristics of, 26, 329, 330
Blackwell, 406
Blackwood, James, 336
Blackwood, John, 35, 141, 152, 390
Bobson, ball-maker, 19, 24, 28
Bombay Club, 27
Boothby, Colonel R.T., 392
Boots, 223
Bothwell, Earl of, 14
Brassy, the, 27, 59, 60, 445
Break-club, 437, 445
Breakdowns, 173, 174
Briggs, Colonel, 395
Broughton, Capt., 350
Brown, 156
Brown, David, record of, 370, 379
Bruntsfield Links, 318
Bulger, the, 405, 445
Bunkers, 41, 144, 147, 415, 445
Burn, Capt. Herbert, 159
Burn, Capt. W., 158
Burns, Jack, performances of, 375, 380
Burton, 41

CADDIES, 8, 17, 24, 36, 42, 273, 274, 293-310, 426, 445
Campbell, Willie, features of his play and record, 156, 347, 368-371, 373, 374, 376, 378, 380
Canada, golf in, 7
Carlyle of Inveresk, 18, 26
Carry, the, 445
Catchpall, 15
Chambers, C. E. S., 40
Chambers, Robert, 1, 79

DOU

Charles I., 16
Chole, the French game, 2; the Belgian game, 2, 4-6
Choulla, 5
Clark, Robert, 29, 390, 391
Cleeks, 55, 64, 65, 445
Club, the, how to grasp, 33; malformations in, 62, 63; other references, 6, 11, 14, 16, 21, 24, 26, 27, 54, 55, 94, 98, 99, 207, 247, 248, 421, 445
Club books to register members' performances, 290
Condie, George, 385, 386, 392
Condie, James, 383, 385
Course, the, 445
Cricketers taking up golf, hints to, 203; the ball, 204; 'quick-footedness,' 204; the swing, 204; clubs, 207; position of feet, 207; wrist stroke, 208
Crosse, 5, 19
Cunningham, James, jun., 406
Cup, the, 446

DALHOUSIE, Earl of, 387
Dalrymple, 19
Definition of the game, 53
Deulin, Charles, 7, 15
De Zoete, Walter, 318
Dickson, club-maker, 17, 19
Dickson, James, 15
Diet, 51, 211, 246, 255
Disappointment swing, the, 161, 165
Divots, 103, 295, 313, 446
Dormy, 446
Double-jointed swing, the, 161, 165
Double shots, 260
Dougall, Captain (now Admiral), Maitland, 354, 390

INDEX

DOW

Dow, Willie, 343, 354, 355
Dress, 167, 168, 276
Driving, 73-100, 177, 193
Driving cleeks, 64 ; clubs, 56 ; Lamb's, 63 ; irons, 66 ; putters, 62 ; 446
Dunn, James, his position as a golfer, 341
Dunn, Tom, 342
Dunn, William, characteristics of his play, 335, 336, 340, 341, 342, 353
Durham, James, 26
Dutch game of kolf, 2
Dutch tiles illustrating the game, 10

Eclipse ball, the, 70, 71, 305
Edinburgh Burgess Golfing Society, 26
Elie Links, 321
Etiquette and behaviour, 256 ; counting an opponent's score aloud, 256 ; touching the sand with the iron, 258 ; double shots, 260 ; ball rolling from its place, 260 ; opponent questioning a penalty, 260 ; laxity in applying rules of game, 261 ; agreement on 'casual water,' 262 ; ball in the burn, 262 ; lost ball, 263 ; clearing putting-green of impediments, 263 ; holing out short putts, 264 ; ball in a carriage, and in a spectator's pocket, 265 ; 'outside bettors,' 266 ; complaining of own bad and partner's and opponent's good luck, 268 ; consoling an antagonist, 269 ; satisfaction with partner, 270 ;

FOR

behaviour on the links, 270 ; conduct towards antagonist in the game, 271 ; replacing divots, 272 ; driving off tee shots, 272 ; caddie favouring ball on windy day, 274 ; relations between partners in foursomes, 274 ; courtesy towards spectators, 275 ; consoling a defeated player, 276 ; dress, 276
Everard, H. S. C., 160, 162, 409, *note*

Fairlie, Captain, 339
Fairlie, Colonel J. O., 386, 387, 349
Fairlie, F. A., 387
Feather balls, 26, 68
Fees, professional, 308
Fergusson, Bob, his matches and methods, 61, 103, 156, 317, 355, 362, 366, 376
Fergusson, Colonel, 20
Fergusson, Mure, 404
Fernie, Peter, 381
Fernie, Willie, matches of, 157, 218, 346, 366, 370, 372, 376-378
Fleming, Hay, 14
Fog, 446
Foozle, a, 124, 446
Forbes, Duncan, of Culloden, 19
Forgan, 79
Form, 170 ; elderly players, 170 ; the golfer's ideal game, 171 ; going off the game, 171 ; to ensure continuing a good game after having developed it, 172 ; history of a man's game, 173 ; break-

FOS

downs, 173, 174; natural and artificial peculiarities, 174; detection and cure of specific faults, 176; bad driving, 177; heeling, 177; slicing, 178, 195–197, 200; 'slow back,' 181; altering position to cure slicing, 182; shortening swing, 185; diagrams illustrative of full and half swing, 186, 187; topping, 187, 188; hooking, 189, 190, 197; 'general debility,' 191; standing too near the ball, 191; smooth swiftness versus abrupt violence, 192; guarding against sway, 192; driving through the green, 193; 'off form,' on changing ground, 193; approaching, 194, 195; forcing approaches, 197; the full swing at all distances, 197; practising approaches, 198; the after swing, 199; lofting, 199; off one's putting, 201

Foster, Norman R., 405, 406

Foursome play, 35, 238–240, 274, 284, 446

French game of chole, 2, 4, 5, **7**

GARRICK, anecdote concerning, 18

Geddes, Tom, 340

Giving odds. *See under* 'Handicapping'

Glennie Challenge Cup, 394, 398, 401, 405, 443

Glennie, George, 134, 140, 141, 315, 328, 388–390

Glossary of technical terms, 445–448

HAN

Gloves, 33, 223

Goddard, W. M., 383, 384, 386

Golfer's Year Book, 387

Gosset, George, 140

Gourlay, ball-maker, 28

Graham, Dr., 27

Grand Challenge Trophy, 404

Grant, David, 375, 380, 381

Grant, Sir Hope, 383

Grassed club, the, 59

Gray, Wilyam, 15

Green, the, 446; passing on, 40; playing through, 37, 100–109, 436

Green-keepers, duties of, 293

Greig, Master, 355

Grip, 81, 117; for putting, 139

Gullane Links, 321

Gutta-percha balls, 68, 70, 446

HAIRT, David, 14

Half one, 446

Half shot, the, 113, 131, 446

Half swings, 161

Half topping, 185, 189

Halved, 446

Hamilton, Gavin, 15

Hamilton, William, of Ayrshire, 334

Hammer-hurling swing, the, 161, 162

Handicap committees, 291

Handicapping, and giving odds, 277; in and out playing, 278; a player's recognised 'game,' 279; odds for different classes of players, 280; matches by holes—eighteen-hole rounds, 280; bisques, 281; proportion of holes to strokes given in a match by holes, 282; winning a 'boohing' match without uttering a 'Booh!' 283; a curious match in which the opponent proved 'Yorkshire too,' 283; single club against a set, 284; three-ball matches, 284; foursomes, 284; medal rounds, 285; difficulties in dealing with unsteady players, 286; handicapping on an average of scores, 287; drawbacks of the handicapper's lot, 287; varieties of the genus handicapped, 287-292; the improving player, 288; 'dark horses' on the golf course, 290; club books to register players' scores, 291; handicap committees, 291; dealing with faulty arithmeticians, 291

Hands, soft, 222, 223

Hay, Sir Robert, 59, 336, 385, 386

Hazards, 144-150, 341, 447

Head, the, 447

Headsman swing, the, 161, 162

Heel, the, 447

Heeling, 177, 178

Henrie, John, 13

Herd, Alexander, 348, 375, 381, 382

Hickory wood for shafts, 64

Hieronymus Mercurialis, 11

History of golf, 1; derivation of the name, 2; the Dutch kolf described, 2; French and Belgian chole, 4-7; quaint account of golf in the 'Philadelphia Times,' 7; on the ice in Holland, 11; the jeu de mail, 11; Holland probably the native seat of golf, 12; early popularity, 13; Sunday playing forbidden in Scotland, 13, 14; a Royal game, 14; prices of clubs and balls in 1503 and 1603, 14; the Marquis of Montrose as a player, 16; caddies, 8, 17; the Duke of York (James II.), 17; betting on the game, 17; anecdote of Garrick, 19; Matheson's 'The Goff,' 19; tradition anent Dame Margaret Ross, 20; 'The Muses Threnodie,' 21; golfing at Leith, 22, 23; women golfers, 23; consecration of St. Andrews Links to golf, 24; course at St. Andrews, 26; Dr. Graham's verses, 27

Hodge, Thomas, 392

Holes, 53, 280, 282, 447

Home practice, 77, 136, 138

Honourable Company of Edinburgh Golfers, 317, 397

Hooked balls, 158

Hooking, 158, 189, 190, 197

Horn, 60, 447

Horne, John, 18

Howdan, Andrew, 14

Howdan, Johne, 14

Hoylake Club, 27

Hoylake Links, features of, 325

Hull, Rev. R. A., 161

Humours of golf, 410; the game open to all ages, 413; pains and penalties of initiation, 414; the intending golfer who 'hired a *bunker* for his exclusive use,' 414; beginners in the horrors of bad bunkers, 415; novel modes of acquiring the golfing maxims, 415; a 'mould of

HUR

form,' 416; apparent meaninglessness of golf to the uninitiated, 416; two Southrons' first impressions of the game, 417; vexations connected with the game, 418; verbal expletives as a vent to irritation at failures, 421; vengeance on faulty clubs, 421; the stage of putting out, 422; facilities for fraud, 424; matches won by singular contrivances, 424; 'diamond cut diamond,' 425; ditto, and one better, 425; that varying quantity the caddie, 426; caddie criticism, 427; the French caddie's congratulation, 427; Long Willie's strategy, 428; 'swinging the *caddie*,' 429; the joys of golf, 429; a New Year Day's 'crack' with the Nestor of golf, 431

Hurry, 237, 243

Hutchings, Charles, 353

Hutchinson, Horace G., 354, 388, 395, 399, 400, 401

ICE, on the, in Holland, 11

Implement to make a ball lift and lie off an iron, 347

India-rubber finger-tips, 223

Indigestion, curious effects of, on a golfer, 51

Innes, Gilbert Mitchell, 64, 159, 362, 390–391

Instructions (elementary) in golf, 73; *driving*, 73; the standard measure of a good golf drive, 74; position for the drive,

INS

75; proper position of right foot, 76–79; distance between golfer's feet, 76; illustrative position-diagram, 77; home practice at position, 77; the golfing drive a swing, not a hit, 79; ball not to be hit at, 79; difference between a hit and a sweep or swing, 80; the swing, 80–95; the grip, 81; upward swing, 83, 86, 87, 95; 'slow back,' 84; 'quick back,' 84; top of the swing, 86; downward swing, 86, 87, 95; 'keep your eye on the ball,' 87; at the end of the swing, 88; preliminary proceedings to the drive, 89; the waggle, 89, 90; angle of arms and inclination of body, 92; swinging with the body a vice, 92; hands to be brought low down, 93; body and members to be in the same relative position when striking as when addressing the ball, 93; 'falling over' the ball as the club comes down to it, 93; suppleness of clubs, 94; the body to turn from the knees, 95; meaning of the word 'swing,' 95; 'don't press,' 95; a golfing fable, 95; 'throw the club at the ball,' 96; practice, 97; 'slogging,' 97; proper horizontal position of the club, 98; club-breaking on the shoulder, 99; accuracy coupled with dash, 99; — *playing through the green*, 100; the downward stroke where there is a lump behind the ball, 100; the swing for the jerking stroke, 101–103; guarding against slicing, 101; average straightness of full iron shots, 102, 103; points to be borne in mind when playing at balls in heavy grass, 104; the ball with a face in front of it, 104; slicing the ball, 104; dealing with the hanging ball, 106; balls lying above facing, and lying below away, 107–109;—*approaching*, 110; meaning of an 'approach shot,' 110; playing short, 110; the three-quarter stroke, 111, 116, 132; the half shot, 113; the wrist stroke, 113; the approach shot to be played off the right leg, 114; position of the right foot, 114; attitude for half shot of medium distance and loft, 115; cutting strokes, 115; running-up stroke with the iron, 116; grip of the club and angle of the arms, 117; true wrist strokes, 120; knee shots, 121; putting cut on the ball, 122; the up and down stroke, 122; professionals' manner of playing iron shots, 123; playing cut strokes when the ground is very hard, 124; when the ground is of loose sand, 124; beginning of the high lofting stroke, 125; exceptionally lofted clubs, 126; difficulty of hitting as wished with a very lofted club, 127; a body stroke, 129; Bob Martin's stroke with his cleek, 129; half shot played off the left leg, 131; cautions respecting the three-quarter shot, 132; the three-quarter stroke with cut, 133; four golden rules, 134;—*putting*, 135; short putts, 135; two methods of putting, 136; chamber practice, 136; playing off the right leg, 137; use of the wrists in putting, 138; home study, 138; the grip for putting, 139; avoidance of jerk, 140; club-head on the ground behind ball before striking, 140; playing off the left leg, 141; relative merits of wooden and iron putters, 141; the style of putting recommended to the learner, 143; drawing-room trials, 143; holing out, 143; 'be up,' 144;—*in hazards*, 144; in a sand bunker, 144; keep the eye on a spot of sand just behind the ball, 146; in hard clayey-bottomed bunkers, 147; the ball clean and smooth on soft sand, 148; whin-gorse, 148; bent grass, 148; long rushes, 149; shots made out of water, 150; dealing with wind, 150; etiquette and behaviour, 256–276; style, 151–169; form, 170–202; nerve and training, 209–223; match and medal play, 225–255; etiquette and behaviour, 256–276; rules of the game, 433–449

Iron, the, 447

Iron putters, 60, 61, 141, 142

JER

JERKING STROKE, the, 101–103
Jeu de mail, 4, 5, 11

KAY, J., 381
Kidd, Tom, 365
King James VI. Golf Club, 322
Kirk, Bob, golfing career of, 148, 354–356, 361, 362, 365, 366
Kirkaldy, Andrew, 348, 381
Kirkaldy, Hugh, 314, 362, 375, 381, 382
Kirkaldy, John, 381
Knee shots, 120, 121, 133
Knuckle Club, the, 26
Kolf, the Dutch game, description of, 2

LADIES, effect of their presence at golf, 48
Ladies' golfing clubs, 27
Ladies' links, 47
Laidlay, John Ernest, 66, 131, 141, 152, 155, 347, 375, 393–396, 400, 403
Lamb, David I., 390, 405
Lamb, Henry A., 63, 159, 160, 390, 401, 405
Lamb's driving clubs, 63
Language, 168
Lauthier, 11
Leitch, D., 382
Leith, golf at, 22, 23
Leslie, 19
Lie, the, 447
Links :—Aberdeen, 321; Alnmouth, 331; Bembridge, 330; Blackheath, 304; Blundellsands, 326; Bruntsfield, 318, 405; Carnoustie, 147, 327, 373, 374; Dornoch, 321; Elie, 321; Eastbourne, 160, 330, 401; Felixstowe, 331, 405; Great Yarmouth, 331; Gullane, 321; Hoylake, 71, 149, 154, 263, 329, 402; Leith, 15, 16; Leven, 365, 373; Littlestone, 378, 381; Luffness, 321; Macrihanish, 322; Malvern, 330, 372; Montrose, 321; Musselburgh, 22, 23, 156, 296, 316, 317, 321, 357, 371; North Berwick, 153, 156, 318–321, 336; Pau, 427; Prestwick, 147, 218, 265, 322–324, 349, 357; St. Andrews, 14, 15, 17, 128, 147, 153, 194, 239, 243, 248, 262, 273, 296, 311–318, 321, 326, 331, 333, 335, 339, 341, 350, 357; St. Rule, 194; Sandwich, 147, 330, 331, 372; Troon, 325, 345, 378; Wemyss, 353; Westward Ho, 147, 149, 326, 329, 372; Wimbledon, 304; Worcester, 330
Links, celebrated, description of, 311–331
Linskill, W. T., 138, 165
Lloyd (the General), 96
Lofting, 66, 99, 199, 200
Lofting iron, the, 59, 66, 67, 200, 243
London Scottish Golf Club, 321
Long Willie, 428
Luce, Siméon, 28
Luffness Links, 321

MACFIE, Allan Fullarton, 66, 92, 138, 152, 160, 398, 399, 401
McGregor, Gregor, 401

INDEX 459

MAC

Machine-made balls, 68
Macpherson, Rev. J. G., 392
Maidment, J., 21
Malformations in clubs, 62, 63
Mansfield, James, 402
Martin, Bob, 59, 65, 92, 129, 316, 370, 373, 378
Mashie, the, 67, 447
Match and medal play, hints on, 225; differences between, 225, 227; fluctuations of the game, 227; effect of winning the first hole, 228; the way to beat a professional, 229; careless strokes, 230; taking the honour, 231, 232; danger of the spirit of emulation, 233; playing 'dourly,' 233, 252; regard the adversary as a nonentity, 234; the match won by the adversary's errors, 234, 250; error of underrating an opponent, 234; 'get inside' the opponent, 235; running out of holing in striving for a long putt, 236; 'be up,' 236; eccentricities in playing, 237; bad results of hurry, 237, 243; duty towards a partner in foursome play, 238, 239; never give up a game, 240, 250; three-ball matches, 241; friendly games, 242; enjoyment in retrospection, 242; playing without reference to partner's performance on medal day, 243; practice strokes, 283; the lofting iron, 243; practising approach putting, 244; over-night practice, 244; scanning the holes on the morning of competition, 245; avoid amiable non-

MOR

golfing friends on the ground, 246; resolve not to be short in approach shots, 247; husbanding drivers for medal day, 247; good effect sometimes of a change of club, 248; no stroke stands by itself, 248; paramount importance of a good tee shot, 249; virtue of deliberation, 249; delusion of 'making up for' badly-played holes, 250; concentration of mind on the stroke being played, 251; cultivate callousness, 251; counting the score, 251; conversation with friends while engaged in the match, 252; swing easy and walk slowly, 253; a generous regimen advocated, 255
Mayne, William, club-maker, 14
Medal play, 225, 447; special rules for, 441, *See* 'Match and Medal Play'
Medal rounds, 285
Melvill, James, ball-maker, 14, 15
Melville, John Whyte, 406–409
Michel, Charles, 2, 5, 6
Miss the globe, to, 448
Mitchell, R. A. H., 56, 204
Molesworth, Arthur H., 161, 360, 400
Molesworth, Captain, 61
Moncrieff, David, 15
Moncrieffe, Sir Thomas, 339
Montrose, Marquis of, 15, 16
Morris, Jamie, 156
Morris, J. O. F., features of his play, 138, 168, 360, 361, 370, 374

MOR

Morris, Tom, old, the Nestor of golf, his history, style, merits, defects, peculiarities, and achievements, 26, 57, 94, 139, 152, 254, 294, 295, 306, 333, 334, 336, 339, 342, 343, 348–354, 359, 365, 366, 391, 397; gives his experiences, 431

Morris, Tom, young, brilliant career of, 87, 90, 134, 137, 141, 155, 156, 193, 306, 314, 333, 345, 352, 354–360, 362, 364, 365, 366, 390

'Mould of form,' a, 416

Mure, W. J., 388

Murray, Sir Patrick, 21

Murray, Wolfe, of Cringletie, 334, 352

'Musselburgh iron,' the, 61

Musselburgh Links, description of, 317, 318

NERVE, 209–224. *See* 'Training'

Niblicks, 55, 67, 448

Nicking balls, 68

North Berwick Links, characteristics of, 318–321

ODD, an, 448

Odds. *See under* 'Handicapping'

Oliphant, R., 383

Orange wood, yellow, for shafts, 64

Outside bettors, 266

Over-practice, 214

PARK, DAVID, 344, 354, 365, 367

PRO

Park, Mungo, features of his play, 345, 359

Park, Willie, junior, record of his achievements and style of play, 345–347, 370, 373, 378, 381

Park, Willie, senior, his golfing record and style, 157, 341, 342–344, 354–356, 359, 367

Park's new patent lofting iron, 200, 380

Partnership in golf, 238

Paterson, John, 17

Patersone, George, 14

Paxton, Peter, 381

Pell mell, 4, 5, 11, 14

Pendulum swing, the, 161, 162

Perspiration in the palms of the hands, 223

Pett, James, club-maker, 16

Philp, Hugh, club-maker, 55, 56

Picking up, 42

Pig-tail swing, the, 161

Pila-Malleus, 5, 11

Pirie, Alexander, 340

Pirie, Tom, 340

Pitcairne, 17

Pitch, melted, for cracks in the hands, 223

Play club, the, 448

Playfair, 383

Porteous, 18

Practice, 77, 97, 136, 244

Practice matches, 212

Pressing, 512

Prestwick Links, description of, 322–324

Pringle, R., 361

Proctor, R.A., 63

Professionals and caddies, 293; duties and qualities of the good green-keeper, 293–296;

PUL

caddies and their badges, 294, 304 ; improvidence of the ordinary professional, 296; caddies as critics, 297 ; a caddie's unfortunate heritage, 301 ; caddies as mentors, 301 ; slavish subordination of players' judgment to caddie's dictation, 302 ; activity in the caddies, 303 ; boy caddies on Southern links, 303 ; bad caddies on metropolitan greens, 304 ; prizes of golf as a profession, 305 ; falling off in professional matches, 306 ; whispers of dishonest play, 306 ; rivalry of the amateur, 306, 307 ; the professional championship, 307 ; points of superiority in the professional over the amateur, 307 ; interest of the game now concentrated in amateur exploits, 308 ; the drink trap, 308 ; fixed professional fees, 308 ; summary of the professional's moral characteristics, 309

Pulling, 197

Purves, W. L., 10

Purvis, Dr. W. Laidlaw, 405

Putters, balance in, 62 ; wooden and iron, 60, 61, 62, 141, 142

Putter-faced clubs, 58

Putting, position and mode of, 44, 135–144, 201

Putting cleeks, 65

Putting-greens, the, 42, 128, 201, 263, 313, 448

Putty, the, 70, 448

QUICK back, 84

RUL

RATHSAY, 19

Rattray, John, 22

Recoil-swing, the, 161, 162

Registration of teeing rights, 36

Resin, powdered, for soft hands, 223

Robertson, Allan, characteristics of his play and record of his performances, 26, 253, 306, 332–339, 340, 342, 348, 349, 357, 388, 398

Robertson, Argyle, 390

Robertson, Robert, 13

Rocketing, 188

Rodger, James, 14

Rodger, Johne, 14

Rogie, Pat, 13

Rolland, J. E. Douglas Stewart, matches and qualities of, 65, 156, 321, 346, 371–373

Ross, A. M., 347, 406

Royal and Ancient Golf Club of St. Andrews, 54, 294, 311, 390, 393

Royal Isle of Wight Club, 330

Royal Liverpool Golf Club, 325

Royal North Devon Golf Club, 327

Royal Wimbledon Club, 328, 405

Rules (St. Andrews) of golf, 433 ; mode and order of playing the game, 436 ; place of teeing and playing through the green, 436 ; changing the balls, 437 ; lifting of break clubs, 437 ; entitled to see the ball, 437 ; clearing the putting-green, 438; lifting walls, 438 ; ball in water, 438 ; rubs of the green and penalties, 438 ;

RUS

ball lost, 439; club-breaking, 439; holing out the ball, 440; unplayable balls, 440; asking advice, 441; parties passing each other, 441; balls splitting, 441; breach of rules, 441; special rules for medal play, 441; local rules for St. Andrews Links:—starting: telegraph board, 442; ball in water, 442; ball lost, 443; medal play, 443; disputes, 443; bye-law, 443; table showing at what holes strokes are to be taken, 444

Rushes, 149

SAND-BUNKERS, 144
Sand-irons, 66
Sandwich Links, description of, 330, 331
Sayers, Bernard, golfing form of, 373, 374–376, 382, 395
Sclaff, the, 189, 448
Scott, Col. Stanley, 16
Sévigné, Madame de, 11
Sharp, Jelf, 387
Silvertown Co. golf balls, 70, 305
Simpson, Archie, record of, 346, 370–372, 373, 378
Simpson, Jack, features of his style, 346, 372–374, 377, 379
Simpson, Robert, 374
Simpson, Sir Walter, 83, 84, 103, 297, 344, 395
Simpsons, the, 156, 321
Skying, 188
Slicing, 101, 104, 178, 182, 195–197
'Slogging,' 97

SWA

Slow back, 84, 181
Soft and cracked hands, remedies for, 223
Spoons, 59, 449
St. Andrews Links, description and characteristics of, 311–318; rules of, 433; local rules for, 442
St. Andrews Mechanics' Club medal, 376
St. George's Golf Club, 331, 405
St. Simon, 12
Stance, the, 449
Stewart, Lieut. James Campbell, 387
Strath, Andrew, 123, 354, 356
Strath, David, his position as a golfer, 103, 306, 356, 357, 359, 362, 364, 365, 367, 376, 390
Stuart, Alexander, 155, 393
Stuart, Queen Mary, 11
Style, 151; vagaries of noted players, 152; the law of imitation, 153; the St. Andrews swing, 153, 155; best examples for the learner, 155; slashing swingers, 156; errors of genius, 157; tendency to 'hook,' 158; playing for a pull on the ball, 159; *tours de force*, 160; half swings, 161; grotesque swings, 161; playing iron approach shots, 166; varieties of putting methods, 166; styles of dress and language, 167, 168
Stymie, 449
Sunday playing forbidden in Scotland, 13, 14
Surprise swing, the, 161, 165
Sway, 192

INDEX

Swing, the, 80, 83, 86, 87, 95, 101, 103, 161, 185, 187, 197, 204, 253, 449; St. Andrew's, 153

TABLE showing at what holes strokes are to be taken, 444
Tait, Professor, 69
Taking the honour, 231
Tee, the, 449
Tee shots, 249, 272
Teeing ground, 449; rights, registration of, 36
Three-ball matches, 241, 284
Three-quarter stroke, the, 111, 116, 132
Thomson, W. C., 390
Topping, 187, 188
Training, 209; loss of nerve, 209; the 'too fine' condition, 210; dietary regimen, 211; attention to be concentrated on the immediate stroke, 211; practice matches, 212; pressing, 212; the courage of despair, 213; practice and over-practice, 214; staleness, 218; habits of professionals, 219, 221; indoor practice, 220; approach putting, 222; a day's hard golf, 222; soft and scratched hands, 222, 223; perspiration in the palms of the hands, 223; gloves and boots, 223; the niblick shot out of sand with a bunker cliff in front, 223; the happy medium, 224

WAGGLE, the, 89, 90
Walker, Rev., 2
Warwick Golf Club, 392
Water, shots out of, 150
Westward Ho Club, 27
Westward Ho Links, description of, 326–328
Whin-gorse, 148, 449
White, Logan, 152
Wimbledon Clubs, 27
Wimbledon Common Links, features of, 328
Wind, 150
Windle-straws, 104, 149
Women golfers, 23
Wood, 383
Wood for shafts, 64
Wooden niblick, the, 60
Wooden putters, the, 60, 61, 141, 142

YORK, Duke of, 11, 17

ZOLA, 7